AN ACCOUNT OF THE KINGDOM OF NEPAL

View of the Temple of Boodhama in Kanahai

AN ACCOUNT OF THE KINGDOM OF NEPAL,

AND OF THE TERRITORIES ANNEXED TO THIS DOMINION

BY THE

HOUSE OF GORKHA.

BY

FRANCIS HAMILTON, (FORMERLY BUCHANAN,) M.D.
FELLOW OF THE ROYAL SOCIETIES OF LONDON AND EDINBURGH:
THE SOCIETY OF ANTIQUARIES, AND OF THE LINNEAN SOCIETY OF LONDON AND OF THE ASIATICK SOCIETY OF CALCUTTA.

ILLUSTRATED WITH ENGRAVINGS.

GYAN

Published by

Gyan Publishing House
5, Ansari Road
Daryaganj, New Delhi-110002
Phone: 011-47034999, 9811692060
E-mail: books@gyanbooks.com

Distribution Network
gyanbooks.com
India, USA, Canada, UK, Australia, France

ISBN : 978-81-212-3015-5 (PB)
First Published, 1819

2nd Impression 2020

Printed at: Gyan Press, Delhi.

An Account of the Kingdom of Nepal
Author: Buchanan

AN ACCOUNT OF THE KINGDOM OF NEPAL,

AND OF THE TERRITORIES ANNEXED TO THIS DOMINION BY THE

HOUSE OF GORKHA.

BY

FRANCIS HAMILTON, (FORMERLY BUCHANAN,) M.D.

FELLOW OF THE ROYAL SOCIETIES OF LONDON AND EDINBURGH;

THE SOCIETY OF ANTIQUARIES, AND OF THE LINNEAN SOCIETY OF LONDON;

AND OF THE ASIATICK SOCIETY OF CALCUTTA.

ILLUSTRATED WITH ENGRAVINGS.

EDINBURGH:

PRINTED FOR ARCHIBALD CONSTABLE AND COMPANY;

LONGMAN, HURST, REES, ORME, AND BROWN;

AND HURST, ROBINSON, AND COMPANY, 90, CHEAPSIDE, LONDON.

1819.

TO

THE MOST NOBLE

RICHARD MARQUIS WELLESLEY, K. G.

&c. &c. &c.

THE FOLLOWING WORK IS INSCRIBED,

AS A MARK OF THE AUTHOR'S ESTEEM,

RESPECT, AND GRATITUDE.

CONTENTS.

INTRODUCTION . . . . Page 1

CHAPTER FIRST.

Of the Tribes inhabiting the Territories of Gorkha.

Original Inhabitants—Hindu Colonies, their period—Brahmans, History—Colony from Chitaur—Colony of Asanti—Success of Colonization in the West, in the East—Colony of Chaturbhuja—Hindu Tribes east from the River Kali—Language—Brahmans, Diet, Festivals, Offspring—Rajputs, adopted, illegitimate—Low Tribes—General Observations on the Customs of the Mountain Hindus east from the Kali—Of the Hindus west from the Kali—Of Tribes who occupied the Country previous to the Hindus—Manners—Magars—Gurungs—Jariyas—Newars—Murmis—Kiratas—Limbus—Lapchas—Bhotiyas 9

CHAPTER SECOND.

Nature of the Country.

Division into four Regions from their relative elevation—First, or Plain Region, or Tariyani—Soil—Productions, Animal and Vegetable—Cultivation—Climate—Rivers—Second, or Hilly Region—Productions—Minerals—Forests—Birds—Vallies called Dun—Cultivation—Climate—Third, or Mountainous Region—Elevation—Climate—Diseases—Cultivation—Pasture—Sheep and Cattle—Minerals—Spontaneous Vegetables—Extent—Fourth, or Alpine Region—Vallies—Mountains—Productions, Mineral, Animal, and Vegetable 61

CHAPTER THIRD.

Laws and Government.

Parts east from the Kali—Courts, and Forms of Proceeding—Punishments—Provincial Government—Revenue and Endowments—Officers of State—Military Establishment—Differences in the parts west from the River Kali—Revenue and Civil Establishment—Military Establishment 101

PART SECOND.

ACCOUNT OF THE PARTICULAR STATES WHICH FORMERLY EXISTED, AND OF THE FAMILIES BY WHICH EACH WAS GOVERNED.

INTRODUCTION 117

CHAPTER FIRST.

OF THE STATES EAST FROM THE RIVER KALI.

SECTION FIRST.

Country of Sikim.

Inhabitants—Government—Extent—History—Geography . . 118

SECTION II.

Dominions of the Family descended from Makanda Sen, Raja of Makwanpur.

General History—Branch of Lohango which occupied the Country of the Kiratas—History—Former Government—Military Force, Police, and Revenue, and Justice—Present State—District of Morang—District of Chayenpur—District of Naragarhi—District of Hedang—District of Makwanpur—Western Branch, which occupied chiefly the Country of Palpa—History—Description—Tanahung Family and its Possessions, and Collateral Branches—Rising, Ghiring, and Gajarkot 128

SECTION III.

Nepal Proper.

Name—History previous to the Conquest by the Gorkhalis—Extent and Topography—Population—Buildings—Revenue—Trade—Coins—Weights—Measures—Agriculture—Tenures—Crown Lands—Lands held for Service—Charity Lands—Tenants—Implements—Crops—Manufactures—Price of Labour—Slaves—Diet 186

SECTION IV.

The Countries belonging to the Chaubisi and Baisi Rajas.

Chaubisi Rajas—Pamar Family, impure Branch—Bhirkot, Garahang, Dhor, pure Branch—Nayakot—Satahung—Kaski—Lamjun—Gorkha, Topography, History—Prithwi, Narayan—Singha Pratap—Bahadur Sahi—Rana Bahadur—Bhim Sen—Royal Family—Kala Macwani Family—Gulmi, Khachi, Argha, Dhurkot, Musikot, Isma—Family of Bhingri and Khungri—Family of Piuthana—Family of Poin—Malihang Family—The Samal Family; Malebum; Galkot; Rugum; Musikot; Jajarkot; Bangphi; Gajal; Dharma; Jahari; Satatala; Malaneta; Saliyana; Dang; Chhilli—The Baisi Rajas—Dalu Dailek—Duti—Yumila—Taklakot, with the adjacent parts of Thibet subject to China 237

CHAPTER SECOND.

Of the Countries west from the River Kali.

Kumau; History, State—Garhawal; History, State—Sirmaur—Twelve Lordships—Besar—Hanur 291

SUPPLEMENT TO THE ACCOUNT OF NEPAL.

Some Information respecting the petty Chiefs who still remain independent to the west of the Dominions of Nepal or Gorkha.

Kangra—History—State—Kahalur—Bhomor—Kottahar—Yasawal—Datarpur —Gular—Nurpur—Chamba—Kullu—Mundi—Sukhet . . 309

Register of the Weather, from February 1802 to March 1803 . 318

Calculation of the Altitudes of some of the Snowy Mountains from the Valley of Nepal. By Colonel Crawford 346

Index 347

DIRECTIONS FOR PLACING THE PLATES.

I.	View of the Temple Bouddhama, to front the title-page.	
II.	View of Kathmandu, to front page .	209
III.	Himaliya Mountains, Plate 1.	at the end of the volume.
IV.	Himaliya Mountains, Plate 2.	
V.	Do. do. Plate 3.	
VI.	Do. do. Plate 4.	
VII.	Do. do. Plate 5.	
VIII.	Map of the Dominions of Gorkha	

AN

ACCOUNT OF NEPAL,

OR OF

THE TERRITORIES OF THE HOUSE OF GORKHA.

INTRODUCTION.

THIS Account, which is intended to describe the country as it stood previously to the war with the British, commencing in the end of the year 1814, is derived chiefly from the following sources.

In the first place, during the years 1802 and 1803, I passed fourteen months in the country, mostly in the vicinity of Kathmandu, the capital; and I was accompanied by Ramajai Batacharji, an intelligent Brahman, from Calcutta, whom I employed to obtain information, so far as I prudently could, without alarming a jealous government, or giving offence to the Resident, under whose authority I was acting.

In the next place, assisted by the same person, I passed two years on the frontier, collecting information, both from the Company's subjects, and from numerous refugees and travellers from the dominions of Gorkha. The following are the persons to whose information I am chiefly indebted:

The account of Sikim is chiefly taken from a Lama, or priest of Buddha, who, with part of his flock, had fled into the district of Puraniya, to escape from the violence of the Gorkhalese, and who constructed a map of the country, which I have deposited in the Company's library. Besides the Lama, I consulted many of the natives of the Company's territory, who had visited the lower parts of Sikim, and several of the Gorkhalese, and other people of Nepal; and Mr Smith, of Nathpur, favoured me with several particulars, collected by a Mr Pagan for the information of government.

Concerning the country between Sikim and Nepal Proper, my information is chiefly derived from the following persons:

1st, Agam Singha, hereditary chief of the Kirats, a tribe bordering immediately on Nepal, and last Chautariya, or prime minister, of the princes who governed that people.

2d, A Brahman, who was the Munsuf, or civil judge of Bahadurgunj, a territory in the district of Puraniya belonging to the Company. His ancestors were hereditary Dewans to the princes who governed the territory between Nepal and Sikim, that is, the Brahman's family managed the princes' revenue.

3d, From Narayan Das, a scribe, (Kayastha,) whose ancestor Janardan accompanied Lohanga, founder of the late dynasty; and whose descendants enjoyed the hereditary office of Neb, or second minister to the successors of that chief, until their final expulsion from the mountains.

4th, A slave of the Raja of Gorkha, who entered into my service in order to bring plants from the Alpine regions; but, finding him very intelligent, and a great traveller, I employed him to construct a map, which I have deposited in the Company's library. In order to enable himself to execute this with more care, he refreshed his memory by several journies in different directions.

5th, A Kirat from Hedang, near the Arun river, gave me

another map, which has also been deposited in the Company's library. It contains only the eastern parts of the territory in question.

These two maps, together with that of the Lama, as might be expected, are very rude, and differ in several points; but they coincide in a great many more, so as to give considerable authority to their general structure; and, by a careful examination of the whole, many differences, apparently considerable, may be reconciled. The general authority of the whole is confirmed by our maps, so far as they go, and by the intelligence which Colonel Crawford obtained in Nepal.

The account of Nepal Proper is chiefly derived from my own observations, assisted by those of Ramajai above mentioned and by some communications with which I was favoured by Colonel Crawford, now Surveyor-General in Bengal. He favoured me, in particular, with several drawings of the snowy mountains; and, by orders of the Marquis Wellesley, then Governor-General, I was furnished with copies of Colonel Crawford's valuable geographical surveys and maps of the country.

In one point respecting these maps, I consider myself bound to do justice to the researches of Colonel Crawford. From a treatise on the sources of the Ganges, given by H. T. Colebrooke, Esq. in the 11th volume of the Asiatick Researches, page 429, &c. it might be possibly inferred, although this, perhaps, was not intended to be expressed, that Colonel Colebrooke and his kinsman were induced to reject the authority of D'Anville respecting the sources of the Ganges, merely from examining the authorities, upon which the course of the Ganges above Haridwar had been laid down in the geographical charts then in use. Now, the fact is, that Colonel Colebrooke had other grounds for rejecting the authority of D'Anville, and especially one of the above-mentioned maps, which had been officially communicated to him by Colonel Crawford. In this map the sources of the Ganges are laid down from the reports of pilgrims; nor has the survey, carried on by the suggestion of Colonel Colebrooke, added any thing material, so far as relates to the general outlines of these sources. By this observation I by no means intend to depreciate the labours of Mr Webb, by whom the survey was conducted; nor the judgment and love of science evinced in the recommendation of Colonel Colebrooke to employ him. So long as the matter rested entirely on the report of pilgrims, doubts would exist; and the survey has not only entirely removed these, but has given us many details of a country previously unknown.

Concerning the country between Nepal Proper and the river Kali, I follow chiefly the authority of the following persons: *1st*, a Brahman, named Sadhu Ram Upadhyaya, whose family was in hereditary possession of the office of priest (Purohit) for the Raja of Palpa, one of the principal chiefs in this district; *2d* and *3d*, Prati Nidhi Tiwari, and Kanak Nidhi Tiwari, two brothers of the sacred order, the former very learned, and the latter a man of business. Their family had been long Mantris, or advisers of the same chiefs, but came originally from Kumau; *4th*, Samar Bahadur, uncle to the Raja of Palpa, now in exile.

Two maps of these parts, now in the Company's library, were prepared by Sadhu Ram and Kanak Nidhi, with the assistance of Kamal Lochan, one of the natives attached to the survey of Bengal, on which I was engaged. Although they differ in some points, they agree in so many more, especially in the eastern parts, that considerable reliance may be placed on their giving some tolerable idea of the country.

Finally, concerning the parts west of the river Kali, in the rainy season 1814 I proceeded up the Ganges, with a view of going to Haridwar, where I expected to procure intelligence; but, fortunately, I met at Futtehgur with a person well qualified for the purpose. This was Hariballabh, a Brahman born in Kumau, but who has been long in the service of the Garhawal Rajas, and has travelled much in the adjacent parts. A map of the western parts of the dominions of Gorkha, now also in the Company's library, was composed by Hariballabh, with the assistance of Kamal Lochan. The same person gave me another map explaining the country, which extends some way west from the Sutluj, and of which a short account will be found in the Appendix.

I regret, that, on the banks of the Karanali, there intervenes a space, with which none of my informants were well acquainted, its communications being entirely with the country belonging to the Nawab Vazir.

I shall have very frequent occasion to mention the account of Nepal by Colonel Kirkpatrick; and, although I often differ from him in opinion, and think it my duty to state these points fully, yet no one can be more sensible, knowing well the difficulties he encountered, of the merits of his work, which is, on the whole, perfectly conformable to his well-known thirst for information and judgment in the acquisition of knowledge. I must here, however, in a general way, caution the reader to place little confidence in the names given in the printed work. I have no doubt, that the numerous errors in the names are to be attributed to the printing of the work having been entrusted to some person entirely ignorant of the native language; and who, therefore, could not be led, by a knowledge of this, to read the names in the manuscript with accuracy. But, besides this source of error, in some degree, perhaps, unavoidable, the printer seems to have been uncommonly careless in reading even those names that are known to Europeans. Thus, (in page 131,) speaking of the birds of Nepal, he has as follows: "The two last belong to the genus of pheasants, the damphia being of the golden, and the monal of the argheer, or spotted sort." There can be no doubt, that Colonel Kirkpatrick wrote argus, and not argheer, which has no meaning.

The utmost negligence may be also observed in a matter of more importance; for, in the route from Kathmandu to Beni, the capital of Malebum, given in page 290, all the stages from Deoralli 1st, to Ragho Powa, both inclusive, are evidently transposed, as going through the territory of Lamjun and Kaski, after having entered Malebum at Kusmachoor, while both Lamjun and Kaski are between Kathmandu and Malebum. I suspect, also, that the person entrusted with the printing has introduced some matter of his own about the Hindu religion, several passages on that subject being unlike the sentiments of a person of Colonel Kirkpatrick's known sense and observation.

PART FIRST.

GENERAL OBSERVATIONS.

INTRODUCTION.

NEPAL, a name celebrated in Hindu legend, in a strict sense, ought to be applied to that country only which is in the vicinity of Kathmandu, the capital; but at present it is usually given to the whole territory of the Gorkha Rajas, which occupies about thirteen degrees of longitude, and five of latitude. It is my intention now to give an account of the whole of this territory, so far as has come to my knowledge.

East from the territory called Nepal Proper, the mountains were chiefly occupied by a tribe called Kirat or Kichak, who, in remote times, seem to have made extensive conquests in the plains of Kamrup and Matsya, now constituting the districts of Ranggapur and Dinajpur. Although these conquests had long been lost to the Kirats, yet Father Giuseppe, who witnessed the conquest of Nepal by the Gorkhalese, and gives a good account of the horrid circumstances attending that event,* considers the Kiratas (Ciratas) in the year 1769 as being an independent nation. Now, although this would not appear to be strictly exact, as the Kirats had then been long sub-

* Asiatick Researches, Vol. II. p. 307.

ject to Rajput princes; yet the Father is abundantly justifiable in what he has advanced; for the Kirats formed the principal strength of these Rajput chiefs, their hereditary chief held the second office in the state, (Chautariya,) and the Rajputs, who were united with them, did not presume to act as masters, to invade their lands, or violate their customs. These Kirats are frequently mentioned in Hindu legend as occupying the country between Nepal and Madra, the ancient denomination in Hindu writings for the country which we call Bhotan.

Towards the west again, the country between Nepal and Kasmir, over which the present rulers of the former have far extended their dominion, in the ancient Hindu writings is called Khas, and its inhabitants Khasiyas. I am told, that, wherever mentioned in ancient records, like the Kirats, their neighbours to the west, the Kasiyas are considered as abominable and impure infidels.

CHAPTER FIRST.

OF THE TRIBES INHABITING THE TERRITORIES OF GORKHA.

Original Inhabitants.—Hindu Colonies, their period.—Brahmans, History.—Colony from Chitaur.—Colony of Asanti.—Success of Colonization in the West,—in the East.—Colony of Chaturbhuja.—Hindu Tribes east from the River Kali.—Language.—Brahmans, Diet, Festivals, Offspring.—Rajputs, adopted, illegitimate.—Low Tribes.—General Observations on the Customs of the Mountain Hindus east from the Kali.—Of the Hindus west from the Kali.—Of Tribes who occupied the Country previous to the Hindus.—Manners.—Magars.—Gurungs.—Jariyas.—Newars.—Murmis.—Kiratas.—Limbus.—Lupchas.—Bhotiyas.

The numerous valleys among the prodigious mountains, of which Nepal in its extended sense consists, are inhabited by various tribes, that differ very much in language, and somewhat in customs. All that have any sort of pretensions to be considered as aboriginal, like their neighbours of Bhotan to the east, are, by their features, clearly marked as belonging to the Tartar or Chinese race of men, and have no sort of resemblance to the Hindus.

The time when the Hindus penetrated into these regions is very uncertain. Bhim Sen, the son of Pandu, is said to have penetrated into these parts, and probably was the first who introduced any sort of improvement. He still continues to be a favourite object with the rude tribes, not only on the mountains, but in their vicinity. Probably at no great distance from the time of that prince, and about the commencement of our era, Sakya, the last great teacher of the Bouddhists, passed through the country, and settled at Lasa, where he is supposed to be still alive in the person whom we call the Grand Lama. His followers seem to have acquired a great ascendancy over all the tribes of Nepal, as well as in Thibet and Bhotan, which they retained until a subsequent colony of Hindus settled in the first of these countries, and introduced the Brahmans, who have had considerable success in destroying the heretical doctrines, although these have still numerous votaries.

Colonel Kirkpatrick, or perhaps rather his editor, seems to have entertained a very different opinion concerning the period when the Hindus penetrated into Nepal. Speaking of Sambhunath, he says, * "After all, it is highly probable that the sanctity of this spot might be safely referred to a period very anterior both to the Newar and Khat Bhotiya dynasties (who preceded the Newars) of Nepaul, since the sacred books of the Hindus leave scarcely any room to doubt, that the religion of Brahma has been established from the most remote antiquity in this secluded valley, where there are nearly as many idols as inhabitants, there not being a fountain, a river, or hill within its limits, that is not consecrated to one or other of the Hindu deities." What idea the author may have held of the terms Hindu and religion of Brahma, I cannot say. If he meant by Hindu whatever colonists may have come from the plains, I agree with him, and have stated, that Bhim Sen and Sakya Singha seem, in early ages, to have penetrated into

* Nepaul, p. 150.

the mountains, and to have introduced civilization. But I think him mistaken, if, by Hindu, he means the followers of the present Brahmans, introduced into India from Saka Dwip by the son of Krishna, contemporary with Bhim Sen; and if, by the religion of Brahma, he means the doctrine taught by these Brahmans, who do not, however, worship that deity. In the first place, I have been assured, that, in the sacred books of the Hindus, that is to say, in the Puranas attributed to Vyas, the Khas and Kiratas, the ancient inhabitants of the mountains, are always spoken of as impure infidels. Again, the number of idols and places consecrated in Nepal to the Hindu gods is no sort of proof that the doctrines of the Brahmans have existed long in the country; for the Bouddhists, who follow the doctrine of Sakya, admit of the worship of the same inferior deities (Devatas) with the Brahmans, both having probably adopted their worship from sects that had previously existed. Farther, the changes in the names of places, since the Hindu conquest, has been rapid almost beyond conception; for instance, the capitals of the three principalities into which Nepal was divided, and which are now called Kathmandu, Lalita Patana, and Bhatgang, and which, in 1802, I always heard called by these names, were, during the Newar government, which ended in 1767, called Yin Daise, Yulloo Daise, and Khopo Daise. * To these circumstances, explanatory of the author's mistake, I must add the statements, which will follow, and which reduce the arrival of the present Hindu colonies to a modern period, or to the fourteenth century of the Christian era.

According to the traditions most commonly current in Nepal, the Hindus of the mountains (Parbatiya) left their own

* Kirkpatrick's Nepaul, pp. 159, 162, and 163.

country in consequence of an invasion by the Muhammedan king of Dilli, who wished to marry a daughter of the Raja of Chitor, or Chitaur, celebrated for her beauty. A refusal brought on the destruction of her father and his capital city; and, to avoid a hateful yoke, many of the people fled to the hills. A somewhat similar story, related in the translation of Fereshtah by Dow, would seem to verify the truth of the tradition, and fix its date to the 1306 year of our era.

In opposition to this tradition, very generally received at Kathmandu, and throughout the eastern parts of the Nepalese dominions, Hariballabh contends, that there was a certain Asanti, a prince descended of Shalivahana in the seventh or eighth generation, and who, therefore, should have lived in about the second or third century of the Christian era, but whom Hariballabh supposes to have lived seven or eight hundred years ago, in which case the Shalivahana from whom he was descended must have been different from the prince whose name has been given to an era. Asanti came to these mountains, and established a kingdom extending from Pesaur to Morang, and having for its capital Karuvirpur, a town near Almorha. His descendants were called Suryabangsi Rajputs, and with them came pure Brahmans, whose doctrines gradually gained ground by the addition of colonists, and the progress of generation. This progress would appear to have been very slow, for I cannot find, even in Kumau, the seat of the first colonists, that there are now any other Brahmans, except those called the Brahmans of Kumau, a colony avowedly introduced from Kanoj by Thor Chandra, who lived after the middle of the fifteenth century of the Christian era, and, therefore, subsequent to the colony from Chitaur. The country had previously been inhabited by Jars, Magars, and other impure and infidel tribes, and great numbers of these continued under the descendants of Asanti as cultivators; but, west of the Soyal, there was no Raja who was not of pure birth, although the barbarous chiefs continued to hold most of the country east from thence, tributary, however, to the descendants of Shalivahana. Hariballabh remembers the names of only the three first of Asanti's successors, namely, Basanti, Dham Deva, and Brahma Deva; but his descendants continued, for a considerable time, to enjoy a supremacy over the chiefs of the hills, although their power was much reduced by family dissensions, and by appanages granted to collateral branches. Various turbulent chiefs, that successively came from the low country, took advantage of this weakness to reduce the authority of the descendants of Asanti to a jurisdiction nearly nominal; and, in the reign of Akbur, the government of Karuvirpur was totally overturned by the petty chief of Kumau, who pretended to be of the ancient family of the moon, and whose ancestors, a few generations before, had succeeded, by an abominable act of treachery, in obtaining a settlement in the hills. Indeed, it is generally admitted, even by themselves, that all, or at least most of the chiefs, who came from the low country, used similar means, that is, entered into the service of the mountaineers, and, having gained their confidence by a superior knowledge and polish of manners, contrived to put them to death, and to seize their country.

This conduct is justified, in their opinion, by their having abolished the impure and abominable customs that previously existed among the mountaineers; and, in conformity with this common principle, all the chiefs west of the river Kali glory in having either totally expelled or extirpated the original inhabitants, and in having established, in its full height, the purity of the Hindu doctrines.

To the east of the Kali river, the chiefs have not been actuated by so pure a zeal, and not only have permitted many of the mountain tribes to remain and practise their abominations, but have themselves relaxed, in many essential points, from the rules of cast, and have debased their blood by frequent intermixtures with that of the mountaineers; while such of these as chose to embrace the slender degree of purity required in these parts, have been admitted to the high dignities of the military order.

Perhaps, in the parts west from the river Kali, the Hindus from the south have not, in fact, been so bad as they pretend; and, although no one is willing to acknowledge a deficiency of zeal, or a descent from barbarians, yet, in fact, they may have permitted to remain such of the cultivators as chose to adopt the rules of purity, and to take the name of Sudras. I have not seen a sufficient number of the people from that part of the country to enable me to judge how far this may have been the case; for all the original tribes of the mountains, as already stated, have strongly marked Chinese or Tartar countenances, when the breed has not been improved by a mixture with people of more elegant features.

According to Sadu Ram and Samar Bahadur, when the colony from Chitaur, mentioned above, arrived at the mountains east from the Kali, in the beginning of the fourteenth century of the Christian era, they found the whole occupied by impure or infidel tribes, nor for some time did any of the sacred order, nor any descendants of the colony, extend beyond the limits of their conquests. Gradually, however, the descendants of the colony, and especially the members of the sacred order, who indulged very much in promiscuous amours, spread wide over the mountainous region, and multiplied exceedingly, introducing everywhere, as much as possible, the modern doctrines of purity and law, modified, however, a good deal, to accommodate it to the licence which the mountaineers exercised in the intercourse of the sexes, and in eating. In this conversion the Brahmans have had great success, and most of the chiefs of the highland tribes have adopted the rules of purity, and are called Rajputs, while various fables and genealogies have been contrived to gratify their vanity, by connecting their history with Hindu legend.

Concerning the colony from Chitaur I received another account, from the Mahanta, or prior of the convent of Janmasthan, at Ayodhya. He alleges, that Chaturbhuja, a prince of the Sisaudhiya tribe, having left Chitaur, conquered Kumau and Yumila, where he established his throne, from whence his family spread to Palpa Tanahung and the Kirats. The supremacy very lately admitted by all the eastern mountain chiefs to the Rajas of Yumila, is a strong presumption in favour of this opinion. Many chiefs, and especially the Palpa Tanahung and Makwanpur families, pretend to be descended of the Chitaur princes; but it is very doubtful whether they have any claim to a descent so illustrious, for the Mahanta said, that, after some generations, all the hill chiefs rebelled, and paid only a nominal obedience to the Raja of Yumila, nor does Samar Bahadur, uncle of the Palpa Raja, claim kindred with that chief, while one of the branches of his family still remains impure. But, if this tradition be well-founded, the Yumila, or Kumau principality, or at least its possession by the Rajputs, must have been subsequent to 1306, which will not admit of above twenty-five generations, instead of the fifty or sixty which the Brahmans of that country allot for the arrival of Asanti. This difference may, however, be explained. Chaturbhuja, as well as a fortunate Brahman, who obtained Malebum, as will be afterwards mentioned, may have married the daughter of the former chief of Yumila, and thus succeeded to the power; and the fifty or sixty generations, in both cases, may include both the original family, and those who succeeded by marriage. But, if the Mahanta is right, the Yumila or Karuvir family, in place of being descended of Shalivahana, was descended of the princes of Ajmir and Chitaur.

In giving an account of the tribes now occupying the dominions of Nepal, I shall first commence with these Hindu colonists, as having acquired the predominance; but I must premise, that very considerable differences prevail in their customs in different parts, and especially that those in the countries east from the Kali differ much from those who live west from that river. I shall commence with the former, with whom I am best acquainted.

The language spoken by the mountain Hindus in the vicinity of Kathmandu, is usually called the Parbatiya basha, or mountain dialect; but west from the capital, it is more commonly known by the name of Khas basha, or dialect of the Khas country, because it seems to have been first introduced into the territory of that name. I have lodged in the Company's library a copious vocabulary of this dialect, from whence the learned may judge how far it is probable that it came from Chitor; for there can be no doubt, that it is a dialect of the Hindwi language, and it is making rapid progress in extinguishing the aboriginal dialects of the mountains.

The character in which this language is written is evidently derived from the Nagri, and may be found in Colonel Kirkpatrick's Account of Nepaul, opposite to page 220; and in the twenty-eight following pages may be seen a short vocabulary.

East from the Kali, the Brahmans, who are of pure birth, are only few in number, there being no means for their subsistence, as they confine themselves mostly to the duties of the sacred order. They are of the Kanoj nation, and the sect of the

Saktis, following chiefly the doctrine of the books called Tantras. Where the chiefs who pretend to have come from Chitaur settled, many of them were men of great learning. In other parts, very few have made any sort of progress in grammar, law, or philosophy; but they are considered as profound astrologers. Although very few have taken service either from men or in temples, they contaminate themselves by uncommon liberties in the gratification of their appetites. They are divided into three ranks that do not intermarry. The highest are called Jayurbedi, from the sacred book which they profess to follow, and they assume the title of Upadhyaya. These are the instructors (Gurus) and priests (Purohits) for Brahmans and Rajputs, and eat goats, sheep, and some kinds of wild fowl, but abstain from venison. The two lower orders are called Kamiya and Purubi, and act as instructors and priests for the lower orders. These not only eat the same animals as those of the highest rank, but many of them rear fowls and swine for their tables.

The sixteen principal festivals observed by the mountain Hindus have been described by Colonel Kirkpatrick, * nor have I any additional information to offer.

All the Brahmans may keep widows of their own class as concubines, and the spurious offspring of such connections are called Jausis. These, having betaken themselves to agriculture and commerce, have become exceedingly numerous, and are reduced to perform every kind of drudgery. Among the poor people whom I observed coming to the markets in the Gorakhpur district, loaded with goods even from the distant hills of Malebum, at least a half stated themselves to be of this class. These, although of illegitimate extraction, are not cal-

* Nepaul, p. 193, 196.

led Khas; but, until the present dynasty seized on the government, were considered as entitled to all the immunities and privileges of the sacred order, as were also the children of Brahmans by widows of their own rank.

The descendants of Brahmans by women of the lower tribes, although admitted to be Khas, or impure, are called Kshatris or Khatris, which terms are considered as perfectly synonymous, and have now formed two tribes, Pauriyal and Sili; but some proper Khatris, called Dewkotas and Lahauriyas, from Bareli and Lahaur, have settled in the country, and intermarry with the Pauriyal and Sili, all of whom wear the thread, and are considered as belonging to the military tribes.

The Rajputs that are, or that even pretend to be, descended of the colony which came from Chitaur, are very few in number; but the families of the mountain chiefs, who have adopted the Hindu rules of purity, and even some who have neglected to do so, are now universally admitted to be Rajputs; and the Chitaur family have so often married the daughters of the former, that several members of it have acquired the Tartar countenance, while some of the mountain families, by intermarriages with pure but indigent Rajputs, have acquired oval faces and high noses. Not only the colony, therefore, from Chitaur, if the Palpa family be such, but all the descendants of the hill chiefs, are now called Rajputs; and, until the absorption of all power in the Gorkha family, the Rajputs held all the principal civil and military offices of the petty states into which the country was subdivided. It would also appear, that, when the princes of the mountaineers were persuaded to follow the doctrines of the Brahmans, many of their subjects or clans were induced to follow the example of their chiefs, and thus have established tribes called Thapas, Ghartis, Karkis, Majhis, Basnats, Bishtakos, Ranas, and Kharkas, all of whom are called Khasiyas, or natives of Khas, but they wear the thread, and live pure like Kshatris, and, in fact, are included among the fencibles or military power of the country, and are very much employed in the government of the family of Gorkha, under which some of them enjoy the highest dignities of the state; for Bhim Sen, who is now vested with the whole power of the kingdom, is by birth a Thapa, as is also Amar Singha Karyi, who commands the army beyond the Yamuna. Among those called Khasiyas, thus adopted into the military order, there may be many others, of which I did not hear; but it would not appear, even when they adopted fully the rules of purity, that the whole of these tribes obtained so elevated a rank, which is almost equal to that of the sacred bastards. The Thapas, for instance, are of two kinds, Khas and Ranggu; yet the latter, although they live pure, and have pure Brahmans to give them instruction, and to perform their ceremonies, are not permitted to wear the military badge, nor to intermarry with those who enjoy this privilege. The Ghartis, also, are of two kinds, Khas and Bhujal. The former are admitted to the military dignity; but the latter wallow in all the abominations of the impure Gurungs, and do not speak the Khas language. The Ranas, also, are divided into two kinds, the Khas and Magar. The latter are a branch of the Magar tribe, and totally neglect the rules of Hindu purity. It is not even, as I have said, all the Rajputs that have adopted the rules of purity, and some branches of the same families were pure, while others rejected the advice of the sacred order, and eat and drank whatever their appetites craved.

All these military tribes, including the Khasiyas, descended of Brahmans or Khatris, who are more numerous than all the others, the Rajputs, Thapas, &c. have again had children by widows of their own cast, and by concubines of lower tribes, and these children are also called Khasiyas, who, although they live equally pure, and observe equally the laws of the Brahmans, are not permitted to wear the thread of distinction; but must toil in ignoble professions. They are considered as of so little consequence, that, of whatever descent they may be by the male line, they may all freely intermarry. They speak the Khas language.

The low tribes, which also speak this language, are all supposed to form part of the colony from Chitaur; but here there is a considerable number of a tribe called Khawas, who are slaves, and accompanied the chief as his domestic servants, having been in slavery at Chitaur. They are reckoned a pure tribe, and their women are not abandoned to prostitution like the slaves of the mountain tribes called Ketis. The Khawas adhered to the chiefs of the Chitaur family, and were employed in confidential offices, such as stewards; while these chiefs soon indulged in the luxury of having mountain slaves round their persons. Next in rank, in the following order, are,

1. Nai, or barbers. A Brahman may drink their water.

2. Karmi, who build and thatch houses, and Chunra, or carpenters. These have degraded Brahmans as instructors.

3. Kami, miners and workers in iron and copper; Sarki, tanners and shoemakers; Damai, tailors and musicians. All these are vile, and have no priests but of their own cast. Any Musulman or Christian, however, who should cohabit with a Damai woman, would suffer death, and the woman would be severely punished; but, according to the Hindu law, a female, however low in rank, cannot for any crime be deprived of life. When any woman has been discovered with a Musulman, the whole kingdom is thrown into confusion. Even if she has been of the lowest cast, she may have given water to some person of the cast immediately above her own. He may again

have given it to a higher, and thus the whole inhabitants may have been involved in sin and disgrace. This can only be expiated by a ceremony called Prayaschitta, in which the prince washes in the river with great ceremony, and bestows large sums on the Brahmans, who read the expiatory prayers proper on the occasion. The expence of an expiation of this kind, which was performed during our stay in this country, was, by my Brahman, estimated at two thousand rupees; but the natives alleged that it amounted to ten times this sum.

Colonel Kirkpatrick * mentions the Dhewars as husbandmen and fishers of the western district, from which circumstance we may conclude that they belong to the Hindu colony; but I did not hear of them, as my account of the Parbatiya tribes was chiefly derived from the central parts. From the condition of similar tribes on the plains, these Dhewars probably belong to the third of the ranks above enumerated, although the Majhis, (Mhanjhees,) whom Colonel Kirkpatrick joins with the Dhewars, were represented to me as a tribe of original Khas, which has been converted by the Hindus, and admitted into the military order.

Colonel Kirkpatrick then states, † "That Nepaul, having been ruled for many centuries past by Rajput princes, and the various classes of Hindus appearing in all periods to have composed a great proportion of its population, we are naturally prepared to find a general resemblance in manners and customs between this part of its inhabitants, and kindred sects established in adjacent countries; accordingly, the differences are so faint as to be scarcely discernible in a single instance." Now, I must here observe, that Nepal, in the proper sense of the word, when Colonel

* Nepaul, p. 185.

† Nepaul, p. 184, 185.

Kirkpatrick wrote, had not been governed for half a century by chiefs, who even pretended to be descended of a Hindu colony, for the Rajas of Nepal were Newars, who deny this extraction. They indeed called themselves Rajputs, that is, the descendants of princes, but so does the king of Ava, although no one ever imagined that he is descended of the Rajputs in Hindustan. I shall afterwards have occasion to show, that the various classes of Hindus, that is, of the natives of India, who have adopted the Brahmans for spiritual guides, have not in all periods composed a great proportion of the population, nor have even entered any part of the country as residents. At present, indeed, in most parts of the kingdom, except in Nepal itself, they, or converts to their doctrine, form a large proportion of the inhabitants; and the more recent the importation, I should expect the greater resemblance between the colonists and the inhabitants of the plains of India; but, in fact, the resemblance, though strong, is not so complete as Colonel Kirkpatrick's short stay amongst them induced him to suppose, as will appear from what I shall afterwards state.

These mountain Hindus appear to me a deceitful and treacherous people, cruel and arrogant towards those in their power, and abjectly mean towards those from whom they expect favour. Their men of rank, even of the sacred order, pass their nights in the company of male and female dancers and musicians, and, by an excessive indulgence in pleasure, are soon exhausted. Their mornings are passed in sleep, and the day is occupied by the performance of religious ceremonies, so that little time remains for business, or for storing their minds with useful knowledge. Except a few of the Brahmans, they are, in general, drunkards, which, joined to a temper uncommonly suspicious, and to a consciousness of having neglected the conjugal duties, works them up to a fury of jealousy that frequently produces assassination. For this they are all prepared, by wearing a large knife in their girdle, and the point of honour requires them never to rest, until they have shed the blood of the man who has been suspected of a criminal intercourse with their wives. The jealous man watches his opportunity for months, and even for years, should his adversary be on his guard; and, having at length found a favourable time, with one stroke of his knife in the throat of his rival, he satisfies his revenge. This is considered as so commendable, that, at Kathmandu, the police, in other respects very strict, does not at all interfere, although the murderer is often actuated merely by suspicion.

The higher ranks, whenever not compelled by the most urgent necessity, conceal their women; and their widows ought to burn themselves with their husbands' corpse. Many, however, refuse, nor did I learn that force is ever used. The custom seems, however, more prevalent than in any part of India where I have been, the vicinity of Calcutta excepted.

The appearance and dress of the lower orders of these Parbatiya Hindus is represented in the plate opposite to page 40 of Kirkpatrick's Nepaul, where the figure, behind those seated, is a porter of this tribe.

In these eastern parts of the dominions of Nepal, the mountain Hindus are far from having extirpated the aboriginal tribes, most of which, until the accession of the Gorkha family, enjoyed their customs and religion with little or no disturbance, and they are still numerous and powerful, as will be afterwards mentioned; but, west from the Kali river, there is a great difference. The whole people in Kumau, and Garhawal at least, as well as their language, are called Khasiyas, as having settled in the Khas country; but all pretend to be descended of colonists from the south, and disclaim every connection with the original impure barbarians. West from Garhawal, the term Khas is altogether rejected, and it is pretended that this impure race never held the country. Each cast, west from the Kali, preserves its race with the utmost care; nor are widows of the high cast permitted to become concubines. Except in a very few places, near the passes through the snowy mountains, the aboriginal inhabitants are alleged to have been obliged entirely to conform to the rules of Hindu purity, and to reject their ancient forms of worship; for I hope that the colonists from the south are not so bad as they pretend, and that religious zeal has not had such a victory over humanity as they allege; for the fear of being thought in any degree contaminated by the infidel Khas, would make them carefully conceal whatever indulgence humanity may have wrung from intolerance. To such a height is caution on this subject required, that the people, who have settled near the passes in the snowy mountains, although acknowledged as of the same tribes with those nearer the plain, and although they use the same language and manners, are called Bhotiyas, and are no longer permitted to intermarry with the people who can have no intercourse with these impure infidels. On account of this strictness, the Rajputs of the western districts are as much courted by those of the plains, as those east from the Kali are scouted.

The mountain tribes, which I consider aboriginal, as I have said, have Chinese or Tartar faces, but each spoke a peculiar language. Some used a written character altered from the Nagri, so as to enable it to express their utterance; others had not the use of letters. Before the arrival of Hindu colonies, they had no idea of cast; but some of the tribes confined their marriages to their own nation, while others admitted of intermarriages with strangers. The women in all seem to enjoy great indulgence, and are allowed, as in Europe, to form a choice for themselves, after they have arrived at mature years.

In all these hill tribes the women were weavers, and seem to have enjoyed great privileges; but the plurality of husbands had not been introduced with the religion of Thibet. Until the arrival of the Rajputs, they seem all to have eaten every kind of animal food, and still do so whenever they are at liberty to indulge their inclinations. They still continue to drink spirituous liquors. Each tribe appears originally to have had a priesthood and deities peculiar to itself, although the worship of Bhim Sen, the son of Pandu, seems to be very general, and to have been that which preceded the doctrine of the Buddhas; but first the Lamas, or, perhaps, rather the Zogis, and then the Brahmans, have made encroachments, and at the same time introduced many new customs. They have not yet introduced the custom of inoculation for the small-pox, and those who are seized are put into a separate hut, to which the friends daily convey water and food, but do not enter; and the sick is allowed to take his chance. They are all very slovenly and dirty.

The tribes, which, on the arrival of the colonies from Hindustan, occupied the country east from the Kali river, (for those to the west have been extirpated or abolished,) were chiefly Magars, Gurungs, Jariyas, Newars, Murmis, Kirats, Limbus, Lapchas, and Bhotiyas. Colonel Kirkpatrick * mentions also people called Nuggerkoties and Hawoos, of whom I have not heard. All these tribes he calls Hindus of the meanest cast; but on what foundation, unless that they are Pagans, and neither Christians nor Muhammedans, I do not know.

The Magars, called Mungurs by Colonel Kirkpatrick, occupied a great proportion of the lower hills in the western parts,

* Nepaul, pp. 184 and 281.

seem to have received the Rajput chiefs with much cordiality, and have now adopted a great part of the ferocious customs of these mountain Hindus. They eat copiously the flesh of hogs, goats, sheep, ducks, and fowls, but now abstain from beef. They are much addicted to intoxication, and are excessively cruel and treacherous; but they are men of great bodily vigour and mental activity. They have, in general, submitted to the guidance of the same Brahmans and Sannyasis that instruct the Rajputs; but formerly had priests of their own tribe called Damis, and seemed to have worshipped chiefly ghosts. They marry only one wife.

The family of Gorkha which now governs Nepal, although it pretends to come from Chitaur, according to Sadu Ram, a good authority, is, in reality, of the Magar tribe; and, at any rate, these people are now firmly attached to its interests, by having largely shared in the sweets of conquest; and by far the greatest part of the regular troops of that family is composed of this nation. Colonel Kirkpatrick * has given a short vocabulary of its language, which has no affinity to the Parbatiya or Sangskrita. In the vocabulary which I have deposited in the Company's library, will be seen a more full specimen of the Magar language, which now, at least, is written in the Nagri character. By many of the soldiery, owing to their frequent absence from home, for the purpose of attending at court, it has been entirely forgotten. In a short time, therefore, it is highly probable that this people may unite with the mountain Hindus, and be considered as one of their casts. When I was at Kathmandu, indeed, I found that many people were then of this opinion; and Colonel Kirkpatrick † in-

* Nepaul, pp. 249—252.

† Nepaul, p. 123.

cludes them among the Kshatriya or military cast. But hitherto the tribe has been so powerful, that many people in the west speak its language although they do not belong to it; and by far the greatest number adhere to the original impurity of life which their ancestors embraced. Before the arrival of the Rajputs, it is said, that this nation consisted of twelve Thums, or clans, the whole members of each being supposed to have a common extraction in the male line; and a man and woman of the same blood could not intermarry. Each Thum was governed by a chief, considered as the head of a common family.

Near the Magars was settled a numerous tribe named Gurung, whose wealth chiefly consisted in sheep, but whose manners are, in most respects, nearly the same with those of the Magars, except that, in the course of their pastoral life, they frequent the Alpine regions in summer, and return to the vallies in winter. The men also employ themselves in weaving blankets; but they are a tribe addicted to arms. A chief who pretended to be of the Hindu colony, and who was Raja of Kaski, having either settled where these Gurungs were the most predominant tribe, in the districts of Gangrong Postong and Argong, or being, in fact, of the Gurung tribe,—these people were strongly attached to his descendants, by whom they were not disturbed in their religious opinions or customs, and they continued to follow the doctrines of Sakya, as explained to them by Lamas of their own tribe, who were supposed qualified to give them instruction, and to direct their ceremonies. These persons are said never to have given themselves the trouble of studying the language of Thibet, and, therefore, were probably not very conversant in the doctrines of Sakya, which they professed to teach. The Gurungs remain in these parts in great numbers, and still adhere to the Lamas; nor do I hear that any of them have been admitted to the dignity of

Khasiya, although perhaps the Ghartis, above mentioned as belonging to that class of Hindus, may be of this race, as one part of the Ghartis, that still remains impure, is said to live among the Gurungs, and to have similar manners. There are, at any rate, several tribes of Gurungs, such as Nisi, Bhuji, Ghali, and Thagsi. The latter live nearest the snow; but all the Gurungs require a cold climate, and live much intermixed with the Bhotiyas on both sides of the snow-covered peaks of Emodus, and in the narrow vallies interposed, which, in the language of the country, are called Langna. The Gurungs cultivate with the hoe, and are diligent traders and miners. They convey their goods on sheep, of which they have numerous flocks.

The Jariyas formed a very numerous tribe, occupying much of the lower hilly region between the Kali and Nepal Proper, south from the Gurungs, and intermixed with the Magars. There can be little doubt that the Malebum family was of the Jariya tribe; but one of the chiefs having an only daughter, gave her in marriage to a Brahman, and from this source spring the families of Malebum, and its numerous collateral branches, with a large porportion of the Rajputs of this part of the country; although, where not of a chief's family, the offspring of a Brahman by a Sudra is reckoned a Khasiya. I have not heard that any of the Jariyas continue to be viewed as impure; and I think it probable, that they have all obtained the rank of Khas, although it is generally admitted, that they had a dialect peculiar to themselves; but of this I could procure no specimen.

The Khas Ranas, there is no doubt, were originally Magars; but whether the Thapas, Karkis, Majhis, Basnats, Bishtakos, and Kharkas, all now considered as Hindus of the Khas tribe, were branches of the Magar race, or Jariyas, or Gurungs, I cannot take upon myself to say. I can only observe, that, in this vicinity, I heard of no tribes but the Magars, Jariyas, and Gurungs, that spoke languages different from the Khas, and that there is no reason to suppose the Thapas, &c. to have come from Chitaur; although, on adopting the religion and laws of that country, they have also adopted its language, but many of them still speak the Magar tongue.

The more fertile part of what is called Nepal Proper, was chiefly occupied by the Newars, a race addicted to agriculture and commerce, and far more advanced in the arts than any other of the mountain tribes. Their style of building, and most of their other arts, appear to have been introduced from Thibet, and the greater part still adhere to the tenets of the Buddhs; but they have adopted the doctrine of cast, have rejected the Lamas, and have a priesthood of their own called Bangras. Their own chiefs, of a family called by the common title of Mal, at the time when conquered by the Raja of Gorkha, had divided into three branches, governing Kathmandu, Lalita, Patan, and Bhatgang. During the government of these chiefs a good many of the Newars had rejected the doctrine of Sakya, and adopted the worship of Siva, but without changing their manners, which are chiefly remarkable for a most extraordinary carelessness about the conduct of their women; neither have they adopted the Brahmans as their priests. Some of themselves, with the title of Achar, have assumed the manners and authority of the sacred order.

Thus the Newars, in point of religion, are divided into two sects. A very small portion has forsaken the doctrine of Buddha, while by far the most numerous class adhere to the doctrines taught by Sakya Singha.

Colonel Kirkpatrick * seems to think, that the worshippers

---

* Nepaul, pp. 149, 150.

of Buddha among the Newars, whom he calls Bahauras, (Bangras,) are only a trifling portion, "who have apostatized in a certain degree from the religious creed of their countrymen at some period subsequent to their conquest of Nepaul, or, at least, to have grafted upon it a considerable portion of the idolatry of Thibet." If this had been the case, we should have found the greater part of the Newars adhering to the Brahmans, which is not the case; and the portion which has adopted the doctrine of the Vedas, rejecting the sacred order of the Hindus, have the Achars as priests of their own. The probable cause of Colonel Kirkpatrick's supposing the followers of Buddha among the Newars to be small in number is explained by another passage, * where the Bangras are called Bhanras, and are stated to be a sort of separatists from the Newars, and to amount to about 5000. He does not seem to have been aware, that these were merely the priests of this sect, and that such a number in the priesthood implies a very large proportion of the sect.

The worshippers of Siva among the Newars in their religious opinions follow the doctrine of the Vedas, as explained by Sankara Acharya; but they do not receive the Brahmans as their Gurus, or instructors, and in spirituals are subordinate to a class of Newars, who are called Achars or Doctors, who are both their instructors (Gurus) and priests, (Purohits,) and who differ in birth and name only from the Brahmans.

Among the Shivamarg Newars, or those who worship Maha Deva, the Achars are considered as the highest cast; but their superiority is not acknowledged by those who worship Bouddha. They officiate as priests (Pujaris) in the temples of Siva and of the Saktis, and read the prayers (Mantras) that are ap-

* Nepaul, pp. 183, 184.

pointed to accompany sacrifices; but they do not kill the animal that is offered. The Achars have among them certain men who perform the ceremonies necessary to free from sin the souls of those who die on certain unfortunate days. This ceremony they call Hom. The Brahmans perform similar rites, which they call Pushkarasanti. The Hindus believe, that if this ceremony is neglected, all the relations of the deceased will perish. By this ceremony the officiating priest is supposed to take upon himself the sin of the departed soul; and if, in its performance, he commits any mistake, he incurs certain destruction from the wrath of the Deity. The office is therefore shunned by men of high rank, both as sinful and dangerous. The Achars who perform this ceremony are called Gulcul, and cannot intermarry with those of the first rank. This inferior order performs also any ceremonies that may be wanted by Newars, who are at a distance from home, and the purity of whose extraction cannot therefore be ascertained. Poor Achars cultivate the land with their own hands, from which they are not deterred by a fear of distressing the ox, as the plough is not used by the Newars. Their women spin and weave, which is the only point in which they seem to differ from the Brahmans; the two casts, however, consider themselves as entirely distinct.

Among the Newars, the Bangras, or Baryesu, are the head of the sect of Buddhmargas, and are much more numerous than the Achars. They are divided into two classes. The first are the Gubal Bangras, who are the instructors, (Gurus,) priests, (Purohits,) and philosophers, (Pandits,) of all the sect, and are priests (Pujaris) at the temples of Buddh, and of some of the Saktis. When they perform any ceremony, they wear a thread like the Brahmans or Achars. They neither eat nor intermarry with any person of inferior rank. The Bakali Bangras work in gold, silver, and copper, and are traders and cultivators. We may thus observe, that the doctrine of cast, and the nature of the priesthood, are essential differences between the religion of the Burmas and that professed by the followers of Buddh in Nepal. The doctrines of these people appeared so shockingly impious to my Brahman, that I could not induce him to converse on the subject with their learned men. These doctrines also are essentially different from those taught by the Rahans, or priests of Ava. The Bangras believe in a supreme being, called Sambhu, or Swayambhu, from whom have proceeded many Buddhs, or Intelligences, which, by the Tartars, are called Bourkans. Among these Matsyendranath has the chief superintendence over the affairs of the world. Under him are a great many Devatas, or spirits of vast power, among whom Brahma the creator, Vishnu the preserver, and Siva the destroyer of this earth, do not bear a very distinguished rank. These spirits are the Tengri of the Tartars, and the Nat of the Burmas, of which the worship is execrated by the followers of Buddha in Ava; but is eagerly followed by most of the Bangras, and still more so by the lower casts of Newars. Sakya Singha is considered one of the Buddhs, who came on earth to instruct man in the true worship, and in Nepal is commonly believed to be still alive at Lasa. His images entirely resemble those of Gautama. As this teacher has admitted the worship of all the Nat, or Devatas, among whom are placed the deities worshipped by the followers of the Vedas, we can readily account for the appearance of these in the temples of the Chinese. The followers of Buddh in Ava reject altogether the worship of these beings, so that, when I was in that country, and was unacquainted with the doctrines of any other sect of Buddhists, I was led into an erroneous opinion concerning the religion of the Chinese, from knowing that they worshipped the same Gods with the Brahmans. This, we see, is allowed by the doctrine of Sakya Singha, nor, on account of finding the images of Vishnu, Siva, or Brahma, in any temple, can we conclude, that it was not built by a follower of Buddh. In fact, even in Swayambhunath, the temple of the supreme deity of the Buddhists, there are a great many images of Siva.

A kind of mixed breed of Newars are, by the Sivamargas, acknowledged as of very high rank. I shall, therefore, mention them in this place, although their pretensions are disputed by the Bangras. They are called Jausi, and are the only cast that ought to practise medicine; but at present all ranks profess that art. The Jausis are descended from the offspring of a Brahman by a Newar woman; and if their mother has been a Bangra, or an Achar, they wear the thread, and act as instructors (Gurus) and priests (Purohits) for their brethren of mixed descent. These privileges are not allowed to such as are descended from low mothers. In imitation of their fathers, the Jausis are mostly Sivamargas; but in other matters, they follow the customs of the Newars.

The next in rank among the Newars are the Srishtas, who form a small cast. They can serve as cooks for all Newars, the Achars and Bangras excepted, which is a sure mark of their transcendent rank. The Buddhmargas and Shivamargas of this cast eat together; but a woman, for her first paramour, always chooses a person of her own persuasion. The highest rank of Srishtas are called Sira, and are mostly traders. A lower class, called Sual, act as porters; and a still lower, called Bagul, cultivate the ground. All these eat together; nor is the difference of class any restriction in their amours.

The persons of the remaining casts are almost entirely Buddhmargas; but, being low and ignorant, they will worship almost any thing that is called a God, which is, indeed, usual with all

Hindus of their rank. Some of our Seapoys, who were Brahmans, immediately on our arrival at Swayambhunath, took flowers and consecrated water, and went round the hill offering some to every image which they saw, and, among others, to that of Sakya Singha. I happened to be standing near it with Ramajaya, my Brahman, who asked them if they knew what they were doing, and informed them that they were worshipping Buddh. At this the poor fellows were much ashamed. However, an old Havildar (serjeant) comforted them, by observing, that, on the march to Bombay, under General Goddard, they had often seen this deity, and that their worshipping him seemed to have been very lucky, as the army had great success.

I shall enumerate the lower casts, according to their respective dignities.

The Jopu Newars were originally all cultivators; but some of them have now become traders and porters.

The Uda were all originally traders, and are nearly of the same rank with the Jopus.

The Bhat procure a living by proclaiming the titles of great men, and singing their praises on all public occasions,—a vanity in which the men of power in India take great delight. The Bhat also beg in the name of the Gods, which, among the Hindus, is always a profession of some dignity.

The three next casts, Got, Kurmi, and Now, are nearly of the same rank.

The Got are gardeners, and one of them, named Balabhadra, whom I employed as a collector of plants, repeatedly told me the following curious circumstances: He said that the Got do not acknowledge the Achars, or Bangras, as their instructors, (Gurus,) but have certain persons of their own cast, who, among their brethren, enjoy this privilege. At certain temples dedicated to Bhawani, which word means merely the Goddess, the Got attend to dance in masks; and, on these occasions, ten of them represent Singhini, Vyaghrini, Indrani, Bhairavi, Bhawani, Varahi, Vaishnavi, Kumari, Brahmani, and Ganesa, while four others represent Mahakal, Nandiswar, Vindhyiswar, and Nasadeva, who are the instructors (Gurus) of the other ten deities. From those who come to worship at the temple, the Got that represent these deities accept of spirituous liquors, which they drink out of human skulls till they become elevated, and dance in a furious manner, which is supposed to proceed from inspiration. In the same manner, they drink the blood of the animals which are offered as sacrifices. In these temples the priests (Pujaris) are Achars, who at the sacrifices read the forms of prayer (Mantras) proper for the occasion, but retire when the animal is about to be killed by the Got who represents Bhairavi. The shrine, in which the images of the gods are kept, is always shut, and no person is allowed to enter but the priest (Pujari) and the Gots, who personate in masks these deities. Once in twelve years the Raja offers a solemn sacrifice. It consists of two men, of such a rank that they wear a thread; of two buffaloes, two goats, two rams, two cocks, two ducks, and two fishes. The lower animals are first sacrificed in the outer part of the temple, and in the presence of the multitude their blood is drank by the masked Gots. After this, the human victims are intoxicated, and carried into the shrine, where the mask representing Bhairavi cuts their throats, and sprinkles their blood on the idols. Their skulls are then formed into cups, which serve the masks for drinking in their horrid rites. I questioned the man repeatedly on the subject, and he always related the circumstances without variation, and declared, that at the last sacrifice, which had been offered nine years previous to our arrival in Nepal, he had represented Bhairavi, and with his own hands had cut the throats of the human victims. My Brahman, however, inquired of several persons, who ought to have known the truth, and who denied altogether the human sacrifices at this ceremony, which is performed in the Ashtami in the month Aswin. All ranks of the natives of Nepal pay so very little attention to the observance of veracity, that I remain in suspense concerning this circumstance. Balabhadra was a mild attentive creature; and although he spoke of the human sacrifice with considerable glee, as being attended with copious potations of spirituous liquor, he was shocked when I asked him if two bulls made a part of the offering.

The Karmi are bricklayers and carpenters.

The Nau are barbers.

Next follow three casts of nearly the same rank.

Songat, or washermen.

Japu, or potmakers.

Hial, or Sial, who are cow-herds.

Nearly of the same rank are the persons, by the Newars called Dhui, but whom the Parbatiyas call Putaul. They are the persons who carry the palanquins of the Raja, and of his family. None but Bakali Bangras will condescend to act as instructors (Gurus) for a cast so low as this is.

All the casts yet enumerated are considered as pure, and Hindus of any rank may drink the water which they have drawn from a well; but the following casts are impure, and a person of any considerable dignity will be defiled by their touch.

The Salim are oil-makers, and weavers of garlands, at which art the Newars are very dexterous, and there is a great demand for their work, as both sexes, of all ranks in Nepal, ornament their hair with flowers.

The Kasulia are musicians, and have a vast variety of ear-rending instruments. The Hindu music, especially that of the martial kind, is said by the natives to be in great perfection in Nepal; and in this holy land are still to be found all the kinds that were to be found in the army of Rama.

Still lower than these are the Kasai, who are butchers, and palanquin bearers for the vulgar. The Chhipi, or dyers, are nearly of the same rank.

Lower again are the two following casts.

Kow, or ironsmiths.

Gotoo, or coppersmiths.

Then follow two military tribes.

Kosar, who are said originally to have been robbers.

Tepai, who can marry, or keep as concubines any Hindu women that have lost cast by eating unclean things.

Then follow three exceedingly low casts.

Puria, fishermen and basketmakers.

Bala, who remove offals and nastiness.

Chamkal, who are dressers of leather and shoemakers.

These casts can scarcely venture to draw near any other Hindu, but would consider themselves as much degraded, by eating, drinking, or cohabiting with a Musulman or Christian; and any of their women who should venture to commit an act of such uncleanness, would be severely punished, as would also be the infidel by whom she had been corrupted. This, however, does not prevent Hindu women of all ranks and casts from being sold as slaves to either Musulmans or Christians. A master or a parent has the power of selling his slave or child, whose consent is not asked, who thereby loses cast, and who has no alternative, but to adopt the religion of her new master. Such incongruities may astonish a person unacquainted with Hindus; and what may add to his surprise is, that, while at

Kathmandu, several Hindus, of high cast, among our followers, chose to embrace the Musulman faith, and thereby subjected themselves to severe restrictions and disgrace.

Musulmans have become pretty numerous, and are increasing, as they are zealous in purchasing girls, and in propagating their sect. Christianity has not been equally successful; and, on our arrival, we found the church reduced to an Italian Padre, and a native Portuguese, who had been inveigled from Patna by large promises, which were not made good, and who would have been happy to have been permitted to leave the country.

These are the various casts of Newars. I shall now give an account of the customs that are common to the whole nation.

All the Newars burn the dead; all eat buffaloes, sheep, goats, fowls, and ducks; and all drink spirituous liquors, to the use of which, indeed, they are excessively addicted. The highest of the Sivamargas kill animals with their own hands; but the higher orders of the Buddhmargs abstain from shedding blood, and from eating pork. They all live in towns or villages, and their houses are built of brick with clay mortar, and covered with tiles. These houses are three stories high, the ground floor being appropriated for the cattle and poultry, the second floor for servants, and the third for the family of the owner. This is in the houses of the wealthy. Among the poor, a number of families live under one roof. The rooms are exceeding low, as I could not stand upright in the principal apartment of what was reckoned the best house in Kathmandu, the palace excepted. At first sight, however, the houses look well, especially to a person coming from the towns of Hindustan. In Nepal, they have numerous large windows, which are shut by wooden lattices curiously carved, and which, in some measure, hang over the street, the upper end of the lattice projecting much more than the lower. Within, the houses are exceedingly mean and dirty, and swarm with vermin, which, added to all manner of filth, including the offals of the shambles, and the blood of sacrifices, that is allowed to corrupt in the streets, renders an abode in any of their towns utterly disgusting.

The following account of the Nepalese, or rather Newar, architecture, I have taken from papers communicated by Colonel Crawford.

The Nepalese possess a great advantage in having an excellent clay for making bricks and tiles; and their workmen are very expert. They use moulds nearly of the size and shape of our common bricks, and have also others for the bricks that are used in cornices and other ornaments. For the fronts and ornamental parts of their best houses, they make smooth glazed bricks, that are very handsome. Their bricklayers and masons are also good workmen, but labour under a great disadvantage, the want of lime. The tiles are flat, of an oblong form, and have two longitudinal grooves, one above and another below, which fit into the adjacent tiles, and the whole are put on with great neatness.

The houses of towns are in general three stories high, though some in the cities and large towns rise to four. The lower story has no windows, and the smoke of their kitchens comes out by the door, which renders the outside, even of their houses, very black and dirty. The windows of the second story are always small and nearly square. In each, a wooden trellis, which is highly ornamented by carving, but which cannot be opened and shut, admits the air and light, but prevents strangers from seeing into the apartment. The third or upper story has large windows, extending a great part of the length of each sitting apartment. Most of these windows have in front a wooden balcony composed of lattice work, in general much carved. This slopes outwards from a bench that is a little elevated from the floor, and joins the edge of the roof, which projects considerably beyond the wall. The bench is the favourite seat of the people, who, from thence, command a view of the street. The rooms are always narrow, the difficulty of carrying large timber from the mountains, perventing them from procuring beams of sufficient dimensions. The beams, which can be usually procured, are fir of about six inches square. These are placed at about a foot distant from each other, and their ends project beyond the walls, so that from the street you can tell the number of beams in each house. The larger houses are square, with an open court in the centre.

In the villages, the houses are built of unburnt bricks, and often also consist of three stories disposed of in the same manner as in towns; but the windows of the upper story are not provided with balconies. Those of two stories are also very common, and one of them is represented by Colonel Kirkpatrick in the plate opposite to page 160.

The temples are of two kinds. One, constructed of solid brick, and peculiar to the worshippers of Buddha, resembles the temples of the same sect in Ava. The other is common to the Bouddhists and followers of the Vedas, and has a strong resemblance to the temples of the Chinese. The temples of this kind are destined to contain idols, and are squares consisting of from two to five stories, each of which is of smaller dimensions than the one below, and the last ends in a point. Each story has a sloping roof, and in some fine temples, these roofs are covered with gilded copper. The lower story is surrounded by a rude wooden colonnade. From the corners, and sometimes all round the edges of these roofs, are suspended small bells with slender clappers, which are considerably longer than the bells, and end in a thin plate shaped like the ace of hearts, so that a strong wind occasions all the bells to ring. The roofs are supported by posts, which project from the middle of the upright wall to the edge of the slope, and are carved with all the distorted figures of Hindu mythology. In the larger temples, these posts on the second story are covered with planks, and on these are fastened all the various offerings that have been made to the Deity, and which form a strange and ridiculous assemblage of swords and shields, pots, pans, spinning-wheels, mugs, jars, buffaloes' horns, looking-glasses, knives, bracelets, &c. &c.

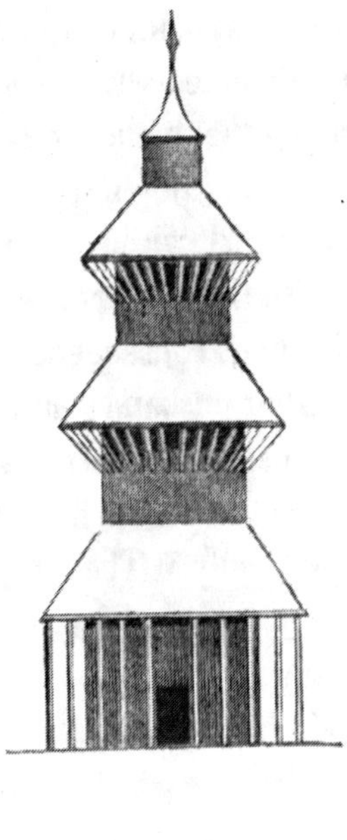

The view given by Colonel Kirkpatrick * of Kathmandu affords a good idea of the place, and shows the strong resemblance of its temples to those of Thibet and China. I cannot but therefore wonder, when he says, † "These edifices appeared to differ nothing in their figure or construction from

* Nepaul, p. 158. † Nepaul, p. 159.

the wooden Mundups, occasionally met with in other parts of India." I have never in India seen any such, either in structure or in materials, every considerable temple there being either of brick or stone.

The Newar women are never confined. At eight years of age, they are carried to a temple, and married, with the ceremonies usual among Hindus, to a fruit called Bel, (Ægle Marmelos, Roxb.) When a girl arrives at the age of puberty, her parents, with her consent, betroth her to some man of the same cast, and give her a dower, which becomes the property of the husband, or rather paramour. After this, the nuptials are celebrated with feasting, and some religious ceremonies. Among the higher casts, it is required that girls should be chaste till they have been thus betrothed; but in the lower casts, a girl, without scandal, may previously indulge any Hindu with her favours; and this licentiousness is considered a thing of no consequence. Whenever a woman pleases, she may leave her husband; and if, during her absence, she cohabit only with men of her own cast, or of a higher one, she may at any time return to her husband's house, and resume the command of his family. The only ceremony or intimation that is necessary, before she goes away, is her placing two betel-nuts on her bed. So long as a woman chooses to live with her husband, he cannot take another wife, until she becomes past child-bearing; but a man may take a second wife, when his first chooses to leave him, or when she grows old; and at all times he may keep as many concubines as he pleases. A widow cannot marry again; but she is not expected to burn herself; and may cohabit with any Hindu as a concubine. The children, by the betrothed wife, have a preference in succession to those by concubines; the latter, however, are entitled to some share. A man can be betrothed to no woman except one of his own cast; but he may keep a concubine of any cast, whose water he can drink. If the woman's cast be lower than his, the children are called Khas, and are considered as belonging to the cast of the mother, but are somewhat elevated on account of their father's birth.

A custom of the Newars, which was observed on the 11th of August by Colonel Crawford, deserves to be mentioned on account of its oddity. Each man on that day purchases a small quantity of boiled rice, mashed into a soft substance, and carries it to the field which he has cultivated. He then searches the field for frogs, and to every one that he can discover he gives a small portion of the boiled rice, at the same time uttering a prayer, and requesting the frog to watch over and protect his crop.

The Newars are a peaceable people, and not so much addicted to assassination as the Parbatiyas; but possess all the other vices of that barbarous race.

Colonel Kirkpatrick * doubts, whether the Newars have at any period been a warlike nation; but the long resistance which they made against Prithwi Narayan appears to me to indicate abundant courage, while his success seems to have been more owing to his cunning, and to his taking advantage of their internal dissensions, than to a superiority in the art of war.

One vile custom of the Newars of Kathmandu has been described by Colonel Crawford, from whose papers I have taken the following account. About the end of May, and beginning of June, for fifteen days, a skirmish takes place between the young men and boys, of the north and south ends of the city. During the first fourteen days it is chiefly con-

* Nepaul, p. 186.

fined to the boys or lads; but on the evening of the fifteenth day it becomes more serious. The opposing parties are drawn up in the broad, level, sandy bed of the river, which runs between the city and Swayambhunath. In the rear of each is a rising ground, which prevents either party from being hard pushed; for, the only weapons used being stones, the ascent gives such an advantage, that the pursuit of the victorious party is usually checked on their reaching the hill of their adversaries. The fight begins about an hour before sunset, and continues until darkness separate the combatants. In the one which we saw, four people were carried off much wounded, and almost every other year one or two men are killed: yet the combat is not instigated by hatred, nor do the accidents that happen occasion any rancour. Formerly, however, a most cruel practice existed. If any unfortunate fellow was taken prisoner, he was immediately dragged to the top of a particular eminence in the rear of his conquerors, who put him to death with buffalo bones. In remembrance of this custom, the bones are still brought to the field, but the barbarous use of them has for many years been abolished. The prisoners are now kept until the end of the combat, are carried home in triumph by the victors, and confined until morning, when they are liberated.

The origin of this custom is attributed to two causes. Some allege, that at one time Kathmandu was subject to two Rajas, and that the skirmishings first arose among their respective followers, and have ever since been continued. Others, with more probability, think that the combat is meant to commemorate a battle between a son of Maha Deva, and a Rakshas, or evil spirit. Colonel Crawford justly gives a preference to this opinion, for, if one of the parties obtain the victory, every thing favourable, seasonable rains, plentiful crops, and fine weather, is augured for the remainder of the year; the reverse is expected should the opposite party gain an advantage.

The territory anciently called Mithila, comprehending much of the northern parts of the district of Puraniya, and all those of Tirahut, belonged for many ages to a dynasty of princes called Janaka, who resided at Janakipur in the low country subject to Gorkha. Long afterwards, in that part of the country there had arisen a dynasty, the seat of whose government was at Garsamaran, through the extensive ruins of which, the present boundary between the Company and the Gorkhalese passes. In the year 1802, when in this vicinity, I heard an imperfect account concerning this dynasty, and have mentioned them in the observations on Nepal, which I then composed. Anxious to procure more accurate information, in 1810 I sent an intelligent Brahman to inquire after traditions, who discovered a person residing at Chotoni, whose ancestors had been registers of Tirahut, and who gave him the following account. In the year of the Bengal era 496, (A. D. 1089,) Nanyop Dev, of the Kshatria tribe, acquired the sovereignty of Tirahut, and was the founder of a dynasty, the princes of which succeeded from father to son in the following order.

Nanyopdev' governed - -	36 years.
Ganggadev' - -	14
Narasingha dev' - -	52
Ramsingha dev' - -	92
Sakrasingha dev' - -	12
Harisingha dev' - -	20
	226

This person had great power, and is universally acknowledged to have settled the customs which are now observed by the Brahmans of Mithila. After his death there was an interregnum of thirty-four years. The greatest difficulty in this succession arises from the two enormous reigns of fifty-two and ninety-two years held in succession by father and son. It is just possible that a grandfather and grandson might reign such a number of years, and the minute distinction of grandson and son may naturally enough have escaped the notice of a Hindu genealogist; but there is reason to suspect, that the accession of Nanyop dev is antedated, for the same authority states, that he took possession of Tirahut on the death of Lakshman Sen king of Bengal, who, it is well known, had conquered it in the 1104th year of our era, or twenty-five years after the accession given to Nanyop, and probably governed it for a good many years. On the death of that warlike prince, it is very likely that Nanyop may have wrested Tirahut, or the western parts of Mithila, from his successor, and may have been the Raja of Oriswa, against whom Laksham II. erected the works of Majurni Khata, for the learned D'Anville places an Oriswa in these parts. When the length of these reigns is thus curtailed, the story may be sufficiently exact.

The account of this dynasty given by Colonel Kirkpatrick* differs considerably from that which I have above stated. He makes Hari Singha (Hurr Sinha) the last king of Gar Samaram, and states, that he was driven from this to Nepal in 1323 by the Patan king Secunder Lodi; but, at that time, according to Dow's translation of Ferishta, Yeas ul deen Tuglick Shaw was the Muhammedan king of India; and the people of Mithila assert, that Hari Singha, their prince, died in quiet possession of

---

* Nepaul, p. 265.

his birthright. The predecessors of Hari Singha at Gar Samaran, according to Colonel Kirkpatrick, were,

Nan Dev, (Nanyop Dev',) who began to reign in the year Sambat 901, (A. D. 843.)
Kamuk Dev, (Gangga Dev'.)
Nersingh Dev, (Narasingha Dev'.)
Ramsing Dev, (Ram'Singha Dev'.)
Bhad Sing Dev.
Kurm Sing Dev.

Nan Dev, the founder of this dynasty, according to Colonel Kirkpatrick, was descended of Bamdeb of the Surijbunsi, (Suryabangsi,) princes of Oude, (Ayodhya;) but in the Pauranic lists of these princes I can find nothing like Bamdeb, unless it be Bhanu or Bhanuman, mentioned both in the Sri Bhagawata and Bangsa Lota among the later descendants of Ramachandra. The objections to this chronology are still stronger than to that which I received, in so much as it makes it commence still earlier.

There is, therefore, great room to doubt, whether in reality Nanyopdev was a Kshatriya. The Brahmans of Mithila, indeed, are totally unwilling to admit, that a person of any lower rank could have authority to settle their customs; but in Bengal a person of the medical tribe obtained this power; and the chiefs of the low tribe called Bhawar trace their origin to a Nanyopdev who brought the stud of the king of Dilli to pasture in the plains of Mithila, then entirely waste. Certain it is, that the Bhawars, about that time, extended their dominion over the Gorakhpur district as well as Tirahut, and that many petty chiefs of that tribe continued to occupy the parts adjacent to the hills until long after; and many of them continue to this day to be objects of worship among the low tribes. These may have been the descendants of collateral branches of the Raja's family, or of the chief officers of their government; and it must be remarked, that many of them assumed the title of Dev, as all the princes descended of Nanyop had done.

After the death of Hari Singha it is in Mithila generally admitted, that a Sivai Singha succeeded; and, although the Bhawars probably then formed the chief population of Gar Samaran and Tirahut, it is probable, as is asserted, that Sivai Singh was a military Brahman of the tribe called Aniwar. It is alleged by the people of Tirahut, that Sivai having had a dispute with a brother, this unnatural relation fled to Dilli, and, having procured an army from the Musulman king, he advanced towards Gar Samaran with an intention of dethroning his brother. Before he had reached the Gandaki, Sivai Singha, having heard of the approach of an army of men that eat beef, was seized with a panic, and after having reigned twenty-two years, resigned his kingdom to Kangkali, the tutelar deity of his capital city. He then dedicated his life to God, and, having assumed the character of a religious mendicant, he passed his days in wandering about the places which are esteemed holy.

It is said, that about this time the unnatural brother of Sivai Singha died, and that the Musulman army, after a fruitless attempt on Gar Samaran, were obliged to retreat, owing, as the Hindus suppose, to the powerful influence of the tutelar deity. The Musulmans, however, seem to have seized on all the country near the Ganges, which afterwards continued subject to them till the establishment of the Company's authority.

About the same time, the inhabitants deserted Gar Samaran, for what reason is not explained. They took with them the image of Kangkali, and retired with an intention of going to

Nepal. On the route they were in danger of perishing from hunger, when Kangkali appeared to one of their chiefs in a dream, and told him, that in the morning she would grant a supply of provisions, and that she gave them permission ever afterwards to use the kind of food which she was about to send. Accordingly, in the morning, a large herd of buffalos appeared, and were killed by the people, who ever since have indulged in that kind of food, which, according to the precepts of their religion, they had formerly considered unclean. They afterwards settled in the valley of Nepal, and are the people now called Newars.

From Dow's translation of Ferishta,* we learn, that Yeas ul deen Tuglick Shaw, king of Dilli, in the year of Christ 1322, on returning from an expedition into Bengal, was passing near the hills of Turhat, (Tirahut,) when the raja of these parts appearing in arms, was pursued into the woods. Having cut down these, the royal army arrived at a fort surrounded by a wall, and by seven ditches filled with water. After a siege of three weeks the place was taken, and the government of Turhat conferred upon Achmet Chan. That this is the same story with that contained in the traditions concerning Sivai Singha and Gar Samaran, I think there can be little doubt, and the Musulman chronology is that upon which most reliance can be placed. Some of the Hindu traditions make Sivai Singha the son of Hari Deva, others make him of another family which succeeded after an anarchy of 34 years; but in both cases the period between 1315, the supposed era of Hari Deva's death, and 1322, the time of Gar Samaran's capture, is too short, and the difference between it and the actual time has probably been added, to make up part of the

* Vol. I. p. 311.

enormous reigns of Narasingha and Ramsingha. At any rate, if the people of Garsamaran retired to Nepal, and became the Newars, the 1322 (or 1323, as Colonel Kirkpatrick has it,) * is the most probable date of the event. There is nothing improbable in the circumstance, and the doctrine of cast prevailing among the Newars is a strong confirmation of their having come from Hindustan.

It must, however, be confessed, that the Newars themselves totally deny this origin, and allege, that the only foundation for it is the resemblance between the names Newar and Aniwar. They consider themselves as the aboriginal inhabitants of the country which they now occupy, and their houses have a great resemblance to those of the Bhotiyas, or people of Thibet, as described by Captain Turner, while in many points their customs resemble those of the other tribes of the Chinese race. It must be, however, observed, that their features are not clearly marked as of that origin, and that many of them have high features, large eyes, and oval faces; but considering the manners of their women, little reliance can be put on this mark, and the truth will be best discovered by an examination of their language, of which I have deposited a copious vocabulary in the Company's library. I think, indeed, that I can trace many coincidences between it and the language of the Murmis, a tribe undoubtedly of the Chinese race, and it appears to me radically different from the Hindwi language, although religion has no doubt introduced some Sangskrita words.

A short vocabulary of this language has been given by Colonel Kirkpatrick, † and may perhaps suffice to decide the language to which it has the greatest affinity. The

---

* Nepaul, p. 265.

† Ib. p. 221—49.

character in which it is written is evidently derived from the Nagri of India, and will be found opposite to page 220 in Colonel Kirkpatrick's Account of Nepaul.

In treating of the Newars, Colonel Kirkpatrick observes,* "That this people differ essentially, so as to prove abundantly that they are an insulated race of men, whose origin is not to be traced to any of the nations immediately surrounding them." Now, if they came from Samaran, as he supposes, they must have been Hindus; and, if they are descendants of Thibetians, intermixed with Hindus, as I suppose, still their origin is to be derived from the nations immediately contiguous. He goes on to observe, "That the Newars are of a middle size, with broad shoulders and chest, very stout limbs, round and rather flat faces, small eyes, low and somewhat spreading noses; yet he cannot agree with those who affirm, that there is in the general physiognomy of these people any striking resemblance to the Chinese features." For my part, I do not well know in what other terms the Chinese features could be better defined, than in the description of the Newars thus given by Colonel Kirkpatrick; and, for a confirmation of a considerable resemblance between the two people, I may refer to the figures given by this author opposite to pages 185 and 187, which, although called merely natives of Nepal, represent in fact Newars. In reality, if the morals of the Newar women had been more strict, I believe that the resemblance between the Chinese or Thibetians and Newars would have been complete; but since the conquest, the approach to Hindu countenance is rapidly on the increase, women in most cases giving a decided preference to rank, especially if connected with arms or religion. Until the conquest, there was

* Nepaul, p. 186.

probably little intermixture, except in the descendants of the governing family, which probably was of a mixed breed between a Thibetian lady and a raja of Banaras, as will be afterwards mentioned; and this family had, I believe, multiplied exceedingly, and composed a numerous and warlike gentry, which, of course, contributed largely to the propagation of the nation.

The assumption of the military dignity, and of the thread, one of its badges among the Hindus, and the title Rajput given to all the chiefs of the mountaineers, seems to have induced Colonel Kirkpatrick to suppose, that the Kshatriya tribe of India formed a large portion of the inhabitants in Nepal. Yet he had with accuracy observed,* that the progeny of a Newar female and one of these Kshatriyas may almost be taken for a Malay, that is, a mixed breed between people of a Chinese race with Hindus and Arabs; and farther, he accurately noticed, that illegitimate persons of the reigning family by Newar women, although he supposes their fathers to have been Rajputs, approach nearer than their mothers to the Tartars or Chinese. The reason of this, I would say, is, that the royal family are in fact Magars, a Thibetian race.

In the more rude and mountainous parts of Nepal Proper, the chief population consisted of these Murmis, who are by many considered as a branch of the Bhotiyas, or people of Thibet; but, although in religion and doctrine they followed the example of that people, and all their priests, called Lamas, studied its language and science, yet it seems doubtful, whether the two nations had a common origin; but this will be best ascertained by a comparison of the languages. For this purpose I have deposited in the Company's library a copious vocabulary of the Murmi dialect. The doctrine of the Lamas

---

* Nepaul, p. 186.

is so obnoxious to the Gorkhalese, that, under pretence of their being thieves, no Murmi is permitted to enter the valley where Kathmandu stands, and by way of ridicule, they are called Siyena Bhotiyas, or Bhotiyas who eat carrion; for these people have such an appetite for beef, that they cannot abstain from the oxen that die a natural death, as they are not now permitted to murder the sacred animal. They have, therefore, since the conquest, retired as much as possible into places very difficult of access; and before the overthrow of Sikim a great many retired to that country, but there they have not escaped from the power of the Gorkhalese, and have been obliged to disperse even from that distant retreat, as they were supposed too much inclined to favour its infidel chief. They never seem to have had any share in the government, nor to have been addicted to arms, but always followed the profession of agriculture, or carried loads for the Newars, being a people uncommonly robust. Their buildings are thatched huts, often supported on stages, like those of the farther India.

The Kiratas, or Kichaks, have been already mentioned as occupying the country east from Nepal Proper. They seem always to have been a warlike and enterprising people, but very rude, although not so illiterate as many of their neighbours. The Lamas have made great progress in persuading them to adopt their doctrines; and the Lamas, who gave them instruction, were skilled in the language of Thibet; but many adhered to their old customs, and the old priesthood continued to perform the ceremonies of all. The Rajputs, on obtaining power, induced many to abandon part of their impure practices, and to employ Brahmans to perform their ceremonies; but in general this compliance was only shown when they were at court. The abstinence from beef, which the Gorkhalese enforce, is exceedingly disagreeable to the Kirats; and, although the Lamas have been banished, this people still retain a high respect for their memory, and a longing after the flesh-pots. Agam Singha, the chief of the nation, now in exile, told me plainly, that, although he received a Brahman as an instructor, it was only because he could not procure a Lama, and that he considered the chief Lamas as incarnations of God.

The Kirats, being vigorous beef-eaters, did not readily submit to the Rajputs. Previous to the invasion of these Hindus they had, it is true, been compelled to retire to the hills; but there, until the vast power acquired by the family of Gorkha, they retained, as I have already mentioned, a great degree of independence.

I have deposited in the Company's library a full vocabulary of the Kirata language. They are said to have had a written character peculiar to themselves; but Agam Singha, their chief, is no penman, and the people with him, born in exile, have contented themselves with acquiring the Nagri character. The Kirats are allowed to marry several wives, and to keep concubines. Their property is divided equally among their sons by wives; but the sons by concubines are allowed a share, though smaller than that given to the offspring of a virgin spouse.

Among the Kirats was settled a tribe called Limbu, the manners of which were very nearly the same, and, indeed, the tribes intermarry; but their languages are said to be different, and it would not appear that the Lamas had made any progress in converting the Limbus. Since the overthrow of the Kirats, and since the reluctance with which they submit to the Gorkhalese has become evident, it has been the policy of the court of Kathmandu to show a decided preference to the Limbus, who have not been disgusted by the loss of power which they never possessed, nor by the banishment of their priests. They are not, however, reconciled to the loss of beef; but are certainly less discontented than any other neighbouring tribe. Their profession is that of agriculture, and they live in huts. I was unable to procure any vocabulary of their language, but Colonel Kirkpatrick * gives a short list of the words of the Limbu tongue, which he calls Limboos. It has no affinity to the Sangskrita.

Another considerable tribe of Nepal, taken in its most extended sense, are the Lapchas, who occupy the country between the Kankayi and Tista, and from that of the Kiratas; but by most Hindus they are included under this odious name. Their manners were very nearly the same with those of the Kirats. The Lapchas are a set of vigorous barbarians, about one half of whom had been deluded by the monkish austerities, and superior learning of the Lamas.

The Lapchas ate beef, pork, and every other thing reckoned abominable, and drank strong liquors without shame. Their women did not marry until after they had arrived at the age of maturity, and had become sensible to the assiduities of courtship. The Lapchas were chiefly armed with swords and bows, with which they shot poisoned arrows. Spears were not in use, being ill fitted for a mountainous country, thickly overgrown with wood, and where men cannot charge in compact order. They had a few muskets, but too large to be fired from the shoulder. They were tied to a tree, and fired by a match.

It must be observed, that the inhabitants of both Thibet, and of what we call Bhotan or Bootan, are by the natives of India called Bhotiyas, and their countries Bhotan or Bhot.

---

* Nepaul, pp. 249—252.

Some of these people, who inhabit near Kathmandu, call themselves Sayn; and the same name name is given by the Newars to the whole nation. Thibet, I am inclined to believe, is a Persian word, totally unknown to the natives. At Kathmandu I had a patient who had been chief of a territory north from Lassa, and who had been dispossessed by the Chinese; and, so far as I could learn from him, the native appellation, at least of the territory subject to Lassa, is Borka, from whence Bhotiya is perhaps a corruption; but I could not ascertain any general name for the countries which we call Thibet. These, however, and also Bhotan, are inhabited by kindred tribes of people, who resemble each other strongly in features, complexion, language, and manners. In the plate opposite to page 40 of Kirkpatrick's Nepaul, are well represented, in a sitting posture, two persons of this nation, although, by some mistake, probably in the publisher, they are called natives of Nepal.

The Lamas are the priests of the sect of Bouddh, in Thibet and the adjacent territories, and are monks, who have nominally at least forsaken the pleasures of the world. They totally reject the doctrine of cast, and a person of any nation may be admitted into the order. The whole, at least of those at a distance, consider themselves as under the authority of Sakya Gomba, who came from India about the time of Jesus Christ, and has ever since resided at Lassa, where he remains in perpetual youth. On this account he is not considered as an incarnation, (Avatar.) There are, however, many personages of this sect who are considered as incarnations of different Budhs, or persons who have obtained divinity. These enter into the bodies of children, and inspire them through life; and when the body dies, the deity enters into another. Of this nature is the Dharma Raja, or spiritual chief of what we call Bhotan; and still more celebrated is the Tishu Lama, who resides at Degarchi, and is the spiritual guide of the Chinese emperors. This class of supposed deities seems to be pretty numerous, as, in the territory of the Lapcha and Kirats, their number would appear to have been at least twelve, as so many were known to my informant, who was only well acquainted with the former territory. The ordinary lamas pretend only to be saints. The best account I have seen of their doctrine is that given by the learned Pallas, which is much more complete than any I could procure in Nepal. The followers of Buddh have had five great lawgivers, and a sixth is daily expected. As each of these is supposed to have been an incarnation of a Buddh or Bourkan, and as all have been usually taken as one person, we may readily account for the difference that prevails in the opinions concerning the era when this sect arose. Gautama is the fourth of those lawgivers, and his doctrine alone is received by the priests of Ava, who reject the fifth as a heretic; but by the Bouddhists of Nepal, Thibet, Tartary, and China, he is named Sakya. Gautama, according to the best authorities, lived in the sixth century before the Christian era, and Sakya in the first century after the birth of our Lord.

Although there is no distinction of cast among the Sayu or Bhotiyas, yet they are not without differences in religious opinions; for some of them in Nepal worship at Swayambhunath, while others prefer a temple of Bouddhama, which is situated near Pasupanath. The doctrine of Sakya Singha differs most essentially from that of Gautama. The Bhotiyas, following the former, worship all the spirits, that by the Burmas are called Nat, a practice which is held in abhorrence by the Rahans of Ava. They also consider the Buddhs as emanations from a supreme deity, view many of their Lamas as incarnations of a

Buddh, and accordingly worship them as living Gods, although they do not consider them as equal to Sakya, who is the Lama of Lassa. There is among the Lamas no prohibition against the laity from studying any character or any book; but they must have wonderfully degraded the human understanding, when they can induce the people to swallow the belief in the deities living among them. It is true, that these are in all probability very much secluded, and rarely shown to the vulgar, except at a very great distance, and in obscurity; but still this seems to be nearly the utmost height of human imbecility.

The belief of Sakya having lived among them since about the commencement of the Christian era, is probably confined to Nepal, and other remote parts, where no means of knowing the contrary exists. Such an absurdity could scarcely pass among actual observers, however degraded in understanding, and in Thibet the Lama of Lassa is probably considered as merely an incarnation of Sakya.

Besides the countries which we call Thibet and Bootan, the Bhotiyas occupy, every where between the Kali and the Tista, the Alpine region adjacent to the snowy peaks of Emodus, on both sides of that chief of mountains, where none of the highland tribes above mentioned can endure the cold of winter any more than the Bhotiyas can suffer the moderate summer heats of Kathmandu. This induces me to think, that the present highland tribes, although of the same race with the people of Thibet, had originally occupied the plains, and, on the invasion of the present Hindus, had retired to the mountains, so far as they considered the temperature of the air tolerable, just as a colony of Hindus had retired to the same quarter, to avoid Mohammedan intolerance. In a region so extended, as that occupied by the Bhotiya nation, it is probable, that there exists a great variety of custom and dialect, for I heard of many different kinds, even among those who inhabit the southern face of Emodus; but the accounts given by people of different tribes and languages, differed so much, that I can say nothing satisfactory on the subject, especially as the season, when I resided on the frontier, was totally insufferable to a Bhotiya, so that I had no opportunity of conversing with them; the Lama from whom I received an account of the Lapchas being by birth a Murmi.

I have already said that the Murmis are by many considered as a kind of Bhotiyas, but this the Lama denied, and the languages seem to have little affinity. I heard, besides, of Khat, Sirmi, and Kutung or Kutiya Bhotiyas, but cannot venture to speak of the nature of these distinctions, farther than to state, that the Khat Bhotiyas are mentioned by Colonel Kirkpatrick * as having long governed Nepal before the Newars, and as at this time occupying the lower parts of Bhotan, (Kachar,) on which subject I have already given my opinion. The resemblance to be traced between the Newar and Murmi languages, induces me to suppose that these two tribes are originally the same, and the historical hints given by Colonel Kirkpatrick induce me to draw the conclusion, that the Newars are Khat Bhotiyas, who have adopted some new customs in consequence of a greater connection with the Hindus. I never, indeed, heard the Murmis and Khat Bhotiyas mentioned as the same; but the former I have often heard named Siyena Bhotiyas, which is very likely to be another appellation for the Khat Bhotiyas, one name implying wild or forest Bhotiyas, and the other implying Bhotiyas who eat carrion like jackalls.

---

* Nepaul, p. 148.

The Bhotiyas, at least the greater part of those in Thibet, neglect agriculture, and, like the Dasnami Sannyasis of Puraniya, chiefly pursue commerce and a life of monkish austerity, but occasionally they wield the sword; and the principal support of the country is in its mines, and its numerous and various herds of cattle. The quantity of grain is said to be very inconsiderable, and both it and the herds of cattle are probably reared by some inferior tribe; but on this subject I have not yet had sufficient information. I have only learned, that the highest and proper Bhotiyas confine their attention entirely to religion, commerce, and arms, and it is in the first alone that they have had much success.

One circumstance relative to the Bhotiyas is remarkable, and seems to me to decide a matter that has long been agitated concerning the natural history of man. All those that I have seen at Kathmandu, not only from the territory of Gorkha, but from Mostong, Kuti, Lasa, and Degarchi, are as black as the natives of Canton or Ava. Climate is not, therefore, able to change the colour of a nation; but it seems to have a greater effect on the temperament. Cold can produce a change of temperament from the melancholic and choleric to the phlegmatic and sanguine, and heat acting on the human frame, is capable of producing a contrary revolution. Hence, rosy cheeks and lips are frequently observed among the mountain Hindus of Nepal, although they are very little fairer than those of Madras.

Such are the principal tribes that occupy the mountains subject to the dominion of Nepal, or rather of Gorkha. In the plains adjacent to the mountains, and subject to the same prince, are several other tribes; but it is my intention to treat of them when I describe the Company's provinces, where the greater part of these tribes is now found.

CHAPTER SECOND.

NATURE OF THE COUNTRY.

Division into four Regions from their relative elevation.—First, or Plain Region, or Tariyani.—Soil.—Productions, Animal and Vegetable.—Cultivation.—Climate.—Rivers.—Second, or Hilly Region—Productions.—Minerals.—Forests.—Birds.—Vallies called Dun.—Cultivation.—Climate.—Third, or Mountainous Region.—Elevation.—Climate.—Diseases.—Cultivation.—Pasture.—Sheep and Cattle.—Minerals.—Spontaneous Vegetables.—Extent.—Fourth, or Alpine Region.—Vallies.—Mountains.—Productions, Mineral, Animal, and Vegetable.

I SHALL next proceed to give a general view of the appearance, soil, climate, and productions of the country, and for this purpose I must divide it into four stages of elevation. My actaul observations are confined to the three lower of these, and I have seen these only in the vicinity of the capital. What I say concerning the highest region is, therefore, entirely from report, and what I mention concerning the others, so far as I write from actual observation, is strictly applicable only to the parts near the capital; but inquiries have enabled me to judge, that a great similarity prevails over the whole territory, and whatever differences have come to my knowledge shall be mentioned either in this part, or when I come to treat of the different principalities, which have now been subjected to the chief of Gorkha.

The lowest region is a part of the great plain of Hindustan. In a few places the Company's territory extends to the foot of the mountains which bound the great plain on the north, which are called Himadri, Himachul, Himalichul, or Himaliya, and which form the Emodus of the ancients: But in most parts the dominions of Gorkha extend about twenty miles into the plain, and it seems in general to have been the policy of the princes of India to allow the mountain chiefs, even when very petty, to retain at least this extent of the low country, as being too obnoxious to their incursions to be of a value adequate to defray the expense of its defence. At times, some of the mountain tribes, which had acquired power, have been able to extend their authority over the plains much farther, and as none of them have ever equalled in power the chiefs of Gorkha, these have for some time been eager in taking every opportunity of encroachment; but although powerful, they have been opposed by a force vastly more formidable than was ever before known in India, and this has checked their power, which might have been very formidable to an undisciplined state however extensive.

This low region is called Tariyani, Tarai, or Ketoni, and, as I have said, is, in general, about twenty miles in width. In this space there are a few scattered small hills, and much poor high land overgrown with trees and bushes of little value; but there is, also, a very large proportion of rich land, and on the whole the soil is much better than in the adjacent parts of the Company's territory.

I do not intend here to enter into a detailed account of its productions; because they are nearly the same with those of the Company's adjacent territory, of which it is my intention to give hereafter a full account, only being less cultivated, there are in the Tariyani more wild beasts, especially elephants and rhinoceroses. The breed of the former is considered as uncommonly bad, and it has been lately remarked to me by Mr Venour, the surgeon at Puraniya, that every one of them has a toe of some one of its feet very much lengthened, which gives the foot an unseemly appearance. So far as I have been able to observe since, the remark of Mr Venour is accurate; but the number of elephants of this kind that I have seen is not great. In the dry season the elephants retire to the lower ranges of hills; but in the rainy season they abandon these forests, and are then very destructive to the crops, which, indeed, prevents the natives from being so attentive to the cultivation of rice as they otherwise would be, so that, although the country is best adapted for the culture of this grain, the farmers content themselves chiefly with winter crops of wheat, barley, and mustard. The Raja reserves to himself the sole right of catching the elephants, and annually procures a considerable number. They are sold on his account at 200 Mohurs, or 86 rupees, for every cubit of their height; but five cubits of the royal measure are only six English feet. As few merchants are willing to give this price for elephants which have not been seasoned, the Raja generally forces them on such persons as have claims on the court, who sell their elephants in the best manner they can. Tigers are not so numerous as might have been expected in a country so uncultivated. Black bears of a great size are more numerous, and are very troublesome. Wild hogs, hog-deer, hares, foxes, and jackalls, are to be found in abundance.

In the waste lands of the Tariyani, the most common trees are the *Palas*, (*Erythina monosperma*, Lamarck,) and the *Simul*, (*Bombax heptaphyllum*, Lamarck;) but by far the greater part of these wastes is covered with long grass or reeds, which once a year are burned, in order to keep the country clear, and to improve the pasture. Owing to the moisture and coolness of the air, the fields, at all seasons, preserve some verdure, but the grass seems to be of a very bad quality, as the cattle, although abundantly supplied with it, are to the last degree wretched; still, however, in the heats of spring, very large herds are sent from the Company's provinces to these wastes. In these, also, there grows a great quantity of the species of *Ischæmum* called *Sabe*, of which ropes are made, and of which a good deal is exported to the territory of the Company.

Before the conquest by the Nepalese, the petty Rajas, who governed its different portions, were so much afraid of their neighbours, that they did not promote the cultivation of this low land. They rather encouraged extensive woods, and contented themselves, in a great measure, with the produce of the forests in timber, elephants, and pasture; even then, however, many rich spots were occupied, and very productive; but they were so buried in the forests as to be little observable. The Gorkhalese, being more confident, have cleared much of the country, although still a great deal remains to be done. Even now they export a considerable quantity of grain; and, were property somewhat more secure, this territory is capable of yielding considerable resources. Its tobacco is said to be uncommonly good, and the reddish cotton wool is said to be very thriving.

In the annexed register of the weather, the state of the atmosphere, during the two months stay which I made in the country, will be seen. The climate is considerably cooler and moister than that in the vicinity of Patna; and the hot winds, according to report, are almost a month later in commencing, than they are at that city. Our residence in the Tariyani was at the most favourable season; but about the time (1st April) at which we advanced towards Nepal, the country becomes very unhealthy, good water for drinking becomes very scarce, and, till the cold season, the people are very subject to fevers and disorders in the bowels, which by the natives of Nepal are attributed to the Ayul, or a poisonous air, which many of them imagine proceeds from the breath of large serpents, supposed to inhabit the forests of the northern mountains. The existence of such serpents in any considerable number, is very doubtful, and rational men assign a more natural origin to the Ayul or bad air. They say, that the ground in the forests, during spring, is covered with fallen leaves, which are rotted by the first rains of the hot season, and, by their putrefaction, corrupt the air. They accordingly allege, that the climate continues healthy, until the first rain after the commencement of the hot season, after which the unhealthy season begins, and continues until the cold weather, although it abates considerably of its virulence with the heavy rains which happen after the solstice.

The Tariyani is intersected by numerous small rivers, which not only serve for watering the crops in the latter end of the dry season; but, when they are swollen by rain, become navigable, and enable the farmer to send the produce of his fields to a good market. These rivers also serve to float down the valuable timber that abounds in the forests, by which the hills are skirted. The term Tariyani, indeed implies the country's being navigable.

Fish are found in abundance in the rivers of the Tariyani; and the mullet, which I call Mugil Corsula, and the carp, which I call Cyprinus Rohita, are of an excellent quality.

Bounding the above mentioned plain on the north, is a region of nearly the same width. It consists of small hills, rising, however, gradually towards the north, and watered by many small rivers, which spring from the southern faces of the first lofty mountains, to which these hills gradually unite.

The channels of these rivers or torrents, even when they have no communication with the high mountains, are filled with fragments of granite and shistose mica; but the hills themselves are in general composed of clay, intermixed with various proportions of sand, mica, and gravel. This mixture contains many masses of rock, and is disposed in strata, that are either horizontal, or dip towards the north with an angle less than 25 degrees. In many places, these heterogeneous materials have been indurated into stone of considerable hardness. But besides those, I observed many rocks in these hills, especially in deep vallies, where they were disposed in vertical strata, running easterly and westerly, and consisting of limestone, hornstone, and aggregates, usually called primitive. These parts abound in incrustations, formed by the deposition of calcareous matter; but I have not been able to hear of the exuviæ of marine animals, except such as are washed down by the Gandaki, and are loose in its channel. The calcareous matter has either formed itself in crusts, covering the surface of rocks, or has assumed the form of the mosses, lichens, and other such plants, that it has covered.

On the bank of the Kosi, near Varaha Chhatra, is found a singular black ferruginous earth, of which the elephant is said to eat greedily, when indisposed; and the natives use it, rubbed with a little water, to supply the place of ink.

The lower part of these hills, and some of the adjacent

plains, are the grand seat of the Sal * forests, among which are many trees of the species of *Dalbergia*, called *Sisau*,† and of the *Cedrella*, which at Calcutta, is called *Tungd*, (*toon* of the English,) but which in the forests adjacent to Puraniya, is called *Chilli kath*. Higher up, the hills are covered with a vast variety of trees, nearly resembling those of *Goyalpara*, of which I intend hereafter to give an account; but in the hills of the North, there are many pines (*Pinus longifolia,*) which the mountain Hindus call *Salla*,‡ and an abundance of the *Mimosa* (*Khoira,*) of which catechu is made. A great many people are employed in preparing this drug. A few of them belong to the company's territory, but by far the greater part are the subjects of Gorkha. Each man pays a duty to the Raja, of from three to five rupees, and during the fair season makes from eight to ten *mans* of the Calcutta weight, which is nearly 82 lbs. The merchants, who advance money for subsistence, usually give the workman four rupees a *man*, that is, from 32 to 40 rupees for six months work; but from this the tax must be deducted. The greater part is sent to Patna and Banaras.

In these woods, a vast number of these kinds of birds which are tamed by the natives on account of their singing or imitating the human voice, form their nests, which are considered as the property of the Raja. These birds are,

Mayna, Gracula religiosa, Latham.

Amrita chela.

---

* Saul, Kirkpatrick's Nepaul, pp. 17 and 35, Shorea robusta, Roxb.

† Sissoo, Kirkpatrick's Nepaul, pp. 17 and 35.

‡ Sulla, Surreen dhool, and Dhoobke, Kirkpatrick's Nepaul, pp. 33 and 43.

Madna } Two parakeets nearly allied to the Psittacus gin-
Kajla, } gianus of Latham.

Tetiya, Psittaca torquata, Brisson.

Chandana, a parakeet not described by Latham.

Sugi, Psittacus gingianus, Latham.

Latkan, a small short-tailed parakeet, nearly allied to the Psittacus galgulus.

The right of taking the young birds from the nest is farmed to men, who again employ people to climb the trees, when the birds are first fledged. These people keep the birds for two months, and then deliver one half to the renter, and take the remainder to themselves. Petty dealers come from the low country, purchase the birds, and disperse them through Bengal.

In several places, these low hills are separated from the high mountains by fine vallies of a considerable length, but a good deal elevated above the plain of Hindustan. In the country west from the Ganges, these vallies are called by the generic name Dun, analogous to the Scottish word Strath; but towards the east, the word Dun is unknown, nor did I hear of any generic term used there for such vallies, although there are very fine ones in that part of the country.

These Duns or Straths are tolerably cultivated by the same tribes that dwell in the great plain of Hindustan. But among the spurs and ridges of these hills, there are many narrow vallies, or what in Scotland would be called Glens, and both these, although their soil is rich, and the surrounding hills, are almost totally neglected. A few straggling villages are however scattered through the woods, especially in the higher parts, and their inhabitants cultivate cotton, rice, and other articles, with the hoe, after having cleared away parts of the forest, as practised by the Garos of Ranggapur. The chief reason of the desert state of this part of the country, seems to be its extreme unhealthiness, and this again, in a great measure, in all probability, depends on the want of cultivation; for Vijaypur Chatra and some other places, that must be included in this division, are abundantly healthy, having been well cleared.

Some estimate of the temperature of this region may be formed from the heat of a spring at Bichhakor, having, in the end of March, been found 74° of Fahrenheit's scale, the latitude being 27° 16′ N.

On arriving at what may be called the mountains, though they are not separated from the low hills by any distinct boundary, we have a very elevated region, consisting of one mountain heaped on another, and rising to a great height, so that, when any fall happens in winter, their tops are for a short time covered with snow. The inhabited vallies between these are in general very narrow, and are of very various degrees of elevation, probably from 3000 to 6000 feet of perpendicular height above the plains of Puraniya. Of course, they differ very much in their temperature; so that some of them abound in the ratan and bamboo, both of enormous dimension, while others produce only oaks and pines. Some ripen the pine-apple and sugar-cane, while others produce only barley, millet, and other grains.

Some estimate of the climate of this region may be formed by means of the accompanying register of the weather kept near Kathmandu, although it is very imperfect, from that want of convenience which must attend travellers in so remote a country. The winter we passed in Nepal, was reckoned uncommonly mild; and in place of the rain, which we had at that season, in most years snow falls at Kathmandu. A more accurate estimate of the average heat of the valley may be obtained from that of its springs, which by repeated trials at a fine spring nearly on a level with Kathmandu, I found to be 64° of Fahrenheit's thermometer; but in a spring near Thankot, the heat in April was $59\frac{1}{2}$°; in one at Chitlong it was a degree lower; and at Bhimphedi, on the skirts of the lower hills, it was 63°. This cold, so uncommon in the latitude of between 27° 30′, and 26° 41′, must be attributed to the great elevation of the country, for the neighbourhood of the snowy peaks of Emodus could produce little effect, as the winds were very seldom from that quarter. We have no data upon which we can calculate the height of the valley of Nepal with any considerable accuracy. The nearest approach I can make to it, is by the difference of the average height of the barometer observed during the month of February 1802, in the Tariyani, and during the February following at Kathmandu. The average height at the former place was 29,60 inches, while at the latter it was 25,25 inches. The difference of the logarithms of these numbers, rejecting the index, and taking only the four next figures, will give 690 fathoms, 4140 feet, for the height of Kathmandu above the Tariyani. The observations with the thermometer, for the proper correction of those made with the barometer, are not complete; but they are not of great consequence, considering that the fundamental observations were not simultaneous, and were therefore liable to great error.

The periodical rains extend to Nepal, and are nearly of the same violence and duration with those in Behar. Colonel Kirkpatrick * thinks, and perhaps justly, that they commence a little earlier. Water spouts are common, which shows that their cause is quite unconnected with the sea.

* Nepaul, p. 171.

On the whole I am inclined to believe, that the climate of the valley is healthful, although, immediately before our arrival, the inhabitants had been much troubled with fevers, and, for the first three months after our arrival, the whole of our native attendants were exceedingly sickly. The complaints to which they were chiefly subject, were fevers of the intermittent kind, and fluxes, attended with a very copious secretion of slimy matter, which, by the natives, is attributed to Bayu or wind; and which was brought on by very slight indulgences in eating. In the fevers emetics seemed much more efficacious than the cathartics which are usually employed at Calcutta; and, indeed, a dose of emetic tartar very frequently cut the fever short, as usual in temperate climates. The fluxes were not attended with much pain, and both these and the tendency in the bowels to the slimy secretions, seemed to require the frequent exhibition of spirituous bitters and small doses of opium. In such cases, I found the chirata tolerably efficacious, but I thought other bitters more powerful, especially the infusion of chamomile flowers, and the compound tinctures of Gentian and Peruvian bark. Our people probably suffered from having passed through the forest too late in the season; but the natives of Hindustan do not support a change of air, and on our first arrival they were not well provided with means to resist the weather, which to them was uncommonly cold.

I have seen no country where the venereal disease is so common as in Nepal, nor so generally diffused among all classes of the people, who are indeed very dissolute. During my stay I had application for medical assistance from all ranks labouring under the venereal disease; and I observed that the men did not consider it as extraordinary or shameful, when they found their wives afflicted with this malady. The dissolute manners of the inhabitants are carried to such a length, that a great many of the young men of rank, by the age of twenty-five, are debilitated, and have recourse to stimulants. The preparation of these forms a chief source of emolument to the medical men, and they are sometimes taken to a quantity that proves fatal.

Cutaneous disorders, and especially the itch, are also very common, and almost as prevalent as in Hindustan. The leprosy, in which the joints drop off, is as common as in Bengal; but in Nepal it cannot be attributed to the lowness of the country, nor to a fish diet, to which the people of Kathmandu have little or no inclination. Some of the persons afflicted with this horrid disorder, I found to be of considerable rank, and quite removed from the want of a nourishing diet. I am almost certain that this disease is not infectious, as I know an instance of a woman, who has lost all her toes and fingers, and who, in that state, has had a child, which she nursed. The child is two years old, and is very healthy. The natives consider the disease as hereditary, and allege that the child will become its victim.

The same kind of swelling in the throat that is common among the inhabitants of the Alps, prevails in Nepal, and, indeed, is frequently seen every where north from Patna. It might at first sight be supposed, that this disease does not derive its origin from the people drinking the water which came from mountains covered with perpetual snow, the cause to which in Europe it has been usually attributed. No water of this kind, however, flows through Nepal; for, although some of the inhabitants of the northern part of Bahar, who live near the Ganduki and Kausiki, drink the water springing from perpetual snow; yet by far the greater part of them drink the water of the various branches of the Vagmati, all of which arise in subalpine regions. It must, however, be observed, that the springs by which these rivers are fed may be supplied by the melted snow, which may sink into the earth of the Himalaya mountains, and not come to light till it reaches the lower hills.

As the seasons resemble those of Bengal, and the periodical rains occupy the greater part of summer, the country is not favourable for many kinds of fruit: the heats of spring are not sufficient to bring them to maturity before the rainy season begins, as is the case in Bengal. Peaches grow wild by every rill; but the one side of the fruit is rotted by the rain, while the other is still green. There are vines, but without shelter from the rain the fruit will always be bad. Two kinds of fruit, however, come to the utmost perfection; the pine apple, in the warmer vallies, is uncommonly fine; and the orange, as it ripens in winter, is nowhere better.

From the abundance of rain in the warm season, the country, considering the inequality of its surface, is uncommonly productive of grain. Wherever the land can be levelled into terraces, however narrow, it is exceedingly favourable for transplanted rice, which ripens after the rains have ceased, so that the harvest is never injured; and, as most of these terraces can be supplied at pleasure with water from springs, the crops are uncommonly certain. This is by far the most valuable land, and is that in which all the officers and servants of the Crown are paid, and from whence all endowments are made. In some parts the same land gives a winter crop of wheat and barley; but in most places this is most judiciously omitted.

Where the land is too steep to be conveniently formed into terraces, or where this operation has been neglected, the fields are called Kuriya,* and are generally cultivated after fallows, by any person that chooses to occupy them, on paying a certain sum by the head, and not according to the extent of land. The hoe is chiefly used, and the produce is rice, sown broadcast, maize, cotton, *kurthi*, *bhot mash*, and *mash kalai*, three kinds of pulse, that, without seeing, I cannot pretend to specify; *ture*, a kind of mustard, which I cannot specify; *manjit*, or Indian madder, wheat, barley, and sugar cane.

The manjit, or Indian madder, seems to be of two kinds; the *Rubia cordata* of Wildenow, and a species of Rubia, not described in the common systems of botany. Both seem to be equally fit for the purpose, and grow in the same manner. It is cultivated exactly as cotton is among the hills. The ground is cleared and laboured in spring, and, when the first rains commence, the field is sown broadcast with rice, having intermixed the seed of manjit or of cotton. When the rice ripens, it is cut. The manjit is allowed to grow four or five years; and, after the second year, the stems are annually cut down to the root. They are four or five cubits long, and lie flat on the ground. When cut, they are stript of the leaves, and rolled up for sale.

Besides these, a most valuable article of cultivation, in these mountainous parts, is a large species of cardamom, of which I have as yet seen no description. The fruit is larger than that of the *Cardamomum minus* of Rumph, and has membraneous angles; but, in other respects, the two plants have a strong resemblance. In Hindustan, the cardamom of Nepal is called the Desi Elachi, while the small cardamom of Malabar (*Amomum repens*, W.) is called the Gujjarati Elachi, as having usually come by the way of Surat. The plant in question is

* Kohrya, Kirkpatrick, p. 94.

a species of amomum, as that genus is defined by Dr Roxburgh, and differs very much from the cardamom of Malabar. The natives call it merely Elachi. It is raised in beds, that are levelled, and surrounded by a small bank, like a field of rice; for it requires to be constantly in water. In spring, cuttings of the roots are planted in these beds, at about a cubit's distance from each other, and must be carefully weeded and supplied with water, so that the soil is always covered two or three inches. In about three years the plants begin to produce, and ever afterwards, in the month Bhadra, give an annual crop. The heads, which spring up among the leaves, are plucked, and, at the same time, old withered stems and leaves and weeds are carefully removed. The capsules are then separated, dried, and packed for sale.

In the country between Nepal Proper, and the Kali river, ginger is also a valuable article of cultivation.

On the whole, one-half of the cultivation among the mountains may be said to consist in transplanted rice. The remainder is composed of the various articles above mentioned, sown on the Kuriya, or steep land. For a more particular account of the agriculture, I must refer to the third section of the first chapter of the second part, where I have detailed all that I know on this subject, so far as relates to Nepal Proper.

The pasture on these mountains, although not so harsh and watery as that of the low country, is by no means good, and seems greatly inferior to that even on the heaths of Scotland.

The Gurung and Limbu tribes, already described, are, however, shepherds provided with numerous flocks. In winter they retire to the lower mountains and vallies; but in summer they ascend to the Alpine regions, which bound the country on the north, and feed their herds on some extensive tracts in the vicinity of the regions perpetually frozen, but which in winter are deeply covered with snow. The sheep which these people possess are said to be very large, and are called Barwal, and their wool is said to be fine. It is woven into a cloth, which is finer than that of Bhotan. The sheep of this breed give also much milk, with which, if I understand the account of the natives right, they make a kind of cheese. Whether or not the Barwal is of the same breed with the sheep employed to carry loads, and afterwards to be mentioned, I do not exactly know.

There is another kind of sheep called San-Bhera, which are never sent to the Alpine pastures.

The cattle of the ox kind resemble those of the low country, and are not numerous.

Buffaloes are brought from the low country and fattened for slaughter, but are not bred. The same is the case with hogs and goats, although the country seems admirably adapted for the latter kind of cattle.

Horses are imported from Thibet, for they do not breed on the south side of the Alps. The same is the case with the Chaungri cattle, (*Bos grunniens*,) and the goat which produces the wool from whence shawls are made.

This part of the country consists in many places of granite, and contains much iron, lead, and copper, with some zinc (*Dasta*) and a little gold found in the channels of some rivers. The specimens which I procured of the ores were so small, that I can say little concerning their nature. The copper ore which I saw adhered to whitish hornstone, or earthy quartz. The iron ore is a dark red stony substance, with a fine grain. I have not seen any of the lead or zinc ores. The following details respecting the management of these mines, will enable the reader to judge concerning their value.

The copper mines seem to be quite superficial, and the ore

is dug from trenches entirely open above, so that the workmen cannot act in the rainy season, as they have not even sense to make a drain. Each mine has attached to it certain families, who seem to be a kind of proprietors, as no one else is allowed to dig. These miners are called Agari. Each man in the month digs, on an average, from two to four *mans* of the ore, that is, about 30 *mans* in the year. The *man* is 40 *sers* of 64 *sicca* weight, so that the total ore dug by each man may be about 1970 lb. This is delivered to another set of workmen, named Kami, who smelt, and work in metals. These procure charcoal, the Raja furnishing trees, and smelt the ore. This is first roasted, then put in water for two or three days, then powdered, and finally put in small furnaces, each containing from two to three *sers*, or from three to five pounds of the powdered ore. Two *sers* of ore give from one to one and a half *ser* of metal, or, on an average, 62½ per cent. The total copper, therefore, procured by one miner's labour is 1232 lb. Of this, the man takes $\frac{1}{3} = 410\frac{2}{3}$ lb. the Raja takes as much, the smelter takes $\frac{1}{5} = 246\frac{2}{5}$ lb. The remainder, $164\frac{4}{15}$ lb. is divided equally between the Raja, the miner, and a person called Izaradar, who keeps the accounts, usually advances a subsistence to the whole party, and often gives loans even to the Raja, the system of anticipation being universally prevalent. The miner, therefore, makes about 465 lb. of copper in the year, and the Raja, for each miner, has as much. The smelter gets about 300 lb. but one smelter suffices for about two miners, so that he makes better wages. It must be observed, that copper bears in India a much greater value in proportion to silver than it does in Europe, so that the profits of the miner are high.

The iron ore is also found near the surface, and the mines of it are nearly on the same footing as those of copper, only the same persons (Kami) dig and smelt, and are allowed one third of the whole produce, while the Raja and superintendent (Izaradar) receive each as much. I have received no estimate of the amount of each man's labour. The iron of different mines is of very different qualities, some being so excellent, that, even without being converted into steel, it makes knives and swords.

Only two mines of lead are at present wrought, because all the metal is reserved for the Raja's magazines; but, so far as I can learn, lead is found in a great many places quite on the surface. These, however, are concealed with care by those who observe them, and who are thus able to work in private.

Colonel Kirkpatrick * was informed, that the people, owing to want of skill, could not smelt their lead ore, and procured the metal from Patna; but it would be extraordinary, if a people who could smelt iron and copper, should be unable to smelt lead. He, in the same place, observes, that the lead of Nepal, as usual, contains silver.

Colonel Kirkpatrick had received information of mines of antimony and mercury, but considered the information vague. I am well assured of the existence of the latter in the form of a native cinnabar, which is called *Sabita* by the natives; and is exported to the low country for sale.

The position of such of the mines as have come to my knowledge, will be seen in the maps.

Mines of sulphur are said to be numerous in these regions. Colonel Kirkpatrick † says, that the government of Gorkha was obliged to desist from working them, on account of their de-

* Nepaul, p. 177.

† Nepaul, p. 177.

leterious qualities. This was probably owing to an admixture of arsenic, which he says is also found.

Corundum of the compact kind, such as is found in the western provinces under the presidency of Bengal, is called Kurran by the Hindus of the mountains, and is found in great quantities on the hills of Isma and Musikot; and at Kathmandu, I was shown some of a coarse nature, said to be brought from the surrounding mountains; but what is most esteemed in that capital is said to come from Thibet. In both the Company's territory and in Nepal, it is always found in detached rounded masses lying on the surface, but often of considerable size. In Nepal, these masses seldom exceed four or five pounds, but in the Company's provinces they are much larger.

I saw masses of the Agalmatolite, used in China to make images, and in Ava for pencils. They were said to be brought from the mountains in the vicinity of Kathmandu.

I have seen very fine specimens of Talc brought from Nepal as a medicine; but I have no information concerning the place where it is found.

On the banks of the Gandaki, at Muktinath, is a precipice, from which the river is supposed to wash the Salagrams or black stones, which are considered by the Hindus as representatives of several of their deities, and which are the most common objects of worship in Bengal, where images are scarce. They are of various kinds, and accordingly represent different deities. Pilgrims, who have been at the place, say, that the stones are found partly in the precipice, and partly in the bed of the river, where it has washed down the earth. On account of its containing these stones, this branch of the river is usually called the Salagrami, and the channel every where below Muktinath, until it reaches the plain of India at Sivapur, abounds in these stones. All the Salagrams consist of carbonate of lime, and are in general quite black, but a few have white veins. Their colour is probably owing to some metallic impregnation, which also occasions their great specific weight. They rarely exceed the size of an orange, and they are rounded, I suppose, by the action of water. Most of them are what naturalists call petrifactions, and by far the most common are Ammonites, half imbedded in a ball of stone, exactly of the same nature with the petrified animal. Others, which are reckoned the most valuable, are balls containing a cavity formed by an Ammonite, that has afterwards decayed, and left only its impression, or they are what Wallerius calls *Typolithi Ammonitarum*. The Ammonites or their impressions are called the Chakras or wheels of the Salagrams, but are sometimes wanting. The stone is then a mere ball without any mark of animal exuviæ. Some balls have no external opening, and yet by rubbing away a portion of one of their sides, the hollow wheel (*chakra*) is discovered. Such Salagrams are reckoned very valuable.

In many parts of these mountains, the substance called *Silajit* exudes from rocks. I have not yet satisfied myself concerning its nature; but intend hereafter to treat the subject fully, when I describe the natural productions of Behar, where I had an opportunity of collecting it, as it came from the rock.

The valley of Nepal Proper, which contains Kathmandu, or, as many call it, Kathmaro, Lalita Patan, and Bhatgang, is the largest in the dominions of Gorkha, and in this plain there is not naturally a single stone of any considerable size. The whole, so far as man has penetrated, consists of what is called alluvial matter, covered by soil. In some places the alluvial matter consists of thick beds of fine gravel and sand, much of which is micaceous. Among these beds are found concretions of the same materials, united into balls, about the size and shape of a turkey's egg. At one end these are generally perforated with a small hole, and some, but not all of them, are hollow. The Newars call them Dungoda; but can give no account of their formation, nor did I observe any thing that could lead to an explanation.

A large proportion of the alluvial matter consists of a blackish substance resembling clay. It seems to approach nearer to the nature of turf than any thing with which I am acquainted, and I have no doubt is of vegetable origin. It is called Koncha by the Newars, who dig out large quantities, and apply it to their fields as a manure. The beds, in which it is disposed, are often very thick and extensive; and it is always much intermixed with leaves, bits of stick, fruits, and other vegetable exuviæ, the produce of plants, similar to those now growing on the neighbouring hills.

The various rivers that pass through the above-mentioned Koncha, have washed from its strata another harder and blacker substance, but still having so strong a resemblance, that it is called *Ha Koncha*. This is most commonly found in the channels of the rivers, and by the natives is supposed to be decayed charcoal; but the great size of some of the masses seems to me incompatible with the truth of this opinion.

A kind of blue martial earth, the earthy blue iron ore of mineralogists, by the Newars called Ong Shigulay, is also found commonly intermixed with the Koncha. It is never in large masses, and, in my opinion, has derived its origin from some vegetable substance that has been gradually impregnated with iron. Cones of the pine may be traced in all stages, from those retaining a half of their vegetable nature, to those entirely converted into martial earth, and only distinguishable by their shape as having once been vegetable productions. The half-formed specimen that I procured is a cone of the *Pinus strobus*; but the more common ones are exuviæ of the *Pinus longifolia*.

In the alluvial matter of the plain of Nepal are also found large strata of clay, fit for the potter and brickmaker.

The greater part of the mountains which enclose the valley of Nepal consists of grey granite, of which the surface is very much decayed wherever it has been exposed to the air. On the south side of Chandangiri, about four miles west from Pharphing, is a very large stratum of fine white sand, which the Parbatiyas call *Seta mati*, or white earth. It seems to me to be nothing more than decayed granite; and I think it probable, that the sandstone found on Sambhu, and the neighbouring hill towards Hilchuck, is composed of this granitic sand reunited into rock. This sandstone is used in a few buildings, but I have seen no large blocks, and the difficulty, or impracticability, of procuring such, has probably occasioned this stone to be in general neglected.

The stone usually employed in Nepal for building is a rock containing much lime, which is so impregnated with other matters, that, though it effervesces strongly with acids, and falls to pieces in a sufficient quantity of these liquids, yet, by calcination, it cannot be reduced to quicklime fit for use. It is disposed in vertical strata, is very fine grained, has a silky lustre, cuts well, can be procured in large masses, and powerfully resists the action of the weather, so that it is an excellent material for building.

Limestone is so scarce, that clay is the only mortar used by the natives. We, however, visited a quarry on the mountain called Nag Arjun, where the people obtain lime for whitewashing their houses, and for chewing with betel. It is a vertical stratum, about two feet wide, and running parallel with the other strata of the mountain. It consists of small irregular rhombic crystals, which agree with the character given by Wallerius of the *Spathum arenarium.*

In the lower part of the hills, which borders immediately on the plain, are found large masses of a hard red clay, considered by some naturalists, to whom I have shown it, as decomposed schistus. It is called Lungcha by the Newars, and used by them for painting the walls of their houses.

The whole of this mountainous region is copiously watered by limpid streams and springs, and the vegetable productions are of most remarkable stateliness, beauty, and variety. Except at the summits of the mountains, the trees are uncommonly large; and every where, and at all seasons, the earth abounds with the most beautiful flowers, partly resembling those of India, but still more those of Europe.

I have already mentioned the vegetable productions of the mountains, so far as they are objects of cultivation. I shall now mention a few of its spontaneous plants that are applied to use.

The timber trees consist of various oaks, * pines, firs, walnut, † chesnut, hornbeam, yew, laurels, hollies, birches, Gordonia, ‡ Michelias, &c. most of them species hitherto unnoticed by botanists; but some exactly the same as in Europe, such as the yew, holly, hornbeam, walnut, Weymouth pine, (Pinus strobus, W.) and common spruce fir, (Pinus picea, W.) As, however, the greater part are of little value, from the inacces-

* Phulaced, Kirkpatrick's Nepaul, p. 79, Bhang, id. p. 81.

† Kirkpatrick's Nepaul, p. 81.

‡ Chillownia, Kirkpatrick's Nepaul, p. 79.

sible nature of the country, I shall only particularize a few kinds.

The *Malayagiri* is a tree, of which I have only seen a branch with leaves, and I cannot with any certainty judge what its botanical affinities may be. It has a pale yellow wood, with a very agreeable scent, and on this account might be valuable for fine cabinet work, and might bear the expence of carriage.

The *Tinmuc*, or *Taizbul* of Colonel Kirkpatrick, * is a species of *Fagara*. In the mountains of Nepal I have only seen the shrubby kind; but, on the lower hills, I observed another species, which grows to be a tree, and which is probably the larger sort alluded to by the Colonel.

The male *Sinkauri*, or *Silkauli* of the mountain Hindus, is a species of Laurus, which is either the *Laurus japonica* of Rumph, † or approaches very near to that plant. Both its bark and leaves have a fine aromatic smell and taste, and this quality in the leaves is strengthened by drying. They are carried to the low country, and sold under the name of *Tejpat*; but the tree is of a different species from the Tejpat of Ranggapur.

The female Sinkauri, or Silkauli, like the male, is another tree nearly related to the cinnamon; but its aromatic quality resides in the bark of the root, which has a very permanent fragrance, and would probably give a very fine oil. The specimens brought from the mountains of Morang, appeared to differ in species from the plant of similar qualities that has been introduced into Ranggapur from Bhotan.

Both male and female Sinkauli are considered by Colonel

* Nepaul, p. 79.

† Vol. VII. p. 63.

Kirkpatrick as one species, which he calls *Singrowla*, * probably by a typographical error.

The *Lalchandan*, or Red Sandal, is a timber tree, the foliage and appearance of which have some resemblance to the Laurels. It seems to be a fine timber for the cabinetmaker, but has little smell, and is not the Red Sanders or Sandal of the shops.

The *Siedburrooa*, mentioned by Colonel Kirkpatrick, † as the plant from which the Nepalese make paper, is a species of Daphne, very nearly allied to that which botanists call *odora*.

The *Karphul*, mentioned also by Colonel Kirkpatrick, ‡ as a small stone fruit, resembling a cherry, is a species of *Myrica*.

The *Jumne mundroo* of Colonel Kirkpatrick § I consider as a species of *Leontice*, although it is a small tree, and has strong affinities with the *Berberis*. Its leaves are pinnated; but each division, as the Colonel notices, has a strong resemblance to the leaves of the holly.

The *Chootraphul* of Colonel Kirkpatrick ‖ is, in fact, a species of barberry, to which the Colonel compares it.

There are two species of the *Chirata*, a bitter herb, much and deservedly used by the Hindu physicians in slow febrile diseases, as strengthening the stomach. The smaller is the one most in request. I have not seen its flowers, but the appearance of the herb agrees with some short notices in manuscript, with which I was favoured by Dr Roxburgh, of the plant sent to him as the Chirata, and which he considers as a species of gentian. The larger Chirata is a species of *Swertia*, but approaches nearer in appearance to the common Gentian of the shops than to any other plant that I know. Its root, especial-

* Nepaul, p. 79. † Nepaul, p. 80. ‡ Nepaul, p. 76.
§ Nepaul, p. 81. ‖ Nepaul, p. 81.

ly, has a great resemblance, and might probably be a good substitute, were not the herb of the smaller Chirata a better medicine. Both species, however, approach so near to each other, that they are often sold indiscriminately.

The dried scales of a tuberous root are imported from these mountains into the Company's territory, and the druggists there call them *Kshir kangkri* or *Titipiralu.* Some people of the mountains, whom I employed, brought me the living bulbs, certainly of the same kind, and these had young stems then very thriving, but which soon withered from the heat. They had every appearance of being a species of *Lilium*, and the people who brought them said, that they were the *Titipiralu*, while the *Kshir kangkri*, according to them, is a plant of the cucurbitaceous tribe. Other hill people, however, brought for the Titipiralu a species of *Pancratium*, which I cannot trace in the works of botanists; but it has a great resemblance to the *Pancratium maritimum.* This is certainly not the plant sold by the druggists of Nathpur.

The same druggists gave me a medicine which they called *Jainti* or *Bhutkes.* Some of the hill people said, that it grows among the mosses, on large stones, on the higher mountains, and is evidently the lower part of the stems of one of the *orchides* of that kind of *epidendra*, which have an erect stem, many of which, I know, grow in Nepal in such situations. Others of the mountaineers alleged that this was not the true Bhutkes, or Bhutkesar, which they say differs from the Jainti; and, in fact, they brought me from the snowy mountains a very different plant, which they called *Bhutkesar.*

Singgiya Bikh, or *Bish*, is a plant much celebrated among the mountaineers. The plant was brought to me in flower, but was entirely male, nor did I see the fruit, which is said to be a berry. So far as I can judge from these circumstances, I suppose that it is a species of *Smilax*, with ternate leaves. To pass over several of its qualities that are marvellous, the root, which resembles a yam, is said to be a violent poison. The berries also are said to be deleterious, but, when applied externally, are considered as a cure for the swelling of the throat, which resembles the goitre of the Swiss, and is very common among the mountaineers.

The *Jhul* is imported by the druggists of the Company's territory, and what was brought as such to me, consisted of four kinds of Lichen, intermixed with some straggling Jungermannias. By far the greater part, however, of the Jhul consisted of two kinds of Lichen, the furfuraceus, and one very like the farinaceus. These grow on stones among the mountains.

With respect to the breadth of this mountainous region, there is reason to think, from the observations of Colonel Crawford, that, immediately north and east from Kathmandu, the horizontal direct extent may be from thirty to forty British miles; but farther west, the breadth of this region probably exceeds that extent. I have, however, no solid grounds for judging; as days' journies, given by travellers on routes, in such a country, can give but a very imperfect notion of horizontal distance.

The alpine region belonging to the chiefs of Gorkha, which bounds the mountainous district on the north, is probably of nearly an equal breadth; that is to say, over a space of thirty or forty miles from north to south, there are scattered immense peaks covered with perpetual snow, before we reach the passes at the boundary of Thibet, where almost the whole country is subject to everlasting winter. Between these scattered peaks there are narrow vallies, some of which admit of cultivation, and, being of the same elevation with the higher parts of the mountainous region, admit of similar productions.

It is indeed said by Colonel Kirkpatrick,* that, in the alpine vallies occupied by the Limbus, there is raised a kind of rice called *Takmaro*, which he thinks may be probably found to answer in the climate and soil of England. Whether or not this Takmaro may be the same with the grain called *Uya*, which will be farther mentioned in the account of *Malebum*, I cannot take upon myself to determine, although I think it probable, from the situation in which both are said to grow, that Uya and Takmaro are two names for the same grain. In this case the grain may probably be rye, although this also is uncertain.

By far the greatest part, however, of the Alpine region, consists of immense rocks, rising into sharp peaks, and the most tremendous precipices, wherever not perpendicular, covered with perpetual snow, and almost constantly involved in clouds. No means for ascertaining the height of the central, and probably the highest peaks of Emodus, have come to my knowledge; but, while at Kathmandu, Colonel Crawford had an opportunity of observing the altitude of several of the detached peaks, the situations of which will be seen from the accompanying map, copied from one of this excellent geographer. The accompanying table also will give the result of his estimate of the height of these peaks above the valley of Nepal. In the five wooden plates, taken from drawings by Colonel Crawford, a view of these mountains from Oba Mohisyu, in the valley of Nepal is represented, and will give an idea of their appearance, as well as that of the valley of Nepal itself, although

* Nepaul, p. 282.

a better judgment may be formed of this from the two copper-plates that will be afterwards mentioned.

The southern face of these alps differs very much from those of Switzerland; for the rains being periodical, and falling in the hottest season of the year, the snow continues almost always stationary. It is only the few showers that happen in winter, and the vapours from condensed clouds, that dissolve in the beginning of summer, and occasion a small swell in the rivers, which spring from the south side of these alps.

The country on the north side of these lofty peaks, so far as I can learn, more resembles Europe. It is exceedingly high and bare, and is far from being mountainous. The rains, however, are not periodical, and the greatest falls happen in summer, so that, although several Indian rivers come from thence, they do not swell much by the melting of snow in the heats of spring.

The ridge of snowy alps, although it would appear to wind very much, has few interruptions, and, in most places, is said to be totally insuperable. Several rivers that arise in Thibet pass through among its peaks, but amidst such tremendous precipices, and by such narrow gaps, that these openings are in general totally impracticable. By far the widest is on the Arun, the chief branch of the Kosi, where Maingmo on the west, and Mirgu on the east, leave a very wide opening occupied by mountains of a moderate height, and which admit of cultivation. Even there, however, the Arun is so hid among precipices, that it is approachable in only a few places, where there are passes of the utmost difficulty. Again, behind this opening in the snowy ridge, at a considerable distance farther north, is another range of hills, not so high and broken as the immense peaks of Emodus, but still so elevated as to be totally impassable in winter, owing to the depth of snow; for the road is said to be tolerable, that is, it will admit of cattle carrying loads. Somewhat similar seems in general to be the nature of the other few passages through these alpine regions.

It is about these passages chiefly, and especially beyond Maingmo and Mirgu, that there is the greatest extent of the alpine pastures, which I have already mentioned; but in every part, bordering on the perpetual snow, these occur more or less.

Colonel Kirkpatrick * thinks, that there two distinct ranges of Emodus or Himaleh; the lower of which, separating Nepal from Thibet, is only streaked with snow, while the highest separates Kuchar, or the lower Bhotan, from Thibet. He also thought, that, from the summit of the Lama Dangra hills above Chisapani, he saw the highest ridge. Now, in the maps which I obtained from the natives, three ridges may in some measure be traced, as proceeding from about the lake Manasarawar, which may be considered as the centre of Emodus. The summits of even the most southern of these ridges, which is probably the lowest, are not covered with mere patches of snow, as Colonel Kirkpatrick seems to have thought, but on them the snow is perennial to a very great extent.

The most northern ridge, which is probably the highest, as it is nowhere penetrated by rivers, approaches Hindustan only at the lake Manasarawar, where the remarkable peak called Kailasa may be considered as its centre. This peak may perhaps be visible from the southward, although there exists no certainty of its being so; but the portions of this ridge, which extend west and east from Kailasa, bordering on

---

* Nepaul, p. 58.

the north, the upper part of the Indus, and Brahmaputra rivers, are certainly invisible from every part of Hindustan, and very little is known concerning them.

The middle ridge of Himaleh, which separates Thibet from Hindustan, taking this word in its most extended sense as including Kasmir, the dominions of Gorkha, &c. extends probably to the Chinese Sea along the northern frontier of the provinces of Quangsi and Quantong, lowering gradually as it advances to the east. Although, so far as connected with Hindustan, it is of enormous height, yet it is perforated by many rivers, such as the Indus, Sutluj or Satrudra, Karnali or Sarayu, Gandaki, Arun, Brahmaputra, &c.

Mr Colebrooke, indeed, * doubts of any rivers crossing this chain; for he says, "It is presumable that all the tributary streams of the Ganges, including the Sarayu, (whether its alleged source in the Manasarawar lake be credited or discredited,) and the Yamuna, rise on the southern side of the Himaliya;" and again he says, "From the western side of the mountains, after the range, taking a sweep to the north, assumes a new direction in the line of the meridian, arise streams tributary to the Indus, or perhaps the Indus itself." On this I would remark, that all the rivers I have enumerated, no doubt, arise from Thibet, and penetrate this chain. If, indeed, the Sarayu, or rather Karnali, arises from the lake Manasarovara, which is undoubtedly on the north side of the Himaleh ridge, how could Mr Colebrooke's position be maintained? He is also probably wrong in supposing that the central Himaliya ridge bends to the north. There is rather reason to think that it passes straight west, after it is penetrated by the Indus, and

* Asiatick Researches, Volume XI. p. 444.

reaches to the Hindoo Coosh of the Honourable Mr Elphinston; while it is the western extremity of the northern ridge, first mentioned, that turns to the north, and separates Samarkhand and Bokhara from Kashgar. These rivers, which penetrate the central Himaliya ridge, do not appear to me to arise from any remarkable ridge of mountains, but spring from detached eminences on the elevated country of Thibet, and pass through interruptions or chasms in the central ridge of Emodus. It is very possible, that Colonel Kirkpatrick saw this ridge from Lama Dangra; but I am very doubtful, whether any part of it is visible from the plains of Hindustan; or, at least, that any of the more distinguished peaks visible from thence belong to it. All the peaks measured by Colonel Crawford were, no doubt, to the southward of the central ridge, and I suspect that all the snow-clad mountains visible from the plains, like those seen by Colonel Crawford, are either detached peaks, or belong to the southern ridge.

There is also reason to think, that the peak measured by Lieutenant Web, and which was one appearing conspicuous from the plains of Rohilkhand,* is that laid down by Mr Arrowsmith, about 40 miles south from Litighat, that is, from the central chain, and must therefore be near the southern edge of the alpine region. Contrary, therefore, to the opinion of Mr Colebrooke,† I think it very much to be doubted, whether the snowy mountains, visible from Rohilkhand, are the highest ground between the level plains of India, and the elevated regions of southern Tartary, by which I presume he moans Thibet.

The third or southern ridge forms the southern boundary of

---

* Asiatick Researches, Volume XI. p. 443. † P. 445.

the alpine region above described. In many parts, the whole space between this and the central ridge is thickly covered with immense peaks, so as to leave no separation between the ridges; but in other parts, there exists an intermediate, more level, and habitable portion, interposed between the central ridge and the southern peaks, which in these parts form a very distinct ridge. This is particularly the case in the Chamba country, towards Kasmir, in the Taklakhar country on the Karnali, and in the Kirata country on the Arun, as will be afterwards described.

Of the productions of this part I shall now proceed to treat, confining myself to those of the southern face, where there are but a very few of the cattle, (Bos grunniens,) whose tails form the Chaungri of India, and the badges by which the Turkish Bashaws are distinguished; nor are there any of the goats which produce the fine wool from whence the shawls are made; nor are there mines of gold, nor, one excepted, of salt, nor of borax. All these, so far as I can learn, are almost entirely the produce of the country beyond the alps.

An account of the Changra or shawl-wool goat has been given by Colonel Kirkpatrick,* who suspects it to be rather scarce, even in Thibet, since it is not without the greatest difficulty that a perfect male of this species can be procured, owing to the jealous vigilance employed by the Thibetians to prevent their being conveyed into foreign countries. The editor, in a note, thinks this opinion unfounded, because Captain Turner brought several of these animals from Thibet to Bengal, from whence he sent a few to England. I do not see that the reasoning of either Colonel Kirkpatrick, or his editor, is here conclusive. If the people of Thibet are jealous, the dif-

* Nepaul, p. 133.

ficulty of procuring a perfect male for exportation can be no proof of the species being scarce. Neither can Captain Turner's having been allowed to bring several of these animals to Bengal be considered as a proof of the want of jealousy. A great many wethers of this breed are annually brought to market at Kathmandu, and may be readily procured, nor does it appear that those brought by Captain Turner were entire males. Those remaining in the Governor General's park in 1803 were all wethers. That both entire males and females may be procured, we know from the exertions of Mr Moorcroft; but that the people of Thibet are very jealous in preserving the monopoly, I have been assured by that gentleman, as well as by the people of Nepal.

I have already mentioned, that I believe sulphur, and perhaps talc, are found in these alpine regions, and there can be no doubt that they abound with Mica (*Abrak*) in large plates, and in rock crystal (*Belor*) of a large size. It is probably in reference to this mineral, that some parts of this great alpine chain, towards the north-west, has been named Belor Tag, although Mr Elphinston gives another derivation, and changes the final *r* into a *t*, in order to accommodate the word to his meaning, which may, however, be quite correct. Besides these mineral productions, the alpine region has several metallic veins, especially lead and zinc, or tutenague.

The most valuable production of the southern face of these mountains is the animal which produces musk, of which vast numbers are annually killed. The only other large animal found there is a kind of wild sheep of great size. The accounts which I have received concerning it are very imperfect, and I have only seen one skin, which was in a very bad state of preservation. It may possibly be the same animal that our zoologists have described by the name of *Argali*.

These frigid regions are the constant abode of two of the finest birds that are known, the Manal * and Damphiya. † To me both seem evidently to have the closest affinity with each other, in size, manners, and form, and the females of the two species are not easily distinguishable; yet the former, (Meleagris satyra, L.) by the best ornithologists, has been most unaccountably classed with the turkey, and the latter (Phasianus Impeyanus) with the pheasant, to which the resemblance is very trifling.

Along with these two fine birds, according to Colonel Kirkpatrick, ‡ is found the *Chakor*, or *Chiukoar*, according to his orthography. He states, that this bird "is well known to the Europeans in India by the name of fire-eater. It is a species of partridge, *(Perdix rufa,)* and derives its English name from its reputed power of swallowing fire. The fact, according to the people of Nepal, is, that in the season of love, this bird is remarkably fond of red or *cheun* (Cayenne) pepper, after eating two or three capsules of which, it will eat a red coal if offered to it." This account of the Nepalese deserves no credit; for, in its native frozen mountains, where is the Chakor to procure Capsicum or Cayenne pepper? and I know that the birds will pick at sparks of fire, where no capsicum has been given to them.

The vegetable productions of these mountains are, however, the greatest object of curiosity, and it is with infinite regret that I not only have not had it in my power to visit them, but that the disturbances existing between the two governments, when I was on the frontier, have prevented me from procuring complete specimens and seeds of many of the most interesting objects, for which arrangements had been made,

* Moonal, Kirkpatrick's Nepaul, p. 131.

† Damphia, Kirkpatrick's Nepaul, p. 131.

‡ Nepaul, p. 131.

when the disputes put a stop to communication. While at Nathpur, I had indeed previously procured young plants of most of the kinds, but although kept in a very cool house, not one of them resisted the summer heats. I shall now mention some of the most remarkable.

The Dhupi is a species of juniper. Its wood has a beautiful grain, a fine mahogany colour, and a remarkably pleasant scent, a good deal resembling that of the pencil cedar, but stronger, and I think more agreeable. Planks of this are sent to Thibet, from whence they are probably carried to China. A man, whom I sent from Nathpur to Thibet, in order to procure plants, says, that the Dhupi grows to be a very large tree, in which case it would be a valuable acquisition in Europe, in the northern parts of which it will no doubt thrive.

The *Thumuriya Dhupi* is another species of juniper, which is a low bush, like the kind common in the north of Europe. Its branches and leaves have an agreeable smell, and are used in fumigations.

The *Hingwalka Chhota saral*, or small alpine fir, so strongly resembles the common fir of the south of Europe, (*Pinus picea*, W.) that I can perceive no difference in the foliage; but I have not seen the cones. There is, however, probably some difference, for it is said never to grow to a considerable size, and the leaves, if I can trust to memory, have a much more agreeable smell than those of the common fir.

The *Hingwalka bara Saral*, or large alpine fir, is in fact the yew tree; and although I have seen it in all its stages, I can perceive no very essential difference between it and the tree of Europe. Its leaves, however, are rather larger, and bent, (*falcata.*) Like the yew in the north of Europe, it grows to a great size.

The *Bhuryapatra* or *Bhurjapatra* is a species of birch, the bark of which resembles that of the tree common in Europe, in being separable into fine smooth layers; but these are of a fine chesnut colour. This bark is imported into the low country in considerable quantity, and is used both in the religious ceremonies of the Hindus, and for constructing the flexible tubes with which the natives smoke tobacco.

The *Sanpati* is a small Rhododendron, which has a considerable affinity with the kinds described in the Encyclopédie by the names of R. lineariifolium and ferrugineum. It is a shrub much like our sweet gale in Europe, and its leaves are very odorous, and, even when dried, retain their fragrance. It is used in fumigations, and sent to the low country.

The *Bhairopati*, although I have not seen the flower, is, I have no doubt, another similar species of the Rhododendron, which has a great resemblance to the kind called Chamæcistus. Its qualities are similar to those of the former, but it is less fragrant. The man whom I sent to Thibet brought, as the *Bhairopati*, a totally different plant, of which the specimens so strongly resemble branches of the Cypressus sempervirens meta convoluta, that I should have no doubt of its being this plant, were it not that the man describes it as a shrub, and that its dried leaves have a disagreeable sulphureous smell. It is, however, the Rhododendron which is always sold in the shops of Hindustan as the *Bhairopati*.

There seems to be some difficulty in fixing the nomenclature of the *Jatamangsi*, a plant celebrated among the natives as a perfume, and of which large quantities are sent from these Alps to the plains of India. What I procured at the shops in Nathpur, and recently imported from the Alps, was the species of Valerian described by Dr Roxburgh in the Asiatick Researches, and supposed by Sir William Jones to be the spikenard of the ancients. As there can be no disputing about taste, I cannot take upon myself to say how far the encomiums bestowed on the fragrance of the spikenard are applicable to this valerian; and the native women, no doubt, consider the smell very agreeable, because most of such as can afford it use oil impregnated with this root for perfuming their hair. All I can say is, that, if this root was the spikenard of the Roman ladies, their lovers must have had a very different taste from the youth of modern Europe. A still greater difficulty attends the nomenclature of the *Jatamangsi*. A person whom I employed to bring me the growing plant from the mountains, produced a root totally different from the former. It strongly resembléd the root of the Anthamantha meum; but when fresh had an uncommonly fragrant smell. From the appearance of the leaves, I have no doubt that it is an umbelliferous plant.

I have already mentioned the doubts that exist about the plant called *Bhutkesar*, which is imported from the mountains, and used as a medicine. What was brought to me from the snowy mountains was a thick woody root, on the top of which were many stiff bristles, and from among these the young leaves were shooting. These were three times divided into three, and resembled these of a Thalictrum, of which I know there are several species in the lower mountains of Nepal.

The term *Bish* or *Bikk*, according to the pronunciation of the same letters on the plains, and in the mountains, is applied to four different plants with tuberous roots, all in great request. I have already mentioned the *Singgiya Bish*, as found on the lower mountains and hills, and supposed it to be a species of Smilax. The others have not the smallest resemblance to it, but are so strongly marked by a resemblance to each other, that I have no doubt of their all belonging to the same genus, although I have only seen the flower and fruit of one. This is called *Bishma* or *Bikhma*, and seems to me to differ little in botanical characters from the *Caltha* of Europe. The *Bishma* or *Bikhma* is also, I believe, called *Mitha*, although I am not certain but that this name may be also given to the following species, which deserves the most serious attention, as the *Bikhma* is used in medicine, is a strong bitter, very powerful in the cure of fevers, while the plant that will be next mentioned is one of the most virulent poisons.

This dreadful root, of which large quantities are annually imported, is equally fatal when taken into the stomach, and applied to wounds, and is in universal use throughout India for poisoning arrows; and there is too much reason to suspect, for the worst of purposes. Its importation would indeed seem to require the attention of the magistrate. The Gorkhalese pretend, that it is one of their principal securities against invasion from the low countries; and that they could so infect all the waters on the route by which an enemy was advancing, as to occasion his certain destruction. In case of such an attempt, the invaders ought, no doubt, to be on their guard; but the country abounds so in springs, that might be soon cleared, as to render such a means of defence totally ineffectual, were the enemy aware of the circumstance. This poisonous species is called *Bish*, *Bikh*, and *Hodoya Bish* or *Bikh*, nor am I certain whether the *Mitha* ought to be referred to it, or to the foregoing kind.

The *Nirbishi* or *Nirbikhi* is another plant of the same genus, and, like the first kind, has no deleterious qualities, but is used in medicine. The President of the Asiatick Society, in a note annexed to Dr Roxburgh's account of the Zedoary, gives the *Nirbisha* or *Nirbishi* as a Sangskrita or Hindwi name of that plant, which has not the smallest resemblance to the *Nirbishi* of the Indian Alps. In fact, the nomenclature of the *materia medica* among the Hindus, so far as I can learn, is miserably defective, and can scarcely fail to be productive of most dangerous mistakes in the practice of medicine. For instance, the man whom I sent to Thibet for plants brought, as the species which produces the poison, that which was first brought to me as the *Nirbishi*, or kind used in medicine.

The *Padam chhal* is a plant with a thick cylindrical root, that is used in medicine, and brought to the low country for that purpose. The specimen that I procured had one large heart-shaped rough leaf, and had somewhat the appearance of an Anemone.

The *Kutki* is another officinal plant with a woody root, and a stem containing many alternate leaves, toothed on the edges, and shaped like a spathula. It has much the appearance of a saxifrage. The roots are brought for sale.

The *Brim* appears to be one of the orchides, and has a root used in medicine.

CHAPTER THIRD.

LAWS AND GOVERNMENT.

Parts east from the Kali.—Courts and Forms of Proceeding.—Punishments.—Provincial Government.—Revenue and Endowments.—Officers of State.—Military Establishment.—Differences in the parts west from the River Kali.—Revenue and Civil Establishment.—Military Establishment.

Having thus described, in a general manner, the inhabitants and country of the territory subject to the chief of Gorkha, I shall now give a similar view of the form of government which existed under the petty chiefs, to whom it was formerly subject, and of the changes which have been introduced since its union under one head.

I shall only premise a very just observation of Colonel Kirkpatrick, who says,* "that the government, taking its colour, for the most part, from the character and temporary views of the ruling individual, must necessarily be of too fugitive a nature to admit of any delineation equally applicable to all periods and circumstances." This may serve to explain many differences between his account and mine, without supposing the information received by either to be erroneous.

The management of affairs in all the petty states was in

* Nepaul, p. 196.

many points the same, and differed chiefly in the names applied to similar officers, and in the nature of the military establishment in the two countries to the east and west of the river Kali. I have already mentioned, that in the former the Hindu rules of purity and law had been established with much less rigour than in the latter; but, in other points, such as the names of officers, and the form of government, the eastern parts followed more nearly the ancient Hindu system, while the western more fully imitated the Muhammedans.

In the parts east of the Kali, for each small territory or manor called a Gang, or, where these were small, for every two or three, there was an officer called an Umra Mukudum or Mahato, and over from ten to twenty gangs there was a higher officer named Desali or Chaudhuri, assisted by a Mujumdar or accountant. In cases of disputes or petty offences, one or other of these officers, called a kind of jury, (Pangchayit,) and endeavoured to settle the affair, so as to avoid farther trouble; but, if one or other of the parties was dissatisfied, he might go to the Raja's court. There an officer, called Bichari in the east, and Darogah in the west, received an account of the affair from the parties, or from the inferior officers, and endeavoured to settle it. If, however, the cause was important, or required severe punishment, or if either of the parties insisted on it, the matter was referred by the Bichari to the minister of the Raja, called Karyi in the east, and Vazir in the west, either verbally or by petition, according to its importance. The minister communicated the affair to the Raja, who ordered the Bichari to try it by a Pangchayit. This kind of jury made a report, saying, that the parties were guilty of such or such a crime. The Raja then ordered whatever punishment he thought fit, but, in doing so, usually consulted an officer called Dharm'adhikar, or owner of justice, who pointed out the law.

The criminal in the east might appeal from even the Raja's decision, to the court called Bharadar, consisting of all the chief officers of government; but in the west, no such court, I believe, existed. Oaths were seldom administered. If the parties, however, insisted on this form, the Haribangsa, a part of the Mahabharat, was put into the witness's hand. Ordeals were seldom used, until the Gorkha family seized the government, since which they have become very frequent.

There were five severe punishments: *1st*, confiscation of the whole estate; *2dly*, banishment of the whole family; *3dly*, degradation of the whole family by delivering the members to the lowest tribes; *4thly*, maiming the limbs; *5thly*, death by cutting the throat.

The people of Gorkha have introduced other capital punishments, hanging and flaying alive. Women, as in all Hindu governments, are never put to death; but the punishments inflicted on them are abundantly severe. The most common is the cutting off their noses. Even those of considerable rank are tortured, by being smoked in a small chamber with the suffocating fumes of burning capsicum, and by having their private parts stuffed with this acrid substance.

There were two kinds of fines; Prayaschitta for the neglect of ceremonies, and those inflicted as punishments for crimes. The latter went to the Raja, and do so still. The former went to the Dharm'adhikar, or chancellor; but having been enormously multiplied since the Gorkha government, their amount is divided into eight shares, of which the Raja takes one, the collector (Gomashtash) one, the Dharm'adhikar one, and one goes to each of five families of Brahmans, named Pangre, Pantha, Arjal, Khanal, and Agnidanda. These families divide their shares equally among their members, who have multiplied exceedingly. Besides the fine, all delinquents in matters of ceremony are compelled to entertain a certain number of these five families; the two first fattening on the wicked of the country west from the Narayani; and the other three on those east from that river. The number to be fed is restricted by the sentence, and the criminal may select those to whom he gives the entertainment, in any manner he pleases, confining himself strictly to the families entitled to participate.

Colonel Kirkpatrick, when he visited the country, thought * that the government, on the whole, afforded considerable protection to foreign merchants, rendering them in all cases as strict and prompt justice, as the imperfect nature of its general polity will admit. This, perhaps, is not saying much, as in the subsequent page he mentions, that the trade between Nepal and Thibet, the principal one in the country, is subject to very enormous, and at all times arbitrary exactions. In fact, all other branches of commerce, so far as I could judge, were in a state of decay, owing partly to these exactions, and partly to the recovery of debts being now very much neglected in the courts of justice, which seems to be one of the causes of the increase of trials by ordeal. A poor creditor, in general, has no resource against a powerful debtor, except sitting Dherna on him; and unless the creditor be a Brahman, he may sit long enough before he attract any notice.

Since the government of Gorkha, there has been usually established a Subah in place of each Raja, and the affairs are generally conducted by these officers as formerly; so far at least as relates to form; but they are not allowed to inflict any of the five severe punishments, without special orders from the

* Nepaul, p. 204.

Raja or court, to whom a report of the case is made. There are, however, great complaints of injustice, the Subahs having power to check all complaints. In the petty states the Raja durst not neglect justice, having no resource except in his subjects' affection. Personal acts of extreme violence, in contests for power, were overlooked in the families of the chief; and no attention was paid to punish assassination, when committed on pretence of revenging injured honour.

The Subahs having no power of inflicting severe punishment, few of these officers have with them a Dharm'adhikar; but, where a person of this kind is allowed, he is appointed by the Dharm'adhikar of Kathmandu. At that city there are now four Bicharis, and these appoint an officer of the same kind for each Subah. Over the Bicharis of Kathmandu is a chief called Ditha, who does not try causes, but watches over the conduct of the court.

The Subah is an officer of revenue, justice, and police, and, in fact, always farms the whole royal revenue of his district. He sometimes collects the different branches of revenue, on his own account, by means of subordinate officers named Fouzdars, and sometimes farms them to Izaradars. The land revenue, under the Fouzdars, is collected by Chaudhuris or Desalis, and other petty officers above mentioned. None of these offices are in any degree hereditary, nor does there seem to be any regular system for their payment. Sometimes the allowances are made in land, sometimes by a *per centage* on the rent, and sometimes by monthly wages. The whole seems to be in a great measure left to the discretion of the Subah, but, under the name of Khurchah, both he, and every man in authority under him, takes from his inferiors as much as he can.

The Subah has under his authority some armed men, and

these are called Seapoys; but they are irregulars, like the Burkandaj, which are employed by the civil authority in Bengal.

The amount paid by the Subah forms by no means the whole of the royal revenue. On a great variety of occasions, besides the presents that every one must make on approaching the court, there is levied a Rajangka, which is a kind of income tax that extends to all ranks, and even to such of the sacred order as possess free lands. A Rajangka is levied at no fixed period, but according to the exigencies of the state; and many districts pay more on this account than the regular revenue, which has been often almost entirely alienated, by giving the lands as religious endowments, to various civil officers, and in military tenure for the support of the army. The Subah does not collect the Rajangka; an officer for that purpose is especially sent from the court.

When Colonel Kirkpatrick visited the country, he learned, on what he considered tolerably good authority, that the revenue which reached the treasury at Kathmandu never exceeded 3,000,000 of rupees, and fluctuated between that and 2,500,000. The subsequent addition of territory, although it has increased the means of supporting a large army, has probably sent little money to the capital.

The ordinary public revenue, consisting of land-rents, customs, fines, and mines, in the east, was divided among the chief, and the principal persons and officers of his family, the chief for his own expence receiving about two-thirds of the whole; but, if there was in the family any estate on the plain, the chief reserved the whole of this for himself, although he sometimes bestowed part free of revenue for services. About a third of the revenue that remained, after grants to the civil and military establishments, was divided as follows: the

Chautariya, or chief councillor, always the Raja's brother in the Indian sense, that is, a near kinsman in the male line, received one-fifth. The Karyi, or man of business, who was always a near relation of the chief, had an equal share. The Raja's eldest son, when married, had as much. The chief's virgin spouse, when she had children, was allowed as much. The Serdar, or principal officer, who was not of the chief's family, received one-tenth. The Jethabura, a councillor, had one-twentieth. Finally, the Kaliya, or secretary, obtained as much. All other officers, soldiers, and even most domestics, were paid in lands, held as long as they performed the duty, and called Jaygirs, a Persian term. The occupants either cultivated the lands themselves, or let them as they pleased. There were, besides, lands appropriated to the support of some temples, and two kinds of free estates granted in perpetuity to individuals. The owners of one kind, called Brittiyas, had no jurisdiction over those living on their estates, which was also the case with those holding Jaygirs; the others, called Bitalpas, administered justice to their vassals. They were all Brahmans, and never were numerous; but by far the greater part of the lands of both Bitalpas and Brittiyas have been resumed by the chiefs of Gorkha, in order to increase the military establishment. In other respects they have not much altered the constitution.

In consequence of their extended dominions, the princes of Gorkha have increased the number of the chief officers of state, and have four Chauteriyas, four Karyis, and four Serdars.

When Colonel Kirkpatrick visited the country the twelve chief officers, according to his orthography,* were reckoned,

---

* Nepaul, p. 201.

one Choutra, four Kajies, four Sirdars, two Khurdars or secretaries, one Kuppardar or storekeeper, and one Khuzanchee or treasurer.

These chief officers now form the Bharadar, or great council of the Raja, which attends him in the Durbar, Rajdani, or palace to transact business, and which frequently acts without his presence. It ought to consist of these twelve members; but some of the places are often vacant, and, at other times, the persons who hold them have so little influence, that they neglect or avoid giving their attendance. At other times, again, on business of the utmost emergency, a kind of assembly of notables is held, in which men who have neither office, nor any considerable influence in the government, are allowed to speak very freely, which seems to be done merely to allow the discontents of the nation to evapotate, as there is not a vestige of liberty in the country, nor does the court seem ever to be controlled by the opinions advanced in these assemblies.

The first rank of councillors is the only one now confined to the prince's family, and is often given to illegitimate kinsmen. The Chauteriya, who is the nearest relation to the reigning prince, is always considered as the prime minister, although he may have little real authority. During our stay in Nepal, the first Chauteriya was a boy, brother to the Raja, and never appeared except on occasions of ceremony, where he was exhibited like a puppet, in the same manner as his sovereign.

The office of Karyi should be held by persons only of a few very distinguished families; but many exceptions have been made of late, and especially in the instance of Bhim Sen, the present ruler of the country, who holds no higher office than this, to which even his birth does not entitle him.

The Serdars are chosen from whatever families the chief thinks proper; but, in public opinion, the giving the office to low men, especially if these are entrusted with much power, is exceedingly offensive.

Every person who has held the office of Chautariya, Karyi, and Serdar, continues to enjoy the title for life; and, whenever a man is appointed to one of these dignities, all his brothers assume the title.

Military officers, named Serdars, frequently are appointed to command over different portions of the country, and, wherever they are, have a jurisdiction in all matters over the Subahs. In particular, their criminal jurisdiction is much more extensive, as they can condemn to capital punishment, without any reference to the court, while the Subah requires an order from thence before he can punish any criminal. Still more are the Subahs under the authority of the higher officers of state, the Chautariyas and Karyis, when any of these eight great officers of state are deputed in command to the provinces. The Serdars who visit the provinces do not always belong to the four great officers of this title, who with the four Chautariyas and four Karyis compose the great council of twelve, which assists the Raja to govern the nation. These great Serdars, like the other great officers of state, are occasionally deputed on high commands; but some Serdars, such as I have before mentioned, are, in general, stationary in different parts of the country, and have authority over all the Subahs and civil officers in their vicinity, although they are properly military men, for such are the only persons, Brahmans excepted, who are considered as entitled to any weight in the state. The Serdar in command at Vijaypur, I understand, receives 7000 rupees a-year, but out of this he pays his establishment. It is to these persons that communications from our provincial officers should be made, as the Subahs are considered as inferior characters.

There are thirty-six families of Gorkhalis, who should hold all the principal offices of government, and, in fact, have always held the greater part of them. A fuller detail of the condition and privileges of these families than I procured may be found in Colonel Kirkpatrick's account.* They are divided into three gradations, and the highest, consisting of six houses, are considered as having an exclusive right to the office of Karyi. When I was at Kathmandu, in 1802, by far the most powerful of these six houses were the Pangres and Viswanaths.

Occasionally a few regulars are sent to act as a guard to the Subahs, but the Telanggas, or regular troops, are entirely exempt from the authority of these officers.

The military force among the petty chiefs was always large in proportion to their means, but consisted of a rabble totally undisciplined and ill armed, although of good bodily endowments. Much order has been introduced by the chiefs of Gorkha, although both in arms and discipline the soldiers are still very far behind Europeans. In Puraniya I was told, that, in that vicinity, that is, in the country of the Kiratas, the lands assigned for the support of the military were given to the officers commanding companies, who were held bound to give regular pay to their men; nor have I any reason to doubt that such a measure has been carried into effect in that vicinity; but I was assured at Gorakhpur, as also at Kathmandu, that each individual in the western parts receives his own lands.

Each Subahdar commanding a company now receives 400 or 500 rupees a-year, and 15 khets or fields, each of which is estimated to produce 100 muris or 234¼ Winchester bushels

* Nepaul, p. 124.

of grain, of which, if the land is let, he will obtain one-half, worth almost 72 ($71\frac{7}{8}$) rupees. For every Pati or squad of from 20 to 25 fuzileers there are one Jumahdar, one Havildar, and one Amildar. The first of these receives 7 fields of land, and 200 rupees in money. A major keeps the accounts of the company, and has Jumahdar's allowances. Each company has five or six squads, besides officers and music. The privates have each three fields, and 25 rupees a-year. Such are the accounts that I received. Those given to Colonel Kirkpatrick * differ somewhat, making the allowance of the superior officers higher, and of the privates lower, than what I have stated.

Each company has a large band of music, amounting to ten men, where there are six Patis or squads. These have instruments of the most hideous noise. Each company has, besides, two flags, and a regular establishment of artificers, so that the army may be considered as perfectly well arranged; but the soldiers are little versed in tactics, and, considering the strong country that they possess, this would be of less importance, were they in habits of more prompt obedience, and more dexterous in the use of their arms; but they do not load with cartridge. They have all firelocks, but these are not in the best condition. They do not use the bayonet, but have all swords, which are, perhaps, better fitted for such a country, and I believe that the men are dexterous in their use. They also have in their belt a large knife or dagger, (Khukri,) which serves as many purposes as that of Hudibras. It is represented in the uppermost figure of the plate opposite to page 118, in the work of Colonel Kirkpatrick. When that

* Nepaul, p. 102.

gentleman visited the country, the troops were irregularly clothed, some in the same company of guards wearing red, some green, and some blue. When I saw them, this irregularity had been remedied, and all were in red, each company having, besides, its peculiar facings; and, although their arms were not clean, they did not appear so bad as when Colonel Kirkpatrick saw them, as he states * that few of their muskets appeared fit for service.

In the vicinity of Kathmandu, Bhim Sen is said to have collected 25 companies, and there are probably 15 at Tamsen, under his father. It is also said, that at each of the capitals of former petty chiefs there are from one to five companies; and a large body, perhaps from 20 to 25 companies, is under old Amar Singha in advance beyond the Yamuna. In the western parts, the old irregulars, I believe, have been entirely discarded, or are only called out occasionally in times of actual hostility, when they are employed to plunder.

In the parts west from the river Kali, almost the whole revenue, whether on the mountains or plains, being reserved under the immediate management of the prince, a fuller establishment was necessary; and that which existed under the petty chiefs, entirely resembled what is described by the late Mr Grant, Sereshtahdar of Bengal, as the proper Mogul system. The actual cultivators, or farmers as they would be termed in England, only they all occupied very small farms, were called Zemindars, and were very moderately assessed. In Almora, (and the other estates did not materially differ,) the rent was fixed by the Visi, which, on an average, may be taken at 10 Calcutta bigahs, or 3⅓ English acres; but the Visis va-

* Nepaul, p. 214.

ried a good deal in size, especially in such as were exempted from assessment, which were in general much larger than such as paid it. The extent of 10 bigahs for the Visi is chiefly applicable to the latter. The rent was paid partly in kind, partly in money. Each Visi in October paid 28 sers of clean rice, (Calcutta weight,) 4 sers of the pulse called Urid, and 2 sers of Ghiu or oil: in May it paid 28 sers of wheat, 4 sers of Urid, and 2 of Ghiu: in August it paid one rupee in money. On each of the two holidays called Dasahara, there was besides a kid offered to the sovereign for every 10 Visis. The possessions of a convenient number of Zemindars formed a gram or gang, and one of them held the hereditary office of Pradhan, entirely analogous to the Umra of the eastern parts. The Pradhan was allowed a deduction of rent, and enjoyed some honourable distinctions, and, when the heir was in any manner incapacitated, a relation was appointed to act for him. The representations of the other Zemindars or farmers in the same gram, were usually considered as the most just criterion of this incapacity. Besides the judicial powers and the magistracy of his territory, the Pradhan kept an account of the other tenants, and of their payments and debts to government, and, receiving what was due, transmitted it to the collector. He was also an agent for the other Zemindars of his village, to represent losses which they had suffered, and to solicit indulgences on the occasion. Over from twenty to fifty Pradhans was another hereditary officer named Kamin, analogous to the Desali of the eastern states. He assisted the Pradhans in settling their accounts, and in obtaining indulgences on account of peculiar losses; and it was his duty, in an especial manner, to protect the Zemindars, and to induce new comers to occupy waste lands. The rents were never farmed out, but were delivered by the Pradhans to the messengers of the collector, or Bandari, who received an account of what was due from the Kanungoe or register, and he made up his accounts from those forwarded to him by the Pradhans. Where the lordship was petty, no other officers were necessary; but where large, the country was divided into pergunahs or taluks, each managed by an officer removeable at will. In the most important of these districts, especially towards a weak frontier, were stationed military officers called Foujdars, who had authority to determine many small suits without appeal, but always with the assistance of a Pangchayit. In the less important stations, the officers managing taluks or pergunahs were on the hills named Negis, and on the plains Adhikars. These also decided causes by means of a Pangchayit; but there was an appeal to the chief's court, in which he sat in person, assisted by his principal officers, the Darogah or judge, and the Dharm'adhikar or chancellor. These often decided the cause without a Pangchayit; but this was only when the parties were obstinate, and would not consent to the use of this kind of jury. The facts in criminal prosecutions were often investigated by the inferior officers and Pangchayit on the spot, and the chief and his chancellor judged from their report, what punishment was due. The Foujdars, Negis, and Adhikars, besides their duties as judges, magistrates, and military guardians of the boundary, which the Foujdars were, received from the Pradhans all the rents, and, having sold those paid in kind, remitted the proceeds to the (Bandari) collector, or rather store-keeper.

About six parts in ten of the whole lands had been alienated to the Brahmans and temples, nor do I hear any complaint in this quarter of the present government having invaded this property; but much of the Zemindary lands have been granted to the soldiers and officers, on the same terms as towards the east, and the Zemindars of such lands have in a great measure been left to the discretion of the new occupants, who have of course raised considerably the rate of rent. In former times the chiefs received the whole proceeds, and paid from thence the whole establishment, civil and military. In comparing the following accounts, therefore, of the states east and west of the river Kali, particular attention must be paid to this circumstance. For instance, the revenue of Gorkha has been stated at 12,000 rupees, and that of Bhajji at 15,000; but the latter, even in comparison with the former, was altogether petty, as this 15,000 rupees was the whole sum destined for the support of the chief and his family, and of his officers, servants, and soldiers; whereas the 12,000 rupees in Gorkha was entirely disposable for the personal expence of the chief, and his children; his kinsmen, and even most of his domestics, as well as the civil and military establishments, being supported entirely by land.

In the western parts, the chief civil authority was held by the Vazir, and the chief military command by the Bukhshi, and both were appointed by the will of the chief; but of course most commonly were conferred on his kinsmen, although some families of Brahmans often interfered. The military were of two kinds. Part consisted of adventurers from the low country, the privates receiving usually five rupees a month, and remaining constantly on duty. The others were selected from the stoutest youth in the families of the Zemindars, and were relieved as often as they pleased, by their parents or kinsmen sending other youths in their place; for no sort of instruction in military evolution was attempted, and the only exercise was shooting at a mark. The privates of this class received daily rations of food, and twice a year from 20 to 100 rupees, according to their supposed intrepidity. Those, however, who received more than 25 rupees were few in number. The whole troops were armed with matchlock, sword, and target.

PART II.

ACCOUNT OF THE PARTICULAR STATES WHICH FORMERLY EXISTED, AND OF THE FAMILIES BY WHICH EACH WAS GOVERNED.

INTRODUCTION.

I NOW proceed to give an account of the various states and principalities which this mountainous region contained, and of the manner in which they became subject to the chiefs of Gorkha; and I shall commence at the Eastern extremity, proceeding westward regularly, so far as I can, without interrupting the account of each family.

CHAPTER FIRST.

OF THE STATES EAST FROM THE RIVER KALI.

SECTION I.

COUNTRY OF SIKIM.

Inhabitants.—Government.—Extent.—History.—Geography.

THE most eastern principality, in the present dominions of Gorkha, is that of the Lapchas, called Sikim. Although the prince of Sikim was a Bhotiya, the strength of his army consisted entirely of the Lapchas, who inhabited the higher mountains between the Kankayi and Tista. The Bhotiyas themselves are a very timid race, entirely sunk under the enervating effects of what they call religion.

Besides the Bhotiyas, who surrounded the prince, and the Lapchas by whom he was guarded, the mountains of Sikim contained many people of the tribe called Limbu, who have been already mentioned. My informant thinks, that of the whole population three-tenths were Bhotiyas, five-tenths Lapchas, and two-tenths Limbus.

The princes of Sikim, as I have said, were Bhotiyas. They were of a family of high rank from Lasa, and took the title of Gelpo. The next person in the state was the chief or Hang of the Lapchas. I suspect that the Gelpo possessed little power, except in matters of religion; for it is said, that his neighbour, the Deva Dharma Raja, although a mere priest, appoints whomsoever he pleases to manage the temporal affairs of his country; but in Sikim the office of Hang is hereditary. I have not learned the succession of the princes of Sikim; but it is probable that the Bhotiyas have governed the country for a considerable time.

At one time the princes of Sikim had extended their dominion far south, into the district of Puraniya, and possessed the low country on the east of the Mahananda, as far as Krishnagunj, a part of the country which was originally possessed by the Koch and Paliyas, the natives of Kamrup and Matsya, now the districts of Ranggapur and Dinajpur. The Rajas of Sikim were driven from the greatest part of this most valuable of their possessions by the Moslems; but they still retained a small space of the plain to the north of the Pergunah of Baikunthapur, when they were attacked by the Gorkhalese. Although the Kankayi, in the upper part of its course, was nearly their boundary, they never would appear to have possessed the plain between the Kankayi and Mahananda; but they were lords of the lower hills, occupied by the tribe called Dimali, who, I am assured, are the same with the Mech, a tribe now confined to the eastern parts of Kamrup or Ranggapur.

The chief who governed Sikim before the year 1782, was by the natives of the Company's territory named Rup Chiring; but the Bhotiya names are so mangled by the Bengalese, that no reliance can be placed on those reported by them. He resided at Darjiling, and had there a fort, or strong house of brick, which an old Bengalese, who visited it about that time, describes as very splendid; but his ideas of magnificence in building are probably rather confined. This prince died about the year 1782, and was succeeded by his son, the Chhawa Raja, which is the name that the low country people give to the heir-apparent of this family. During his time, and, as would appear from a letter addressed by Mr Pagan to Colonel Ross, in the month of September, (probably of 1788, for there is no date in the letter,) the Gorkhalese invaded Sikim. Their troops consisted of about 6000 men, of whom 2000 were regulars, and were under the command of Tiurar Singha, Subah of Morang. He met with no opposition until he approached Sikim, the capital, in defence of which the Rajah ventured an engagement; when, after an obstinate resistance, he was completely defeated, owing, in all probability, to the 2000 fusileers. The Gorkhalese, however, suffered much, although they immediately laid siege to the capital. This happened shortly previous to the 28th October 1788, as, in a letter from Mr Pagan of that date, he mentions, that he had just received accounts of the entire conquest of Sikim by the Gorkhalese, who, in this report, had considerably magnified the extent of their victory.

The Raja of Sikim retired towards the frontier of Thibet, in order to reassemble his army, and to solicit assistance from Lasa andTasasudan. At the latter place was soon concluded a treaty, by which the Sikim chief engaged to pay the Deva Dharma Raja a certain tribute, on condition of his being restored to his dominions by the exertions of that prince. This negociation is said to have been facilitated by an open boast made by the Gorkhalese, that they no sooner should have conquered Sikim, than they would attack the Deva Dharma Raja, a kind of policy of which the Gorkhalese are fond, when they have no sort of intention of putting their threats in execution.

The Raja, strengthened by a considerable force of the Deva Dharma's troops, and a party of Bhotiyas from a province of

Thibet, named Portaw, returned towards the capital, and, about the beginning of December, compelled the Gorkhalese to raise the siege; and, after losing many men in a skirmish, to retire towards Ilam on the Kankayi, where they had erected forts to secure a communication with Morang. It must be observed, that, at this time, the Gorkhalese had invaded the province of Kutti in Thibet, and had there met with a repulse; and that a body of the troops of Thibet had penetrated through a pass in the mountains to the eastward of Kutti. These troops seized on the passes of the Kosi and Arun rivers, thus intending to cut off all communication between Kathmandu and the army in Morang; an excellent plan, and very easily practicable.

The Gorkhalese commander, far from being dismayed, seems soon to have dispossessed these troops, and gave out that he had retreated from Sikim merely on account of the severity of the cold.

From the reports of the natives, there is reason to suppose, that about this time the Sikim Raja died, leaving his son Kurin Namki, an infant. The war was chiefly conducted by Yuksu-thuck, the Hang or chief of the Lapchas, who was next in rank to the Raja. This man, by the natives of the low country, was called Chhatrajit, and was a person of barbarous energy. He seems to have headed the army in the field, while his brother Nam-si (Lamjit of the Bengalese) defended the capital. They were sons of Lang-cho, son of De-sha, both of whom had held the office of Hang.

Soon after these advantages over the Gorkhalese, the troops of the Deva Dharma Raja retired; for they are allowed no pay, and the country was too poor to admit of plunder. By a letter from Mr Pagan, this would appear to have happened before the 29th March 1789. On this the greater part of the people of Sikim submitted to the Gorkhalese; but the Raja fled to Tankiya in Thibet, and the chief of the Lapchas retired to a stronghold situated between the two branches of the Tista; from which he has ever since annoyed the Gorkhalese. This place, called Gandhauk, has annexed to it a territory of considerable extent, and affords the Raja a revenue of about 7000 rupees a-year, which is all that he possesses; but, being a man of high birth, he lately obtained in marriage a daughter of the chief minister at Lasa, with whom, in 1809, he returned to the petty dominion, which the vigour of his minister has retained.

Both the Deva Dharma Raja and the government of Lasa seem to have been most seriously alarmed at the progress of the Gorkhalese, and applied to the Emperor of China for his interposition. In the meanwhile, the Deva Dharma Raja is said to have sent an embassy to Kathmandu, offering as a sacrifice the part of Baikunthapur, that had been given to him by Mr Hastings; but the interposition of the emperor came in time to save this, and the Gorkhalese have ever since abstained from giving him any molestation. The people of Thibet were not so fortunate, and were compelled to cede to the Nepalese a part of Kutti, which now forms the government of Kheran or Kheru, on the head of the Sankosi, and some Bhotiya villages near the Arun, which are now annexed to the northern part of Vijaypur, and with that form the government of Chayenpur. By a letter from Colonel Ross, dated in the end of December 1789, it would appear that our government had received intelligence of every thing having been settled by the interference of the Chinese, and that a Gorkhalese envoy had been dispatched to pay homage to the emperor.

The Lapchas were, however, not so easily managed. Part

under their chief Nam-si maintained an absolute independence, and the remainder have been so troublesome, that the Gorkhalese have judged it prudent to give them a governor, or, at least, a collector of their own. This person, named Yu-kang-ta, and called Angriya Gabur by the Bengalese, is nephew of the Lapcha chief, who has so gallantly defended the remnant of the principality. In 1808, I found that he was in possession of the whole civil government, and had agreed to pay annually a fixed sum as tribute. The Subah of Chayenpur was, however, in military authority over him, and there were Gorkhalese troops at Sikim and Darjiling, the two chief places in the district.

On the return of the young Raja to Gandhauk, he brought with him as an escort 500 Bhotiyas of Thibet; and an insurrection seems to have been meditated. In the end of 1809, a person calling himself Dihit Karan, a relation of the chief of the Kirats, came to Lieutenant Munro, then stationed at Sannyasikata, and informed him that he had been sent as an embassador by the Chinese general, (Vazir,) who had arrived with 15,000 men and 40 guns to restore the Prince of Sikim, and that he was on his way to Puraniya, to proceed from thence to Calcutta. From the information of his nearest relations, there is reason to think that Dihit Karan had died before this time, and the messenger did not go to Puraniya. It is probable that he merely came to sound Mr Munro, whether or not there was any actual appearance of hostility between the British government and the Gorkhalese. The only troops that had come were the 500 armed Bhotiyas; but with even these the enterprising Lapcha is said to have determined to proceed, and a good many Gorkhalese soldiers marched in that direction. At this time the Lapcha died, and after a little skirmishing things were amicably adjusted, the Sikim Raja retaining Gandhauk alone.

The map of this country drawn by the Lama, and mentioned in the Introduction, although very rude, as might be naturally expected, will enable scientific men to throw considerable light on the geography of that country, hitherto almost unknown, and more reliance is to be placed on most of the Lama's positions, than on those given in the map of the countries east from Nepal, which has been mentioned in the same place, except towards the south-west corner, for the Lama was better acquainted with the other parts of the country than the person who constructed the map to which I have alluded. His scale is an inch to the day's journey. His angular lines represent mountains, and, beginning at the north, we find Khawa karpola, that is, the mountain white with snow, or the highest ridge of Emodus, which separates Sikim from the dominion of Lasa. According to the map, this ridge is penetrated by three rivers. That on the west is the Kankayi; but it seems doubtful whether or not this actually rises from beyond the highest peaks of Emodus, for, in another map, which will be afterwards mentioned, its source is made to come from a lower range of the snowy mountains, which by some is called Mirgu; and this opinion is strongly confirmed by its size, when it enters the plains. The Kankayi would appear to run in a narrow valley between two ridges of mountains, and for some way down the whole valley belonged to Sikim. In this are two Golas or marts, Bilasi and Majhoya. To these marts the low country traders carry rice, salt, extract of sugarcane, hogs, dry fish, tobacco, spirituous liquor, and various cloths. Formerly they took oxen for slaughter, but, since the conquest, this has been prohibited. They procured in return cotton, Indian madder, (Manjit,) musk, and Thibet bull-tails, (Chaungris.)

Farther down, the Kankayi formed the boundary between the Kirats and Sikim, until it reached the plain, the whole of which, as far as the Mahananda, belonged to the Vijaypur Rajas, while all the low hills belonged to Sikim. These low hills are not represented in the map, although they are of very considerable size, such as the greater part of the mountains of Scotland or Wales; but, near Emodus, these appear like mole-hills. The hilly country, I am told by the traders, commences at what they call six coses north from Sannyasikata, and extends about eighteen coses farther to Siumali, another mart, which the low country people name Dimali.

The hills south of Dimali are thinly inhabited by the Mech or Dimali, who cultivate cotton, rice, and other articles, in the same manner as the Garos, which will be described in my account of Asam. This kind of country extends from the Kankayi to the Tista, everywhere, probably, about the same width; but the coses, in all likelihood, are very short, twelve of them being reckoned a day's journey, and, in such roads, twelve miles is a long journey, and will give no great horizontal distance.

Between the Mahananda and Tista the Sikim Raja possessed a low tract, four or five coses wide, which is inhabited by Koch, and cultivated with the plough. The chief place in it is Dabi, on the east bank of the Mahananda. This part is not noticed in the Lama's map.

Siumali, or Dimali, according to the Bengalese, is a custom-house on the east side of the Bala kongyar river, but the Lama places it on the west, and is probably more correct, the Bengalese concerning such points being uncommonly stupid. At this custom-house or mart is a Lapcha collector, appointed by Yu-kang-ta. He has with him four Bengalese writers, to assist him in collecting the duties. The custom-house consists of a square surrounded by buildings, in which the traders and their commodities are received, for there is no house near, except those of the collector and his assistants. The traders from the low country take up salt, tobacco, cotton cloth, goats, fowls, swine, iron, and occasionally a little coral, and broad cloth. They bring back Indian madder, (Manjit,) cotton, bees-wax, blankets, horses, musk, bull-tails, (Chaungris,) Chinese flowered silk, (Devang,) and rhinoceroses horns.

North from the mart, half a day's journey, on a hill at the source of the Bala kongyar, is the residence of Yu-kang-ta, the Lapcha chief, who now collects the revenues for the Gorkhalese. By the natives it is called Sam-dung, but the Bengalese call it Nagrikoth. They describe it as a very large building, with several stories, and it was represented to Mr Monro as a fort of some strength. Both accounts are, however, doubtful, as I learn that it is roofed only with thatch. Two days' journey east from this, at the source of the Mahananda, is Satang, another Gola or mart; but, of late, Siumali has engrossed almost the whole trade.

Immediately north from these places the Lama lays down a high ridge of mountains, extending from the Kankayi beyond the Tista, and on this he says that Dalimkoth, belonging to Bhotan, is situated, and he makes it communicate with the snowy mountains, both at the Kankayi and to the east of the Tista. All the rivers between the Kankayi and Tista spring from the south side of this chain, and between its two arms is included the greater part of Sikim, watered by various branches of the Tista, and forming, as it were, a valley; but the whole of this space is extremely mountainous, though there is much cultivation carried on with the hoe. The great articles of cultivation are rice and Manjit.

Beyond Sam-dung and Sa-tang one day's journey, and on the other side of the first high mountains, is Darjiling, which would appear to be the chief fortress of the country, as it is there that the Gorkhalese troops are mostly stationed. From thence to Sikim, the capital, is six days' journey, and the snowy mountains are about the same distance still farther north. Sikim is on the west side of the Jhamikuma river, which arises from the south side of the snowy mountains, and, opposite to the town, divides into two branches, which surround an immense mountain, on the top of which there is a small level and strong-hold named Tasiding. The descent from this to the river is reckoned half a day's journey on each side. Some way below this, the river receives from the west a branch named Rainam, that rises from the mountains, by which the Kankayi is bounded on the east. The united streams are called the Rimikma, which soon joins the Tista.

The great river Tista arises in the dominions of Lasa by two branches, called the Greater and Lesser Tista, and passes through the snowy mountains. The western branch forms the boundary between the dominions of the Gorkhalese and the petty territory of Gan-dhauk, which still remains to the Raja of Sikim. This poor prince possesses also a small portion beyond the lesser or eastern Tista, which, however, in general, forms the boundary between him and Bhotan, or the country of the Deva Dharma Raja. On its east side is Dam-sang, a fortress belonging to the last-mentioned prince. The united stream of the two Tistas forms the present boundary between him and Gorkha.

The only route between Sikim and Thibet is by a passage through the snowy mountains, named Phakali, and this is seven days' journey from Jang-chim, in the north-east part of the Sikim territory, so that, the route being through the territory of the Deva Dharma Raja, the people of Sikim were entirely dependent on this prince for a communication with Thibet.

SECTION II.

DOMINIONS OF THE FAMILY DESCENDED FROM MAKANDA SEN, RAJA OF MAKWANPUR.

General History.—Branch of Lohanga which occupied the Country of the Kiratas.—History.—Former Government.—Military Force, Police, and Revenue, and Justice.—Present State.—District of Morang.—District of Chayenpur.—District of Naragarhi.—District of Hedang.—District of Makwanpur.—Western Branch, which occupied chiefly the Country of Palpa.—History.—Description.—Tanahung Family and its Possessions, and Collateral Branches.—Rising, Ghiring, and Gajarkot.

The next principality to that of the Lapchas was that of the Kiratas, which fell to the lot of a family that pretends to be sprung from the Rajas of Chitaur, although its claims, as I have said, are by no means well substantiated, and the different branches of the family differ much in the account of their genealogy.

In the account of the Newars, I have mentioned, that the tribe called Bhawar or Bhar has many territories, which had been subject to a powerful chief, whose capital was Garsamaran in Tirahut, and the dominion of these Bhawars extended once all over Gorakhpur. Garsamaran was destroyed in 1322 by the Muhammedans, and in its vicinity a state of anarchy, under petty chiefs, prevailed for twenty-four years, while the Muhammedans seized on the parts towards the Ganges. About 1306, the Muhammedans had destroyed Chitaur, and expelled from thence the Chauhan tribe, called also Sisaudhiyas, because they had been settled in a town of that name before they occupied Chitaur.

In the account given of the mountain Hindus, I have mentioned, that these Chauhans are said to have retired to the mountains, and founded the dynasties of Karuvirpur and Yumila; but another family pretends also to be descended from the Rajas of Chitaur, and to have long occupied a great extent of country to the east, south, and west of Nepal Proper. In the eastern parts of this dominion, it was said, that the first chiefs of this family, who came to the parts of which I am now treating, were Jil and Ajil Rays, sons of Buddhi, brother of Chitra Sen, Raja of Chitaur, and son of Pratap Sen, son of Udayraj Sen, of the Sisaudhiya tribe of the Kshatriya race. These two adventurers, with 700 soldiers of fortune, entered into the service of Karma Singha, a person of the impure tribe of Bhawar, which is very numerous in the low country subject to Nepal. This chief resided at Rajpur, on the west side of the Gandaki or Salgrami, where that great river enters the plains, and he had subject to him many of his countrymen, who chiefly cultivated the low lands, and some Kirats, and other barbarians, who occupied the adjacent hills, and formed his military power. He is said to have had two brothers, Nandakumar, Raja of Nandapur Tisuti, near Bhawara, (Bawara R.) in Tirahut, and Sarandeo, Raja of Belka on the Kosi.

For twenty-two years the Hindu nobles served this low man, but were then able to cut him off, and Ajil Sen assumed the government. He was succeeded by his son Tula Sen ; and it must be observed, that all the princes of this family are called Sen, which I shall for the future in general omit, although among the natives, in speaking of them, it is always annexed. Tula built on the hills the fortress of Makwanpur, (Mocaumpour, R.) since which time the principality has been often called by that name, but it seems then to have extended only from the large Gandaki to the Adhwara River. He was succeeded in regular lineal descent by Dambhal, Gajapati, Chandra, Rudra, and Mukunda, by which time the principality had been extended far towards the west, over the mountains of the Magars and Gurung.

In the western parts of the territory belonging to this family, I procured a manuscript said to have been composed by Rana Bahadur, late Chautariya of Palpa, and one of its descendants. He states, that the first of his ancestors, who came to this country, was Rudra Sen, the son of Chandra Sen, Raja of Chitaur, descended of Ratna Sen, first Chauhan chief of that city ; but I think that this account is not tenable, and Samar Bahadur, the brother of Rana Bahadur, gives one totally different, and, in my opinion, more probable. He says, that Ratna Sen, instead of being the first Raja of Chitaur, was the last of these princes ; and that Naya Sen, his eldest son, settled at Prayag or Allahabad, which he seized with 20,000 men, and he considers Tutha Sen, Ribeli Sen, Dimirawa Sen Udayarawa Sen, Udayachanda Sen, Jagadbrahma Sen, Dharma Pala Sen, Aneka Singha Sen, Ramraja Sen, and Chandra Sen, the father of Rudra Sen, not as Rajas of Chitaur, as his brother's manuscript represents, but as chiefs of the colony from that city, which settled in the vicinity of Nepal. Tutha

Sen, he says, having been driven from Prayag, seized on the country adjacent to the hills of Butaul, and afterwards seized on the principality of Champaranya, the capital of which was Rajpur. Now, this seems highly probable, for Chitaur was taken in about 1306, and Garsamaran, of which Champaranya was originally a dependency, did not fall until 1322, while an anarchy prevailed throughout the territories of Garsamaran until 1346, that is to say, until these were mostly reunited under the colony from Chitaur, 40 years after the fall of that city. It is, therefore, unlikely, that the chief who left Chitaur should have seen his family established in a new dominion; but, that it should have been his son who accomplished this event, as Samar Bahadur says, is highly probable. Tutha's first acquisition on the hills seems to have been Rishiyang, now an inconsiderable place between Butaul and Palpa. His son founded Ribdikot in that vicinity, of which it continued to be the capital, until Palpa was founded by Rudra Sen. It must be observed, that the accounts procured in Puraniya and Gorakhpur differ totally as to names, until the time of Chandra Sen, after which they agree tolerably well, and Rudra was probably the first of the family, as his descendant alleges, who assumed the title of the Palpa Raja. It is agreed by all, that the Makanda Sen, the son of Rudra, possessed very extensive dominions, and might probably have founded a kingdom equal to that which the Gorkhalese now enjoy, but he had the imbecility to divide his estates among his four sons. The accounts concerning these sons differ somewhat. According to what I heard in Puraniya, Manik, the eldest son, obtained Palpa, Bhringgu received Tanahung, Rajpur the original possession of the family, was given to Arjun, and Makwanpur, with its hardy mountaineers, fell to the lot of Lohangga. But the account given in the manuscript of Rana Bahadur, which here, I think, deserves most credit, is, that the eldest son was Binayak, who communicated his name to a large territory on the plain west from the Gandaki, which he received as his patrimony; but this territory is now most commonly called Butaul, from its chief town, and in the low country the chiefs are commonly called the Butaul Rajas. The second son, Manik, obtained Palpa; the third son, Bihangga, (Bhringga of the Puraniya account,) obtained Tanahung, and Lohangga, the fourth son, obtained Makwanpur.

I shall now return to the Kiratas, the nation next to the Lapchas, when they were about to receive Lohangga as their chief.

At that time the country between the Kosi and the Kankayi, and on the plain so far as the Mahanandah, was subject to Vijayanarayan, whose ancestors are said to have come from Kamrup. From his title, one might be led to suppose that he was of the Vihar family; but one of this race, who was in my service, denied any such relation; and, indeed, as Vijaya is said to have been the seventh prince of his family, he could scarcely have been descended of the grandson of the Koch Hajo, ancestor of the chiefs of Vihar. The natives allege, that the title of the chiefs of this family was Harbhang Raja, and that the title of his minister was Bharbhang Mantri. Harbhang Bharbhang, in the provincial dialect, implies foolish, similar to the notions entertained by the Bengalese of Havachandra and Bhavachandra of Kamrup, which may perhaps serve to connect the history of the two dynasties. Not that these princes seem to have been more foolish than their neighbours, but they probably had some customs, that appeared extraordinary to their subjects. Two dynasties are mentioned as having preceded that of the Harbhang Rajas; *1st*, That of Kichak Raja, contemporary with Yudhishthir; and, *2d*, That of the Satya Rajas, in whose time probably the power of the Kirats or Kichaks was at the greatest height.

I have received three accounts of the manner in which Vijayanarayan was overthrown. The first was given me orally by Agam Singha. He says, that the ancestors of Vijayanarayan originally possessed only the low country called Morang; but that this prince took into his service his ancestor Singha Ray, the son of Khebang, who was Hang or hereditary chief of the Kirats, that occupied the hills north from Morang. When the needy mountaineers had for some time been accustomed to the luxuries of the plains, the Raja built Vijayapur, and took the title of Vijaya Bharati, or victorious over the earth. He soon after took occasion to put the mountain chief to death, under pretence, that he, being an impure beef-eating monster, had presumed to defile a Hindu woman. Baju Ray, son of the mountain chief, immediately retired, and, going to the Rajput chief of Makwanpur, promised to join him with all his Kirats, if that prince would enable him to destroy the murderer of his father. This was accordingly done, and the Hang was constituted sole Chautariya or hereditary chief minister of the principality, which dignity his descendants enjoyed, until its total overthrow, and Agam Singha, the last possessor of the office, accompanied his master, when he fled for refuge into the Company's territory, and now lives with the mother of that unfortunate youth.

The second account was given by the Munsuf of Bahadurgunj, mentioned in the Introduction. He nearly agrees with the Kirat chief, but says, that the new dynasty was formed in a manner entirely peaceable. Vijayanarayan having died without heirs, the Kirat chief, who was the second person in the government, invited a brother of the Palpa Raja to take possession of the government.

The third account was communicated to me in writing by Premnarayan Das, mentioned also in the Introduction. The scribe says, that one day Vijayanarayan went to Varahachhatra, a place of pilgrimage on the Kosi, where Vishnu is worshipped under the form of a boar. Here he found a Sannyasi, Ramanath Bharati, who, warned by a dream, had come from Surya kunda, and had taken up his residence in a hut near the place of worship, where he was assiduous in prayer. The Sannyasi having been insolent to the Raja, a circumstance not at all improbable, the prince had the audacity to kick him down the hill, and to burn his hut. The god then appeared to the saint in a human form, and gave him authority of speech, (Bakya Siddhi,) by which all men would obey his command. Bharati then went to the poor chief of Makwanpur, who, having been kind and attentive, was commanded to take possession of the dominions of Vijayanarayan, and was informed how it might be done.

The account of the Kirat is evidently the most credible, although it is not unlikely that Ramanath may have been disgusted, and might have been employed to gain over the people, and to negociate between the Rajput and Kirat; but the scribe alleges, that these barbarians were not elevated to the first office of the state until a later period. However that may be, in the remainder of the history, I shall follow chiefly his account, although even there it differs in some particulars from the accounts that I received both from Agam Singha, and from the Brahman.

Lohangga, on crossing the Adhwara, first subdued a petty chief of the Magar tribe. He then took possession of a small territory on the plain, belonging to an Aniwar Brahman. Then he destroyed Mohan Thakur, another chief of the last mentioned tribe, and seized on his territory, which now forms the district of Mahatari. He in a similar manner seized on Korani, belonging to a Bhawar, and probably a descendant of Nandakumar. (p. 129;) on Khesraha, belonging to Raja Langkeswar; on Rampur belonging to Raja Muzles; on Pokhari, belonging to Raja Karabandar; on Jhamuna, belonging to Raja Roja; on Jogoda, belonging to Raja Udaygir; on Dhapar, Kalisa, and Belka koth, belonging to Raja Karnadeo; on Samda, belonging to Ballabh deo; and on Karjain, belonging to Dullabh deo, a brother of the two last mentioned chiefs, who were descended of Saran deo, brother of Karma Singha and Nandakumar, (p. 129,) as I am informed by Gauri Chaudhuri, their representative, and now Zemindar of Dhapar, in the district of Puraniya. All these were petty independent chiefs, whose territories now form Pergunahs in the Subah of Saptari, belonging to Gorkha, or in the adjacent parts of the Company's territory. The rapacious chief now made an attack on the hill Gidha, but here he was opposed by a devil, (Dano,) who killed a number of his troops, and prevailed, until the holy man Ramanath ordered the god Ramkrishna to cut off the devil's head, which was accordingly done. The Raja then descended to Meghvari on the banks of the Kosi, where he learned that Vijayanarayan had died. He, therefore, left one-half of his troops at Meghvari, and, advancing with the other, took quiet possession of Vijayapur, (Bissypur, R.) The nature of these transactions strongly confirms the account given by Agam Singha, as the force of the petty district of Makwanpur seems to have been totally inadequate to effect such conquests; but the junction of the Kirats will readily account for the success.

Agam Singha says, that during these wars, his ancestor Baju was killed, and was succeeded by his son Bidyachandra, who relinquished the title of Hang, and in its stead took that of Chautariya, and who, like all his successors, assumed a Hindu name, and adopted some degree of purity in his manner of life.

Lohangga had now acquired a very extensive territory, reaching from the Adiya on the west to the Mahananda on the east, and from the alps of Bhot to Julagar near Puraniya. When the Sannyasi had placed the Raja on the throne, he wished to return to his native country, but, at the intercession of the prince, he remained some time longer, having been appointed priest (Mahanta) to a temple (Math) erected at Varaha Chhatra, and well endowed. According, indeed, to my authority, the priests, his successors, seem to have held a distinguished place in the state; but, since the conquest, they have sunk into insignificance, although the Gorkhalese still allow them ample endowments.

Lohangga had two sons, Raghav' and Bhagawanta, but rationally left the whole of his dominions to the former, who, by all other persons except the scribe, is considered as having been the founder of the family in these parts, and as a brother of the Raja of Palpa. In his reign Ramanath delivered over his office to Jagamohan, and disappeared; but he promised his successor to favour him with an annual visit.

Harihar', the son of Raghav', extended his dominions to Gondwara, and took the title of Hindupati, or chief of the Hindus. His wife, Jagamata, having been delivered of a daughter of most extraordinary beauty, he, in his joy, called to her by her name; but, as it is totally contrary to Hindu law for a man to call his wife Mata, that is, mother, he was under the necessity of divorcing her, which will, perhaps, show that his civilians had a considerable skill in discovering legal pretexts for the actions of their prince. The chief was soon after supplied with other wives, for, having made war on the Vihar Raja, and taken that prince in battle, his anger was pacified by obtaining Mahisi and Maheswari, two beautiful daughters of the descendant of Siva. By Mahisi the Morang Raja had four sons, Chhatrapati, Padma, Pratap, and one who died an infant. Maheswari bore only one son, named Subha, to whom his father intended to leave the whole of his dominions, and, in order to secure his authority, gave him immediate possession of the territory of Makwani.

After this, Harihar seems to have fallen into a state of dotage, and his three sons by Mahisi rose upon their aged parent, and put him in confinement. In this difficulty he applied to Adanuka, the wife of Chhatrapati, one of these unnatural sons, and promised, if she would procure his release, that he would leave the whole of his kingdom to the child with which she was then pregnant. This lady, who seems to have possessed great abilities, persuaded her husband and his two brothers to release their father, on condition that the whole kingdom should be divided into four equal shares, one for each brother. The three sons of Mahisi then went and attacked their brother, in order to compel him to agree to this engagement, but they were defeated with great loss, and retreated to Phulwari, on the Kamala river, where Adanuka was delivered of a son, whom his grandfather immediately created king of all the territories east from the Kosi, while he left all on the west of that river to his son Subha. The father and uncles of the infant had probably been too much weakened by their defeat to venture on any farther enterprise of villany.

I shall now follow the history of Subha, who soon after these events fell sick, and sent for Ganggadhar, the successor of Jagamohan as priest at Varaha Chhatra. This person informed the Raja that he was just about to die, but, as he himself had forty years of life to spare, he would transfer them to the prince, for whom he had a great regard. The Raja accepted the offer, and soon after the priest went and buried himself alive, (Samadi,) a manner of taking leave of the world which is considered as very laudable, and to this day is occasionally practised at Varaha Chhatra. The Raja, on the strength of this accession of life, married a young Rajput named Amarawati, by whom he had two sons, Mahapati and Manik.

Subha Sen had governed thirty-one years of his additional life, when he had a dispute with Pradyumna Upadhyaya, a Brahman of Tanahung, who was his Dewan, or minister of finance. This traitor entered into a conspiracy with a certain officer named Parasuram Thapa, and, in order to induce this man to rebel, did not hesitate to give him his daughter in marriage, although the fellow was of the spurious breed called Khas, descended by the father's side alone from the sacred order; and this would appear to be considered as by far the most reprehensible part of the Brahman's offence. Having seized on the old Raja, their master, these traitors intended to deliver him up to Isfundiyar khan, the Nawab of Puraniya. By this time Indu Bidhata, the infant who had been made Raja of Marang, had grown up, and, hearing of his uncle's misfortune, led an army against the Nawab and the traitors, and was accompanied by his brother Budha Sen. Having obtained a victory, he restored his uncle; but, while they were still in the midst of their joy, Kalu Upadhyaya, a relation of the treacherous Brahman, contrived to seize on both the uncle and nephews, and again delivered them to the Nawab, who had made the most liberal promises. It was on this occasion that the Moslems reduced the greater part of the low country of Morang, and, in fact, they settled some free land on the family of the traitor, but to no great extent, and vastly less than was expected. One of his descendants is now the Munsuf at

Bahadurgunj, mentioned above as one of the persons from whom I received information respecting this principality.

The unfortunate Subha and his nephews were sent to Dilli, where Muhammed Azim, then emperor, deprived them of cast by a curtailment of which the faithful are proud.

Prabodh das, the then Neb, or second hereditary minister of the family, fled with the two sons of Subha Sen to the Kirats, and his descendant, who gave me the written account, alleges that it was then only that the chiefs of this tribe were elevated to the dignity of Chautariya; but in this, I imagine, he is mistaken.

Mahapati, the eldest son, was placed by the Kirat Bidyachandra Ray on the throne of all that remained to the family east from the Kamala river, while the smaller portion west from that river was given to his brother Manik, to whom Prabodh das adhered; but a Kirat of the same family with Bidyachandra acted as the Chautariya of Manik, and Mahapati had a Neb of the family of Prabodh das.

Mahapati married, but neglected his wife, and had eighteen illegitimate children. Mahapati means elder son, and I was assured by the Munsuf of Bahadurgunj, that his real name was Mandhata. Here, indeed, I must follow chiefly the authority of the Munsuf; for the descendant of Prabodh das is little acquainted with the history of the eastern division, while the Munsuf was naturally unwilling to speak of the western.

Mandhata governed eighteen or twenty years, and left his territory to his natural son Kamdatt. I am informed by a Brahman, who had resided long in these parts, and by an intelligent Kirat, that Kamdatt lived on very bad terms with Bichitra Ray, the Kirat Chautariya of this part of the principality, who drove Kamdatt to Lasa, and placed on the throne

Jagat, a younger but legitimate son of the western branch of the family. This prince reconciled the Chautaryia to Kamdatt, and while Jagat reserved to himself the country between the Kamala and Kosi, he gave all the territory east from the latter river to his kinsman Kamdatt. Thus the principality became divided into three shares.

Soon after this Bichitra the Chautariya died, and was succeeded by Budhkarna his son, with whom Kamdatt continued to live on the worst terms; sometimes the one, and then the other, being under the necessity of flying from Vijayapur, which was the seat of government. On one of these occasions Kamdatt came to the Company's territory, and applied to Ghanasyam Upadhyaya, of the family of the traitor who had betrayed Subha Sen. The Brahman took him to Calcutta; but, receiving no countenance from the Governor-General, they returned to the frontier, where they raised some men, with whom Kamdatt recovered the government of Morang. Kamdatt still farther enraged the Kirat by putting his brother to death, on which event Budhkarna applied to the legitimate heir of the family, then in exile, who recommended an alliance with the Sikim Bhotiyas. Budhkarna having gone to that country, and having formed an alliance with its rulers, ten men were sent by them under pretence of adjusting the differences between the prince and his minister. These ruffians, having been admitted to a conference without suspicion, rushed on Kamdatt and put him to death. Budhkarna then placed on the throne of Vijayapur the legitimate heir, Karna Sen, whom the Gorkhalese had then expelled from the middle principality. He died in about eighteen months afterwards, in the year 1774, leaving an only son, a boy, under the charge of his widow, and of his Chautariya Agam Singha, decended in the fifth degree from Bidya Chandra, who was contemporary, according to Agam Singha, with the first Rajput prince of this country. In the same year the Gorkhalese attacked Vijayapur, and the widow fled with her son, and accompanied by Agam Singha, to the Company's territory.

The widow, her son, and minister, settled near Nathpur; while Budhkarna, after some fruitless engagements, went to Calcutta to solicit assistance, but without success. He soon after came towards the frontier, at Chilmari in the Company's territory, from whence he was carried off by a party of Gorkhalese soldiers disguised like robbers. He was taken to Vijayapur, where, under pretence of avenging the death of Kamdatt, the slender claim which the Gorkhalis used to cover their unjust attack on the infant son of Karna Sen, he was put to the most cruel tortures, which continued three days before he expired.

The jealousy of Prithwi Narayan of Gorkha did not permit him to view the poor child, then five years old, without anxious fears. His first plan was to endeavour to inveigle him into his power, by promising, on condition of an annual tribute, to restore his inheritance. He next offered to hold the territories of the youth from the British government, and to pay an annual sum; for he was cruelly alarmed lest the governor should interfere. At length he is alleged to have calmed his fears by a stratagem worthy of his savage nature. A Brahman was hired to insinuate himself into the favour of the mother, to whom he represented himself as a person skilled in the inoculation for the small-pox. Having gained the mother's consent, he performed the operation; but the small-pox did not appear; in its stead most dreadful ulcerations took place, and the child perished of a wretched disease. It is in general believed that poison was used instead of matter, and that the perpetrator was hired by Prithwi Narayan;

for, immediately after the operation, the Brahman disappeared, and is supposed to have retired to Nepal. The character of the prince does not leave much room to think that he would hesitate about employing such means.

The unfortunate widow, deprived of her only hope, seems to have harboured views of revenge. She sent to Mukunda Sen, the Raja of Palpa, and, as I have said above, of the same family with her husband, in order to request one of his sons, whom she might adopt, and to whom she might transfer the right to the middle and eastern divisions of the principality. The Raja accordingly sent Dhwajavir, one of his younger sons, who came to Puraniya in the year 1779, and sent letters to the Deva Dharma Raja, to Sikim, to the Chaubisiya Rajas, and to the Governor of Bengal, soliciting aid, but without the least probability of success. He had remained about three years at Puraniya, and had formed a friendship with Madrapate Ojha, a Brahman, who managed the estate Dhumgar, within nine coses of the frontier of Morang. He had also formed a friendship with a Ganes Bharati Mahanta, a priest, who lived between Puraniya and Dhumgar. This man, in the year 1782, promised, that, if the youth came to his house, he would adopt him as his pupil, (Chela), and lend him money, of which the young man was in much need. On his arrival at the residence of this priest, various delays and frivolous excuses were made to avoid the performance of the promises; and the youth was tempted, by an invitation from his friend Madrapati, to advance to Dhumgar, where he and his attendants were entertained eight days, in the office where the rents of the estate were collected. In the night of the eighth day the party were suddenly awakened by the approach of a body of men; and, on looking out, perceived that these were armed, and had surrounded the house. The party in the office now looked for their arms; but these had been removed in the night without their knowledge. They soon learned, from the language of the people by whom the house was surrounded, that they were Gorkhalese soldiers, who ordered them, in opprobrious language, (Nekal Bahenchod,) to come out. Several who went out were killed, but the Raja remaining within, and all his people invoking the protection of the Governor and of the Company, as usual in such cases, the soldiers entered, and said, there is no Governor nor Company can now give you any assistance. The Raja soon received a cut in his forehead, and then acknowledged himself, asking them, whether they intended to carry him away or to murder him. They replied, that they came for his life; on which he began to pray, and held out his head, which was cut off with a sword. During the confusion a Brahman escaped, and repaired to Madrapati, who replied with the utmost composure that he could give no assistance. The Raja had with him thirty-four people, of whom fifteen were killed, eleven wounded, and four carried away. Among the killed were Ripumardan, a natural son of Karna Sen Raja of Morang, and a messenger from the Sikim Raja, with five of his attendants. The soldiers were disguised like robbers, and took away such property as they found with the Raja, more probably to show what they had effected than for the sake of the plunder, as they gave no disturbance to the people of the village. From all the circumstances attending the event, few doubt that the scheme was preconcerted, and that the Mahanta and Brahman were the agents of the Gorkhalese, to decoy the youth within their reach.

The poor widow was now totally helpless. She was originally allowed a pension of 100 rupees a month; but for many years this has been withheld, and the Zemindars in the Company's territory are giving her great trouble respecting some lands, which had been granted her free of rent. Her sister-in-law died in the year 1810, in Tirahut, where she had some villages, which she left by will to the unfortunate old lady; but I am told that the Raja of Darbhangga has seized on them as Zemindar, although his claim is probably dubious, the grants having been made before the decennial settlement.

Having thus traced the fate of Mandhata and his descendants, I return to his brother Manik, who procured the share of the principality that is west from the Kamala river.

By the Munsuf of Bahadurgunj, Manik is said to have governed his country quietly for twenty years. Although his share of the principality was one of the most productive of revenue, as including a large portion of the plain, he had little power, few of the hardy Kirats being under his authority; but then he was exempted from the dangers arising from the turbulence of these mountaineers. He left four sons, Hemkarna, Jagat, Jaymanggal, and Vikram. The first succeeded his father, and Jagat, as I have mentioned, was placed by the Kirats in the government of that part of the principality which is situated between the Kamala and Kosi.

Kemkarna had a son, Digbandan, and a daughter, Maiya Saheb, of most extraordinary beauty. About this time first rose to notice Prithwi Narayan Saha, whose ancestors had held the petty territory of Gorkha, in some measure dependent on the Palpa Rajas, the kinsman of Kemkarna. This person had by various means acquired some little power, and had induced the people of Lalita Patan to choose his brother Dalmar-dan Saha for their king; for they had fallen into anarchy, and had displaced their lawful sovereign of the Mal family, which had long been in possession of the three principalities into which Nepal Proper had been divided. Prithwi Narayan, about this time, offered himself as a suitor for the beautiful daughter of Hemkarna, but was rejected with scorn, as a match far beneath her rank. Soon after, however, he was the fortunate suitor, but I do not exactly know the period. Hemkarna having died, was succeeded by his son Digbandan, a very weak prince, in whose affairs his brother-in-law, Prithwi Narayan, soon began to interfere; and by his courage, liberality, and strength of understanding, totally drew to himself the minds of the soldiery. In the year 1761 he openly attacked his brother-in-law, and took him and his family prisoners. The chief persons that had resisted his attack he put to death, some by the sword, some by the rope, and some by flaying them alive. Their children he delivered to the most vile and abominable tribe, (Sarki,) to be educated in their odious profession, as outcasts. The captives he conducted to Nepal, the open attack on which he then commenced; for, until then, he had contented himself with seizing on the passes, by which the valley is surrounded, and with fomenting dissensions among the three divisions of the principality. In 1769, having completed his conquest of Nepal Proper, he attacked the petty Rajas west from Gorkha, usually called the Chaubisiya, or Twenty-four. For some time he had rapid success, but in an engagement with the Tanahung Raja, he was so roughly handled, that he was compelled to relinquish these conquests. In the mean while, his brother-in-law Digbandan, his wife, and seven sons, were kept in close confinement, and were only prevented from starving, by a pittance sent to them by their kinsman the Palpa Raja. What became of the remainder of these unfortunate persons I cannot say; but in the year 1780 Bhubar, one of the sons of Digbandan, effected his escape to Betiya, in the Company's territory, where he was kindly received, and two villages, free from the obligation of paying any revenue, were granted to him. He died lately, and has left two sons, one of whom in 1810 was eight, and the other five years of age; and these are the undoubted legal heirs to the whole principality founded by Lohangga Sen.

I have already mentioned, that Budkarna, the Kirat chief of the eastern division of the principality, discontented with the illegitimacy and temper of Kamdatt, invited Jagat, a younger son of Manik, to assume the government, which he accordingly did, but he seems to have been a person of moderation; he contented himself with the middle portion of the principality, situated between the Kamala and Kosi, and allowed Kamdatt to retain whatever was beyond the latter river, for a maintenance, but not as a sovereign. Jagat usually resided at Chaundandi and Shikarmari, and died in peace. He had no son, and his dominions went to his brother Vikram, who left them to his son Karna Sen. In 1773 Prithwi Narayan, having somewhat recovered from the defeat which the Tanahung Raja had given him, attacked Karna Sen, and took his dominions. The fugitive prince, as I have mentioned, was received by Budkharna, the Kirat, as sovereign of Morang; but I have already given an account of the miserable events that immediately after happened.

Having now detailed the first origin and total overthrow of the principality founded by the Rajput Lohangga, I shall mention what I have learned concerning the nature of the government, which his descendants administered.

The Raja, in most cases, seems to have given himself very little trouble about the affairs of government, but was surrounded by Rajputs and Khas much attached to his person and family, and by Brahmans; by whom both he and his guards were duped, and who seem to have been the most active intriguers of the court.

Next in rank to the Raja was the Chautariya, who, as I have said, appears to me to have always been a Kirat of the family, that had governed his nation before the union with the Rajputs. The Kayastha alleges, indeed, that this was not the case; but he appears to me to be either mistaken, or to have made his representation from hatred to the Kirats, by whose power the Rajas and their Hindu adherents were very much controlled; for, setting aside the evidence of Agam Singha, a plain unaffected man, but who may however be supposed to be influenced by vanity, the Kayastha pretends, that, until a late period, the office of Chautariya was held by the family of the perfidious Brahman, who delivered Subha Sen to the Moslems; but the descendant of that person does not pretend that his ancestors ever enjoyed the dignity of Chautariya, and says, that they held the lucrative appointment of Dewan, which will be afterwards mentioned. The Chautariya signed all commissions and orders, while the Raja applied his seal. The Raja might punish the Chautariya in whatever manner he pleased, and even put him to death; but he could not deprive him of his rank, nor his son of the regular succession. This power of punishment, however, must have been very much limited, as the Kirats seem to have been entirely guided by their chief; and they composed almost the whole strength of the state. The Chautariya was allowed one-tenth part of the whole revenue.

The ancestor of the Kayastha held, by hereditary descent, the office of deputy (Neb) Chautariya, and seems merely to have been the person appointed by the Hindu Raja to carry on the writings necessary to be executed by the chiefs of the Kirats, who, if we may judge from Agam Singha, were no great penmen.

Next to the Chautariya was the Kazi or Karyi, to whose office the Raja might appoint any person that he pleased. The Karyi was usually the most active person in managing the affairs of government, and received one-sixteenth of the profits of the whole country.

Next to these was the Dewan, whose office, as I have stated, was hereditary in a family of Brahmans. The Dewans managed the whole collections of the territory on the plain, and probably made much more than either Chautariya or Karyi, which, joined to their birth, gave them great influence. When the principality subdivided, each Raja had his Chautariya, Karyi, and Dewan, who formed his council.

The regular military force consisted of two kinds. First, The Rajputs and Khas, who generally resided near the person of the Raja, and formed his immediate security. They were by no means numerous, and were usually paid in money. The other branch of the regular army was more numerous, and consisted chiefly of Kirats. They were under the orders of Serdars, but the number of men under each of these was not defined; each was appointed to command a number proportioned to the supposed extent of his abilities. The Serdars could at pleasure be removed, or the number of their troops altered. Each Serdar, in proportion to the extent of his command, received a quantity of land in the hills, which he subdivided among his officers and soldiers, reserving a share for himself. He might at pleasure appoint new soldiers, or remove old ones; but he received no regular tribute from the lands, although all his men made him presents. When called upon by the Raja, he was bound to appear in the field with his stipulated number of men; and a few Kirats, in their turn, were always on duty at the residence of the prince. When on actual service, the men were allowed subsistence. The Kirats seem to have been chiefly armed with swords and bows, their arrows being poisoned. The Rajputs had fire-arms. It is said, that there were in all 90,000 Kirats able to carry arms; but not above 5000 or 6000 were considered as regulars. The others paid rent.

In the hills the management of the police and the collection of the revenue was entrusted to officers called Subahs, who accounted to the Dewans for the revenue, but as commanding the militia, were subject to the Serdars. There were also Zemindars, who appear to have held the property of the soil, but were allowed to retain only a small portion (15 to 20 bigahs) of good land, fit for transplanted rice, and for this they were held bound to pay three rupees a-year, and to appear in the field as a militia, when called upon by the Subah. The Zemindar, however, as lord of the soil, was entitled to cultivate, without additional burden, as much as he pleased of any ground not fit for transplanted rice, and no one could cultivate such without giving him a present. Every family, except the Zemindars, who cultivated this kind of ground, paid three rupees a-year to the Raja, and the men, when required, were bound to appear in the field. All the land fit for transplanted rice, except that held by the Zemindars, was Melk or free of revenue. Part had been granted to Brahmans and temples, and part to various officers of the state, none of whom were paid in money; but by far the greater part was given to the Serdars, for the support of their men. Over every three or four villages the Subah appointed a deputy, called a Duyariya.

In the hilly part of the country, much of the cultivation was carried on by Adhiyars, who gave to the soldier, officer, or Zemindar that employed them, one half of the produce for rent. Each family of this kind paid a rupee a year to the Raja. All persons not employed in agriculture (Sukhvas and Khosvas) paid eight anas for ground-rent, and two anas for holidays. No casts were exempted.

In the level country the lands were cultivated by tribes, who had little or no turn for military affairs, and paid a rent in money, which was collected under the Dewans by Fouzdars, who managed districts (Garhis) by means of Chaudhuris, who held manors, (Pergunahs,) and under these by Mokuddums, who held villages, (Gangs.) In some places the word Pergunah had not been adopted, but the Chaudhuri held the space between two rivers, which is called a Khari.

Independent of the Dewans was a register called Suduriya, and, wherever there was a deputy of the Dewan, the register had also a deputy. In fact, the Mogul system of finance had been completely introduced, while in the mountains the Hindu system of military tenure seems to have been more completely retained.

The trial of civil causes was conducted at the capital by four Bicharis, who appointed a deputy for the jurisdiction under each Subah, and for each subdivision; and these judges seem to have had a much greater authority than is usual in Hindu or Muhammedan governments. Under the Bicharis and their deputies were petty officers, named Duyariyas, who arrested offenders, and decided petty suits. These were assisted by Kotwals, or messengers. The reason of the attention paid to suits seems to have been, that the Raja took one-fourth of all property recovered by legal process, and allowed the judge a share; of course, the complainant usually gained the cause. The principal chance which the defendant had was giving a bribe higher than the share that the judge would legally receive; but the Raja was a check on this kind of gain.

In the hilly country there were no duties levied, except at custom-houses placed on the passes towards the plain, or towards the dominions of Lasa. On the plain there was a vast variety of duties, similar to those now exacted, and which will be afterwards detailed.

I shall now proceed to consider the present state of this principality, in the footing on which it has been placed by the Gorkhalese.

In the first place, it has been divided into districts.

The eastern division of the principality, founded by Lohangga, together with the part of Sikim, and a portion of Thibet, that have been conquered, are now divided into two districts, (Zilas,) Morang and Chayenpur, each under the management of a Subah.

Morang, in a general sense, extends in the low country from the Tista to the Kosi, for the level country, that formerly belonged to Sikim, has now been annexed to this district. Its extent, therefore, from east to west, is rather more than 87 miles. On the low hills, it extends from the Kankayi to the Kosi, which is about 48 miles. It includes very few or none of the mountains, and none of the Alps.

The most remarkable places are as follows:

Vijaypur, the residence of the Subah, and of a former dynasty of princes, is situated on the higher part of the low hills, and is in so much exempt from the unhealthy air of that region called Ayul, that the people, they say, can eat three-fourths more there than they can in the lowlands; a manner of measuring the salubrity of different places, which is in common use among the natives, but, I suspect, is rather fanciful. The fort is always garrisoned by regulars, and a Serdar very commonly resides in it, superintends the conduct of the neighbouring civil officers, and watches over the frontier.

Samrigarhi is another small fort still occupied.

Chaudanda, until the division of the principality founded by Lohangga, was most commonly the seat of government. It is now almost entirely deserted.

Satya Raja is a ruin, which is said to have been the residence of a dynasty, that governed the country before the ancestors of Vijaynarayan.

Kichak jhar is also a ruin, which is said to have been the residence of Kichak, the brother-in-law of Virat, king of Matsya, celebrated in Hindu legend. I am assured by the people of the vicinity, that in a very thick wood at Kichak jhar there are ruins.

At Sorahbag was the residence of the wife of Vijaybharat, the last king of the dynasty, which preceded Lohangga.

Varaha kshetra is a temple dedicated to Vishnu, in the form of a boar. During the government of the former dynasty, the priests (Mahanta) of this temple seem to have had great weight; and their successor enjoys some land, and the whole duties collected at a neighbouring custom-house, (Chatra Gola.) The place is still frequented by a good many pilgrims, but the number has, of late, considerably diminished. This is a place where holy persons sometimes bury themselves alive, and on such occasions, are supposed to be endowed with the gift of prophecy. The buildings are not considerable, and, of late, have become ruinous.

The market places (Hats) are 24 in number, as will appear by the map.

The Golas, or custom-houses, are frequently changing, and, of late, have mostly been placed near the frontier, and removed from the hills.

At present, Morang is divided into three Taluks, or districts. Each is under the charge of a deputy collector, or Fouzdar. The first has under him one Chauduri, or Zemindar; the second has four Chaudhuris; and the third three Chaudhuris. The land, under this Subah's authority, is divided into Pergunahs.

1.	Nangang and Dhapar, land rent,	Rupees 5,000	Sayer, 1,300
	Beli,	600	
2.	Futchhari,	4,500	1,000
	Gogra,	7,500	
	Hathiya Simar,	450	
	Mangar,	250	2,500
	Beliya,	700	
	Kuthar, Bariyati,	12,500	
3.	Harchand garhi,	14,300	1,600
	Kerayan,	1,125	
	Atmauza,	7,000	1,100
	Mechpali and Latang,	400	
		R. 54,025	R. 7,500

Total land rent,		R. 54,025
Do. Sayer,		7,500
Kascharai, or rent for pasture,		24,000
Khayer Sal, or duty on Catechu,		3,000
Kathmahal, or duty on timber,		38,000
Chiriyamahal, or duty on birds,		500
Customs at the Golas,		
Chatra, (given to a temple,	R. 1,500)	
Vijayapur,	2,000	
Raksa,	300	
Latang,	600	
Rotoya,	1,000	
		4,400
	Total Rupees	131,425

The land rent is levied by so much on each crop, by a bigah of nine common cubits the Katha, equal to 72,900 square feet. The following was the rate at the time when I procured the account; but the chief of the village, (Mokuddum,) for every hundred bigahs that pay rent, is allowed five free of that charge.

Rate in the year Sambat 1868, A. D. 1810.

	By the country measure.		By the Calcutta measure.	
	Rupees.	*Anas.*	*Anas.*	*Pies.*
Sali or rice, ...	3	5	10	5½
Maruya and Mustard, ...	2	11	8	6
Cotton and patuya or corchorus, .	2	4	7	0
Kitchen gardens and tobacco, . . .	5	0	15	9½
Sugar-cane, ...	4	0	12	7½

No other crop pays any thing, and the tenantry pay no ground rent for their houses. The Calcutta Biga is one-third of an English acre, and the rupee weighs 179½ grains of silver; it is divided into 16 anas, and the ana into 12 pies.

The settlement in the year Sambat 1846, soon after the conquest, was considerably lower, but more crops were included.

The duties called Sayer include a capitation on artists, a duty on the sale of oxen and buffaloes, on marriages, on the contract with a concubine, on grain exported, on all things sold at Hats or markets, and on adulterers.

The duty on Catechu I have already explained.

The management of the mines is not entrusted to the care of the Subahs.

The whole amount which the Subah collected in the year 1809-10 is said to have been 131,425 rupees, out of which the Subah pays 80,000 rupees to government; and his share of the Rajangka, and presents to the twelve great officers of state, usually amount to 20,000 rupees more; but this is probably compensated by similar exactions that he makes from his inferiors. He, however, incurs a heavy expence in furnishing the regular troops with provisions, which he must do at a price fixed by government, and which is always far below the market price; but he squeezes a great part of this from the neighbouring tenantry. Colonel Kirkpatrick * esti-

* Nepaul, p. 42.

mates the nett revenue of this territory, which he calls East Turrye, at from 125,000 to 150,000 rupees, including, perhaps, Rajangka and mines.

Each village (Gang) is under a Mokuddum, who has five *per cent.* of the land free of rent; a Patwari or clerk, who has one-half ana on the rupee of rent, and two anas a-year on each house, both from the tenants, and gives one-half of this to his superiors, the Mohurers, who are registers to the Fouzdars, and to the Kanungo, who is register to the Subah. The messengers (Gorayits) from every house get about two loads of the ears of rice, which give about one *man* (82 lbs. avoirdupois) of grain; so that, neither on account of the village establishment, nor on that of the Kanungoes or his clerks, (Mohurer,) is there any deduction from the above sum; but the Subah pays several heavy establishments.

At his chief office, it amounts to about 3500 rupees a-year. There are, besides the Fouzdars, Chaudhuris and armed men, at the three subordinate divisions for the land rent and sayer.

The Subah, being a merchant of Banaras, keeps the Catechu at his own disposal, and, besides the duties, has probably much profit on this article as a merchant.

The duties on timber are formed in three lots, to three Fouzdars, and the nett proceeds only have been included.

The rents on pasture are farmed on the same plan to two Fouzdars.

His whole establishment, therefore, does not probably exceed 7000 rupees a-year.

Two captains (Subahdars) have lands in the district for the maintenance of 300 men.

The Subah, as judge, receives 25 *per cent.* on all sums recovered in his court, but the greater part of this goes to the Raja. The Subah, however, always receives presents from the defendant, when the suit is given in his favour, and he has fees in the management of the police. The avowed profits, in the management of justice and police in the year 1809-10, are said, in even numbers, to have been 15,000 rupees.

The inhabitants of Vijaypur, towards the east, are chiefly Koch or Rajbangsis, who are considered as the same, live on the plain, and speak the dialect of Bengal; on the lower hills are many Mech. Both these tribes are original inhabitants of Kamrup. In the western parts, most of the cultivators are of the Gangaye cast, who speak the dialect of Mithila, and adhere to the doctrines of purity, as established in that country. On the hills, the people are mostly Khas, or a mixed breed between the mountain Hindus and natives, with some Rajputs, and some Magars, who have been lately introduced.

The northern part of the eastern division of the principality, founded by Lohangga, has been lately formed into a distinct district, and its Subah resides at Chayenpur. The hilly parts of Sikim, so far as has been subdued, and a portion of Thibet, bordering on the Arun river, have been annexed to the jurisdiction, which is bounded by the Sengkhuya Arun, and Kausiki on the west, and by the Tista on the east, extending between 80 and 90 miles in these directions, and perhaps about 60 or 70 from north to south. It consists altogether of lofty mountains, rising, in many parts, to the most tremendous Alps.

The land revenue, I am told, is very trifling, the whole almost being held by military tenure; but I did not learn the particulars. The chief revenues are the customs at Golas, mines, and capitation, (Rajangka,) but the two last are not collected by the Subah. There is no Sayer.

The forts are Chayenpur, about two or three coses from the

Arun, Changiya, Hedang, a large place towards the frontier of Thibet, Darjiling, and Sikim.

The Golas, or custom-houses, are Ilam, Majhuya, Bilasi, Tangting, Huchi-Mechi, Dimali, and Satang, all in the territory formerly belonging to the Sikim Raja. The Gorkhalese have no connection with Thibet in that quarter, because the route is still in possession of the Sikim Raja. Chayenpur, however, has a considerable trade with Thibet by that part of the country which is near the Arun. Hatiya on the Arun, and Alangchang on the Tamar, are at present the marts established for this commere. Formerly it was carried on at Pakang in the middle between the two rivers. People can pass to the two former all the year; the trade at Pakang was confined to summer. The goods imported at these places from Thibet are salt carried on sheep, gold, silver, musk, and musk-deer skins, the tails called Chaungris, blankets, borax, Chinese silks, and medicinal herbs. The goods sent from Chayenpur are rice, wheat, maruya, (Cynosurus corocanus,) uya, a grain, oil, butter, iron, copper, cotton cloths, broadcloth, catechu, myrobalans, (harra bahara,) planks of the Dhupi, pepper, and spices, indigo, tobacco, hides, otters' fur, sugarcandy, and extract of sugarcane, occasionally some pearls.

The route from Vijaypur to Pokang is said to be as follows in days journies:

1. To Mulghat on the Tambar river. The road hilly, but not mountainous. Much cultivation. No river of note.

2. To Dhankuta, or Dhankot. The same kind of country. Cross the Tambar.

3. To Ukhaliya. Country more hilly, and less cultivated. Several small rivers, especially the Mangmay.

4. To Jaresang, a town in a plain well cultivated country.

5. To the Leghuya river, where there is a fine valley. The road passes over low hills.

6. To Dobhang. The road hilly, but in many parts cultivated. Cross the Piluya river below Chayenpur Fort. Dobhang is situated on the Soyeya river, near where it joins the Arun.

7. To Tamlingtar, a smooth road fit for horses. It stands between the Soyeya and the Arun, which are about $1\frac{4}{5}$ coses distant from each other. This is the largest place in the district, and is said to be about the size of Kirtipur, in the valley of Nepal, which, I suppose, may contain 6000 people; but Tamlingtar is not built with brick, as is the case with Kirtipur. The plain round it is very considerable, extending twelve coses north and south, and four coses east and west. The plain is bounded on the west by the Arun, and is not quite so cool as Kathmandu, nor is it fully cleared.

8. To Tamling, a smooth road fit for horses. Tamling is about three coses east from the Arun.

9. To Segeya, a smooth road fit for horses. The country is well cultivated. Segeya is a day's journey east from the Arun.

10. To Lum, a good road.

11. To Jupha, a very hilly road with steep ascents and descents, but much cultivation.

12. To Jholangghat, on the Arun, where there is a bridge suspended by rattans.

13. To Hedang, the route being on low hills by the west side of the Arun. West from Hedang two days journey, is Meyangma, a snowy mountain, and at the same distance east is another named Mirgu.

14. To Komba, a village of Bhotiyas, at a distance from the Arun, and formerly at least the residence of a Lama, who was supposed to be an incarnation of God.

15. To Chamtang, another village inhabited by Bhotiyas, and at a distance from the Arun.

16. To Seksula, or Seksura, on the Arun. Some accounts place it on one side, and some on the other of the Arun. It is a village of Bhotiyas, and part may be on each side of the river, which is crossed on a bridge of rattans.

17 and 18 to Pokang. The country is not very hilly, but so high and cold, that it is frequented only in summer by shepherds and traders who attend the mart.

From Seksula, proceeding on the west side of the Arun, you have,

17. Hatiya, a Bhotiya village, where there is a mart.

18. Chipachintang, another Bhotiya village belonging to Gorkha. A little way beyond it is Manigumba, a village subject to Lasa.

The Arun here would seem to pass through the highest ridge of the snowy mountains. The Kirat, who gave me the map of the eastern parts of the principality, names the portion of these mountains towards the east Papti, and says, that between it and Mirgu, mentioned above, there is a large valley; but, except near the Arun, it has no regular inhabitants. In summer it is frequented by shepherds alone; but he would not appear to have been acquainted with its eastern parts; for, though he admits that the Tambar rises from Papti, and afterwards passes through Mirgu, he knew nothing of the Gola that is there, and is called Alangchang. South from Mirgu is another high ridge; but the snow that occasionally falls on it in winter soon melts. The Kirat calls it Ichhanglima; I have no doubt that it is the Phakphok of the map made by the slave; for the Kirat says, that the Kankayi rises from Mirgu, and passes through a gap in Ichhanglima. The slave in his map says that Phakphok is the proper source of the Kankayi, but admits, that it receives a stream from the snowy mountains. The Kirat alleged that the hollow between Mirgu and Ichhanglima is overgrown with immense forests occupied by elephants and rhinoceroses, which is scarcely reconcileable with its necessary elevation; and the compiler of the other map represents it as a well inhabited country, which is the most probable account, as the Kirat had not visited that part.

On the west side of the Arun, again, the Kirat places Syamphelang as the highest ridge of snowy mountains, and he seemed to think, that the very highest peak visible, and bearing about N. by W. from Nathpur, was part of this mountain connected with this, but leaving between them the valley watered by the Tarun, is another snowy mountain, which the Kirat calls Meyangma, but which the slave who constructed the map calls Salpa pahar.

The inhabitants of the eastern parts of Chayenpur have been already mentioned. In the western parts the most numerous tribe is Kirat, next Limbu, then Magar, lately introduced as soldiers, then Khas and Rajputs. There are also Murmis, and towards the N. W. Bhotiyas.

The middle part of the principality of Lohangga has also been divided into two districts under Subahs. The first comprehends the southern portion called Saptari, but the low land between the Rato and Kamal, named Mahatari, which formerly belonged to the western division of the principality, has lately been placed under the authority of this Subah. His jurisdiction, therefore, on the plain extends about 100 miles from east to west, and its width there is nearly the same as that of Morang; so that it possesses more level land. Very little of the hilly country belongs to it, as Kotang and Makwanpur come far down and meet at the Kamal.

The most remarkable places in this district are Naragarhi, a small fort on the plain, where the Subah usually resides; Bhemagarhi, another similar place, where he occasionally resides; and Janakpur, a place of pilgrimage noted in Hindu fable, and already mentioned as the seat of a very ancient dynasty. I am told that there are no remains of former power or greatness.

There are ten market-places.

The Golas, or custom-houses, are placed in the map.

The land-rent is collected by two Fouzdars, one for Saptari, the other for Mahatari; but these also collect some trifling dues which have not been let with the sayer or duties on markets; for there is no regular system of finance. These dues are those on marriages, (Bihadani,) on contracts of concubinage, (Sagora,) and a fine on adulterers of rupees $2\frac{10}{16}$. levied by the collector, besides the fine that goes to the Raja; for the man who has farmed the duties on the markets takes a part of the fine, amounting to rupees $2\frac{10}{16}$. The following will show the sums collected on these heads in the year Sambat 1867, (A. D. 1809.)

ZILA.	SAPTARI.	Land-rent.	Marriages.	Concubines.	Adulterers.
Pergunah,	Khalisa,	10,015	75½	50	25
	Jagadal,	2,485	25	12½	—
	Pakri,	13,345½	55½	25	30
	Majhumna,	754½	15	5	—
	Rayjhumna,	941½	25	7½	10
	Pakuya,	655½	10	5	5
	Gudagari,	501½	25	7½	20
	Rampurbehara,	481	—	5	—
	Mahishan,	501½	20	5½	—
	Khonjvaghni, Majhoya, Dhanchhoyar, Vihar,	Totally waste.			
	Total	29,881	251	123	90

ZILA.	MAHATARI.	Land-rent.	Marriages.	Concubines.	Adulterers.
Pergunah,	Mahatari,	9,115½	103	50	25
	Korari,	10,025	40¼	10	16
	Khesraha,	11,212	50	25	—
	Pihan,	7,855½	80	40	65
	Total rupees,	38,208	273¼	125	106

The establishment is nearly similar to what is maintained in Vijaypur. A great part of the rents are farmed. The rent is paid by so much a bigah for each kind of crop. The bigah is of the same size as in Morang. The following is the rate:

	According to Country measure.		According to Calcutta measure.	
	Rupees.	Anas.	Anas.	Pice.
Rice. (Sali,)	4	10	14	7¼
Mustard, (Turi,) } Corocanus, (Maruya,) }	3	10	11	6¾
Cotton,	3	12	11	10
Tobacco and Kitchen Gardens,	5	0	15	9½

All ranks pay the same rate. Tradesmen pay a ground rent for their houses of rupees 5. 10. included in the land-rent, and a capitation tax to the Sayer of rupees 1. 10. Those who have regular shops in the market-places pay to the Sayer rupees 7. 10, and nothing for ground rent. Washermen, barbers, tailors, and shoe-makers, pay no capitation.

The Sayer, consisting of the capitation on tradesmen, and of the duties levied on goods sold, and grain exported, is farmed to two men for Saptari, one paying 3254 rupees, and the other 3135½; and for Mahatari, to one man paying 6595½.

The rents on the pasture of buffaloes is farmed at 1431 rupees for Saptari, and 3956$\frac{4}{5}$ rupees for Mahatari.

Theduty on those who make catechu is farmed in Saptari for 1015 rupees, and in Mahatari for 1212 rupees.

The duties on timber are farmed in Saptari for 2462 rupees, and in Mahatari for 2225 rupees.

The duties on boats loaded with timber are farmed in Saptari for 2441 rupees, and in Mahatari for 345.

The duty on birds for both is farmed at 698½ rupees.

The duties levied at the Golas, or custom-houses, have been farmed for three years at 100,000 rupees, or 33,333⅓ a year; but in this bargain are included the duties at Varaha kshatra and Vijaypur, for which the renter pays 1500 rupees annually to the priest of the former place, and 2000 to the Subah of Morang; so that the customs here are actually farmed at 29,833 rupees a-year. The person who has farmed these rents, Achal Thapa, resides at Bhangraruya on the Kosi, and has endeavoured to secure a monopoly; but his plans have not been very successful, add he will be a heavy sufferer by the interruptions of commerce that have ensued in consequence of the disputed frontier.

The total revenue collected by the Subah is as follows:

Land-rent and several casualties,	Rupees 68,957
Pasture,	5,386
Catechu,	2,227
Timber cutters,	4,687
Duties on boats loaded with timber,	2,786
Duties on birds,	698
Customs at Golas,	29,833
Duties on markets or Sayer,	12,985
Total,	127,559

Exclusive of the Rajangka or income tax, he pays to the Raja 58,000 rupees a-year.

There is very little land granted for the support of the

army, or officers of government, and no great religious establishment.

At Jaleswar, in Mahatari, south from Janakpur, the Raja has a manufacture of saltpetre and gunpowder.

There is only one mine of iron at Sisuya, near the Kosi.

The Tharu cast, resembling, in its manners, the Gangayi of Morang, composes the greatest part of the population on the plain. Next to these, are nearly equal parts of the impure Bhawars, and of the military and agricultural tribe of Brahmans, called Aniwar, both of whom have, at different times, been sovereigns of the country. Immediately under the hills are many Batars, who speak the Hindwi language. The lower hills are occupied by Sringguyas, a branch of the Limbu tribe, and by Magars, and Rajputs or Khas. The Magars have been lately introduced.

The northern parts of this middle division of the principality of Lohangga, form the jurisdiction of the Subah of Khatang, who possesses an extensive region of mountains, bounded by the Arun on the east, and on the west by the Tamba Kosi, which separates it from the territory of Bhatgang, one of the three principalities into which Nepal Proper was divided. Towards the south it descends to the Kamal, which, in part, separates it from Makwanpur. On the north it is bounded by the snow hills, which separate it from Thibet or Lasa, and, in this part, advance far south.

The land revenue has been almost entirely granted to the different officers of the Gorkhalese government, and there is no Sayer, nor customs, so that the Raja chiefly receives the income tax, (Rajangka,) fines, and the profits of mines. The Subah pays only 12,000 rupees a-year, and about 8000 rupees as Rajangka. This district maintains two companies of 120 fusileers each.

The forts are Hedang, where the Subah resides; Chaudandi, where the Rajas formerly lived; Rawa, near the junction of the San and Dudh Kosis; Chariyagarbi, on the Kamal; and Hatuya, at the junction of the San Kosi and Arun, where a Serdar often has a military station.

At the temple of Siva in Kalesi, where the Dudhkosi and Sankosi unite, is a very great fair in February.

With Thibet there are two routes of communication.

On the Dudhkosi is Lamja, to which the Bhotiyas come at all seasons. The Alps extend two day's journey beyond it, on the banks of the Dudhkosi; afterwards there is a plain country. The road from Kalesi to Lamja Gola is as follows:

One day's journey to Rawa, a large town with a fort. The country fully occupied.

One day to Hakula, a large village. The country here, also, is well inhabited.

One day's journey to Jubing, a large village.

One day to Ghat, a village inhabited chiefly by Bhotiyas, the climate being too cold for the mountain Hindus.

One day's journey from thence to Lamja, also inhabited by Bhotiyas. The imports are as usual from that country, but there are no duties.

The other route to Thibet, from this district, is towards Dudhkunda, a place in Thibet, where there is a very great annual fair. The road, commencing at Lengleng, at the junction of the Tamba and San Kosi, is as follows:

One day to Namari, a large village.

One day to Jirikampti, where the Raja of Gorkha has 10,000 or 12,000 cows on fine plain land, kept waste on purpose.

One day to Gama, a large village inhabited by Bhotiyas.

One day to Goyang, a similar village.

One day to the snowy mountain Pangmo. Dudhkunda is a little way among the Alps, but is subject to Thibet.

The commerce by the Tamba kosi goes by Phala, a Gola or custom-house in the former territory of Bhatgang.

The roads from the San Kosi to the mountains are difficult, but, for a part of the way, people can ride on horseback.

From Chatra to Nepal the road is rather better, but, in many places, the rider must dismount. After, however, passing the falls of the Kosi at Chatra, the San Kosi is navigable in canoes, to the junction of the Risu, where it turns to the north. The Arun is navigable to Hedang.

The best route, by land, from Chatra to Nepal, is as follows:

On the first day's journey, cross the Kosi to Mayna, and then the San kosi to Lasuniya.

A day's journey from Lasuniya to Kuta.

One day's journey to Khatang, which may be five or six coses north from the San kosi.

From Khatang to Kamtel, one day.

To Halesi, at the junction of the Dudhkosi, one day.

To Teliya, about three coses from the San kosi, one day.

To Bangnam, on the west of the Lekho, one day.

To Chupulu, one day.

To Mantali ghat, on the Tamba kosi, one day. The village is on the west side.

To Puchi ghat, on the San kosi, one day.

To Dumja, on the Rusi, one day.

To Dapcha, on the north side of the Rusi, one day.

To Banipa, at the head of the Rusi, on the hills that bound the valley of Nepal, one day.

The mines in this district are numerous, as will appear from the map.

There are no markets, (Hats,) but some shops in all the towns.

The chief place in Khatang is Dalka, on the Tamba kosi, upon a plain extending to Puchigat, on both sides of the Tamba kosi, and about a cose in width. This valley extends down the San kosi, from one-half to one cose in width. Dalka is a town like Timmi, in the valley of Nepal, which, I suppose, may contain 4000 people, and is chiefly inhabited by Newars, and built of brick. At it there is a celebrated temple of Bhim Sen, one of the sons of Pandu. The Pujari is a Newar, and the temple is considered as the eastern boundary of Nepal Proper.

The most valuable district which the Raja of Nepal possesses, is that which formed the western division of the principality, founded by Lohangga, although the district called Mahatari has been separated, and annexed to the Subah of Saptari. The Subah of this district resides usually at Makwanpur, on the hills, but, in the cold season, he visits the plains and resides at Baragarhi, from whence he is often called the Baragarhi Subah. His jurisdiction extends from the Rato, on the east, to the Trisul Gangga, and Gandaki, on the west; and from the Company's territory, on the south, to the San kosi, and Rusi, on the north. In some parts, towards the north, this boundary was disputed between the Rajas of Patan, in Nepal, and the Rajas of Makwanpur. One would naturally have supposed, that the boundary would have been determined by the mountain called Lama dangra, which extends from the Trisul gangga to the Arun, and which, except by the Vagmati or Vagwati, is crossed by no river, all those from its north side falling into the Trisul gangga, Vagmati, or Kosi. In fact, where I passed this mountain at Chisapani, a little above the fort, I was shown an old wall on the summit, which was said to have been the boundary; but I am told, that the copper mine on the north side of the hill belongs to Makwani, and that the boundary goes thence obliquely towards the north-east, so that it includes many villages between Lama Dangra, and the Rusi, and San kosi rivers.

When Colonel Kirkpatrick visited Nepal, * it would appear that the Subah of Makwanpur, or Baragarhi, governed the whole country from the Kosi to the Gandaki, divided into five Zilas, which he names Subtuni, (Saptari,) Mohtuni, (Mahatari,) Rohuttut or Rohtut, Bareh, (Baragarhi,) and Persa, (Pasara.)

One-half of this territory is on the level country, called Tariyani, and is exactly on the same footing with the level of Morang, Saptari, and Mahatari.

About one-fourth of the district consists of low hills, very thinly occupied; and one-fourth consists of high mountains.

The most remarkable places of strength are the fort of Makwanpur, where the Rajas formerly dwelt; Hariharpur, commanding the Vagmati; Sinduli, (Seedly R.) and Chisapani, commanding two passages through the mountain called Lama dangra; Chayenpur, on the San kosi; and Kumbi, Gar Pasara, Kurarbas and Baragarhi, commanding the plain. Chisapani, the most important, and Gar Pasara, both of which I have seen, are altogether contemptible; and it is probable that the others are still worse. Baragarhi, (Bharra Gharry,) according to Colonel Kirkpatrick, † is a mean place, containing 30 or 40 huts, and its fort is not more respectable than Gar Pasara. In the whole district, there is not one considerable town.

At Hethaura, Sinduli, and Bichhakhori, customs are collected, but none of them are marts for the sale of goods. On the plain country are several markets, (Hats,) but I have not learned the names nor situations of the whole.

---

* See his Account, p. 40.

† Nepaul, p. 13.

I did not learn the particulars of the revenue of this district, but was told at Kathmandu, in a general way, that the Subah pays annually 100,000 rupees. Colonel Kirkpatrick * estimates the money annually remitted by the Subah at 200,000 rupees; but then this Subah held also Saptari, which, paying now 58,000 rupees, should leave 142,000 for the present territory; but, in what Colonel Kirkpatrick states as the remittance, the Rajangka was perhaps included. There are, besides, many mines. The greater part of the hills has been granted in Jaygir to various officers. The plains alone are rented on account of the court.

On the plains, the population consists chiefly of Tharus and Aniwars. The great cast on the hills is the Murmi, and this is also the case on the north of the valley of Nepal. About the forts are some Rajputs, many of the spurious breed of Khas, and a good many Magars.

The inhabitants of this part of the Tariyani, which I had an opportunity of seeing, are quite the same in their circumstances, language, dress, persons, and customs, with the Hindus of the northern part of Behar. The peasantry are extremely nasty, and apparently indigent. Their huts are small, dirty, and very ill calculated to keep out the cold winds of the winter season, for a great many of them have no other walls but a few reeds supported by sticks in a perpendicular direction. Their clothing consists of some cotton rags, neither bleached nor dyed, and which seem never to be washed. They are a small, hard-favoured people, and by no means fairer than the inhabitants of Bengal, who are comparatively in much better circumstances.

---

* Nepaul, p. 41.

Having finished my account of the principality, founded by Lohangga, the youngest son of Mukunda, in the eastern parts of the territory, now subject to Gorkha, I proceed to give an account of the territory adjacent to the west, which fell to the lot of the other branches of the same family.

Makunda Sen the 1st, when he provided for his sons, gave Champaranya to his brother, who left it to his son Rama Singha, descended of whom was another Makunda Sen, whose son, or grandson, is supposed to have been destroyed by the ghost of a Brahman, whom he had offended, and the country now belongs to the Raja of Betiya. This is an account given by Samar Bahadur. Others say, that Rama Sen, or Rama Singha, was a son of Makunda the 1st, who obtained Tilpur and Rajpur, both in the Company's territory, as I intend hereafter to describe.

I have already mentioned, that Binayak, said to be the eldest son of Mukunda, received the territory on the plain now called Butaul. Jasu Sen, the son of Binayak, did nothing worth remark, but left his patrimony to his son Damodar Sen, who, in the same manner, begat Balabhadra Sen, and he begat Ambar Sen, who succeeded to Palpa, the line of Manik having failed. He was succeeded by his son Gandharba Sen, who begat Udyata Sen, but survived his son, and was succeeded by Makunda Sen, his grandson, who had wars with most of his neighbours, conquered Gulmi, and recovered some of his dominions that had been seized by the Raja of Gorkha. In the course of his wars with a Muhammedan Nawab, he took some guns and flags, as trophies of victory. He had five sons. 1. Mahadatta S. who succeeded. 2. Suravir S. 3. Karuvir S. 4. Chandravir S. And, 5. Dhwajavir S. Mahadatta had three sons. 1. Prithwi Pal S. 2. Rana Bahadur S. And, 3. Samar Bahadur S. Prithwi Pal S. succeeded his father, and left one son named Ratna Sen, who is the present representative of the family. This is the account contained in the manuscript composed by Rama Bahadur, already mentioned. I shall now give some farther detail.

Gandharba Sen of Palpa and Binayakpur made a considerable addition to his dominions, having, with the assistance of his allies, the Rajas of Gulmi and Kachi, seized on the territories of an impure Magar chief, who resided at Balihang. This chief, of whose family there are no remains, had large possessions, both on the hills and plains, especially on the latter. These were divided among the three allies, Palpa taking the best share. There was a small territory, however, called Khidim, about the division of which the three chiefs could not agree. After much squabbling, it was determined that it should be given to a Brahman, whose descendants held it, until the country was seized by the late Raja of Gorkha and Nepal, who gave it to his father-in-law, the Raja of Gulmi.

Makunda Sen the 2d held Binayakpur Palpa and a great part of Balihang, and was at the head of an alliance of petty chiefs, composed of Gajarkot, Rising, Ghiring, Argha, Kachi, and Gulmi, which last, after a vain attempt at conquest, he was obliged to relinquish. Narabhupal, Raja of Gorkha, had married his aunt, daughter of Gandarbha, and he received kindly at his court his cousin Prithwi Narayan, the son of Narabhupal, while that chief was a young man, very slenderly provided. One of Prithwi's most early acts was to subdue the three first mentioned allies of Makunda; but from their territories he was soon expelled, and this is what in the manuscript is called recovering part of his dominions from Gorkha. After the death of Prithwi Narayan, his son Singha Pratap showed so much favour to a Swarup Singha, whom he had raised from a low rank to the important office of Karyi, that, on account of the envy which was excited, the favourite was under the necessity of flying to the Company's territory. There some European gentlemen took notice of him, and supported him with money. Having introduced himself to the unfortunate widow of Karna Sen, chief of the eastern branch of the family, whose only child, as I have already mentioned, had been poisoned by the intrigues of Prithwi Narayan, Swarup obtained authority from this lady to proceed to Palpa for assistance; and having gone there, Makunda gave him his youngest son Dwaja vir to be adopted by the old lady, and to assert the claims of his family. The melancholy fate of this youth has been already detailed. At the time of his murder Swarup Singha was at Calcutta, soliciting assistance. On his return he was invited to Kathmandu, and all envy, it was said, having died away, large promises were made, and the mother of the Raja's heir gave an oath, that he should meet with no harm. Immediately, however, after his arrival he was confined, and in less than a year he was killed.

Makunda Sen procured from the Nawab Vazir a grant of the extensive estate of Tilpur, and of that part of Rajpur, which is on the west side of the Gandaki, and had once, as lately mentioned, belonged to a branch of his family; but in the latter he never acquired proper authority, owing to the intrigues of the Kanungo, or register.

This enterprising chief married the eldest daughter (Maha Kumari) of his ally the Raja of Argha, and on this occasion presented his father-in-law with an estate situated on the plain, and called Tuppah Bandar; although he continued to pay the revenue to the Nawab. This was part of the spoil taken from Balihang by his grandfather.

Mahadatta Raja of Palpa was very much in favour with

Asofud Doulah, the Nawab Vazir, who confirmed to him all his hereditary or acquired lands on the plains, at an easy rate; and, going there frequently to hunt, seems to have amused himself with the Raja's children. The youngest son Samar, a lame but shrewd man, seems in particular so have attracted his notice, and he bestowed on him the title of Nader Shah, by which he is much better known than by his proper name.

Mahadatta also entered into the strictest alliance with Bahadur Sahi, younger son of Prithwi Narayan, and regent of Gorkha during the minority of his nephew Rana Bakadur. In order to cement the friendship, Mahadatta gave his daughter in marriage to the regent, which, on account of her birth, was considered as a very honourable connexion for the chief of Gorkha. These friends soon entered into a most iniquitous combination. The Gorkha family had hitherto entirely failed in all their attempts to extend their dominions to the west, and, if Palpa had continued to assist the neighbouring Rajas, it is probable, that their resistance to Gorkha might have been continued with success; but the father and son-in-law agreed, that they should make a common cause, and divide the spoil. This scheme completely succeeded, and Damodar Pangre, a Khas by birth, but representative of one of the chief families in Gorkha, and a most gallant officer, was sent in command of the regent's forces. After the conquest, Damodar took for his master the lion's share, but allowed Mahadatta to retain as master Gulmi, Argha, and Kachi, three of the states that had been long in alliance with his family, and which he was bound to protect, not only by the duty of alliance, but of kindred, for the Raja of Argha was his uncle. The other three allies, who had been saved by his father, were abandoned to the power of Gorkha, and annexed to Nepal. Mahadatta was very soon forced to eat the fruit of his villany. Damodar advanced the conquests of his nation to the west, and, having subdued Kumau, all resistance to his force on the hills was in vain, and Mahadatta was soon deprived of all the hope of protection, that he might have had from the power of his son-in-law the regent, the young Raja of Gorkha having put his uncle to death. The friendship of the Nawab Vazir, however, saved Mahadatta, nor was any encroachment made on Palpa, so long as he lived.

Prithwi Pal succeeded his father, when very young, and was endowed with great personal vigour, nor was he, I believe, at all scrupulous about means; but he seems to have been rash and credulous, which rendered him totally unable to resist the wiles of the people of Gorkha, who were afraid to use open violence, on account of his connexion with the Nawab Vazir. They did not therefore molest his ancient dominions, nor any of the territory that he had acquired on the plains, all of which was tributary to the Nawab; but, immediately after his accession, Rana Bahadur, king of Gorkha and Nepal, compelled the Raja of Palpa to restore the mountains of Gulmi to Siddhi Pratap, the legal heir of that country, whose sister Rana Bahadur had married.

When Rana Bahadur of Gorkha determined to place the sovereignty in the hands of Yudda Vikram Sahi, his illegitimate son, he invited Prithwi Pal to perform the ceremony of Tika, under pretence that he was desirous of obviating the defects of his son's birth, by having the mark of royalty placed on his forehead by a person of Prithwi Pal's high rank; for, among the hill chiefs he was considered as the most eminent by birth, and the Raja of Yumila had been expelled from his dominions; nor did the Gorkha family, after the acquisition of Nepal, acknowledge the superiority of its chief. The real object, however, of the invitation, was in all probability to have power over Prithwi Pal; for he remained in a kind of confinement until January 1803, when the noble and high-spirited lady, wife of Rana Bahadur, who then governed Nepal, had the magnanimity to allow him to return to his own territories, although his father had treacherously stript her's of his dominions, and, although there is strong reason to suspect, that Damodar Pangre, discontented with the illegitimacy of Yuddha Vikram, had entered into a conspiracy to dethrone that young prince, and to place Prithwi Pal on the throne of Nepal.

When Rana Bahadar had returned from Banaras, had assumed the management of affairs, as regent for his son, and had put to death Damodar Pangre, and the other discontented nobles of his kingdom, his first care was to secure Prithwi Pal. He accordingly sent an embassy to that chief, requesting his sister in marriage, and making the most profuse offers of increasing the territories of his future brother-in-law. The lady was sent, accompanied by her brother Rana Bahadur, for Prithwi Pal was suspicious; and, although invited, did not attend. The lady and her brother were most kindly received by Rana Bahadur of Gorkha, who said to the chief of the same name, I have been a king, and should therefore think myself degraded by worshipping you, (according to the Hindu custom,) when I received your sister from your hands; it will be therefore highly agreeable to me, if your brother, who is a prince my superior in birth, would attend to give away his sister. The Guru, or spiritual guide of the Palpa Raja, was in the suite of the princess, and was dispatched in order to persuade Prithwi Pal, in which he succeeded, by declaring, that Rana Bahadur had before him taken the most solemn oaths to do his guest no injury. Whether Rana Bahadur had actually done so, or whether the Brahman was bribed, and told a falsehood to obtain his end, I cannot take upon myself to say, either circumstance being abundantly compatible with the characters of the persons; but Prithwi Pal had no sooner reached Kathmandu, with about 400 attendants, than these were disarmed, he and his principal officers were put in close confinement, and no more mention was made of the marriage. No one can pity the fate of Prithwi Pal; as, in order to ingratiate himself with his intended brother-in-law, he took with him, and delivered to Rana Bahadur, the widow and only surviving son of his friend Damodar Pangre; who, when that gallant veteran and his elder sons had been murdered by the tyrant, had fled to Palpa for refuge. The Raja of Gorkha was, however, afraid of driving the Palpa family to extremities, and compelling it to seek refuge in the territories of the Company, whichha d received from the Nawab Vazir the sovereignty of the low countries belonging to Palpa, and might be disposed to give its powerful support.

When mortally wounded by his brother, the Raja of Gorkha placed the authority of the kingdom, and the protection of his son, in the hands of Bhim Sen, a very vigorous rash young man, who, owing partly to the moderation of the Company's negociations with Rana Bahadur, by him attributed to fear, and partly to the hope of protection from the Chinese, seems to have beheld the British government with contempt. One of his first measures, about the end of June 1804, was to put the Raja of Palpa and all his officers to death. It is said by some that, under pretence of the conspiracy to which I have alluded, he inflicted most severe tortures on the unfortunate chief; but others maintain, that his throat was cut, like that of the others, without any form of investigation or delay. Bhim Sen acted with the utmost promptitude in obtaining his object. His father, Amar Singha, was raised to the English rank of general, sent with a considerable force, and in less than a month from his son's elevation, took possession of Palpa without resistance; nor did he hesitate to advance into the low country, which belonged to the Raja of Palpa, as a subject of the Company. Had Bhim Sen confined himself to the hills of Palpa, it is almost certain that he would have met with no disturbance from the British government; but he still perhaps congratulates himself on having understood the British government better than Rana Bahadur; for, although he has not been allowed to keep undisturbed all the low country that was subject to Palpa, he has for some years held a considerable portion.

On the approach of General Amar Singha to Palpa, in July or August 1804, the widow of Prithwi Pal, with her son Ratna Sen, his uncle Samar Bahadur, usually called the Lal Dewan, or Nader Shah, and his grand-uncle Suravir, who held the office of Chautariya, fled to a house which the family had at Madhuvani in Tilpur. The unfortunate lady died there, and the Raja was removed to Gorakhpur, where he has ever since remained, but in such constant apprehension of assassination, that it has been judged necessary to have his house secured by a guard of regular seapoys. The Company have allowed him a pension in lieu of the profits which he would have had from his remaining estates, of which the collector has assumed the entire disposal; for owing to the encroachments made by Amar Singha, and the devastation that has followed in what remains, it is altogether impossible for him to fulfil the engagements into which his father's agents entered with Mr Rutlege, the gentleman who had the management of the country ceded by the Nawab vazir to the Company. This pension was altogether inadequate to support the number of persons by whom he was followed; and even his venerable grand-uncle Suravir, son of Makunda Sen, suffered such mortifications, that he had determined to perish on the place where his son had suffered death, for this youth had accompanied his cousin Prithwi Pal. The old man, after taking an affectionate leave of some of the family adherents in Tilpur, and weeping with them a whole day, went to Palpa and presented himself to Amar Singha, who was moved with compassion, and said, though we have killed your son, and overthrown your family, we will do you no injury, but will provide for you in a manner very different from your friends the English. There has accordingly been settled on him an income sufficient to supply his wants. I am not sure that this has proceeded from generosity; but it has produced some effect on the minds of the populace. If it was intended to lull the fears of the family into a fatal security, it has hitherto completely failed.

The extent and boundaries of Palpa will be better seen from the maps than explained by description. The country, independent of Butaul, is in general lower and warmer than the valley of Nepal Proper. The greatest crop is transplanted rice, next to that broad-cast rice, then maize, then the pulse called urid, almost equal in quantity to the maize, then the Lathyrus sativus, called dubi kerao, then the Eleusine corocanus, or maruya, then the Ervum lens, or masuri, then four kinds of sesamum, and the cruciform oil seeds, like mustard and rape, then three kinds of the pulse called kurthi, and then a little of the grains called sama and kodo. Much ginger is reared. The sugar-cane grows very large and juicy, but is eaten without preparation.

When the colony from Chitaur first took possession of Palpa, it belonged to a Magar chief, and the people were of that tribe. Brahmans, but mostly of the spurious breed called Jausi, are now the most numerous class; next to these are the Khas; and the Magars only occupy the third place.

Since the Raja of Gorkha and Nepal has seized on this country, the seat of government has been removed to Tansen, a town at some distance west from Palpa, with a tolerable road between them. This is now the residence of the General Amar Singha, formerly called Thapa, and the Subahs, or civil officers, governing the petty principalities to a considerable distance, are under his authority. He has with him a large force of regulars, (fourteen or fifteen companies,) which he has for some time been assiduously increasing, and to enable him to put this measure into execution, a great part of the free land has been resumed. The plan adopted on this occasion was to say to the Brahmans who held the land, " you are impure fellows, who have degraded yourselves by doing many things totally inconsistent with the character of the sacred order. It is impossible, therefore, that you should, as such, be permitted to hold lands; and if you presume to act in the character from which you have degraded yourself, you shall be scourged. For a subsistence, therefore, betake yourself to cultivation, or other drudgeries, for which alone you are now fit, and do not bring a disgrace on the character of the sacred order." In these degenerate days perhaps there is not one Brahman out of fifty who either does not do what he ought to shun, or who does not omit to do what he ought to perform; and all will admit that degraded Brahmans are unworthy of holding such possessions. If the Brahmans, however, were to be the judges of the quantum of such transgressions necessary to occasion the forfeiture of free lands, such an event would seldom indeed happen. But the lay rulers of Nepal judged more strictly; and as they knew that whatever proofs they might bring would produce no conviction, they probably deemed it quite unnecessary to put the parties to any trouble, or to go through the farce of a trial, where the measure to be adopted was predetermined; nor are the chiefs of Nepal men against whom any complaints of injustice are made by those under their authority.

There are many routes from the plain into the hills of Palpa; but, except by a few smugglers, most of these have been deserted since the conquest, for which there seem to be two reasons. The Nepalese are desirous of having only a few open routes, by which an army from the low country might penetrate into the hills, and they think that in a few years the neglected routes will be either altogether forgotten, or be so overgrown with woods as to prevent access. The few remaining roads will then be easily guarded by a small force. But besides the military point of view, they are desirous of having few passages as a point of economy in collecting the customs. Accordingly, so far as they can, they have stopt every pass, except that by Butaul, which, of course, has become a considerable mart, although most inconveniently situated. It stands on the plain, but in a recess of the mountains, and is so dreadfully unhealthy, that no one resides there in the rainy season. The Rajas had a house called Nayakot on a hill overhanging the town, or assemblage of huts; but I am told, that this castle is not sufficiently elevated to be exempt from the effects of the insalubrious air.

The Palpa Rajas possessed also a very important mart in the hills. It is called Rerighat, and is situated on the bank of the Narayani. The best, or rather the only tolerable roads passing through the country either from the east and west, or from the north and south, pass this route; and it seems to be of equal importance either in a military or commercial view. During the cold season there is at Rerighat a fair (Mela) which lasts for three or four months, and is frequented by a great number of traders from all parts of the mountains. The road from

Butaul to Rerighat by Morihang, Mosihang, and Tansen, was said to be far from difficult; but what idea a mountaineer annexed to a difficult road is not easy to determine. Some of them say, that loaded oxen could pass; others say that they could not. It is generally admitted, that the easiest route from Rerighat to the plains would be east through Tansen, Rampur, Nayakot, and Dewghat, but this road is at present stopt.

Loaded canoes, I am assured, can pass up the Gandaki, or Narayani, all the way to Rerighat, except at a narrow rapid between two rocks at a place called Gongkur, a little above Dewghat. There they must be unloaded and dragged up empty. Timber in floating down this passage is apt to fall across the channel, and to stick between the rocks; but this may be obviated by tying a rope to one end of the logs so as to allow them to float end on. Canoes can ascend to Dewghat with little difficulty. There are, indeed, three rapids; one above Bhelaunji to which large boats can go with ease; a second at the junction of the Arhung; and a third at Khairiyani, near Dewghat; but in the dry season canoes or small boats may be dragged up loaded. In floods the navigation is altogether unadvisable, the river being then of tremendous rapidity.

Near Tansen, the present capital, there was formerly a mine of iron, but, since the conquest, copper has been discovered in the same place, and now, it is said, the mine produces that metal to the value of 50,000 rupees a-year. In the small territory of Khidim lately, as I have said, annexed to Palpa, is a mine of lead.

I received very little information concerning the Tanahung branch of this family. It is said to be descended of Bihangga, or Bhringga, son of Makunda Sen, who lived ten or eleven generations ago. After some generations the then chief of Tanahung, it is said, gave Rising as an appanage to a younger brother, although, as I shall afterwards state, there may be some doubt entertained on this point. Afterwards, on the failure of the Champaranya, or Rajpur branch of this colony from Chitaur, the then Raja of Tanahung secured a part called Ramnagar, which is situated in the district of Saran, under the protection of the Company, and is now all that belongs to the family. No chief resisted with such gallantry and effect the rising power of Prithwi Narayan of Gorkha as the Raja of Tanahung, by whom the forces of that perfidious prince were defeated in a most decisive battle; nor was any attempt afterwards made to extend the dominions of Gorkha to the west until the Raja of Palpa was gained, as I have already mentioned. How the overthrow of Tanahung took place I have not learned; but the Raja made his escape to Ramnagar, and retains only what he held of the Company. His country, that was formerly independent, consists of two portions; one on the hills that surround Gorkha on the west and south, and one in the valley of the Raputi, which is adjacent to the southern portion of what is on the hills. This valley is inhabited by the ordinary Hindus of Mithila. It contains three Pergunahs or baronies, Chitan, Belan, and Sengjhayat, of which the two former contain a good deal of cultivation. The road through them along the Raputi to Hethaura is tolerably level, and might be easily made good; while I understand that from Ramnagar by Bakraghat there is a pretty good road to Chitan over the low hills, by which the valley is bounded on the south. The direct road from the plain to Hethaura by Bichhakhori is, I know, very difficult; but some allege, that there is along the banks of the torrent, in which the road now goes, a very good route, which has been shut up by the present government of Nepal. Colonel Kirkpatrick describes another route through these hills; but, from all accounts, it is more difficult than any of the others.

The mountains of Tanahung were inhabited by the same races as Palpa, and nearly in the same proportions. Its southern division contained three towns, Yogimara, Upadrang, and Kavilas; the first of which is said to be large, and a military station of some importance, although I did not learn the title of the officer commanding, nor the extent of his force. The circumstance of the military station, however, strongly confirms the statement of Samar Bahadur, who alleges, that by these three towns is one of the easiest routes to Nepal, of which the following is a detail given by Sadhu Ram.

From Sivapur Ghat on the Gandaki, in the Company's territory, to Bhelongji in Nepal, the distance is 2½ coses, very bad road, but large boats can go up the river. From Bhelongji to Benmohar the distance is 3 coses, the river having some rapids. Near Benmohar the Raputi joins the Gandaki or Narayani; and there is a road through a level country, partly cultivated, to Hethaura. From Benmohar to the Arung Dumohan the distance is 3 coses. At this place also are some rapids. From Arun Dumohan to Leraghat is a distance of 3½ coses without rapids. From Leraghat to Dewghat are two days' journey, having the cultivated lands of Chitan to the right, and Nawalpur, the residence of a Subah, to the left. From Dewghat to Kavilas is one day's journey east through a hilly country, in some parts cultivated. Kavilas is a village near the Trisul Gangga, which is larger than the Narayani above Dewghat. From Kavilas to Upadrang is a day's journey through a hilly country. Upadrang is a town and military station, with the Trisulgangga one-quarter cose to the north. It must be observed, that Kanak Nidhi reverses the situation of the two last places; but Sadhu Ram's position is supported by Colonel Kirkpatrick. From Upadrang to Yogimara, or Yogimaya, is a day's journey east. Yogimara is a large village on a hill one-quarter cose south from the Trisulgangga. From Yogimara to Chitlang, in the lesser valley of Nepal, is two days' journey; and the road seems to pass through the valley, which Colonel Kirkpatrick calls Doona Baisi, and fully describes.* From his account it would appear, that, from this valley, besides the route leading to Chitlong, there is another leading to Thankot in the greater valley of Nepal, and avoiding the difficult passage of Chandangiri, which lies between Chitlong and Kathmandu. Samar Bahadur says, that on the whole route there is no great ascent; but the Brahman Prati Nidhi alleges, that the route is both circuitous and steep. At any rate, it has been stopt by the present government of Nepal.

In the western wing of Tanahung were the capital and Bandi, two places of some consequence. The two maps differ a good deal in the details of this principality; nor do I know to which the preference should be given.

The mountains of Tanahung contained mines of iron, but no others.

It was said, by Samar Bahadur, that Rising, Ghiring, and Gajarkot, formerly belonged to Tanahung, and were given as an appanage to a younger brother, among whose descendants they were afterwards subdivided, and the three chiefs, to whom they belonged, are universally looked upon to be of the same family; but here a great difficulty occurs. The Tanahung family, as well as the Palpa branch, is very generally admitted to be descended of the Chitaur family, and to be

* Nepaul, p. 85.

of the highest and purest tribe on the hills, east of the river Kali; but these three petty chiefs wallow in all the ancient abominations of the mountaineers. That Samar Bahadur was mistaken, I see no reason to suppose; especially as these three chiefs were in league with his family, and as Rising seems to have belonged to his ancestor Makunda the 1st, who founded at the Dewghat, in that territory, a celebrated temple, where he died. I shall not take upon myself, however, to say, whether we are, from the circumstance, to infer, that the whole members of this family have no just claim to be descended from the Chitaur colony, but were impure mountaineers, who had this pedigree invented to flatter them, when they turned from their impure ways, and were induced to follow the Brahmans. It is possible, that the first chief of the Rising family, who obtained that country as an appanage, may have been of illegitimate birth, and that, his mother being impure, he may have been brought up in a hankering after the flesh-pots, from which it has been impossible to wean his descendants.

Rising, as I have said, was given by a Raja of Tanahung to a younger son. The territory was always petty, and, according to Prati Nidhi, Dewghat seems to have been resumed by Tanahung; but Sadhu Ram alleges, that so long as the principality of Rising continued independent, Dewghat was its port, and enjoyed some trade, which has been stopt by its present rulers. The image of Siva, contained in the temple, is called Makundeswar, from the founder. There is a great assembly of votaries on the Sivaratri, and another on the Khichri. Some of this family are said to remain, but where, I have not heard. The country and its inhabitants do not differ materially from Palpa, but it contains no mines.

Ghiring and Gajarkot, which belonged to two collateral

branches of Rising, were still more petty than that state, but did not differ in any other considerable respect.

SECTION III.

NEPAL PROPER.

Name.—History previous to the Conquest by the Gorkhalis.—Extent and Topography.—Population.—Buildings.—Revenue.—Trade.—Coins.—Weights.—Measures.—Agriculture.—Tenures.—Crown Lands.—Lands held for Service.—Charity Lands.—Tenants.—Implements.—Crops.—Manufactures.—Price of Labour.—Slaves.—Diet.

I MUST next proceed to describe Nepal Proper, which is bounded on the east, south, and south-west, by the territory above mentioned. I have to regret, that various restraints, by which my inquiries were checked, while at Kathmandu, prevented me from obtaining much information that I was anxious to procure. In particular, I obtained little or no information concerning the history of the princes who governed Nepal at the time of the conquest; except that the Newars had been long subject to a family of their own nation, all the members of which assumed the name of Mal, and, for some time previous to the conquest, had separated into three lordships, Kathmandu or Kathmaro, Lalita Patan, and Bhatgang, which circumstance greatly facilitated the enterprise of the chief of Gorkha.

Nepal is a country celebrated in Hindu fable, and is said to be written thus in the Purans, attributed to Vyas; but in the country itself, it is commonly said, that its proper name is Niyampal, derived from a certain Niyam, a Muni, or very holy person, the Nymuni of Colonel Kirkpatrick.* This, however, is probably some modern conceit, as the Brahmans of both south and north agree in writing the name Nepala, or Nepal, and as the fables on which this etymology is built, as Colonel Kirkpatrick justly observes, † merit no attention.

As I myself procured little or no historical account of Nepal Proper, previous to its conquest by the Raja of Gorkha, I might altogether refer on the subject to Colonel Kirkpatrick's account, contained in his eighth chapter; but for the sake of connection, and in order to communicate my opinions on the subject, I shall here give an abstract of Colonel Kirkpatrick's account, referring to his own work for particulars.

Colonel Kirkpatrick ‡ quotes books, which he calls Hurrumunt Khund and Ooter Khund, probably portions of the Sri Bhagwat, for copious details concerning Nepal, during the time that it continued one of the favourite haunts of the Hindu deities, that is, during the Satya Yug, or Golden age; nor have we any reason to regret, that, instead of detailing such idle fables, he has contented himself with a mere reference to this work. Afterwards he goes on to give a series of princes, who are said to have governed Nepal in subsequent ages, commencing with Niyam Muni, or as he writes Nymuni. In this part of his work Colonel Kirkpatrick quotes no authority; but, as he brings the lists down to the termination of the Newar dynasty in 1767, his authorities are probably quite modern,

* Nepaul, p. 256, &c. † Nepaul, p. 169. ‡ Nepaul, p. 255.

and, as he supports the doctrine of the Newars having come from Gar Samaran, which they deny, his authorities must be founded on the legends of the Brahmans, much of which probably may be inventions perfectly recent, but some foundation may have been taken from ancient works, mangled to suit them for modern systems of Hindu chronology.

However this may be, Niyam Muni and his eight descendants are said* to have governed during the Treta and Dwapar Yugs, or the Silver and Brazen Ages, which, according to the present system, lasted for many hundred thousand years. The eight successors of Niyam Muni governed † four hundred and ninety-one one-third years, which requires rather an unwarrantable stretch of faith to believe; but, even admitting this, what remains to Niyam Muni is altogether beyond measure. This, perhaps, is owing to the works originally consulted having been composed before the present system of chronology was invented. It is more to the purpose to observe, that these princes have Sangskrita names, and therefore probably came from the plains; and that, except Niyam and his immediate successor, all of them are called Gupt; which shows that they were of the cow-herd tribe.

This dynasty was deprived of power by Bhul Singh of the Rajput tribe, and descended of Mehip Gopal, who came from Semrounghur (Gar Samaran) and Jamnukpou, (Janakipur.) He and his two descendants both having Sangskrita names, governed a hundred and eleven seven-twelfth years. Gar Samaran, it must be observed, was not built for many ages after the time of this dynasty; but Bhul Singh may have come from Janakipur, which was in the vicinity of the place where Gar Sa-

* Page 169. † Page 256.

maran was afterwards built. Whatever title these princes may have assumed, there is no reason to suppose that they were of the ancient Kshatriyas, descended of the sun, who resided at Janakipur, and governed Mithila, as no such name as Mehip Gopal appears in any list of the princes of Mithila that I have seen. Indeed, the title Gopal rather implies, that, like the former dynasty, the descendants of Mehip belonged to the low tribe of cow-herds.

This dynasty, whatever may have been its origin, was expelled by the Kerrats, (Kiratas,) of whom 27 princes governed 1630 years. The names of these princes, as might be expected, from what I have said of the tribe Kirata, are entirely barbarous.

The barbarian Kiratas were expelled by Nevesit, a Chetree (Kshatriya) of the Surejbunsi (Suryabangsi) race, of whose descendants 33 princes governed 1702 years. These princes had Sangskrita names, although Colonel Kirkpatrick,* speaking of one of them, who built the temple of Sambhunath, says, that they were Thibetians, who, after having been expelled by the Newars, obtained the name of Khat Bhotiyas, which they preserve to this day. Many of them took the title of Burmah,† on which account Colonel Kirkpatrick calls them Burmahs, probably meaning Varmas; and it is probable that these are the Varmas celebrated in the Purans, and had no connection with the Burmas of Ava, as Dr Leyden supposed.‡ Both, indeed, were of the sect of Buddha, who are usually called Brahmas by the Hindus, and the word Burma, Burmah, or Birmah, is probably a corruption of that appellation.

The Ahirs, (Ahiras, another name for cow-herds,) who were

---

* P. 148. † P. 265.

‡ See his Treatise on the Languages of Eastern India, in the 10th volume of the Asiatick Researches.

originally the sovereigns of Nepal, then recovered their dominions, and three of them governed 175 years. These must have been descendants of Niyam Muni. They have Sangskrita names, with the addition of Gupt, to mark their descent and tribe.

After these the Burmahs, descended of Nevesit, again recovered Nepal, and during 46 reigns governed $1869\frac{1}{8}$th years, which, by some error in the printing, or addition, is made $2869\frac{1}{17}$ years. Three sons of the last of these 46 princes governed successively, but the length of their reigns is not stated. One of them left a daughter, named Suttey Naik Deby, (probably Satya Nayeka Devi,) and married to Harrir Chander Deo, (probably Harihara Chandra Deva,) Raja of Banaras, by whom she had a daughter, Raj Letehmi, (Raya Lakshmi,) who was queen of Nepal.

This lady was succeeded by Hurr Singh Deo Raja of Semrour, (Hari Singha Deva of Samaran,) who introduced the Newars, and * expelled the Thibetians, now called Kath Bhotiyas, who since occupy chiefly the mountains near Kuti. This event happened in the Newar year 444, (A. D. 1323.)

The length of time allotted in the preceding account to these reigns is quite inadmissible, and on an average, I think, that more than ten years should not be allowed for each. According to this, we may form the following estimate.

Niyam and his eight descendants would govern 90 years, beginning A. D. 33, nearly about the time that Sakya introduced the doctrine of the Buddhas into these mountainous regions, and it was he who probably introduced Sangskrita names, and any considérable degree of civility among the mountain tribes. We know abundantly, that most of the

---

* P. 148.

successors of Niyam continued to adhere to the doctrine of Sakiya, as the Kiratas Burmahs and Newars occupy by far the greatest portion of the subsequent space, and were no doubt of the sect of Buddha.

The three descendants of Mehip Gopal would govern 30 years, beginning A. D. 173.

The Kiratas would govern 270 years, commencing A. D. 303.

The Bhotiyas, descended of Nevesit, would govern at first 330 years, beginning A. D. 473.

The descendants of Niyam Muni, after recovering their old patrimony, would govern 30 years, beginning A. D. 803.

The Bhotiyas would again govern 490 years, beginning A. D. 833.

In the account of the Newars I have already stated, that this people totally deny their having come from the plains, or that their princes were descended of Hari Singha of Gar Samaran, and the people of Mithila, in which Gar Samaran is situated, altogether deny that Hari Singha ever left their country. I am therefore inclined to suppose, that the Mal family, which afterwards governed Nepal, are in fact the descendants of the last queen of the Burmah race, who, under the influence of her father from Banaras, may have introduced the doctrine of cast, and other customs, in which the Newars differ from the Thibetians, and thus separated their subjects from that portion of their tribe who retained their ancient customs, and who were afterwards distinguished by the name of Khat Bhotiyas.

Jat Mull, according to Colonel Kirkpatrick,* in the sixth generation from the founder of the Newar dynasty, was a

* Page 268.

great conqueror; but divided his kingdom into the three principalities which existed when the country was conquered by the Gorkhalis. Runjeet Mull (Ranjit Mal) of Bhatgang, in the seventh generation from Jat Mull, entered into a league with Prithwi Narayan of Gorkha against Kathmandu, which ended in the total subjugation of his house in the year 1767, so that thirteen generations held the government for 444 years, which coincides very exactly with the calculation of the venerable Herodotus.

The finest parts of Nepal consist of two delightful vallies separated from each other by the mountain Chandangiri; but these vallies, called Great and Little Nepal, do not include the whole of Nepala Desa, which is one of the fifty-six regions of Hindu geography. It extends also a considerable way over the countries watered by streams which run from the outside of the mountains that inclose the greater valley, and which fall into the Gandaki on the west, and the Kausiki on the east. The real boundaries are four celebrated places of pilgrimage; Nilkantha, eight days' journey north from Kathmandu; Nateswar, three days' journey south; Kaleswar, two days' journey west; and Bhimeswar, four days' journey east. The whole territory between these places is holy ground, and is properly called Dhama. This holy land, according to the Brahmans, is inhabited by 5,600,000 Bhairawas and Bhairawis. The former are male spirits of Maha Deva, or Siva, and the latter are female spirits of the Sakti, who is the wife, the mother, and the divine power of that deity. The whole territory within these boundaries was not, however, subject to the Newar chiefs who governed Nepal, and a large part in the vicinity of Nilkantha in particular, until the rise of the house of Gorkha, was subject to Thibet.

Nilkantha is a place much frequented by pilgrims, and which

would seem to possess many natural curiosities. I therefore shall here annex an account of the best route to it, in hopes that it may be of use to some fortunate traveller, who may procure access to visit the Alps of Nepal. The traveller ought to proceed to Yogimara, the route to which I have mentioned before.

From Yogimara it is one day's journey north and east to Mahes Domohana, a large village on a hill, at the junction of the Mahes with the Trisulgangga. The Mahes rises at Bhenhongga, a village three coses west from Kirtipur, in the greater valley of Nepal.

From Mahes Domohana to Devighat is a distance of 2½ days' journey, with not above two or three villages on the whole route. Devighat is a large village, where the Tazi or Tadi joins the Trisulgangga, and where there are annually several assemblies for the people to bathe at the junction of the streams. Kanak Nidhi, it must be observed, places a Devighat much lower down, at the junction of the Trisulgangga with the Gandi, but the Devi Ghat at the junction of the Tadi and Trisulgangga, or Daiby Ghaut, as he calls it, is that described by Colonel Kirkpatrick,* at considerable length. It is dedicated to Maha Maia, or Bhawani, concerning whom, Colonel Kirkpatrick, or his editor, seems to have fallen into several errors, saying, "that Bhowani is Daiby, (so "he writes the words,) in her character of universal mother, "or in other words Nature." Now, Devi and Bhawani have exactly the same meaning, that is, the Goddess; and Maha Maia is not universal mother, but great mother; nor is Bhawani ever worshipped as the Genetrix naturæ, as universal mother might imply, but as the Sakti, or power of Siva, who

* Nepaul, page 119.

is the God of destruction, and her worship is entirely that of fear.

North from this Devighat, six hours' (two pahars) journey, is Nayakot, a town of Nepal Proper, situated on a hill, on the east side of the Trisulgangga. It contains about 12,000 houses, mostly occupied by Newars, and is built of brick like Kathmandu. The Court often retires here in the winter, the situation being warmer than Kathmandu. The town is situated on a hill, overhanging a valley, which Colonel Kirkpatrick * estimates to be 2200 feet lower than Kathmandu, on which account, it is not habitable after the middle of April, being subject to the Ayul.

From Nayakot north, one day's journey, is Dhayabung, a village chiefly inhabited by Bhotiyas, and situated on a high hill at the Bitrawati ghat. The Bitrawati comes from the east, and has a course of four or five hours' (1½ pahar) journey in length.

North from Dhayabung, one day's journey, is Dhunchi, a Bhotiya village, on a large hill, south from the Trisulgangga.

From Dhunchi east, one day's journey, is Dhimsa, a large Bhotiya village, not now subject to Gorkha. From Dhimsa to Gosaingsthan there are no inhabitants, and the country is covered with snow. Three hours' journey from Dhimsa, the pilgrims come to Ganes Gongera, where there is an image of Ganes, to which the pilgrims resort. They then proceed about seven or eight hours' journey (two or three pahars) to Bara Nilkantha, where, during the fair, there are many shops. There are eight springs, one of which is hot, and emits a blue flame from its surface. East from thence one-half cose, is a pool called Gaurikunda. Another pool, named Suryakunda, is about one-half cose farther east; and immediately beyond that,

---

* Page 115.

rises the immense peak of Gosaingsthan, from the east-side of which a branch of the Kausiki issues. On a mountain south from Gosaingsthan, and called Mahamandal, are found lead, zinc, or tutenague, mica in large plates, and rock crystal.

From Dhunchi there is a road to Kerung, one day's journey north. This has lately been ceded to the Chinese by the governors of Nepal.

Considerable illustrations of this route up the Trisulgangga, by Nayakot to Nilkantha, and Kerung, * may be found in the 5th Chapter of Kirkpatrick's Account of Nepaul, page 107, &c.

I have already given an account of the Newars, and of the mineral productions of the valley of Nepal, and now proceed to treat of some other circumstances, relating partly to the former, and partly to the present state of things, when Nepal has become the seat of a foreign government; although by this arrangement, I must here detail much of what I have to state concerning the family which now reigns, and to which I must afterwards return.

The following is the route to Kathmandu, by which I went to that city, and which is the one most frequented by merchants from the low country, especially by those trading to Patna, which is the principal mart for this commerce.

From the Company's boundary near the Bera river is about ten miles to Gar Pasara, over an open plain, little of which is cultivated. An old fort, and many plantations of Mango trees, show that formerly it has been in a better state. We crossed the Bera, and passed some way along the banks of another river. Even in the end of March, these rivers are full of water, and contain no large banks of sand, as is usual in India. With industry, they might be applied most advantageously to irrigate

* Kheero, Kirk.

the fields. The water is dirty, and owing to the quantity of rotten vegetable matter which it brings from the forest, and which at this season is little diluted, it is reckoned very unwholesome. Gar Pasara is a small village with a large tank. Near it is a brick house built by Singha Pratap, the present Raja of Gorkha's grandfather, who in the cold season sometimes resided in the Tariyani, on the improvement of which he bestowed considerable attention.

From Gar Pasara to Bichhakor is about fourteen miles. The three first miles are clear, the remainder passes through a stately forest, with little or no underwood, but some long grass and reeds. For seven miles the ground in the forest is nearly level, and a very little trouble would make the road fit for carts. The remaining road passes along the lower part of some small hills, which are rather stony, and it crosses the rough and wide channels of some torrents, which in the cold season are perfectly dry; yet a small labour would render the whole way from Gar Pasara to Bichhakor passable for carts. At present it is perfectly good for laden cattle. There is no water by the way. Bichhakor contains about a dozen huts, and affords no supplies except wood and water, of which last there is a very fine spring, and several small streams in a very wide stony channel, the only clear place in the vicinity.

Bichhakor derives its name from the place abounding in scorpions. There is no cultivation near it, and the only inhabitants are a few Parbatiyas, or mountain Hindus. They reside at the place to collect some duties, and for the accommodation of travellers, and by long habit have become inured to the climate, and enabled to resist its baneful influence, which, from the end of March, till the beginning of December, is exceedingly destructive to all strangers. The temperature of the air at Bichhakor is sensibly cooler than at Gar Pasara, and we found the heat of the spring to be 74° Fahrenheit's thermometer, which may be considered as the average heat of the place.

From Bichhakor to Hethaura is about sixteen miles. For the first seven miles the channel serves as a road; but both sides consist of low steep hills and precipices; the former covered with thick woods, among which are many pines. The ascent on the whole is considerable, but is nowhere steep; and with a little pains, the road might be made very good for loaded oxen, or even for light carriages. Even now, cattle convey along it on their backs the usual burthen of grain. About seven miles from Bichhakor, the road proceeds to the right from the channel, through a very strong pass called Chiriyaghat, or bird passage. It is commanded by two hills, which are less than a mile from the river, and which, although steep, are not high. The road between them is narrow, but in other respects is not bad. Colonel Kirkpatrick * considers Chiriyaghat as the name of the whole ridge, and not as that of the pass, as the name would seem to imply, and as I understood. From Chiriyaghat to Hethaura, the road is very good for loaded cattle, and might be easily rendered fit for carts. It descends gently through a country that rises into small swells, and has few trees, but is intersected by several dry water courses. About a mile from Hethaura, the Karara, coming from the east, passes the road. The ford is perfectly easy, and the road from thence to Hethaura is good, leading through a stately forest. From Chiriyaghat to Hethaura, there is no water except the Karara, a dirty black stream, which it is unsafe to drink, being black and unwholesome.

* Nepaul, p. 22.

The route to Hethaura above described by Gar Pasara, or as he writes it Goolpussra, * or Goorpussra, † according to Colonel Kirkpatrick, possesses decided advantages over that by the Bhareh pass, situated farther east.

Hethaura stands on a fine plain, about a mile wide, and is bounded on the north by the Raputi, and on the south by the Karara. The soil of this plain is good, but none of it is cultivated, and most of it is covered with stately forests of the Sakhuya or Sal, which are kept clear of underwood, by burning at this season the fallen leaves and dry grass. This is done to all the forests in the neighbourhood, and every night of my stay, the surrounding hills were illuminated in a very grand manner.

The Raputi is a beautiful rapid clear stream, which, having come from the north, turns here to the west, and after having been joined by the Karara some way below, passes till it joins the Gandaki, through a valley, the lower part of which is cultivated, but all near Hethaura is waste, although the plain there would admit of a considerable extent of cultivation, should ever the jealousy of the Nepal government be so far removed as to allow the forests to be cleared. This, however, is not likely soon to be the case, as these forests increase the insalubrity of the air at Hethaura, which is one of the most important stations that could be chosen by invaders coming from the south. All kind of stores and provisions can be transported to it with ease, and it is a fine situation, admitting of a large camp. This might be secured by taking Makwanpur, a fortress situated about five miles to the eastward on a high hill. The people of Nepal are very jealous concerning Makwanpur, Hari-

* Nepaul, page 14.

† Nepaul, page 30.

harpur, and Sinduli, as the possession of these would give an enemy the entire command of the Tariyani.

The heat at Hethuara is much more temperate than that of the Tariyani; bnt, as the warm season advances, the air becomes exceedingly unhealthy, which seems to be chiefly owing to the want of cultivation.

For the accommodation of merchants, Hethaura has a brick building, which surrounds a square court. There are also a few shops.

From Hethaura to Bhimphedi is a distance of about eighteen miles, leading through a narrow defile, between high and steep hills, overgrown with thick woods. The Raputi winds through the defile in an extraordinary manner, so that it is crossed twenty-two times by the way. It is a strong, rapid, clear stream, not too deep to prevent it from being easily forded, so far as the water is concerned; but the channel is filled with rounded slippery stones, that render the fords very bad; when we went, bridges had therefore been constructed of trees laid from stone to stone, and covered with earth, so that cattle might have passed with tolerable ease, nor is the road very bad. From Hethaura to Bhimphedi is usually reckoned one day's journey; but in returning, I halted by the way, on a clear space, called Maka Paka, which, although of small extent, and uneven, afforded abundance of wood and water; while at Bhimphedi the supply of the latter is scanty, and it is practicable from Maka Paka to go over the hill of Chispani, and in one day to reach the fine rivulet called Panauni, which is on its north side. Between Maka Paka and Kethaura are a few cleared spots, like it cultivated by rude tribes, who shun all communication with travellers, and dwell in the recesses of forests which protect them from the Gorkhalese.

About fourteen miles from Hethaura, and a little way from

Maka Paka, the road leaves the immediate bank of the Raputi, and ascends a very steep and strong bank, called Dokaphedi, from whence to Bhimphedi there is a fine level.

At Bhimphedi, the valley of the Raputi entirely ceases, and the high mountains called Lama Dangra divide it from the country on the north watered by the branches of the Vagmati. A large channel, one of the branches of the Raputi, passes Bhimphedi; but in the dry season it contains no water, and the inhabitants receive a scanty supply from a small spring. Water, however, might probably be procured in abundance, by digging wells in the channel of the torrent.

The height of Bhimphedi, above Hethaura, is very considerable, and the influence of the Ayul is much later in extending there, owing to the coolness of the air. At sunrise, on the 8th April, while the thermometer in the air was at 67° of Fahrenheit's scale, it sunk to 63° upon being immersed into the spring. This may be considered as the average heat of the place, which is about 27° 30′ of north latitude. Here the mercury in our barometer sunk out of sight below the scale, which descended only to twenty-six inches; nor during our stay in Nepal did the mercury ever reach that height. At Bhimphedi, the vegetable productions put on a strong resemblance to those of Europe. It is a small village inhabited by Parbatiyas, and where some public buildings have been erected for the accommodation of passengers. Some shops afford grain, and such articles of consumption as Hindu travellers usually require.

From Bhimphedi to the copper mine (Tamrakhani) on the Panauni, is about 5½ miles over the chain of mountains called Lamadangra, and by the pass called Chisapani. The mountain is of great elevation, and very steep, but not very rugged; nor are the woods thick, although the trees are lofty. Except in steepness, the road is not bad.

About a mile and a half from Bhimphedi, I came to a fort called Chisapani, considered as the bulwark of Nepal; but it is by no means fitted to inspire us with respect for the skill of the engineers of Gorkha. It is situated on the declivity of the hill, so that an assailant might go round by the right, and when he had got above it, even with musquetry, the garrison could not show their faces on the works. Its form will be understood from the sketch.

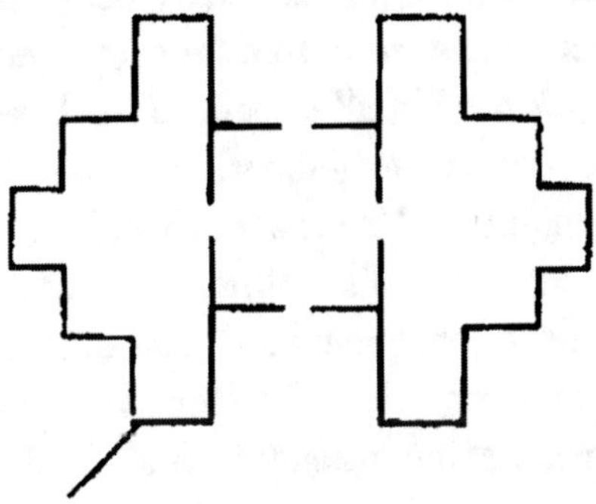

The center in which the gates are is commanded by the two wings. The whole is built of brick, without any ditch. The wall on the upper side is about thirteen feet high; but on the lower front, the height of the parapet being carried round on a level, the elevation may be eighteen feet. This fort is always guarded by a company of seapoys; and, if fully garrisoned, might contain two hundred men. Round the fort a space has been cleared from trees; bat so steep is the hill, that an enemy resting at the edge of the forest, and within two hundred yards of the fort, is not from thence visible. Immediately above the fort is a small village and market, (bazar;) but the Hindu engineers have been so improvident, that the only supply of water is about half a mile higher up the mountain. There, near the road, is a small spring of fine clear water, like that at Bhimphedi. It is called Chisa Pani, or the cold water, and is reckoned unwholesome, probably from people having suffered by drinking it rashly, when they have been heated by ascending the hill: for being a pure spring, it is probably excellent water.

For about a mile beyond the spring, the road continues to ascend, although with a more moderate declivity than below the fort. At the summit of the hill are some old fortifications, which were said to form the boundary between Nepal Proper and Makwanpur. The view from thence is said to be very grand, but a thick haze in all directions hindered me from seeing any thing except the neighbouring hills.

From this summit to the Panauni river, there is a very steep descent of about two miles through a beautiful forest of oaks, which is clear from underwood, and ornamented with the purple flowers of a large rhododendron, and with innumerable parasitical plants, having splendid and odorous flowers. In this forest, on account of its northern exposure, the pine does not thrive. The road over this mountain called Chisapani, is on the whole fatiguing; nor will it admit of any load being transported by cattle. To conduct a road over such a mountain, with proper slopes, so as to enable carriages to pass, is a work not to be expected from the natives, who, even if they were able to contrive such a work, would be afraid to put it in execution; as they would consider it as likely to afford too free an intercourse with their more powerful neighbours; and jealousy of strangers is the predominant principle in the Nepal government.

The Panauni is a clear rapid stream, with various branches, which come from the west and north, and water the country called Lahuri, or Little Nepal. All these branches unite where the road descends from Chisapani, and run to the east to join the Vagmati. Having crossed the Panauni twice, and observed in its channel numerous large masses of grey granite, I halted to breakfast at a small village named Tamra Khani. Near it is a productive copper mine, which the jealousy of the people hindered me from seeing, nor could I procure any of the ore, except a few small fragments. Tamra Khani, or the copper mine, is a small village inhabited by mountain Hindus, (Parbatiyas,) and situated in a very narrow part of the valley, which is straitened by an insulated hill on the north side of the river. Although its situation is low, yet being subject to continual high winds, this place is by the natives considered as very cold.

From thence I proceeded about six miles, and having at first followed the principal stream of the Panauni, and then one of its branches, I halted a little beyond Chitlong, after having had a good view of Lahuri Nepal. Except in dimensions, this so much resembles the larger valley, that I need not take up much time in its description. The road through it frequently crosses the river, and ascends a steep hill above a village named Marku; but this might be in a great measure avoided. The whole valley is not only clear of woods, but very bare. Its surface is extremely uneven, but is finely watered by numerous springs and rivulets, so that it is well cultivated, and produces much grain. The whole appearance of Lahuri Nepal, and its vegetable productions, strongly resemble those of the wilder parts of Britain; and, during my stay, I was entertained with the note of an old acquaintance, the cuckoo. The air of the higher part of the valley where we encamped is much cooler than that of Kathmandu, and was so sharp to our relaxed habits, that our winter clothing became comfortable, although Chitlong is situated nearly in twenty-seven degrees and a half of north latitude. I judge from the temperature of the springs, as they issue from the earth, that its mean heat is 58½ degrees of Fahrenheit's scale. The winters, however, are never severe; and at that season the fields produce a crop of wheat, while in summer they yield one of rice. The great inferiority of this country, when compared with the mountains of Europe, consists in its pasture, which is very poor. It is, however, of a more nourishing quality than the rank grass of the Tariyani; for the cattle of Chitlong are in excellent condition when compared with those below the mountains.

Lahuri Nepal formerly belonged to the Raja of Lalita Patan. Its chief town called Chitlong, is well built, and its inhabitants are mostly Newars.

From Chitlong is about four miles to Thankot in the greater valley of Nepal. The road is very bad and rough, and conducts through forests over a mountain named Chandangiri, and nearly as difficult of ascent and descent as Chisapani. It derives its name, signifying sandal mountain, from one of the fables in the Hindu mythology, which states, that the goddess Parwati, the wife of Siva, rubbed herself with the powder of this fragrant wood while she sat on the mountain. Colonel Kirkpatrick calls this Chandraghiri, or the Mountain of the Moon.* On the highest part of the pass a house has been built for the accommodation of passengers. In the wooden carved work of this building are some very indecent figures, which by the natives are considered as fit ornaments, even in places erected from religious motives, as all these houses for the accommodation of travellers are.

Thankot is a small town, finely supplied with wood and water. It stands on a rocky eminence at the south west corner of the valley of Nepal, in a district separated from the

---

* Nepaul, p. 66.

other parts of the plain by a low ridge of hills. On the most conspicuous part of this ridge stands Kirtipur, a considerable town. This part of the valley seems to be a good deal elevated above the portion which contains Kathmandu; and I found the heat of a spring in a small wood above Thankot to be 59½ degrees of Fahrenheit's thermometer. From Thankot to Kathmandu is about seven miles over very uneven cultivated fields, with no roads but foot-paths.

The larger valley of Nepal is somewhat of a circular form, and is watered by numerous branches of the Vagmati, which flow from the surrounding hills towards the centre, and unite into one stream a little way south from the capital. From the place of junction the Vagmati runs south, and goes to the Tariyani, after having forced a passage through the mountains. Taken in the largest sense, therefore, the valley of Nepal comprehends all the grounds watered by these branches of the Vagmati, and, according to this definitjon, it is about twenty-two miles from east to west, and twenty miles from north to south. This extent is every where bounded by a chain of hills, all of which are steep, and some of them rise into high mountains. Of these the most remarkable are Shiva, or Siwapuri, on the north, Nagarjun on the west, Chandangiri on the south-west, Pulihu on the south east, and Devikot on the east. It must be observed, that from these hills, various branches reach a considerable way into the plain, and separate from it small vallies, most of which are considerably elevated above the general level, and from these vallies issue the various streams by which the country is irrigated. The larger valley, reduced by these branches, may be about fourteen miles each way. A person placed in the centre of this extent would consider the whole as one great level, but on travelling about, he frequently comes to very deep hollows, excavated by the various branches of the river, which flow with a very gentle current in large sandy channels. Except after heavy rains, these are almost always fordable, and are commonly sunk fifty or sixty feet perpendicular below the general level of the plain.

It appears evident to me, that Colonel Kirkpatrick * judged rightly in supposing that this valley has formerly been a lake, which has gradually deposited all the alluvial matter that now forms the different substrata of the plain. The extent of the lake may in all places be traced by that of the alluvial matters, above the edges of which generally appear irregularly shaped large stones, which, having rolled down from the hills, stopped at the water's edge as usual in the lakes of hilly countries. The memory of the lake is preserved in the fables contained in the books of the natives, which mention the deity by whom the mountain was cleft to drain off the water, together with numerous circumstances connected with this event. The following is an account of these fables that was communicated to me by Colonel Crawford. When the valley of Nepal was an immense lake, an incarnation of Buddha was born in that country. A petition was therefore made to the gods requesting that the lake might be drained, that the valley might be filled with inhabitants, and that thus the number of the followers of Buddha might increase. The gods attended to this petition, and ordered Menjoo Dev' to evacuate the waters by making a cut through the mountains. This he performed with one blow of his scimitar, and ever since, the waters of the Vagmati have flowed through the gap, which he then formed. The spirit who had presided over the lake was a large serpent, who, finding his water become scanty, and the dry land

* Nepaul, p. 170.

beginning every where to appear, became exceedingly wroth, but he was pacified by the gods, who formed for his residence a miraculous tank, which is situated a little to the southward of Lalita Patan. This tank has a number of angles, all of which cannot be seen at once from any station; they can only, therefore, be numbered by walking round the tank; the miraculous nature of which, in the opinion of the natives, is fully demonstrated by no two persons who make the attempt to number these angles, being able to agree concerning this important point.

The Brahmans, it must be observed, have invented another story, equally extravagant, and attribute the blow which cleared the valley to Anirudhra, the grandson of Krishna, who at the same time killed Sangkhasur, who until then had been lord of Nepal.

The Vagmati must always have flowed from the valley, to carry away the vast body of water collected in the rainy season, and which evidently was confined by a narrow ledge of rocks, which crosses the channel of the river, where it enters the southern mountainous district. At that time the bottom of the lake must have been a smooth cavity, and it must have been surrounded by small narrow glens, pouring their streams into the lake, as they now do into the valley. As the river gradually wore away the rock, over which it must have been precipitated in a cataract, the water in the lake would subside, and the various streams running from the glens would form deep excavations in the soft matter that had formerly been deposited by the water; and this operation would go on, till the ledge of rock was entirely worn away, and a stop was put to the sinking of the river, by the immense mass of rock opposed to its influence.

While the lake existed, there must have appeared in it two

islands, which now form hills. The one is called Sambhunath, or rather Swayambhunath, as being, in the opinion of the Bouddhists of Nepal and Thibet, a favourite residence of the Supreme Being. It is an elegant hill, with two peaks occupied by religious buildings, and covered with the most stately trees. It is a conspicuous object from almost every part of the valley, and every where appears to great advantage.

The description given of the Temple of Buddha on this hill by Colonel Kirkpatrick* is not very accurate, and the drawing is bad, especially in representing the upper part quadrangular, while in reality it is round. It is generally admitted to be the most ancient temple or edifice in Nepal, and, indeed, Colonel Kirkpatrick states, that it was built by Maun Deo, (Mana Deva,) who, according to him, was the sixty-first prince of the country, before the year of Christ 1323. Allowing ten years for each reign, this would place the building of the temple in the beginning of the eighth century, which, from its appearance, is fully as early a date as can be admitted.

The other hill is larger, but not so high, and is greatly celebrated among the followers of the Vedas. It is venerated as being the residence of Siva, under the name of Pasupatinath, and of his wife, under the name of Guhyiswari. The hill is covered with trees, and has a temple dedicated to each of the deities. These temples are frequented by great numbers of pilgrims, who, by visiting the holy place, expect to be ever afterwards secured from being born an animal lower than man. The hill, in a large part of its circumference, is washed by the Vagmati, which is there a holy river; and all the Hindus of Nepal wish to expire with their feet immersed in its stream,

* Nepaul, p. 147, &c.

Engraved by J. Hawksworth

View of Kathmandu and Lalita Patan from the West.

and are desirous, that after death they should be burned on its banks.

The two copperplate engravings, taken from drawings by Colonel Crawford, will give an idea of the scenery in the valley of Nepal. No. 1. represents the temple of Bouddhama in Kasacheit, the most favourite place of worship with the Khat Bhotiyas, or ancient inhabitants of the country. In the distant parts of the back ground are peaks of the Himaliya mountains rising through the clouds. No. 2 gives a distant view of Kathmandu towards the right, and Lalita Patan towards the left, with the temple of Jagannath between them, and in front of Lalita Patan, the Queen's Garden, in which the British Embassy was lodged. The town of Kirtipur is seen on a hill behind Kathmandu.

In Nepal Proper, the Parbatiyas are not near so numerous as the Newars. The valley of Nepal seems to be exceedingly populous; but when the natives, as usual, talk of 18,000 houses in Kathmandu, 24,000 in Lalita Patan, and 12,000 in Bhatgang, they certainly grossly exaggerate. The persons of all ages and both sexes may in these towns amount to such numbers, and in Kathmandu may perhaps somewhat exceed this calculation. There are, besides, in this small valley several other considerable towns, such as Timi, Kirtipur, Dewapatan, Sangghu, and Thankot.

Colonel Kirkpatrick observes,* that "we are altogether unfurnished with any documents that would warrant our hazarding even a conjecture on the number of people, the materials we possess for judging of the population of the valley of Nepaul itself being at the best extremely vague, and enabling us only to state it loosely at about half a million." In p. 161,

* Nepaul, p. 183.

he reckons 48,000 or 50,000 people in Kathmandu, which seems to me considerably exaggerated.

The Parbatiyas do not, like the Newars, delight in towns and villages, and, except the followers of the court, few reside in Kathmandu, or other cities of Nepal; neither are they so much addicted to large brick buildings; for the princes of the Gorkha family, although they have united very extensive dominions under their authority, have been contented with the palace of the petty chief of Kathmandu, or Kathmaro, as it is often called. This, indeed, is a large building, but of so singular a form, that our terms of art could not be applied to describe its architecture. It possesses no magnificence, and seems to have been inferior to the palaces of Lalita Patan and Bhatgang. All the three, however, are works of astonishing magnitude, considering the small extent of country subject to the princes by whom they were built. The great families of Gorkha have occupied the best houses of the Newars, or have built others in the same style, some of which are mansions that in appearance are befitting men of rank. The greater part of the Parbatiyas, however, retain their old manners, and each man lives on his own farm. Their huts are built of mud, and are either white-washed or painted red with a coloured clay. They are covered with thatch, and, although much smaller than the houses of the Newars, seem more comfortable, from their being much more neat and clean. Their usual form may be seen in the foreground of the copperplate No. 1.

Near the palace of Kathmandu is the shrine of Tulasi Bhawani, (Toolaja Bhowani,*) who, with Gorakhanath, is the tutelar deity of the reigning family. There is no image of this

* Kirkpatrick's Nepaul, p. 191.

deity which is represented by a Yantra, or cabalistical figure. In order to impress the subjects with awe, no person is admitted into this shrine except the Raja, the Rani or Queen, the Guru or spiritual guide of the prince, and the Pujari or priest, who is always of the Guru's family. In order probably to add more to the awe of the place, Prithwi Narayan is said to have offered some human sacrifices; but the deity is reported to have reprimanded the prince in a dream, and ever since the victims offered have been buffaloes, sheep, and goats. After the proper ceremonies have been performed, the throat of the animal is cut, in the outer part of the temple, before the multitude, and the blood is carried into the shrine by the priest, or by the prince.

Colonel Kirkpatrick * describes the twenty most remarkable temples of Nepal, excluding the two greatest, Sambhunat and Bouddhama, as being heterodox; but he was not aware, that the same reason should have induced him to exclude the temples of Matsyendranath, (Mutchendernath,) and Gorakhnath, (Goorukhnath.) I may, however, refer to his account for all that requires to be mentioned on this subject.

Nepal Proper is immediately under the management of the Bahradar, or great officers of the court. Kathmandu, for the support of the court, pays annually 18,000 rupees, Lalita Patan pays 18,000, Bhatgang 14,000, and Kirtipur 7000.

About three years ago, a kind of perpetual settlement was made on these crown lands. Each farm was assessed at a certain quantity of grain, which the farmer might either pay in kind, or in money, at the market price. Much benefit would have resulted to the Company, had Lord Cornwallis adopted such a plan. A very large portion of Nepal Proper has been

---

* Nepaul, p. 188—192.

alienated, either in fee or in charity lands. A fine town, named Sangghu, is the Jaygir, or jointure lands of the Maha Rani, or Queen Regent, and is worth annually 4000 rupees. Dewa Patan, a still larger place, belongs entirely to the temples of Pasupatinath and Guhyeswari.

The trade of Nepal was formerly pretty considerable, although the territories of the Raja produce few articles for exportation, except iron, copper, and drugs. At present the defects in the police, and the total want of credit, partly owing to the weakness of the law, and partly to the falsehood of the people, have in a great measure put a stop to the commerce which passed through the country. Its nature was as follows:

Some merchants of Kasmir carried their manufactures by the way of Ladak to Kutti, and other towns in Thibet, in order to procure the wool produced in these countries by the Shal goat. These manufactures were partly used in Thibet, partly sent to Siling or Sining, on the western frontier of China, by the way of Digarchi and Lassa, and partly sent to Patna by the way of Kathmandu. These Kasmirians have factories at Lassa, Siling, Patna, and Kathmandu. They brought from China such goods as answered for the demand of Nepal and Kasmir, among which tea and silks were the principal articles; and from Patna they carried to China otters' skins, to the annual amount of about 50,000 rupees. These otters' skins are procured in the neighbourhood of Dhaka in Bengal.

Again the merchants of Bhot or Thibet brought for sale to Kathmandu paper, coarse woollen cloths, horses, Shal goats, common goats, sheep, Chaury cattle, chauries, (changwari or chaungri,) musk, salt, sal ammoniac, hurtal or yellow arsenic, borax, quicksilver from China, gold-dust, silver, preserved fruits, such as almonds, walnuts, raisins, and dates, and drugs, such as Indian madder or manjit, chirata, and charas, or extract of hemp. Formerly the Lamas of Digarchi (Teeshoo) and Lassa sent much bullion to the mint at Kathmandu, and made a very liberal allowance for having it coined; but the rapacity of Rana Bahadur induced him to alloy the money, which of course put an entire stop to this source of wealth. Of these articles, the greater part of the musk, chaungris, hurtal, borax, and bullion, are sent to Patna, or the low country. From thence again are brought up buffaloes, goats, broad-cloth, cutlery, glass ware, and other European articles, Indian cotton cloths, mother of pearl, pearls, coral, beads, spices, pepper, betel nut and leaf, camphor, tobacco, and phagu, or the red powder thrown about by the Hindus at their festival called Holi. Most of these articles, together with many utensils of wrought copper, brass, bell-metal, and iron, are sold to the merchants of Thibet.

The borax and salt are said to be brought from a lake, which is situated nearly north from Kathmandu, about fifteen days' journey beyond the Brahmaputra. They are conveyed to Nepal on the backs of a large kind of sheep, of which many have four horns, and which seem to be the common beasts of burthen in all the countries towards the sources of the Indus, Ganges, and Brahmaputra. The annexed figure represents a wether of this breed. Each wether, according to what I heard, carries about eighty pounds weight; but Colonel Kirkpatrick * states the load at forty-two pounds, which is more probable. These sheep are about the size of the larger breeds in England.

Captain Turner † describes a sheep used in Thibet for carrying burdens, but that is probably different from what I have mentioned, as he takes no notice of the sheep of this breed having four horns, and states them to be of a small size. Each carries only from twelve to twenty pounds.

In Nepal accounts are kept thus: 4 Damas = 1 Paisah; 4 Paisahs = 1 Ana; 8 Anas = 1 Mohur. The Ana is an imaginary money. The coin called a Mohur varies in its rate of exchange, but is commonly worth 34 Paisahs. The Paisah always exchanges for 4 Damas. On Prithwi Narayan's accession, he called in all the gold and silver money and recoined it, so that I could procure no pieces of a more ancient date than his reign. Ever since that period the value of the coin has continued the same, and is as follows.

Gold coins are called ashruffies; but the full ashruffy is not coined. The fractions in use are halfs, quarters, and eighths. The half ashrufty is by the Court paid away at the rate of 14 Mohurs; and at this value it is a legal tender of payment be-

---

* Nepaul, p. 134. † Embassy to Thibet, p. 302.

tween man and man, unless silver has been specially stipulated. In the market, howeve , the half ashruffy usually exchanges for 12½ Mohurs. It weighs 84¼ grains; and, according to an assay made at Calcutta, is worth nearly three Calcutta rupees, or nearly six shillings and threepence at the mint price.

The coins analogous to the rupee of Hindustan and its fractions are collectively called Madarmali. Colonel Kirkpatrick writes this word * Mehnder mulie, applies it only to the Mohur or Mohr, as he calls it, and says that the word is derived from the name of a prince. The integer is called Pura Rupiya, or Du Mohur, and is seldom seen The half is called the Mohur, and is the common silver currency in the country. When new it weighs 84¼ grains, and is worth six anas, 10⅝ pies, or $\frac{43}{100}$ of the Calcutta rupee. The quarter is called Adha Mohur; the eighth is called Suki.

Besides the Madarmali, there is a wretched small silver coin called Dama, of which the value in exchange is variable; but commonly 136 Damas are given for one Mohur.

The copper coins are Paisas, Half-Paisas, and a few Quarter-Paisas. These last are of the same value with the Dama, but the minute silver coin is considered as more convenient than the Paisa of copper. I am indeed persuaded that no great inconvenience arises from a very minute coinage in circulation; and that, without any loss, we might entirely dispense with the use of a copper currency.

The weights in use are founded on the Paisa, but these are by no means uniform. On an average, however, they may be taken at 162 grains Troy weight.

---

* Nepaul, p. 217.

72 Paises = 1 Ser = lb. avoirdupois 1.666.
3 Sers = 1 Dharni = lb. 4.998.

The Dharni may therefore be considered as equal to five pounds avoirdupois. It is also divided into two Bisulis, and four Barapuls.

Grain is always sold by measure.

8 Manas = 1 Pathi = 152 cubical inches.
20 Pathis = 1 Muri = Winchester bushels $2\frac{344}{1000}$.

The whole lands in Nepal have long been divided into what are called Khets or fields, each of which is estimated in ordinary seasons to produce 100 Muris, or 234½ bushels of Paddy, or rice in the husk. About the year 1792 Ranjit Pangre, then one of the Karyis, by the orders of Rana Bahadur, made a survey of the valley; but the result has been kept secret. The people know only that he estimated each of their possessions at a certain number of Rupinis, and that on an average twenty-five of these formed one Khet. They also observed, that in good soils he used a rod seven cubits and a half in length, and in bad soils he employed one nine cubits and a half long. Some people who had resided at Patna informed my Brahman, that the Rupini was nearly of the same size with the Biga of that city, which is one-third of an English acre; and this is the only foundation that I have for the calculations which I have made.

It must, however, be observed, that, according to the information received by Colonel Kirkpatrick, * the average Rupini contains only 3¾ Katahs of the Calcutta measure, or only $\frac{3}{16}$ of what was reported to me; and if his information is considered more likely than mine to be correct, all the statements which

---

* Nepaul, p. 95.

I have subsequently given, concerning the produce of an acre in Nepal, must be augmented in that proportion. For instance, I have stated the rice in the husk produced by an acre to be about 28 bushels; but, according to the information given to Colonel Kirkpatrick, it ought to be almost 150 bushels. This induces me to place no great confidence in part of the information given to the Colonel; for, as I shall afterwards have occasion to state, I have no doubt that the crops of rice near Calcutta are more abundant than those of Nepal.

In Nepal the pastures and forests are in general commons, and any person that pleases may use them; but some forests are reserved for the Court. Although these forests contain many oak, chestnut, pine, and yew trees, none of these are by the natives esteemed of much value; but for carpenter's work a preference is given to the Champa or Michelia, which is certainly a good kind of timber.

Nothing is paid for pasture; but, as it is very scarce, and as the Newars do not employ cattle in agriculture, very few are bred in the country. A few milch cows are kept in the towns, and still more in the narrow vallies inhabited by Parbatiyas, who use cattle in their ploughs. Buffaloes and goats are imported from the low country; and horses, chaungri-cattle, shal-goats, common goats, and sheep, are brought from Bhot. They become tolerably fat on the pasture of the hills, which, although scanty, seems to be nourishing. Captain Knox killed two female buffaloes, that had been fattened entirely on grass; and they made tolerable beef.

No taxes are paid to government for houses.

The arable lands are partly retained as the immediate property of the Court, for defraying the household expences of the Raja. The whole of the rice land near Nayakot is reserved as the Raja's proper farm, and is cultivated by his servants and slaves, under the superintendency of a steward: and the same management is observed with a considerable number of fruit and flower gardens, in the valley of Nepal, and with an extensive pasture on the banks of the Kosi. The produce is not sold, but serves for the consumption of the Court, and for distributing in charity at temples, and to religious mendicants. By far the greater part, however, of the lands reserved for the use of the Raja, is let to tenants, as I have before mentioned. The extent of these has at different times varied; but I believe they have never produced a net income of more than a million of mohurs. The only other public revenues are the fines levied from offenders, which are sometimes considerable; the customs, which are very trifling; and some small profits arising from the mines, from elephants, and from the sale of Sal or Sakhuya timber, from the forests below the mountains. The demands on the treasury, however, are very few; for not only every officer, civil and military, and every soldier, but even the private servants, and principal slaves of the Raja, are paid by lands granted for their support.

The lands thus granted in feu for service are called Chakran, and in general are resumable at pleasure, and follow the office of the person by whom they are held; but some branches of the Royal family, and some of the families of distinction, have enjoyed certain lands ever since the time of Prithwi Narayan, and it would not be safe to attempt a resumption of such property. Some persons have even been permitted to alienate such lands by sale; but to do so, the consent of the Court must be obtained. I procured no information on which I could attempt to calculate the amount of these two kinds of Chakran lands.

Another kind of property, which pays no rent nor tax, and which is not resumable, is called Khairat zemin, or Charity land, which is the Birtha or Brhemoter land of Colonel Kirkpatrick, (p. 92, 93.) This is of two kinds; part belongs to Brahmans Baras, or Achars; and another part has been granted for the support of temples. The whole amount of this kind of land is not equal to that reserved by the Crown for its own purposes.

The Khairat that is given to religious men is of two kinds. The first is called Yamapatri, which is given when the Raja bestows Dhana in order to procure the remission of his sins. This can never revert to the Crown, but, in case of the family to which it was granted becoming extinct, it goes to the temples of Pasupanath and Changgu Narayan. The second kind of Khairat given to religious men is bestowed on account of their piety and learning; and, on failure of heirs, reverts to the Crown. This kind may be sold, if the proprietor obtain the consent of the Raja.

The lands belonging to the temples are in fact held by the priests, (Pujaris,) who are bound to defray the expences of worship. They are removable at the pleasure of the Raja.

This Khairat or Brhemoter land, Colonel Kirkpatrick says, is also divided into two kinds, Koos Brhemoter and Soona Brhemoter, the owners of which are perhaps the same with those called to me Bitalpas and Brittiyas, mentioned in page 164, although this is not very certain. The Koos Brhemoter land, according to the Colonel, is rarely bestowed but on Brahmans, and that with a very solemn investiture. Land of this kind is rent-free, saleable, and hereditary, but for certain crimes it may be forfeited. Presents are often given, especially on the accession of a new Raja. The Soona Brhemoter has been granted to certain Newars, and other natives of countries subjected by the Gorkhalis, and continued by the conquerors for a considerable fine under each succeeding prince, but it is saleable and hereditary.

Landholders, who do not cultivate their own estates, in general let them for one-half of the grain produced. Money rent can seldom be procured, and is very low. It varies from four to twelve anas a Rupini, which produces at least four Muris of Paddy, one half of which, or the rent usual when paid in kind, is worth about fifty anas, and if it be good land, it produces also a winter crop.

Most great proprietors, however, like the Raja, employ stewards with their servants and slaves, to cultivate some land for supplying their families. The great, therefore, seldom go to market, which, among a lawless people, is an advantage for the lower classes, although it subjects travellers to great inconveniency from the want of markets. It is besides alleged, that the lower classes, in the vicinity of these farms, often suffer by being compelled to labour without an adequate remuneration.

When lands are alienated by sale, they bring from 1600 to 2000 Mohurs a Khet, which high price is owing to the very small quantity of land that is brought to market.

The persons who rent lands from the owners are of two kinds: first, the Kuriyas, who occupy free (Khairat) land, are exempted from any services to government, except the repairing of roads, and the attending on armies employed on certain duties; and, secondly, the Prajas, who occupy the crown land, whether that be held by the Prince, or granted in Jaygir. The Prajas are bound to perform various services at the call, both of government and of their immediate masters. The rent which both usually pay is one-half of the produce, with an annual fine of between two and three rupees for each Khet. Where the land is tolerable, these terms are considered as favourable for the tenant, and enable him to support a family with ease.

The following is the account which my Brahman gives of the agriculture of the Newars.

The hoe used by the Newars has been represented by Colonel Kirkpatrick, (in the uppermost figure of the plate opposite to page 100 of his Account of Nepaul,) but the figure is not good. It seems a very awkward instrument, as the blade is fixed by a long neck, so as to stand parallel to the short handle, at about the distance of six inches. The labourer, therefore, must either stoop exceedingly, when at work, or must sit on his heels, which is the most usual posture. Still these people use it with great dexterity, and one man in three days digs up a Rupini. After each hoeing, the women and children break the clods with a wooden mallet fixed to a long shaft, which does not require them to stoop. Almost the only other implement of agriculture these people have is the Khuripi, or weeding iron, and some fans for winnowing the corn. In Nepal, however, they have in some measure made a further progress than in India, as they have numerous water-mills for grinding corn. The stones are little larger than those of hand-mills, and the upper one is turned round by being fixed on the end of the axis of the water wheel, which is horizontal, and is placed under the floor of the mill, with which the stones are on a level. This wheel consists of six blades, about three feet long, and six inches broad, which are placed obliquely in the axle-tree. On these blades, the water falls down an inclined plane of about eight or ten feet in perpendicular height. The hopper is a basket perforated at the bottom, but has no contrivance to shake it. The people at one of the mills which we examined said, that, in one day, it could grind twelve *Muris*, or rather more than twenty-nine bushels.

In Nepal, rice is the great crop, and the ground fit for it is of two kinds, which differ in the manner, and in the time of their cultivation, so as to make two harvests of rice: but no one field, in one year, produces two crops of this grain.

Colonel Kirkpatrick indeed mentions,* that some fields yield two crops of rice successively, the one coarse, and the other fine, besides affording in the same year a crop of wheat. This, however, I presume, does not allude to Nepal Proper, but to some of the warmer vallies in the dominions of Gorkha; as where he goes on, in the 99th page, to describe the expence of cultivation, he mentions the ploughings, an operation which is not employed in the agriculture of the Newars.

The first kind of ground produces the crop called Gheya, is the highest, and there is no necessity for its being absolutely level, as the fields are not inundated. From the 13th of March to the 11th of April, this ground is hoed; and, having been well manured with dung collected in the streets, it is hoed again. A week after this, the field is hoed two or three times, and is well pulverized with the mallet. About the 12th of May, after a shower of rain, the field is slightly hoed, and the mould is broken, and smoothed with the hand. Small drills, at a span's distance from each other, are then made by the finger, which is directed straight by a line. At every span-length in these drills are placed four or five seeds of the rice, called Uya Dhan, which is the only kind cultivated in this manner. The seed is covered by the hand, and a very small quantity only is required. In about five days the young corn comes up in small tufts, just as if it had been transplanted. From the 13th of June to the 15th of August, when the corn is about a cubit high, the weeds are removed with the spud. About the

* Nepaul, p. 98.

latter period, slugs, worms, and insects, fill all the moister fields in Nepal, and in order to be rid of them, the farmers keep a great number of ducks, which, at this season, they turn into the fields, to devour the vermin. The Gheya crop ripens about the 1st of September, and by the middle of the month the harvest is finished. The ears only are cut off, and next day the grain is beat out, and generally dried in the streets. Very little of the crop is made into Hakuya, a process that will be afterwards mentioned. After the Gheya crop has been cut, the field is in general cultivated with radishes, mustard, or some other crop, that is usually sown about the time.

By far the greater part of the rice ground, and that the lowest and the best, is of the kind which produces the crop of rice called Puya. The kinds of rice which are cultivated in this crop are very numerous, and it would be tedious to mention their names, as I have no observations to make on any one in particular. The fields which produce this crop must be perfectly level, as they are inundated during the greater part of the process of cultivation. Therefore, as the plain is by no means even, it has been divided into terraces. So much pains has been bestowed on this part of agriculture, that on the steep descents leading down to the rivers, there have been formed many terraces not above two feet wide. The numerous springs and rivulets that issue from the surrounding hills have been conducted with great pains to irrigate these terraces, and have been managed with considerable skill.

The cultivation of the Puya crop commences between the 13th of May and 12th of June, during which the field is hoed two or three times, and manured with dung, if any can be procured. At any rate, it is always manured with the kind of earth called Koncha, which I have already described. The banks that confine the water are then repaired; and about the

12th of June, when, either by the rain or by the irrigation from aqueducts, the fields have been inundated, and the soil has been by the hoe reduced to mud, the seedlings which have been raised in plots sown very thick, are transplanted by the women. The men perform all the other parts of the labour. This is a time of festivity as well as of hard work; and the people are then allowed a great freedom of speech, to which they are encouraged by large quantities of intoxicating liquors, in a share of which even the women indulge. The transplanting ought to commence from the 12th to the 15th of June, and ought to be finished by the Amavasya of Asharh, but this is a moveable feast. On the Krishna Chaturdasi, which happens on the day preceding the Amavasya, the Maha Rani or Queen, with her slave girls, (Ketis,) transplant a small plot within the palace, and it is reckoned an unlucky circumstance when this is not the last planted field in the valley. The fields are always kept under water, and weeds are not troublesome. The few that spring up are removed by the spud. This crop begins to ripen about the 15th of October, and by the 1st of November the harvest is completed, after which a considerable portion of the land is cultivated for wheat or other winter crops.

The Puya rice is cut down close by the ground. The finer kinds of rice are immediately thrashed, as is likewise all that which is intended for seed; but the greater part is made into what is called Hakuya. This is done with a view of correcting its unwholesome quality: for all the grain produced in the valley of Nepal is thought by the natives to be of a pernicious nature. The manner of preparing Hakuya is as follows: The corn, immediately after having been cut, is put into heaps, ten or twelve feet diameter, and six or eight feet in height. These are covered with wet earth, and allowed to heat for from eight to twelve days, and till they may be seen smoking like lime-kilns. After this the heaps are opened, and the grain is separated from the straw by beating it against a piece of ground made smooth for the purpose. Both grain and straw are then dried in the sun. The grain is called Hakuya, and the straw is the fuel commonly used by the poor, for fire-wood is very dear. According to the accounts received by Colonel Crawford, this manner of preserving rice was discovered by accident. Many years ago one of the towns was besieged by an enemy that came so suddenly as not to allow the citizens time to gather in the crop, which had just then been cut. The citizens, rather than allow the enemy to benefit by their corn, determined to throw it into the water and cover it with earth. In this manner it remained about a week, when the enemy were compelled to retire. When the grain was taken up it was found to have begun to rot, but necessity having compelled the people to eat it, they found, to their astonishment, that it was much better and more salutary than the grain which had been prepared in the usual manner. It is only the Newars that eat this Hakuya.

The crops of rice in Nepal appeared to me very poor when compared with those of Bengal; and, if my Brahman was rightly informed concerning the extent of a rupini, they are really so. The rupini produces four muris of paddy, or $9\frac{576}{1000}$ bushels, but near Calcutta the biga (supposed to be of the same extent) of good ground produces often 640 sers, or $19\frac{82}{100}$ bushels. The difference of price, however, in the two countries makes the value of the produce in Nepal the greater of the two. I have already stated that the value of four muris of paddy in Nepal is usually 13 M. 2 A. 2 D., or about $5\frac{3}{4}$ rupees. But near Calcutta in harvest the usual price of 640 sers of paddy, is 5 rupees 5 A. 4 P. If no error has been made in estimating the extent of a rupini, the acre of good land in Nepal produces rather more than 28 bushels of paddy, or rice in the husk.

Immediately after the Puya crop has been cut, the ground is formed into beds by throwing the earth out of parallel trenches upon the intermediate spaces. On these about the middle of November is sown wheat, or sometimes a little barley. These ripen without farther trouble, and are cut from the 12th of April to the 12th of May. The seed for a rupini is stated to be one pati, and the produce is stated to be two muris. This would make the seed about the fifth part of a bushel an acre, and the produce about fourteen bushels; but this seems to me greatly exaggerated. I have never seen more wretched crops, and most of the fields of wheat are quite choked with hemp, *(Cannabis sativa,)* which in Nepal is a troublesome and useless weed. The wheat and barley are mostly used for making fermented or distilled liquors.

Pangdu Kodo, or Maruya, is the *Cynosurus Corocanus* of Linnæus, of which I saw much growing on some of the higher parts of the plain. It seems to thrive well. The Maruya is sown from the 13th of June to the 14th of July, and twenty days afterwards is transplanted. It is ripe about the middle of September, and produces four muris a rupini.

In thrashing this corn, Colonel Crawford saw the Newars using a kind of flail, an implement which I have never observed in India. Three pieces of Bamboo, about eighteen inches long, were fastened together in a parallel manner, at aoout a finger's breadth asunder, and then fixed to a peg, which passed through a hole in the end of a longish pole that was a little bent. The instrument seemed to require considerable dexterity in its management, but appeared to answer the purpose intended.

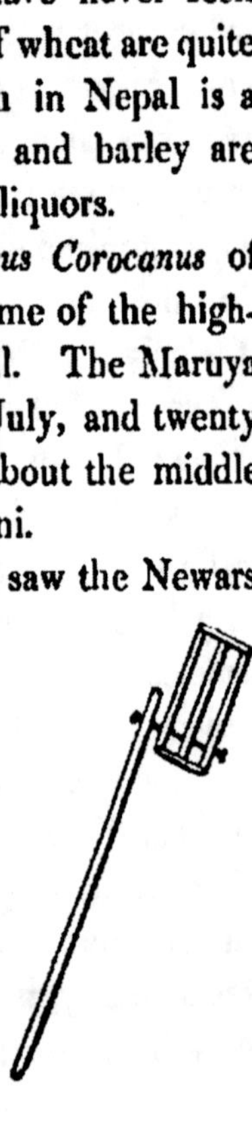

The Sana Kodo of the Parbatiyas is probably the Paspalum kora of Wildenow. It also is transplanted, ripens in October and November, and produces as much as the Pangdu Kodo.

The Muccai and Muruli of the Parbatiyas are both by the Newars called *Kaunguni*, and are varieties of the *Holcus sorghum*. They are chiefly planted in the small vallies that open into the plain, and on high terraces, that have a bad supply of water.

The Urid, or Kala Mas of the Parbatiyas, is by the Newars called May; and Dr Roxburgh, in his manuscripts, calls it *Phaseolus minimoo*, from its Telinga name. In Nepal this is the most common pulse. It is sown about the 1st of July, and reaped about the 1st of September. A rupini produces about ten patis, or an acre about three bushels and a half.

The Seta Mas of the Parbatiyas, or Chica May of the Newars, Dr Roxburgh has raised from seed, which I sent from Nepal. He thinks it a new species, which he calls *Phaseolus ocultatus*. It is sown about the 1st of July, reaped the 1st of October, and produces the same quantity that the urid does.

The Lato, Rato, or Ruta mas of the Parbatiyas, is by the Newars called Hayngu may. It also appears to Dr Roxburgh to be an undescribed species, and he has given it the name of *Phaseolus calcaratus*. It is sown and reaped at the same time with the preceding, and yields the same produce.

The Lal mung of the Parbatiyas is also called Hayngumay by the Newars. The seeds of this plant, which I sent to the botanical garden, show it to be a *Phaseolus*, that is by Dr Roxburgh considered as a nondescript, and he calls it the *Phaseolus racemosus*.

The Mung of the Parbatiyas, and the Muk or Mugy may

of the Newars, is the Dolichos Mungo of Linnæus. Three manas are sown on a rupini about the 1st of July, and about the 1st of November produce eight patis.

The Seta, and Cala Bhot Mas of the Parbatiyas, are called Musa and Gya by the Newars. They are two varieties of the *Dolichos soja*, the one of which has yellow flowers and white seeds, and the other has black seeds, and purplish flowers. The former is ripe about the 1st of November, the latter about the 1st of September. Their seed and produce are equal to those of the mung.

The Mosuri of the Parbatiyas, and Mosu of the Newars, is the *Ervum lens* of botanists. About the 1st of November two manas are sown on a rupini; and about May produce twelve patis.

The same is the case with the Pea, or *Pisum arvensis*, called Kerao by the Parbatiyas, and Caigo by the Newars.

The mustard called Sarishi by the Parbatiyas, and Turi by the Newars is mostly cultivated as a pot-herb. It is sown about the middle of October, and is cut before it flowers. Another, which by the Newars is called Ika, is the *Sinapis ramosa* of Dr Roxburgh. About the 1st of February two manas are sown on a rupini, and about April produce two muris of seed. The ground is afterwards cultivated for rice.

Sesamum is called Til by the Parbatiyas, and Hamo by the Newars. It grows commonly wild as a weed, but very little of it is cultivated.

The sugar-cane is planted in considerable quantities, and seems to thrive. The Newars make a very little extract, soft sugar, and sugar-candy; but a large proportion of the cane is eaten without preparation. It is planted about the 1st of April, and is cut, from the middle of November to the middle of May. The juice is generally expressed by a lever.

Ginger, the Puli of the Newars, is planted about the 1st of April, and dug up in October or November.

The common radishes are by the Parbatiyas called Mulu, and by the Newars Kipo, and are very much cultivated. They grow in vast abundance all the year, except from the 15th of November to the 10th of February. In order to procure a supply of this useful article, for three months of winter, a large quantity is sown about the 1st of September, and pulled about the 1st of November. The roots are then buried in a pit for six or seven days, during which they seem to undergo a kind of half putrid fermentation; as when they are taken out of the pit, and dried in the sun, they exhale a most powerful stench. These dried roots are called Sinky, keep all winter, and, although offensive to the smell, enter largely into the diet of the poorer Newars. These, owing partly to the great quantity of sinky and of garlic which they eat, and partly to the dirtiness of their linen, exhale a worse smell than any people I have ever been among.

Methi, or Fenugreek, grows at all seasons, except from the 15th of November to the 12th of January. It is used only as a pot-herb, and is the one most commonly consumed in Nepal.

Khira, or cucumbers, grow to great perfection, and with another cucurbitaceous plant called Kangkari, are ripe from the 13th of June to the 15th of August.

The garlic is planted about the 1st of January, and is taken up from the 12th of April to the 12th of June.

Bera, or the Solanum Melongena, is sown about the 1st of May, and is ripe about the 1st of October.

In the hilly parts of the country, the common potatoe (Solanum tuberosum) has been introduced, and grows tolerably: but it does not thrive so well as at Patna, owing probably to a want of care.

The Sakarkandh (Convolvulus batatas) succeeds better. It is planted about the 1st of April, and is taken up from the middle of October to the middle of December.

Most of the European kitchen vegetables have been introduced: but they are only to be found in the gardens of men of distinction, and in very small quantities.

When Colonel Kirkpatrick visited the country,* the only kitchen vegetables (meaning, I presume, European) were cabbages and peas, both of which were of the worst kind. They had, he says, the Thibet turnip, but cannot raise it any more than the potatoe, without receiving the seed annually. This, compared with what I observed, indicates some degree of progressive improvement.

None of their fruits are good, except the oranges and pine apples; but both of these are in great perfection. The peach is every where wild, and is also reared in gardens: but it does not ripen till long after the rainy season has commenced, and is generally half rotten before it becomes soft. At Kathmandu the Plantain tree (Musa) dies to the ground in winter, but the roots are not killed, and in the spring send up fresh stems. Some good plantains come from Nayakot, and other valleys, that are situated lower than the capital is.

Such is the account I could procure of the cultivation in the plains of Nepal. On the sloping faces of the hills, bounding the smaller vallies in its vicinity, I observed another mode of cultivation. The soil there is not formed into terraces; but in April is pared and burned, and then is sown with Sama,

---

* Nepaul, p. 181.

or the *Panicum Italicum*, with Tangni or Kakun, which is the *Panicum colonum*, and with Kaungni, which is the *Holcus Sorghum*. When the soil is in heart, these produce very good crops, and once in the three or four years the field is allowed a season's fallow. This seems to be the kind of land which Colonel Kirkpatrick calls Kohrya.*

In Nepal, the Gangja, Charas, or Cannabis sativa, as I have already mentioned, is a common weed: but in that country it is not cultivated, although much used for the purpose of intoxication. The dried leaves are brought from the Tariyani, but are reckoned heating, and are not so much used as the extract, which is called Charas: of this Thibet produces the best. The proper manner of preparing Charas is by making incisions into the stem, and collecting the juice, in the same manner as opium is produced from the capsules of the poppy. A coarser kind is prepared from the expressed juice of the hemp.

Colonel Kirkpatrick † gives a different account of the manner of preparing this drug, which, he says, is procured by rubbing the leaves of the plant Jeea, until the resin adheres to the fingers, from which it is scraped off with a spathula. The plant called Jeea is no doubt the *Cannabis sativa*, nor can much reliance be placed on the information which the Colonel received on this subject: as the person who gave it has evidently been inaccurate, when he stated concerning the Gangja and Subje produced from the same plant, that the former is prepared from the flowers, and the latter from the leaves; while, in fact, the one is the dried plant, and the other the expressed juice.

The dose of Charas is from ten to twelve grains made up into a pill, which is smoked like tobacco. The dried leaves, or Gangja, are taken in the same manner, and both produce vio-

* Nepaul, p. 94.

† Nepaul, p. 142, 143.

lent intoxication. While we were in Nepal, a shopkeeper, who attended the camp, smoked so much Charas that he died. From the accounts given me by those who saw him, he became stupid, but not irrational, and complained of nothing except thirst, for which he two or three times drank water. As it was not looked upon as any thing extraordinary, I did not hear of the circumstance till some hours after the man's death. He did not intend to kill himself; but, in the course of his indulgence, repeated the dose too often.

Two kinds of coarse cotton cloth, called Khadi and Changa, are woven by the Newar women of all ranks, and by the men of the Parbatiya cast, called Magar. The cotton grows in the hilly parts of the kingdom, and is sufficient for the consumption; but none is exported from Nepal Proper. These cloths constitute the dress of the middling and lower classes of people, although woollen would be better fitted for the cold of a Nepal winter. All those, however, that are not very poor, can afford to have woollen blankets, which are manufactured by the Bhotiyas, who even in summer wear no linen. The whole dress of the higher ranks in Nepal is imported, and consists chiefly of Chinese silks, shals, and of the low country muslins and calicoes. The military alone wear European broad cloth.

In Lalita Patan and Bhatgang there is a very considerable manufacture of copper, brass, and Phul, which is a kind of bell-metal. The bells of Thibet are superior to those of Nepal: but a great many vessels of Phul are made by the Newars, and exported to Thibet, along with those of brass and copper. Iron vessels and lamps are also manufactured for the same market.

A very strong paper, remarkably well fitted for packages, is made at Bhatgang, from the bark of a shrub, which I call the *Daphne papyrifera*. The supply, however, is not adequate to the demand, and not only the paper, but a considerable quantity of the raw material is imported from Bhot. The bark is exceedingly strong and pliable, and seems to be the same with certain tape-like bandages, employed by the Chinese in tying many of their parcels.

At Kathmandu the common daily hire for a labouring man is two anas. Merchants pay three Mohurs for every porter who brings a load from Hethama, and five Mohurs from Gar Pasara. The porter takes three days to come from the former, and five days from the latter; but he must return empty; the hire is therefore four anas a day. The usual load is twenty Dharnis, or a hundred pounds; but some strong men carry a half more. They carry their loads in a basket called Doka, of which a representation is given in the plate opposite to page 39 of Kirkpatrick's Nepaul. Persons of rank, who do not choose to walk or ride on horseback, usually travel in what is called a Dandi, which is a hammock suspended on a pole, and carried by from four to six men, as represented in the plate opposite to page 39 of Kirkpatrick's Nepaul. When a woman goes in a Dandi, a cloth thrown over the pole conceals her from view. This conveyance is well fitted for a mountainous country, where few of the roads will admit of the use of a horse. For a Dandi, to convey them from Kathmandu to Gar Pasara, merchants pay twenty-four Mohurs: carpenters and blacksmiths receive three anas a day: bricklayers two anas and a half: goldsmiths, for every two Mohurs weight of gold they work up, are allowed four anas: for working silver, they receive one-sixteenth part of the metal. According to the fineness of the work, the labourers obtain from one to two Mohurs for every Darni of copper which they manufacture.

The want of labouring cattle among the Newars renders the operations of husbandry so tedious, that at many seasons every person in the family capable of labour must be employed; and as no one can be left to take care of the young children, these must be carried to the field. As this is often at a distance from the house, the poor villager may be often seen carrying his infants in two baskets suspended over his shoulder by a bamboo. In these baskets some food also is taken, as the family does not return until night. An oblong mat also forms a usual part of what is carried into the field. This mat defends the children as well as the victuals from the sun and rain, and is sometimes used by the labourers for the same purposes, especially when they are employed in weeding the rice fields. As that operation is performed during the rainy season, the labourers would suffer considerably, unless they kept off the water by a mat tied over their heads and covering their backs, while their arms are left at liberty.

In Nepal most of the domestic servants are slaves. A male slave is called a Keta, and costs about thirty Mohurs. A female is called Keti, and costs about the same price; but, if young and handsome, she will bring ten Mohurs additional. There are some Brahmans who are slaves even to Rajputs: but they are not degraded by the name Keta, and are employed in great families, either as cooks, or in the service of the private chapels. All other ranks are sold for common slaves: and persons of the best families have often been degraded by the Rajas, and given to the Damais or Tailors, by which they lose not only their liberty, but their cast, which is of more importance to a Hindu. In general, however, among the higher tribes, the cast of the slave is respected, and no duty is imposed on him, by which that would be injured. It is reckoned very disgraceful for any persons but those of the lowest rank, to sell their children to any person of impure birth, or who is an infidel. Still, however, this is occasionally done by persons of high birth, who happen to be in necessitous circumstances; nor do the parents on this account lose cast. They would, however, inevitably become outcasts, should they ever afterwards admit their child into their house, even were he to be set at liberty by his master. Most of the slaves, it must be observed, have been born free. A few have been degraded, and sold by the Raja on account of crimes alleged against them: but by far the greater part have been sold by necessitous parents. All the Ketis, even those belonging to the Queen, are prostitutes, and therefore seldom have children. The masters in general do not give their slave girls any other allowance than a small quantity of rice; and a great many of them are so obdurate, that even this allowance is stopped, when sickness prevents the slave from working. The poor creatures are therefore forced to sacrifice their chastity, in order to procure clothing; and beggary is the usual resource of those who are old and infirm. The Ketis of the court, indeed, are allowed some privileges, and have a considerable influence among the young men of family. In the day time they attend the Maha Rani or queen; and when she goes out, some of them armed with swords follow her on horseback, and form her body guard. They are well dressed, and ride astride like men. They are allowed to carry on intrigues with any person of good birth: but the young Rajputs of the guard are their usual favourites. Some Brahmans and Bankers from the low country, induced by the beauty of these girls, have formed connexions with them; but they have in general paid dearly for their indulgence. Fidelity to one mistress is not a virtue among such men, and the Ketis of the court think the whole corps bound to punish any infidelity against one of their number, nor will the police interfere to prevent them from plundering the delinquent of his whole property. The slaves of private persons are not only ill fed, but are hardly wrought. The common duties imposed on them are to wash, to bring fire-wood from the mountains, to clean the cooking utensils and the house, and to carry the umbrella.

Rice is the great article of support in Nepal. Along with their rice the poorest people eat raw garlic and radishes; they also fry radishes, fenugreek, or lentiles, in water mixed with salt, capsicum, and turmeric. To these, people in more easy circumstances add oil or ghiu; and those who are rich add a great deal of animal food. Even the poorest are able occasionally to sacrifice a pigeon, a fowl, or a duck, and of course they eat these birds. No Hindu eats any meat but the flesh of sacrifices; for he considers it as a sin to kill any animal for the purpose of indulging his appetite; but, when a sacrifice has been offered, the votary may without blame eat what the Deity does not use. We observed, that even the Rajputs in Nepal were so fond of animal food, that, to the utter astonishment of our low country Hindus, they drank the blood of the sacrifices as it flowed from the victim.

Section IV.

THE COUNTRIES BELONGING TO THE CHAUBISI AND BAISI RAJAS.

Chaubisi Rajas.—Pamar Family, Impure Branch.—Bhirkot, Garahang, Dhor, Pure Branch.—Nayakot.—Satahung.—Kaski.—Lamjun.—Gorkha, Topography, History.—Prithwi Narayan.—Singha Pratap.—Bahadur Sahi.—Rana Bahadur.—Bhim Sen.—Royal Family.—Kala Macwani Family.—Gulmi, Khachi, Argha, Dhurkot, Musikot, Tama.—Family of Bhingri and Khungri.—Family of Piuthana.—Family of Poin.—Malihang Family.—The Samal Family; Malebum; Galkot; Rugum; Musikot; Jajarkot; Bangphi; Gajal; Dharma; Jahari; Satatala; Malaneta; Saliyana; Dang; Chhilli.—The Baisi Rajas.—Dalu Dailek.—Duti.—Yumila.—Taklakot, with the adjacent parts of Thibet subject to China.

Immediately west from Nepal Proper is a country of considerable extent, which had long consisted of 24 petty estates, whose chiefs were collectively called the Chaubisi Rajas. Yet it would not appear that they were all connected by any common union for defence, by a common extraction, or by any other tie. They all, indeed, acknowledged the superiority of the Yumila Raja, of whom some account will be afterwards given; but besides these 24 chiefs, he had many others in similar dependence, which, however, conferred very little authority on the superior, whose power seems chiefly to have been confined to exhort his vassals in the support of a balance of power, and to confer the mark (Tica) of supreme authority on the heirs of each chief. His superior rank was, however, never disputed, and his call seems long to have met with a good deal of attention, when directed to procure assistance, in preventing one chief from swallowing up the dominions of another. The 24 chiefs, according to Kanak Nidhi, were the Rajas mentioned in the following list; but other lists differ considerably.

1. Piuthana	9. Palpa	17. Gajarkot
2. Malebum or Parbat	10. Garahang	18. Rising
3. Galkot	11. Poin	19. Ghiring
4. Isma	12. Satahung	20. Tanahung
5. Dhurkot	13. Birkot	21. Lamjun
6. Argha	14. Nayakot	22. Gorkha
7. Khachi	15. Kaski	23. Tarki
8. Gulmi	16. Dhor	24. Musikot

Of the other lists, which I received, it would be useless to give a detail, but I shall mention that given to Colonel Kirkpatrick, * referring to the names given in my list by prefixing the number. (21) Loomjoong. (15) Kashki. (20) Tunhoo or Tunnohoo. (3) Gulkoat. (2) Purbut or Mullibum. (14) Noakote or Nuwakote. (11) Pyoon. (12) Luttohoon. (10) Gurhoon. (18) Reesing. (19) Ghering. (16) Dhoar. (9) Palpa. (8) Goolmi. Wigha. (7) Khanchi. Dang. (24) Musikote. (1) Purthana. Jhilli. Suliana. (5) Dhoorkote; and (4) Isma. He thus omits Gorkha, Tarki, Gajarkot, and Argha of the list which I have given; although I suspect, that his Wigha is no other than Argha, for in page 288, he reckons Urghaloor as one of the 24 chiefs, and in page 297 he speaks of the territories of the Urgho Raja. I have indeed little doubt, that

* Nepaul, p. 284.

Wigha is a mistake of the editor for Urgho, and that Urghaloor was originally written Urghapoor, poor or pura being a common termination of the names of Indian cities. Gorkha was probably omitted by the Gorkhali who gave him the information; as its being included would have been acknowledging the former supremacy of Yumila, which the chiefs of Gorkha now wish to disavow. In place of Tarki and Gajarkot, Colonel Kirkpatrick's list introduces Dang and Jhilli, (Chhilli,) both of which I have placed in the class containing twenty-two chiefs, although perhaps on slender grounds.

Several of these chiefs had entered with others into leagues for mutual defence, as the interpositions of Yumila, although of some weight, were by no means sufficient to procure security. The leagues were sometimes connected by a common descent in the chiefs, and such were called Athabhai, or eight brothers; while other leagues were composed of chiefs who were of different origins. Such leagues were called Satbhai, or seven brothers.

Among the leagues I heard of the following:

I. Lamjun was at the head of a league composed of Tanahung and Kaski; but Tanahung was followed in war by Dhor, and Kaski by Satahung, without any reference to the union of these states with Lamjun.

II. Birkot was at the head of a league containing Garahang, Poin, and Nayakot.

III. Palpa was at the head of a league composed of Gajarkot, Rising, Ghiring, Argha, Kachi, and Gulmi.

IV. Malebum had in alliance Gulkot.

V. Piuthana had in alliance Musikot and Isma, and also the two petty chiefs of Khungri and Bhingri, who, although their territories were surrounded by those of the Chaubisiya Rajas, were not included in the number of these chiefs.

Gorkha, I was informed, was always completely unconnected, and independent of all these alliances; nor did I learn that Dhurkot or Tarki were in a contrary situation.

I shall now proceed to give an account of the chiefs who governed this assembly of states, and of their countries.

I have already given an account of the family of highest rank, including the Rajas of Palpa, Tanahung, Rising, Ghiring, and Gajarkot; because this family possessed also large estates to the east of Nepal Proper. It therefore remains to describe the other 19 states.

I shall first mention the family which at present has obtained almost universal empire over the mountains north from the Company's provinces, and does not content itself with a gentle rule, such as that exercised by the Rajas of Yumila, but has seized the entire dominion and power of the conquered countries, and assumes a menacing countenance even to the Company.

The family pretends to be of the Pamar tribe; but it is alleged, as I have already explained, that this is a mere fable, and that, on the arrival of the colony from Chitaur, this family were Magars. One of its branches, however, has long adopted the Hindu rules of purity, and has intermarried with the best families, although not without creating disgust; and the other branch remains in primitive impurity, although we have seen that the same is the case with the Chauhans, who long pretended to a great superiority over the chiefs of Gorkha.

The first persons of the Gorkha family, of whom I have heard, were two brothers named Khancha and Mincha, or Nimcha, words altogether barbarous, and in no manner resembling the high sounding titles of the family of the sun, from whom the Pamars pretend to be descended. From whence these persons came, I did not learn; but Khancha was the founder of the impure branch of the family, and Mincha was the chief of Nayakot.

The impure branch of the family possessed Bhirkot, Gharahang, and Dhor, which afterwards separated under three chiefs of the same house; but Bhirkot seems to have been the head of the whole, as its chief was at the head of a league containing Nayakot, the most ancient family of the pure descendants of Mincha. Bhirkot is a very petty state, consisting entirely of mountains, and containing neither mines nor mart of any consequence.

The same is the case with Garahang, whose chief adhered to the league with his kinsman of Bhirkot. The capital, (Rajdhani or Durbar,) of the same name with the country, is situated on the top of a hill, with no water nearer than a cose. In such a situation, only 60 or 70 huts surrounded the chief's castle, which was built of brick.

The impure chief of Dhor did not join in the league of his kinsmen; but followed in battle the pure chiefs of Tanahung. His country was as petty and as mountainous as that of his kinsmen, but contained some iron mines.

I now return to Mincha, whose descendants were reclaimed from their impurity by the Brahmans.

Mincha was Raja of Nayakot, and the chiefs of this place, although they lived pure, continued to the last to follow in war the impure representative of Khancha, who governed Bhirkot. Nayakot was very petty; but, besides the capital, contained a town of some note, named Limi, but no mines of any consequence.

A collateral branch of the Nayakot Rajas obtained a similar state called Satahung, which, besides the capital, contained a town called Gengdi. The capital, of the same name with the territory, is situated on a hill, and contained about 250 thatched huts, besides the brick castle of the chief. In the whole territory there might have been 1500 houses. The Raja's share of the land revenue amounted to 2000 rupees a-year. He followed in war the chief of Kaski. The most numerous tribe among his subjects was the Khasiya.

A second collateral branch of the Nayakot family was Kaski, a more powerful state than that of the chief from which it sprang. I believe that the territory of this chief towards the hills was much wider than is represented in the map of Kanak, for I was informed, that Gorkha had no communication with the Bhotiyas, his country being narrowed there between Kaski and Nepal. It may, however, have happened, that the want of communication was owing to the impracticability of the mountains, and not to the shortness of the frontier. The chiefs of Kaski leagued with Lamjun, a collateral branch of their own family, but had as a follower in war their kinsman of Satahung. Although adjacent to the mountains covered with perpetual snow, the southern parts are rather warmer than the valley of Nepal Proper, but the parts adjacent to the snowy peaks were inhabited by Bhotiyas, and next to these were some Gurungs. The warmer parts were occupied by Brahmans, Khasiyas, and the persons of low tribes necessary as artisans. The mountains here formed an uninterrupted and impenetrable barrier towards the north. The chief possessed some mines of copper; and, besides the capital, there is a considerable town called Pokhara, which is a mart frequented by merchants from Nepal, Palpa, Malebum, &c. and afforded duties that in so poor a country were reckoned considerable. The capital by Colonel Kirkpatrick * is called Buttolachoor, is situated among hills on the Seti river, (Saite, K.) which is very deep but narrow.

Kaski, the ancient capital, Colonel Kirkpatrick places 7 coses

* Nepaul, page 290.

west from Buttolachoor, with Surrungkoat, a large town with a fort on a hill between them.

The chief of Lamjun was descended from a younger son of Kaski, and was originally powerful, the sum appropriated from the land revenue, for his family expence, being 22,000 rupees a-year; and he was not only followed in war by his kinsman the chief of Kaski, but by the Raja of Tanahung. Lamjun, after the loss of Gorkha, was a cold country bordering on the snowy peaks of Emodus, and inhabited by Bhotiyas, with some Brahmans and Khasiyas in the warmer vallies. It contained no mine of any importance, nor any town of note, except the capital; and the chief advantage, after the loss of Gorkha, that the Raja enjoyed, was the commerce with Bhotan or Thibet, which was carried on through a passage in Emodus called Siklik. Many goods were conveyed by this route to Lamjun, and from thence, by the way of Tarku, Tanahung, Dewghat, and Bakra, into the low country; but this trade has been interdicted by the present government of Nepal, which is very jealous of the Raja of Tanahung, to whom Bakra still is secured by the Company's protection. Siklik, however, is still the residence of a Subah or civil governor, and is probably the place called Seshant in the map of Kanak. The name merely implies a frontier place, but among the hills is used to imply a place inhabited by barbarians; that is, such as reject the doctrines of the Brahmans. In both meanings the term is applicable to Siklik, as its inhabitants, Bhotiyas and Gurungs, adhere to the Lamas, and it is the frontier town towards the empire of China.

One of the Lamjun Rajas, according to Prati Nidhi, had a younger brother named Darbha Sahi, who as usual held the office of Chautariya; but rebelled, and took to himself Gorkha, the southern part of the principality, paying 12,000 rupees of the 22,000 that came to the chief for his support.

Gorkha is rather warmer than the valley of Nepal, and its chief inhabitants were Brahmans and Khasiyas, in about equal numbers, with rather fewer Magars, the Brahmans being the chief cultivators, and the Khas and Magars the fighting men. The capital Gorkha is situated on a very high hill, and was the only place of note in the territory. It is said to contain about 2000 houses, and the temple of Gorakhanath, who is one or the tutelar deities of the reigning family. From this circumstance we may perhaps infer, that the proper name of the place is Gorakha, and that, previous to having adopted the doctrines of the Brahmans, this family had received the Zogis, or priests of Gorakhanath, as their spiritual guides.

Colonel Kirkpatrick * states the old boundaries of Gorkha to have been the Trisulganga (Tirsoolgunga) on the east, and the Marichangdi (Mursiangdi) on the west. In place of the former he should have stated the Gandi; but from what he says, (in page 122,) it would seem that he confounded the Gandi with both the Setiganga and Trisulganga.

Nara Bhupal or Nribhupala, according to Prati Nidhi, was the sixth or seventh in descent from Darbha. The account which I received in Nepal does not materially differ. The first chief of Gorkha was, however, there called Rama Sahi, whether a different name for Darbha, or his son, I do not know, but his descendants were as follows: 1. Puran. 2. Chhatra. 3. Dambar. 4. Virbhadra. 5. Prithwi Pati. 6. Nribhupal. These chiefs entered into none of the leagues formed by their neigh-

* Nepaul, p. 123.

bours, trusting to their own vigour chiefly, for their country was very poor.

The chiefs of Gorkha being cut off from any direct communication with either the low country or Thibet, and having no mines nor other productions as a basis for commerce, were considered as insignificant, but Nribhupal procured in marriage, first, a daughter of the Palpa family; and, secondly, a daughter of the sixth son of the chief of Malebum, both of whom added much to his dignity.

His eldest son Prithwi Narayan (Purthi Nerayn in Kirkpatrick) was a person of insatiable ambition, sound judgment, great courage, and unceasing activity. Kind and liberal, especially in promises to his friends and dependants, he was regardless of faith to strangers, and of humanity to his enemies, that is, to all who opposed his views.

When a very young man, he visited Banaras, and having met with what he considered insolence at some (Chauki) custom-house, instantly put the officers to death. He was concealed from the police by a (Vairagi) person dedicated to religion, who, induced by most abundant promises, conveyed the highland chief in safety to his cousin, Makunda Sen, Raja of Palpa, by whom he was very kindly received, and furnished with the means which enabled him to undertake his first enterprises. I have already mentioned the manner in which he repaid this friendship, and in which he conquered the countries that the Chitaur colony held on the east of the Gandaki. Some account of the invasion of Nepal by this chief is given by Colonel Kirkpatrick, * and in the Asiatick Researches will be found a more full narration by an eye-witness of the manner in which he acquired that country,

* Page 270.

to which he immediately transferred the seat of government, although his nobles and soldiers despise the name of Nepal, and call themselves Gorkhalis. I have also mentioned his total failure in an attempt to extend his dominions to the west, towards which, during the remainder of his government, and that of his son, the Marchangdi continued to be the boundary to the west, as it had been in the time of his ancestors.

The Vairagi, who had saved the life of Prithwi Narayan at Banaras, no sooner heard of the conquest of Nepal, than he repaired to that country, and reminded the chief of his promises. These the chief did not attempt to deny; but said, that, as the promises had been extorted by fear, he would give nothing. The Vairagi, having assembled 500 of the religious order of Nagas, attempted to use force; but the whole horde was taken, and put to death, an event of great use to Bengal, which these ruffians had been in the habit of plundering.

Prithwi Narayan, besides his personal endowments, was much indebted for success to the introduction of firelocks, which until his time were totally unknown among the hills; and, so far as he was able, he introduced European discipline, the value of which he fully appreciated. His jealousy of the European character always, however, prevented him from employing any of them in his service, and he is said to have strongly recommended to his successors to follow, in this respect, his example. How far this may have been judicious, I cannot say; but it has certainly prevented his troops, although in many respects well organized, from making considerable progress in tactics, or in a dexterous use of their arms, and these are probably much more defective than his descendants and their officers think.

Prithwi Narayan died about the year 1771, and left two legitimate sons; Singha Pratap, who succeeded his father, and

Bahadur Sahi, who, after his brother's death, was regent of the kingdom during his nephew's minority, although he had excited the jealousy of Singha Pratap, and had with difficulty saved his life by living in exile.

Singha Pratap's attention, as I have mentioned, was chiefly directed to secure the conquests towards the east, in which, as I have said, he seems to have had as few scruples as usual in his family. He died in 1775, at Devighat, and left his kingdom to his son Rana Bahadur, placed in charge of his uncle Bahadur Sahi, a very active enterprising prince, and of his mother Rajendra Lakshmi, a princess of a similar character.

Two such enterprising personages could not agree: and, until the princess's death, there were constant disputes, sometimes the one, and sometimes the other, acquiring the ascendancy, and then confining or banishing their adversary. Yet it is alleged, that in times of reconciliation, marriage had been proposed between them, the custom of the lower casts of Hindus, at least, not only permitting, but requiring a younger brother to espouse his elder brother's widow. That such a proposal should ever have been made, being contrary to the customs which at present prevail among the high casts, is rather improbable; and, perhaps, owes its origin to a desire of flattering Rana Bahadur, whose treatment of his uncle required an apology. The people of Palpa indeed allege, that, during the life of Singha Pratap, a more criminal intercourse had actually taken place between the two regents, and that it was to revenge the disgrace thrown on his family, that Rana Bahadur proceeded to extremities against his uncle. Were this true, the attempt to unite their differences by a marriage might be supposed possible: but I attribute the origin of such a story to the disappointed hopes of the Palpa family, which, after having entered into an iniquitous league with Bahadur

Sahi, found itself in consequence reduced to a state of dependancy.

I have already mentioned the manner in which Bahadur Sahi thus connected himself with the Palpa family, and the success that attended Damodar Pangre, the officer who was most judiciously employed, and who then held the office of Karyi. Except Palpa, and its share of the spoil, this officer speedily reduced the whole country from Gorkha to the boundary of the country called Garhawal, the capital of which is Srinagar. At the same time, the dominion of Gorkha was extended over the Sikim Bhotiyas of the east, as I have already mentioned; and several other chiefs of the Bhotiya nation towards the north were reduced to obedience.

So far the greatest success had attended the regent, when he was tempted to adopt a very rash measure. Sumur, a discontented brother of the Tishu Lamas from Digarchi, came to Nepal, and told the needy chief wonderful stories concerning the wealth of the convent, in which the Tishu Lama, spiritual guide of the Chinese Emperor, resided. Inflamed with a desire for plunder, and without having the slightest pretence or intercourse with that priest, a large body of Gorkhalis (it is said 7000) overcame all the obstructions of a long and very difficult route, and succeeded in carrying back a large booty, although closely pursued by a Chinese army, that came to the assistance of the Lama. This army having been greatly increased, about the time when Colonel Kirkpatrick visited Nepal, advanced to Dhayabung, and compelled the regent to submit to several indignities, although it had suffered severely from the climate, and the poverty of the country. For the particulars, however, I may refer to the Account of Colonel Kirkpatrick, * and of Captain Turner, † whose opportunities

* Nepaul, Appendix, No. 1. by Mr Duncan.

† Embassy to Thibet, p. 437.

of acquiring information were superior to mine. So far as I can learn, the people of Gorkha were very much discontented with the regent for submitting to the indignities which the Chinese demanded; and they seem to have thought, that the invading army had been reduced to a situation rather to offer than demand submission. The submission was, however, not impolitic; for I believe, that the tribute agreed upon has never even been demanded, much less expected, and the Gorkhalis are in the habit of saying, that, should they have any dispute with the English, their only formidable neighbour, they will claim the protection of the Chinese, with whose influence over the Company they seem to be much better acquainted than one would have expected. The Chinese general consented to move back on receiving a supply of grain for his army, and fifty virgins as an homage for his sovereign; but no stipulation was made for the restoration of the plunder of Digarchi. It was given out at Kathmandu, that the virgins threw themselves from the precipices on the route, and perished rather than submit to the embraces of infidels defiled by every impure food: but I have since learned, that their sense of honour did not carry them to such lengths, and that the Chinese placed them in a convent near the frontier. The people of Thibet procured no satisfaction for the injury, and Chinese garrisons having been placed through their country, they have become more subject than ever to that empire, and most of their petty chiefs have been put to death or banished, while the Chinese have since extended their conquests still farther west. The dominions of Nepal are therefore the only thing that separates them from the British power, and saves them from political discussions, managed free from the control of their own forms, and from exposing to their officers and people the view of a nation far their superior in power.

It is alleged, that at length the regent's ambition overcame his sense of duty, and that he intended to keep his nephew in confinement, and seize the government. The people of Palpa allege, that he had secured the assistance of his brother-in-law Mahadatta Sen. Certain it is, that he was suddenly dispossessed of power by his nephew, and died in confinement, some say by the Raja's own hand, while others assert that he was starved to death.

Bahadur Sahi, although a prince of great vigour, is supposed to have been uncommonly superstitious; yet from some anecdotes related by Colonel Kirkpatrick,* it would appear, that he was very capable of evading with skill the performance of troublesome ceremonies, and that he could speak on religion with the popish missionaries without harshness, but with a considerable quickness of repartee. His superstition was probably, therefore, of that nature which is usually assumed by princes placed in difficult situations.

Rana Bahadur received little or no education from his guardians, but was allowed to indulge in every vice, surrounded by minions and young profligates of the court. These not only assisted him in the pursuit of low vices, but encouraged his natural propensity to cruel diversions. He had no sooner secured his rights to the throne, and assumed the power of the state, than he showed the restless ambition of his family by an attack on the Yumila Raja, whom all the mountain chiefs acknowledged as their liege lord. The Yumila chief, although he had been thrown off his guard by all manner of professions, having an extensive territory, made a stout resistance, but was finally compelled to seek refuge in the country of the Vazir.

---

* Nepaul, p. 120.

Rana Bahadur had married a daughter of the Gulmi Raja, to whom he showed some favour, compelling the Raja of Palpa to give up to that chief several estates, of which he had been stript by Mahadatta Sen; but, perhaps being disgusted by his wife's having no children, he soon neglected that virtuous and high-minded lady, and very openly cohabited with other women. He first had a son by a common slave girl, and then one by the daughter of a Brahman. This gave great offence to the sacred order, but the ungovernable fury of the Raja's temper hushed all complaints. As a means of disturbing him, however, the skilful in astrology (Jyotish) published a prophecy, foretelling that the Raja would not long survive his beauteous favourite of the sacred order, who would soon be seized with a disease. As the latter circumstance happened, the Raja, who, like other Hindus, had no doubt in the science, was in the utmost consternation. Some of the learned took immediate advantage, and informed him, that, by certain ceremonies performed before a certain image, his favourite might be restored to health. The Raja, caught by this device, advanced what was held to be a very large sum, it is said 100,000 rupees; but without effect, for his favourite died in a few days. The Raja's ungovernable temper now fully disclosed itself. He not only scourged the Brahmans to make them disgorge his money, but he took the image, and, grinding it to pieces with excrement, threw the fragments into a river. His fears, however, were not abated, and the people, disgusted and terrified at his violence, were ripe for change. It was judiciously suggested to him, that, as he could not expect to survive long, he should endeavour to secure the government to the son of his favourite, by placing him immediately on the throne, (Gadi,) and by making all ranks take the oaths of fidelity to the child. The Raja approved entirely of this measure, and determined to end his days at Banaras, and thus to secure a place in heaven. Every step, however, was taken to secure the young Raja's authority. The Raja of Palpa was invited to place the mark of royalty (Tika) on his forehead, and some of the conquered chiefs, I believe chiefly those descended of Khancha and Mincha, were induced to be present, and promised an annual pension, on condition of their acknowledging the legitimacy of their illegitimate kinsman: and so much weight has been attached to this acknowledgment, that the pensions, I am told, are still continued.

Before all these ceremonies had been performed, much time had elapsed. Although, therefore, every preparation had been made for the Raja's departure for Banaras, and although he had conferred the regency on his surviving favourite the slave girl, his wife having refused to accept of the office, and having insisted on accompanying her lord, Rana Bahadur, no longer called Raja but Swami, finding himself very well, seems to have repented of what he had rashly done, and suspecting some trick, was inclined to resume the government. Both people and chiefs were, however, in general averse to this measure, as the violence of his temper was universally feared. The chiefs, therefore, under the direction of Damodar Pangre, informed him, that they, having sworn obedience to the young Raja, would support his government. The Raja fortified himself in the town of Lalita Patan, near the capital, and most of the eastern provinces were disposed to support his authority; but Damodar had shown such prudence and mildness, when he conquered the west, that the people of that quarter were determined to adhere to his cause. Sadhu Ram alleges, that on this occasion, in the country between Gorkha Proper and Garhawal, including Palpa, in the strictest friendship with Damodar, 17,000 men of the sacred order, and an equal number of the military tribes, were ready to support this officer. After some skirmishing, Damodar's party being evidently the strongest, Rana Bahadur retired privately to Banaras with the character of insanity; but, except in an ungovernable ferocity and cruelty of temper, and in a credulity, evidently the fault of education, he seems to have been abundantly judicious, and in fact finally overreached all his adversaries.

Rana Bahadur having incurred a considerable debt to the British Government, which supplied his wants at Banaras, a treaty was entered into for a gradual repayment, and for the residence of a British officer at Kathmandu; and Captain Knox, with whom I went, entered their territory in February 1802. We had been there only a few days, when the officers, who came to meet us, and who were very friendly disposed, were thrown into great trouble by the arrival of the princess, Rana Bahadur's wife. The unprincipled chief had connected himself with one of these frail but pure beauties, (Gandharbin,) with which the holy city abounds, had stript his wife of her jewels to bestow them on this wanton companion, and finally had turned his wife out of doors. As the slave regent had the meanness to seize on the income of the town, assigned for the princess's dowry, the poor lady was reduced to the utmost distress, and conceived that we were her enemies, being on an embassy to the low woman, by whom she had been so shamefully used. She therefore stirred up to destroy us a certain Masan Raut, who had under him many thieves and robbers, with whom he plundered the borders. We received, however, timely notice, and our guard being all night under arms, no attempt was made, although the sentries saw hovering round parties of men, who, no doubt, had come in the expectation of finding some unguarded part.

As might have been expected, under such circumstances, the

slave girl's regency had been from the first marked with weakness. The two most powerful chiefs then in Nepal were Brahma Sahi of the royal family, and Damodar of the house called Pangre, which, ever since the conquest, has been the most powerful family among the Gorkhalis. Damodar had strengthened his influence by the marriage of his sister into the distinguished family of the Viswanaths, and had procured the command of most of the fortresses, which he intrusted to the care of his own dependants. The eldest of his nephews, of the Viswanath family, was then a fine young man named Kritimohun. Him the regent appointed Karyi, and in his abilities reposed the highest confidence, which was supposed to have been increased by her regard for his person. Far from supporting his uncle, this rash young man removed all the adherents of the Pangre family from the command of the fortresses, and gave them in charge to dependants of his own, and of Rudravir his illegitimate brother. In the meanwhile, envy raised against him many enemies, and he was assassinated by persons of a rank too elevated to be publicly mentioned. Among these was Sri Krishna Sahi, one of the legitimate princes of the royal family, who was compelled to fly into the Company's territory; but the principal odium and suspicion fell on Damodar Pangre, the young minister's uncle. As the regent never liked this chief, the circumstance was made a pretence for attempting his ruin, and for the elevation of Brahma Sahi to the principal authority in the government. This personage having joined with two brothers of the Viswanath family, and with Sher Bahadur, illegitimate brother of Rana Bahadur, seized on the two sons of Damodar Pangre; but the old man could not be touched; he was too much versed in affairs, and was too strongly supported by his friends, and especially by two warlike brothers. With these he retired from court; an when Captain Knox approached the frontier, in the beginning of 1802, was living in sullen retirement. At this time an apparent reconciliation took place between Brahma Sahi and Damodar Pangre; both came to receive the English embassy; and the sons of Damodar were liberated. The probable cause of this reconciliation was the elevation of a low man to the principal confidence of the regent, while the charge of her conscience and heart was in possession of a young Sannyasi or religious mendicant, one of the finest formed men that I have ever seen. Both circumstances gave offence to the people.

On our arrival in the valley of Nepal, in April, we found a young illegitimate Raja, about six years of age, whose nominal chief minister, Chautariya, was an illegitimate brother, two years older than himself, and son of the regent slave girl, who had in fact given the whole power to a very low person, which occasioned universal disgust. Damodar Pangre, who had met us on the frontier, did not accompany us to the court, for what reason I do not exactly know; but it is probable that he scorned the low favourite, who had been raised to the chief authority in the kingdom. The only man of weight at the court was in fact Brahma Sahi, descended of the royal family; but whether or not legitimate, I cannot say. He was, however, highly respected by the people, and has fewer of the vices of his family than usual, with much good sense and moderation.

Soon after our arrival we learned, that the distressed princess, spouse of Rana Bahadur, terrified at the thought of remaining in the unhealthy forests during the rainy season, deprived of means to support her in the Company's territory, and probably encouraged by Damodar Pangre, intended to come up to Nepal without leave; for the regent could not bear the approach of her former mistress, and yet would not give her the stipulated dower. People were therefore sent, who brought up all the male attendants of the princess in irons; and it was hoped, I believe, that she would perish in the woods. Necessity, however, added boldness to her measures, and she advanced with ten or twelve female attendants to Chisapani, a fortress commanding the entrance into Nepal. It was evident, however, that the commiseration of the people was daily gaining strength, and the timidity of the regent gave daily an increase of power to the princess. An additional company of Seapoys was sent to Chisapani, as if soldiers were the proper persons to stop the progres of a few helpless women. The officer commanding had received positive orders to refuse the princess admittance; but he contented himself by executing merely the letter of his orders. He took in all his garrison, shut the gates, and allowed the lady and her attendants to walk quietly round the walls. Much anxiety was now evident at the capital, and another company of Seapoys was dispatched to Chitlang, with positive orders to prevent the princess from advancing farther; and, if the arrears of dower had accompanied the officer, I do not believethat she would have made any attempt; but the sordid dispositions of the regent and her favourite did not suffer them to part with money. The officer commanding the company met the poor princess and her attendants on the road, and, being a man of true honour, with a good deal of difficulty mustered courage to disclose his orders. When he had done so, the high-born lady, unmoved by fear, pulled out a dagger, and saying, will you presume to oppose the lawful wife of a Gorkhali Raja, while going to her own estate? she struck him on the arm; on which, although wounded, he immediately retired, quite ashamed of the service on which he had been employed; and his men required no orders to follow his example. The princess that morning entered the valley of Nepal, and halted about five miles from the capital. No sooner was this known than she was joined by Damodar Pangre, and all ranks flocked to pay their respects, and among them all the officers of government, except the low favourite, who immediately fled towards Thibet.

The regent, thus deserted, retired with the Raja and her son to the sanctuary of a temple, taking with her all the money in the treasury and the jewels of the crown. Next day the princess entered the capital, and, after a short negociation, took upon herself the regency, and settled on her base-born rival an income, which, had she received, she would never have given any trouble. In the whole transaction, indeed, she showed great magnanimity; and the only stain on her character, so far as I know, during so difficult a scene, was her conduct to the wife of the low man, whom the late regent had elevated to the office of Serdar. This unfortunate woman was put to the torture, to make her disclose where her husband had concealed his treasure; but, I believe, the treasure was imaginary, and the report of his having accumulated wealth arose, I imagine, in base minds, envious of his sudden rise, and anxious to gratify their envy by misrepresentations to the princess regent. The man, indeed, bore on the whole a good character; and the meanness of his birth and education, with some low conduct, arising more from these misfortunes than from any inclination to evil, are the only things for which I ever heard him blamed.

The new regent placed in her chief confidence Damodar Pangre, the officer in the country of by far the highest reputation; and although she consulted him chiefly, she expressed great anxiety for her husband's return. She also showed the utmost jealousy of the British embassy as likely to interfere with that event; and in the end of March 1803 we left the capital. It was probably at the instigation of Damodar, that the Palpa Raja, as I have mentioned, was allowed to return home. Whether or not these chiefs had entered into any conspiracy, as has been hinted, I do not know; but it is generally believed, that Damodar, so far as he was able, opposed the return of Rana Bahadur, which certainly was neither desirable for Nepal nor its neighbours. The natives in general believe, that he wrote a letter to a gentleman of rank at Banaras, requesting his influence to keep Rana Bahadur at that city; and that this letter, by the treachery or mistaken policy of the gentleman, came into the hands of this ferocious chief. He instantly departed by post, and was in the dominions of Nepal before any one suspected that he had left Banaras. He was cordially received by his faithful wife, although he did not fail to send to Banaras for the wanton beauty, by whom he had been there captivated, and who must have cost him great sums, if we can judge from the style in which she now lives at Banaras, to which she returned on his death.

On his approach to the capital, Rana Bahadur was met by Damodar Pangre, at the head of a large body of armed men. This certainly had an alarming appearance, and the intention of a man so prudent and reserved as Damodar must always remain uncertain; but the prince, supported by the advice of Bhim Sen, a young attendant, showed no sign of fear, and called aloud to the officers and men, "Now show whether you will have me or Damodar for your lord?" on which the whole joined him, and the gallant veteran, and his eldest son, were bound.

Rana Bahadur contented himself with the title of Swami or Lord, and, finding that the oath of fidelity had still a considerable influence among the troops, acted merely as regent for his son; but, in action, he never hesitated to assume the full power of the prince. Soon after, having shown the letter to Damodar, he delivered him and his son to the public executioner. As leading to the place, the young man proposed resistance, and a sudden attempt might have put them in possession of arms, which, with their known courage, and the veneration for their character, where no higher authority was present, might have overcome the guard. The old general, however, recommended submission, lest their attempt might have proven totally fatal to their house. He appears to have here also acted with his usual judgment; as his only surviving son was spared by Rana Bahadur, when treacherously delivered up by the Palpa Raja, as I have above mentioned; and the young man, I believe, now holds the office of one of the Karyis, the whole soldiery viewing the family with affection, and considering it entitled to have one of its members always in possession of that dignity.

Immediately after this, Rana Bahadur determined to enlarge his dominions, and with that view entrusted Bara Amar Singha with a large force. This officer Rana Banhadur, when he arrived from Banaras, found in confinement, in which he had been placed by his old commander, Damodar Pangre, and, on this account, he was justly considered as more faithful to the prince. He rapidly seized on Garhawal, and extended the power of Gorkha beyond the Yamuna; where, had it not been checked by Ranjit Singha, the Sikh chieftain, it would soon have extended to the boundary of Kasmira.

I have already mentioned the arts by which Rana Bahadur inveigled Prithwi Pal, and the chief officers of that prince, into his power; in which he showed no symptoms of insanity, unless a shameless perfidy be considered as such. His career, however, was then near a close. Most of the chief officers were disgusted, and kept in constant terror by the remembrance of Damodar Pangre's fate, with whom most of them had been intimately connected; and each daily expected, that this connection might be made a pretence for his ruin; for the regent or lord consulted only a young man named Bhim Sen, vigorous, ambitious, and unprincipled as himself. A conspiracy is said to have been formed with a view of placing the Palpa Raja at the head of affairs; and Sher Bahadur, an illegitimate brother of the regent, who long had held the high office of Chautariya, is supposed to have been concerned. In order to remove his brother from such dangerous enterprises, the regent ordered him to join the army in the field, but he declined. The regent was then very angry; and, while in full court, sent for his brother, with orders to bring him by force if he declined. Sher Bahadur followed the messengers into the court, and being asked, if he would join the army, declined by saying, we are sons of the same father, go you and I will follow. What may be exactly meant by this phrase in an ambiguous language, I cannot say; certainly, however, it so enraged Rana, that he ordered his brother for execution; but, while no one was aware, the brother drew his sword, and gave the regent a mortal blow. He was instantly put to death by Bhim Sen, into whose hands the regent, before he expired, delivered his son, the Raja, and commanded all persons to obey his authority.

When the Raja expired, Bhim Sen immediately retired to another room, commanding a view of the court, in which the guard was assembled, and, having addressed the soldiers, and received a promise of their support, he immediately surrounded the hall, in which the court was assembled, and put to death all the most active persons, under pretence, at least, of the conspiracy, and there is reason to suspect, that what he alleged was not destitute of foundation. On this occasion, Bidur Sahi, an illegitimate son of the royal family, then one of the Chautariyas, Narasingha Karyi, Tribhuvan Karyi, and about fifty military officers, were killed. On the same day he put to death the Palpa Raja, and his chief officers, as has been already mentioned; and his father, Amar Singha, immediately seized on the dominions of that chief. Some variations are told in the circumstances of this event, but the above I consider as the best authenticated.

Rana Bahadur, although he could not treat his wife with kindness, nor even decency, does not seem to have been altogether unmoved by her noble conduct; and, after his return from Banaras, had enlarged her father's dominions. Fortunately for Bhim Sen, the high-spirited lady accompanied the body of her faithless husband on the funeral pile, and freed the new regent from her presence, which might have been very troublesome. For his subsequent conduct in seizing on her father's petty states, which was done when he seized Palpa, it will be difficult to account, except on the principle of insatiable rapacity. The tragedies of his first day's government of course stopped all observations on his conduct. Disliking to have at the capital a person so venerable, and of such high rank as Brahma Sahi, he induced that chief to accept the government of Kumau or Almora, the most honourable in the kingdom, and augmented in dignity by the new title of Raja. Brahma Sahi, exempt from ambition, and knowing from his character that he was safe from danger, accepted the office as more suited to his great years, than the dangerous intrigues of Kathmandu. The remote government of Saliyana is occupied by his brother Rudravir, but the youngest brother Kasthadal, and all his legitimate male issue, are held at Kathmandu, no doubt as hostages; for all the family is suspected not only of disaffection, but of being too friendly to the English. Kasthadal, however, is now one of the Chautariyas. The command of the army in the west has been continued to Bara Amar Singha, whose birth gives him no pretension to raise disturbances; but who has good abilities, and there is reason to believe is firmly attached to the present ruler. Bhim Sen, himself, now in the vigour of youth, and of the most determined courage, has probably very ambitious views. Whether or not he may think these promoted by his disputes with the English, I do not know; but the Raja approaches manhood, and the objections to his succession are very numerous, while the disputes with the English have been a pretence for assembling a very large force, (twenty-five companies under the son, and thirteen companies under the father,) and for thus attaching to his family a very large proportion of the army. The army in the west is under the command of Bara Amar Singha, father of Ranadhwar, the chief confidant and coadjutor of the young minister.

From the following genealogical table of the legitimate descendants of Narabhupal or Nribhupal, composed in spring 1803, it will appear, that the line of Prithwi Narayan ended in Rana Bahadur; nor do I know what has since become of the other branches of the family. They were in obscurity when the table was composed, and their condition since has probably in no way been altered, at least for the better; and at any rate, they are distant relations to Rana Bahadur, nor are they descended from Prithwi Narayan, the favourite hero of the nation. Every male of the family, legitimate or not, takes the title of Sa, Sahi, or Saha, which is always used in conversation and writing, but need not be repeated in the table.

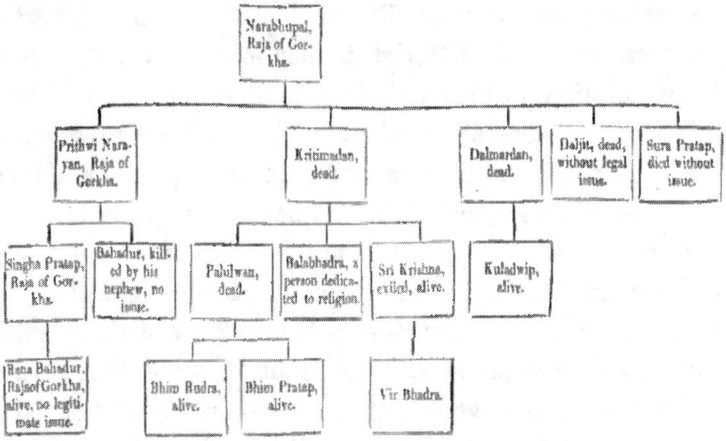

There was another family, which contained six petty chiefs, Gulmi, Khachi, Argha, Musikot, Dhurkot, and Isma; all of whom, except Musikot, had adopted the rules of purity, and took the title of Sahi, or Saha, like the chiefs of Gorkha; but it is not alleged, that the two families had any connection, except by marriage, and two of the branches of the family, of which I am now giving an account, Gulmi and Musikot, called themselves Kala Makwani, although no one knows from whence they came, nor the origin of the appellation. The Rajas of Gulmi, Khachi, and Argha, followed Palpa in war; Dhurkot stood independent; and Isma and Musikot followed Piuthana.

It is probable, that Gulmi was the original seat of the family, as Khachi and Argha are acknowledged to be collateral branches; but with the claims of the other three chiefs I am not acquainted. Gulmi, the capital of the state so named, is situated on a hill, the ascent of which is said to be three miles in length. The castle is built of bricks, and covered with tiles. The town contained 500 houses, mostly thatched. There is no water within a quarter of a mile of the town. A part of the great mart, called Rerighat, mentioned in the account of Palpa, belonged to the chief of Gulmi. His territory contains mines of zinc, (dasta,) cinnabar, (sabita,) and copper, of which one is on a hill, called Chandrakot, and another on Arakul Pahar, near the former. These mines would appear to be valuable. The allied chiefs of Palpa, Gulmi, Khachi, and Argha, as I have mentioned, about the beginning of the eighteenth century, destroyed the Magar chief of Balihang, and divided among themselves his dominions, both on the hills and plains. The division seems to have given rise to sundry bickerings. The capital, which was situated on a hill near the plains, and fortified, fell to the share of Palpa; but Gulmi and Khachi received a large share of the plains. Makunda Sen of Palpa, about the middle of the last century, contrived to seize on Gulmi, by the intrigues of a Brahman, named Kanak Nidhi, who gives me the account, and he delivered the fortress to an officer of his master's, named Kirtibamb Thapa; but that person very soon restored the place to its lawful owner. I have already mentioned the base manner in which Mahadatta of Palpa joined with his son-in-law, Bahadur Sahi of Gorkha, and how he obtained Gulmi, Khachi, and Argha, as the dear bought fruit of his perfidy. These, however, he was allowed to possess, so long as he lived. Siva Saha, the dethroned chief of Gulmi, retired to Ramnagar, where he found refuge with the exiled chief of Tanahung, and while there, gave his grand-daughter in marriage to Rana Bahadur, the young Raja of Gorkha and Nepal, who no sooner obtained the government, than he compelled Prithwi Pal to restore the hills of Gulmi to his wife's father; and when he returned from Banaras, and had secured Prithwi Pal in confinement, the original possessions of the Gulmi family were augmented by the whole of the hills of Balihang; but this flourishing state lasted only for a few weeks, as, on the death of Rana and his high-minded spouse, all her father's possessions were seized by the rapacious Bhim Sen, who now governs Nepal. Sidhi Pratap, the chief of Gulmi, is supposed to be still in the mountains; but others allege, that he has died without issue. He is supposed to have been about the thirtieth chief of his race.

In Gulmi and Balihang one-half of the people are Khasiyas, one-eighth Brahmans, of whom many are of pure birth, (Upadhyayas,) and few illegitimate, (Jausi.) The remainder of the population consists of impure tribes of cultivators and artificers.

The principal crop in these hills is the rice, which is reaped in the beginning of winter, (Aghani.)

The chief of Khachi, a younger branch of Gulmi, profited much by the spoils of Balihang, and had a fine territory on the plain adjacent to his hills. In the latter were no mines, except one of iron; but at the foot of the hills was a considerable mart, called Barakadwar, the trade of which, however, has been almost totally forced to Butaul, since the chief of Gorkha has seized on both countries. It is said, that there is a still more important pass, called Khor, four coses east from Barakadwar. This is said to be the easiest of all the ascents to the mountains, and leads to the town of Khachi, from whence there are routes in many directions leading to places at a great distance, without any very difficult ascent or descent. The town of Khachi, which was the capital, stands on a hill plentifully supplied with water. The town contained about 300 houses, mostly thatched; that of the chief was built of brick. The Raja's share of the land revenue on the hills, besides the lands for supplying the officers and soldiers, amounted to 4000 rupees a-year, and from the plain he annually procured from

500 to 1500 rupees, according as the cultivators were discontented or satisfied. Some of the officers had lands free of rent on the plains; but, as usual among the mountaineers, the whole revenue from the plain went to the chief. On the hills of this state 5-16ths of the people were Khasiyas, Brahmans and Rajputs 3-16ths, and low cultivators and artisans 8-16ths. The last Raja's name was Durgar Sahi, who was expelled by Mahadatta of Palpa, as already mentioned. I have not heard of his subsequent fate.

Argha belonged also to a collateral branch of Gulmi, which is supposed by some to have become extinct; but others allege, that the son of the last chief is now in Nepal. It had a small territory on the plain, bestowed by Makunda Sen in consequence of a marriage; but both hill and plain were seized by his son, as I have mentioned. Argha, the capital, is on a hill, four coses in ascent, on the summit of which, round the chief's castle, are about 150 houses, while there are 350 about the middle of the ascent. The houses have mud walls and thatched roofs. Water is plenty at the lower town, but is a quarter of a mile distant from the upper. The hills possessed no mines, nor any considerable mart. The Raja's share of the land rent amounted to about 4000 rupees a-year, and the whole of his territory might contain 5000 houses. Not above 100 of these belonged to Brahmans, and the number of Rajputs was quite trifling. One half of the people were Khasiyas, the other half impure cultivators and tradesmen.

Concerning Dhurkot I learned nothing but what has been already mentioned, and that its chief had one iron mine. It was rendered subject to Gorkha by Damodar Pangre.

Musikot was the residence of the chief of this name, who had a brick-house on a hill close to the Barigar river, and, unlike the other chiefs of his race, rejected the pure doctrines of the Brahmans. The house of the chief was surrounded by 400 houses of his subjects, mostly thatched. He had no possessions on the plain, and his whole territory might contain 3000 houses, of which 5-16ths were occupied by Rajputs, 1-16th by Brahmans, mostly of spurious birth, (Jausis,) 4-16ths by Khasiyas, and 6-16ths by impure cultivators and tradesmen. Most of the Rajputs were of the Raja's family, a circumstance uncommon on the hills, where the governing families seem seldom to have propagated to nearly such an extent, and were often rather weak. The Raja's share of the landed revenue was estimated at 2000 rupees a-year. There was no great mart, but near the Barigar there is a mine of copper. The great crop here, also, is winter rice. When Damodar Pangre seized the country, the chief and many of his family went to Kathmandu, where a great part has obtained service.

Isma, the last chief of this family, resided at a fortress of the same name, situated on a lofty hill, of very difficult access, three coses in ascent. Horses could not ascend more than half way, where there were about 250 houses. Round the castle, on the summit, were 50 or 60. These houses are thatched huts, with walls of stone or planks. On the hill are several springs of water. The Raja had no possessions on the plain, and his subjects might amount to 2500 houses, from whom his share of the rent might amount to 2000 rupees. One half of his subjects were Khasiyas, 1-8th pure Brahmans, (Upadhyayas,) 1-16th bastard Brahmans, (Jausis,) 1-16th Rajputs, and 1-4th low cultivators and tradesmen. The country contained neither mines nor marts. It must, however, be observed, that both in this country and in Musikot, Corundum (Kuran) is found in detached masses, either on the surface or mixed with the soil. Some of it is bluish like lead, and some is of a copper colour. The pieces seldom exceed 4 lbs. or 5 lbs.

in weight. It affords no revenue. The chiefs of this family waged a constant war with their kinsman of Musikot, and the twenty-third or twenty-fourth of them married a daughter of Makunda Sen of Palpa, so that Mahadatta leagued with the chief of Gorkha to destroy his nephew.

The Raja of Piuthana, among these petty chiefs, was a person of some consequence, and was followed in war by Isma and Musikot, two chiefs of the last mentioned family. He was also followed by the chiefs of Khungni and Bhingri, whose countries were surrounded by Piuthana; and I think, that in all probability these two belonged to the Chaubisiyas, although they are not mentioned in Kanak Nidhi's list; and I must confess, that the latter I have heard arranged with the twenty-two Rajas. All that I learned concerning these chiefs is, that they were of the same family, followed Piuthana in war, and were very petty. The situation of their countries will be seen in the maps.

Piuthana had no mines of value, but it possessed a considerable tract on the plain, and paid the revenue of this through the Raja of Bangsi, after Mahadatta of Palpa had been freed from that vassalage by the Nawab Vazir. This territory on the plain, called Siwaraj, is, therefore, claimed by the Bangsi family; but is in possession of the Raja of Gorkha. The chief of Piuthana pretends to be a Chandel Rajput, nor had his family subdivided into different branches. The town, from whence he derived his title, is situated on a hill, the ascent to which is two coses in length. Round their chief's house, which was built of brick after the fashion of Kathmandu, were about 400 houses, mostly mud-walled huts with thatched roofs. The Jimri, called Rapti in the low country, passes on its south side. The whole territory on the hills and plains contained about 2500 houses, of whom 5-16ths were Khasiyas, 3-16ths Brahmans, one-half low cultivators and tradesmen. There were a very few

Rajputs and Newars. Manik Chandra possessed this country in quiet, and was succeeded by Mati Chandra, who retired without a struggle, when attacked by Damodar Pangre. Rudra Chandra, his son, now resides at Ramnagar with the Tanahung Raja, for the people of Gorkha seized on Siwaraj, when they took possession of Piuthana, although it then belonged to the Narwab Vazir, and should now form a part of the Gorakhpur district. They at first cajoled the Bangsi Rajah, promising to pay more than the chief of Piuthana had done; but, after the first year, he got nothing. The present representative of the family, in 1814, was about twenty-eight years of age, and is supposed to be the twenty-fifth chief of his race. If so, his pretence to be a Chandel is probably ill-founded, as no true Rajputs are said to have settled so early in these hills.

Poin was a very petty chief, who followed in war the impure chief of Bhirko but was himself pure, and called himself a Sirnet, saying that he came from the mountains south-west from the Yamuna. Poin is situated on a high hill, where much snow falls, and there is intense cold. At this capital were only 120 houses, and the whole in the territory amounted to only 2000; but there were iron and copper mines in the country, and the Raja, for his share of the revenue, had 4000 rupees a year.

In the list of the twenty-four Rajas given by Kanak Nidhi, a Tarki Raja is mentioned; but I heard no account of any such person, nor does any such place appear in the maps. In place of Tarki I suspect, therefore, we must introduce the very petty chief of Malihang, usually called the Sat Bisi, or seven-score Raja, because his revenue amounted to 140 rupees a year; a poverty which renders St Marino an empire.

There remain two countries, Malebum or Malebamba, and Galkot, which, by all the authorities that I consulted, were included among the Chaubisiya or twenty-four Rajas, and, therefore, I shall treat of them here, although I suspect an inaccuracy. It is said, that there was a certain impure chief of the Jariya tribe, who had very extensive dominions. The daughter and heiress of this chief married a Gautamiya Brahman, and by him had twenty-two sons, each of whom obtained a share of his grandfather's dominions, and among these, besides Malebum and Galkot, are the northern Musikot, Jajarkot, Jahuri, Baphi, Rugun, and Salyana, all reckoned in a class called the Baisi or twenty-two Rajas. I have not been able to procure a complete list of these chiefs, some of whose dominions extend farther north than the knowledge of my informants; but I think, that the above mentioned circumstance of the twenty-two descendants of a common origin must have given rise to the classification, and that Malebum and Galkot in fact belong to the Baisi, thus making room for Khungri and Bhingri in the Chaubisiyas, among whom they are placed in the maps. The same conclusion may be drawn from a circumstance stated of Nag Bamba of Malebum; who is said in his wars to have led twenty-two chiefs to battle.

The Brahman common ancestor of this family settled first at Takam, where his father-in-law probably resided, and this place is in Malebum, or Parbat, as the country is often called, on account of the immense mountains that it contains. This division of the grandfather's estate was always by far the most powerful, and was probably the share of the eldest son. The Brahman was named Dimba Ray, which savours rather of a barbarous race. On his marriage he called himself a Samal Rajput, and all his descendants have imitated his example, although, according to the custom of the country, they should be reckoned Khasiyas, being descended of a Brahman father and impure mother. I have never before, nor any where else, heard of a Gautamiya Brahman; and the Gautamiya tribe of the plains is a spurious branch of the Gautama Rajputs, formerly very powerful near Allahabad; and I suspect that Dimba Ray belonged to this race.

Some generations after the fortunate marriage of this chief, the seat of government was removed from Takam to Dhoral Thana, usually called Malebum, and situated at the junction (Beni) of the Mayangdi, Mehagdi of Kirkpatrick, with the Narayani. On this account the town is often called Beni Shahar or Beniji, while Dhoral is the name of the castle by which it is commanded; Malebum is a term applicable to both. Nag Bamba was then Raja, and he was a person eminent for strength and courage. A prize-fighter (Mal) from Dilli, who had previously overcome all those in three principalities that dared to engage him, was conquered by Nag Bamba, on which occasion the king (Padshah) sent him the title of Nag Bamba Mal. This chief and his allies had afterwards a long continued war with his sovereign lord, the Raja of Yumila, who wished to possess himself of Thenikot.

Long after this Raja Male Bamba Mal communicated his name to the principality. His son was Saha Bamba Mal, who was succeeded by his son Kirti Bamba, reckoned the sixtieth in descent from Dimba, but more probably from the first of the barbarian race from whom Dimba procured the country. The government of Kirti Bamba gave great dissatisfaction to his officers, who wished to dethrone him, and to place in his stead his own son Nrisingha Mal, then a child. This gave Bahadur Saha an opportunity of conquering the country with little difficulty. The Raja with his son retired to Balirampur, in the dominions of the Nawab Vazir, where the father shortly died, and the son, unable to suffer the heat, retired to the hills, and lives near Bhirkot on a small allowance from the Raja of Nepal.

Parbat or Malebum is a very elevated cold country, one-fourth of the whole being occupied by mountains covered with perpetual snow. It contains the remarkable hot springs of Muktanath, with mines of sulphur, cinnabar, iron, and copper, and some allege of zinc, (Dasta,) although by others this is denied. The mines of copper are said to be twenty-five in number, and produce a great revenue, besides what is used in the country and Thibet, sending large quantities to the plains of India. It also has three mines of Abrac or mica, and several places abound in rock crystal, (Phatik.) The crystals are said to be sometimes found as thick as a man's thigh, but their usual size is five or six inches in length. Gold also is found in the sands of several rivers, especially in the Krishna Gandaki or Narayani, the Bakhugar or Bathugar, the Modi, and the Mayangdi.

The upper part of the river, which in the plains of India is called the Gandaki, is called Kali, and, rising near a place called Damodur kund, runs through the territories of a Bhotiya chief, called the Mastang Raja, who is, or at least when I saw him in 1802, was tributary to Gorkha; but there is reason to think, that since that time the Chinese have compelled the Raja of Gorkha to cede both Mastang and Kerung. On passing the highest peaks of Emodus, the Kali enters Malebum, and receives from the east a small stream called the Narayani, which rises near the perennial snow from the warm sources of Muktanath, a very celebrated place of pilgrimage. The usual love of fable multiplies the number of these sources to 1000; but Sadhu Ram, who has visited the place, reduces the number to seven, and the most remarkable is the Agnikund or spring of fire, which is in a temple. The spring is not remarkably copious, but is perennial, and issues from among stones, accompanied by a flame, which rises a few inches. The water falls immediately into a well (Kund) or cistern, which is about two feet wide. On the whole, so far as I can understand the description, it entirely resembles the Sitakunda near Chitagang, that is, the water has no connexion with a subterraneous fire, and the flame is occasioned by the burning of an inflammable air, that issues from the crevices of a rock, over which the water has been artificially conducted. The streams of the Kali and Narayani unite at Kagakoti, take the name of Narayani, and are also called Krishna, Gandaki, and Salagrami, from the number of stones of that kind, which the channel contains.

Concerning these places Colonel Kirkpatrick states, * that four journeys beyond the capital, is situated Muktanath, within half a mile of which the Gandaki takes the name of Saligrami. It rises north from Muktanath; and not far from Kagbeini (Kagakoti) in the direction of Mastang, a place of some note in Upper Thibet, and twelve days' journey from Malebum. Three days' journey beyond Muktanath is Damodarkund, a celebrated spring or natural reservoir. The breadth of the Narayani at Beni, the capital of Malebum, is said not to exceed thirty yards wide. Colonel Crawford laid down the upper part of this river's course, from the authority of a Lama, who accompanied the Mastang Raja, which is better than that received by Colonel Kirkpatrick.

Thakakuti, some way below Kaga Koti, is the chief mart for the trade with Thibet through Mastang, and may contain one thousand houses. The Narayani is no where fordable below

---

* Nepaul, p. 287.

this place, and is crossed in some places on wooden bridges, (Sangga,) and in others on jholas or bridges of ropes made of rattans connected by cords of tough grass. Thakakuti is situated in a fine valley extending from Dhumpu to Kaga Koti, which is compared to the valley of Nepal, but is not so wide, and the hills around are covered with perennial snow. The plain is sandy. Danakoti, some way below Dhumpu, is a place of some trade. There is there a bad hill, but except over that, oxen could, with some difficulty, carry loads all the way from Rerighat to Kaga Koti. Goods are, however, conveyed mostly, if not entirely, on men's shoulders, or on sheep. Dhorali, the former abode of the Rajas, with the adjacent town of Beni, is still the most considerable place in Malebum. Kusma on the Modi, near its junction with the Narayani, has some commerce, but the great route of trade goes through the hills straight from Dhorali to Rerighat, and from thence to Butaul, without at all following the course of the river. Baglungchaur, according to Colonel Kirkpatrick, * is a large town and frot situated in a valley, and very opulent and populous.

In the whole country it is supposed, that there are 100,000 families, of whom three-fourths are Gurungs, occupying chiefly the country west and north from the capital, which is called Seshant. This country is cultivated with the hoe, and the crops are, 1. Barley. 2. Uya, which, I presume, is rye, the natives saying, that it is neither barley nor wheat, but has a resemblance to both. It must, however, be confessed, that it may merely be the kind of rice called Uya, which is reared on the high uneven land, that, in treating of Nepal Proper, I have mentioned in the account of agriculture; for the natives

* Nepaul, p. 289.

speak of the objects of natural history with such a want of precision, that much reliance cannot be placed on their comparisons. 3. Maruya, or Eleusine Corocanus. 4. Kanguni, (*Panicum Italicum*;) and, 5. Phaphar, said by some to be a species of Amaranthus, called Amardana in the low country; but others say that this is a mistake. The other crops are inconsiderable. The other part of the country, south and east from the capital, is called Khasant. One half of its inhabitants are Brahmans, mostly of the bastard (Jausis) race, who plough and carry burthens; one-fourth consists of Khasiyas, who call themselves Khatris; and one-fourth consists of other Hindus of a lower birth, but called also Khasiyas. Very few of even these spurious Hindus have settled among the Gurungs, and very few of the latter have remained in the Khasant. The houses in both parts have in general stone walls, and are thatched. Some of those belonging to the Gurungs have two stories.

Galkot, which belonged to a chief of the same family with Malebum, is a territory of small extent, but contains three mines of copper, and one of iron, which would be very productive, were there a sufficient number of miners, (Agari;) but there are only a few, and these have an exclusive right to work the mines. Although a cooler country than the valley of Nepal, it is the best cultivated in these parts, partly with the hoe, partly with the plough. Except in Malebum, the latter alone is used in all the territories hitherto described. The Raja's share of the revenue, including the mines, amounted to 3500 rupees a year. The whole number of inhabitants were reckoned at 3000 houses, of whom a half were low tribes of cultivators and tradesmen; one-fourth Khasiyas, and one-fourth Rajputs and Brahmans. The chief's house called Galkot was on a hill, the ascent to which is reckoned five coses long.

Around it were 500 houses, mostly thatched huts. Colonel Kirkpatrick * calls Galkot a considerable fort and town. The Raja, on being attacked by order of Bahadur Saha, submitted quietly, and remained in the country.

As I have said, these two last chiefs have been included among the Chaubisiya or twenty-four Rajas, agreeable to the reports I heard; although I think it probable, that they actually belonged to the Baisi or twenty-two Rajas.

At Rugun resided one of the twenty-two Rajas, whose territory was adjacent to Malebum on the west; but my informants had very little knowledge of that part of the country.

West from Rugun is Musikot, the chief of which also is said to have been one of the twenty-two Rajas.

West again from Musikot is Jajarkot, whose chief also belonged to the same class, and to the alliance, at the head of which was the chief of Malebum.

South from Jajarkot is Bangphi, which belonged to another of the twenty-two Rajas.

In the same direction I heard of Gajal, Dharma, and Jahari, three petty states also in alliance with Malebum, and probably belonging to three of the twenty-two Rajas, but that was not stated. Their situations are not placed in the maps, and Dharma may perhaps be a tribe of Bhotiyas, that was formerly subject to Yumila, and bore the name of Dharma.

In the maps again, I observe Satatala among the twenty-two Rajas; but I procured no verbal account of the place, and its name implies seven petty districts, so that, in place of being one petty state, it should have perhaps been marked as seven.

Malaneta is near it, and belonged to a chief of the Male-

---

* Nepaul, p. 288.

bum family, who lived in strict alliance with the Raja of Saliyana of the same race. The Malaneta Raja had no mines nor plain country, and was very poor.

Saliyana is also called Khasant, 10-16ths of its inhabitants being Khasiyas, or bastards of various kinds, 2-16ths are pure Brahmans, (Upadhyayas,) 1-16th bastard Brahmans, (Jausis,) and 3-16ths consist of various impure tribes. Saliyana, the residence of the chief, is situated on a large hill, and his house was built of brick, and covered with tiles. The other houses were mostly mud-walled huts. The air there is cool, although not so cold as Kathmandu. The Raja fortunately held some part of the plain belonging to the Nawab, and in a valley, between the mountains and a low ridge of hills, had a considerable mart called Jara Pani, or cool water, a tempting name on the burning plains of India. It is ten coses north-east from Balirampur, and is still a considerable thoroughfare, although not so great as Butaul. The Raja possessed also several mines, yet he was so poor, that, when the late chief married a daughter of Prithwi Narayan's, the young lady complained bitterly to her father, that he had bestowed her on a chief unable to give her food. Prithwi promised to give her the estate of the neighbouring chief of Dang, but died before this was accomplished. It was, however, done by Bahadur Saha, the lady's brother, and she and her two sons enjoyed their estates quietly, until Rana Bahadur was murdered. Bhim Sen, the present violent ruler, did not respect the daughter of the favourite hero of his country; but, when he seized Palpa, seized also on her estates, carrying her and her younger son to Kathmandu, where he allows them a very scanty subsistence. The eldest son fled to his estates on the plain, fortunate in having the protection of the Nawab Vazir, with whose dominions the chiefs of Gorkha do not interfere. Why they respect them more than the Company's, I do not exactly know; but that they do so is certain. This branch of the Malebum family is supposed to have governed for about 50 generations.

The Raja of Dang, the next neighbour to Saliyana, has adopted the rules of purity, and is connected by marriage with the Palpa family; but, whether he was reckoned one of the twenty-two Rajas, I have not learned, although, from his situation and family, being a Samal, that is, of the Malebum race, I think it highly probable. By Colonel Kirkpatrick, however, as I have already mentioned, he and the next chief of his family are both classed among the twenty-four Rajas. The chiefs formerly lived on a high hill called Dang; and, until deprived of this part of their estate, they had there a house called Chaugora; but for some generations they had withdrawn to Phalabamb, which was not on the plain, but on a hill immediately overhanging it. This town is now often called Dang, and consists of huts with mud or wooden walls, the Raja's house alone being built of brick. On the hills were several mines of iron; but the most valuable part of the chief's estate was on the plain, and consists of Pergunah Tulasipur, belonging to the Nawab Vazir. A part of this, called the Bhitari Tarai, is separated from the great plain of India by a small ridge of hills. The valley between this small ridge and the mountains is about six coses wide, and belongs partly to Saliyana, partly to Dang. I have already mentioned, that Bahadur Saha took the hills of Dang, and gave them to his sister, the Rani of Saliyana, but New Dang, or Phalabamb, was protected by the Nawab Vazir. Nawab Singha, who was deprived of his estates, was reckoned the fortieth chief of his race. He retired to a house called Barapate, twelve coses north from Tulasipur, and he usually resided there, although he had a house at Tulasipur. His son Dana Bahadur is now Raja of Tulasipur, and is said to have about 25,000 families of vassals. Among these are a few Upadhyayas, Jausis, and Khasiyas near Phalabamb; but the most numerous casts are Brahmas, Puns, and Ales, all impure: there are a good many Majhis and Darwes, both pure, and some Ghartis, partly Misal and partly Bhujal, both impure. Some Ghartis, who are pure, are called Khasiyas.

Chilli is a very small territory, partly on the plains and partly on the hills; but it produced, as the Raja's share, 2500 rupees a-year. The chief's residence was on a hill, the ascent to which may be 1½ cose in length. There is round his house a small town containing two hundred houses. He is of the Samal tribe, that is, of the Malebum family, and is a branch of the Dang chief's house. Being nearly connected with the Gorkha family by marriage, when his estates were seized, he went to Kathmandu, and procured the whole to be restored without even tribute. If Bhim Sen has respected them, he is the only chief from the Tishta to the Yamuna, that has retained his estates or power.

According to my ideas, Malebum, Galkot, Rugum, Musikot, Jajarkot, Banghpi, Gajal, Dharma, Jahari, Satatala, Malaneta, Saliyana, Dang, and Chilli, are fourteen of the twenty-two chiefs, so that there are still eight wanting; but Satatala, implying seven petty divisions, may account for six of these, and the two remaining may be Dalu Dailek, or Bilaspur and Duti, although I did not hear any such thing mentioned, and neither Raja is of the Malebum family.

By Colonel Kirkpatrick * the twenty-two Rajas are called

* Nepaul, p. 283.

Bansi, no doubt by an error of the editor for Baeesci, or twenty-two. Unfortunately the list, which he procured, is as imperfect as mine, and is as follows.

1. Jumla, (Yumila,) 2. Jajurkote, (Jajarkot,) 3. Cham, 4. Acham, 5. Roogum, (Rugum,) 6. Musikote 2d, (Musikot,) 7. Roalpa, 8. Mullyanta, (Malaneta,) 9. Bulhang, (Balihang,) 10. Dylick, (Dulu Dailek,) 11. Suliana 2d, (Saliyana,) 12. Bamphi, (Bangphi,) 13. Jehari, (Jahari,) 14. Kalagong, 15. Ghoorikote, 16. Gootum, 17. Gujoor, (Gajal ?) 18. Darimeea, (Dharma.) Of these the 1st, so far as I could learn, belonged to neither the twenty-four nor the twenty-two Rajas, but to the common chief of both classes, and the 9th, according to the information which I received, belonged to the class containing twenty-four chiefs. The 10th number confirms my conjecture concerning Dalu Dailek being one of the twenty-two chiefs. No. 3, 4, 7, 14, 15, and 16, are probably six of the seven chiefs, which in my list were included under the common name Satatala. Or if Satatala be considered as the proper name of one territory, the above-mentioned places would serve to complete the list. I have heard nothing myself concerning these places, and can find almost nothing in Colonel Kirkpatrick's work. From a route, however, which he gives,* it would appear that Chhamkote, probably the capital of Cham, is about thirty-one miles road distance west from the Karnali river, (Kurnali Kola,) and that Acham is thirty-two miles farther west. Both territories are west from Yumila, and in the route are said to have belonged to its chief. Acham he reckons seventy-two B. miles in a straight line from Duti, (Dhotee,) and about twenty-four from Yumila, four miles road distance, on long routes, giving only one in a direct line.

* Nepaul, p. 297.

The country between the Beri and Dalu Basandra, by Sadhu Ram, was called Bilaspur, while by the two Nidhis it was called Dalu Dailek, a name which should be preferred, as farther west there is another Bilaspur. The chief town is at Mathagari, where the government of Nepal, since the conquest, has built a fort. It is probable that Mathagari is the name of this fort, and that the former town was called Bilaspur, but I did not hear this mentioned. This capital contains about one hundred and fifty thatched huts. The chief's house is built of stone, and partly thatched, partly covered with tiles. The chief was called a Khas, but he rejected the rules of Hindu purity, and was probably one of the real ancient Khasiyas. When attacked by the forces of Bahadur Saha, he retired to some strongholds and began to plunder, on which all persons of his family that could be caught were put to death. This so terrified the chief that he fled; but to what place my informants do not know. There are in the country many Khasiyas, who, I presume, live impure like their former master. There were scarcely any pure Brahmans (Upadhyayas) in the country; but about one-eighth of the people were considered pure, and were called Jausis and Rajputs. The most remarkable thing, by far, in this petty territory is the place of worship called Dalu Basandra. There are three springs (Kunds) supposed to issue from the head, navel, and feet of Vishnu, (Sirasthan, Nabhisthan, and Padukasthan.) The central one is about 1½ cose from each of the extreme springs. At each place, according to Sadhu Ram, who once performed the pilgrimage, there is a small natural pool without any building. The water springs from the sand in the bottoms of the pools, and is very hot. Above the small holes from whence the water issues, of which there are several in each pool, a flame appears on the surface of the water.

West from Dalu Basandra was rather a considerable chief,

called the Duti Raja, who, according to Prati Nidhi, pretended to be of the family of the Sun; but, according to Hariballabh, the chiefs of this state were of a collateral branch of the Shalivahan family. According to Prati Nidhi, they had governed for about 40 generations, when Vishnu Sa, the son of Pradipa Sa, was dethroned by order of Bahadur Sahi. He was carried to Nepal, but Prati does not know what has been his fate. According, however, to Hariballabh, the chief who was expelled was Dip Sa, the son of Krishna Sa, the son of Mahendra Sa. He resided some years at Pilibhit, where he died, leaving three sons, who have retired to Mahmudi, in the Nawab's country, in great distress, the army of Gorkha having seized the whole of their lands on the plains, as well as on the mountains. I have, however, heard it stated, that very lately the heir has been taken into favour, and restored to his estates, on condition of paying an annual tribute. The country extended to the Kali-nadi, or Black-water, which separated it from Kumau, and through its centre passes the Setigangga, or White River. On the banks of this is a fine valley, two coses long and one broad, in which stands Dipal, the capital, surrounded on three sides by the river. It contains about 400 houses built of stone, and roofed with the same material. The Rajas possessed some territory on the plains. Of the whole population, pure (Upadhyayas) Brahmans composed a fourth, the bastard Jausis an equal share, Khasiyas 3-16ths, and low labourers and tradesmen 5-16ths. The principal crop was winter rice, the second Urid, the third Kurthi, and the fourth barley; all the others were small. The oil-seed chiefly reared was the Til, or Sesamum.

To the north of all these petty chiefs, and reaching within two days' journey of Dipal and Mathagari, is an extensive country called Yumila, which, towards the west, was once bounded by the territory of Gar, or Garhawal, the capital of which is Srinagar; and towards the east by Mastang, as it extended to Kagakoti on the Narayani, at the northern extremity of Malebum; but towards the east it was much straitened by Jajarkot, which extends to within a few coses of Chhinachhin, the capital. Large territories also had been gradually seized from its prince, by the chief of Kumau, who had extended his dominions to the snowy mountains.

The chief of Yumila was a Rajput, and he was long acknowledged as the supreme lord or king over all the mountain chiefs towards the west; at least, as all my informants from that quarter declared, and they extended his authority to the east also; but this was entirely denied by Hariballabh, and in these parts his information is more to be trusted than that of the others. We may safely, however, conclude, that his superiority was acknowledged everywhere between the Kali river and Nepal. His authority, however, was still more limited than that of the late Cæsars of Germany, his subjects frequently levying war, not only against each other, but against their sovereign; nor was there any assembly of states from which he could obtain assistance against a common enemy. His power probably resembled that possessed by those who were called the sovereign kings of India, before the Muhammedan conquest, and consisted in three privileges. Each chief sent him an annual embassy, with presents; he bestowed the mark of royalty (Tika) on each heir, when he succeeded; and he had a right to interfere in keeping the stronger from overrunning the weaker, and to exhort all chiefs to preserve the balance of power. Except persuasion, however, no means seem to have existed to enforce co-operation. Still, however, the evident common benefit of such a power seems long to have given it some effect; although, in the struggle for universal dominion by the chiefs of Gorkha, it never seems on any one occasion to have been employed.

Etawargiri is a merchant nominally dedicated to religion, (Atithi,) who was born at Chhinachhin, and who still adheres to the Raja. He left the country when very young, but has since made three journeys thither to purchase horses, there being at the place several merchants of this order, who deal to a considerable amount. They carry up metals, spices, and cloths; and bring down cow-tails, salt, horses, a woollen cloth called Pheruya, medicinal herbs, musk, &c.

Etawargiri, setting out from Tulasipur, in the dominions of the Vazir, crossed the Bheri, and proceeded through Jajarkot, the territory of which reaches within three coses of Chhinachhin; but from Jajarkot to the boundary took him nine days over a hilly country. At the boundary he entered a fine plain cut with deep ravines, like that of Nepal, but well cultivated. It is said to extend eight coses from north to south, and fifteen from east to west. It is cultivated by the plough drawn by oxen, and produces much wheat, barley, *phaphar*, and *uya*; with some *urid*, peas, lentiles, and maize, and a little transplanted rice. Sugar-cane, *kodo*, (*Paspalum frumentaceum*, Roxb.) and *chana*, (*Cicer arietinum*, Lin.) will not grow there, for there is snow in winter. In this level part of the country, each ploughgate of land is said to pay ten rupees a-year; but in the high poor parts of Yumila, one rupee is the rent.

According to the accounts which Colonel Kirkpatrick received,* this valley is nearly of the same extent as that of Nepal, but is rather more contiguous to the Himaliya mountains, and more chequered with low hills. The ridge of mountains immediately to the north is called Seela pahar, (Sweta pahar, white mountain,) and makes part of the greater Himaliya.

* Nepaul, p. 292.

Chhinachhin is a large scattered place. All the houses are built of brick or stone, and have flat roofs. The two most remarkable temples at Chhinachhin, at least in the opinion of Etawargiri, belong, of course, to Siva. The one is called Chandranath, the other Bhairav'nath. In the daily market are exposed for sale the birds called Manal and Dhangphiya, mentioned above, (page 95,) and another called Chakuri, which I do not know, unless it be the Chakor, mentioned in page 95. These are commonly eaten. There are also exposed for sale many sheep and goats, loaded with salt, musk, medicinal herbs, and a seed called Bariyalbhera. Near Chhinachhin there are some of the cattle whose tails form the chaungri * chamar, or changwari, of the vulgar tongue, and the chamari of the Sangskrita, and they are very numerous in the hilly parts. Sadhu Ram says, that in Bhot there are three kinds of cow; the Changwari, the Lulu, and the Jhogo. The tails of all the kinds are bushy from the root, but those of the changwari are the most valuable. None of these kinds of cattle have the undulated dew-lap of the Indian cattle.

Besides the plain on which Chhinachhin is built, the Rajas held a very great extent of narrow vallies and mountains, many of the latter perpetually covered with snow. Towards the east, the country extended fifteen days' journey to Bhot. I know from other circumstances, that it reached to Kagakoti on the Narayani, which is said to be about nineteen miles east from Butaul, and Chhinachhin is nearly north from Dalu Basandra, which, according to the map that I procured, is 124 miles west from Butaul; the fifteen days' journey gives, therefore, 143 miles direct distance, or about 9½ miles for each. Chhinachhin, at this rate, allowing it to be six miles from the boundary,

* Chowri, Kirkpatrick's Nepaul, p. 133.

would be about ninety miles north from Jajarkot, which is nearly north from Dalubasandra, and Jajarkot, according to the map deposited in the India House, is 108 miles from the plains of India. But to admit these situations as accurate, we must suppose, that the snowy mountains take there a great bend to the north, which is not said to be the case, and we must, therefore, allow that Jajarkot stands much farther south than it is placed in the map; and that Yumila is much nearer Jajarkot than Etawargiri supposes.

Colonel Kirkpatrick gives a route from Beni, the capital of Malebum, to Chhinachhin, the two places lying east and west, distant by the road 250 coses. Their actual distance, by the native maps, being about 143 miles, will give, on a long route, rather more than half a mile (0.57) of direct horizontal distance for the cose of road distance.

One of the most important productions of Yumila is salt, which is said to come from a place called Mukhola, reckoned ninety or a hundred miles road distance from Chhinachhin, towards the north-east. It is said, that, at Mukhola, there is a large space, containing many pools, that in winter are covered with snow. When this melts in spring, the water is thrown out, and cattle are turned into the muddy pools to tread the bottom with their feet. As summer advances, a crust of salt is formed, and removed. I do not understand the nature of such a process, and suspect some mistake, as the dialect spoken by Etawargiri was not clearly understood by any of my people, much less by myself.

About half way between Chhinachhin and Mukhtanath is a frontier fortress of Yumila called Tibrikot. It is remarkable for a temple of the goddess Tibrisundari.

About one-fourth of the people in this country are Brahmans, Rajputs, and Khasiyas, who follow the doctrines of the present Hindu law. The Bhotiyas are on the whole the most numerous tribe, and with Gurungs, Rohanis, Khatis, and Rahals, all impure mountain tribes, make up the remaining three-fourths, who chiefly adhere to the Lamas. The language spoken at Court was the Khas, but differed very much from that of Palpa or Gorkha; even the titles of the chief officers of government were totally different, although the same forms of administration were established. For instance, the Chautariya of Palpa was in Chhinachhin called Hitan, and the Karyi of the former was the Bist of the latter.

According to Hariballabh the Rajas of Yumila were of the Suryabangsi tribe, and were admitted to be pure, so as to intermarry with the chiefs of Kumau and Garhawal. They had penetrated into the northern hills about 500 years ago; but, as I have above mentioned, were far from having expelled or persecuted the ancient inhabitants. It was said by the Mahanta of the Janmasthan at Ayodhya, that they first settled in the Almora country, and thence removed to Yumila; and as the Duti Raja, acknowledged to be of the Shalivahan family, is also called a Suryabangsi, I think it probable, that the Rajas of Yumila are the descendants and representatives of Asanti and Basanti, and this will explain the vassalage to them, which all the eastern chiefs avowed, although the people of Kumau, by whom the Yumila chiefs were stript of the best part of their dominions, deny this vassalage, and pretend to know nothing of their descent.

When Rana Bahadur attacked the country, it is universally admitted, that he was opposed by Sobhan Sahi; but, according to Etawargiri, this person was Raja, while Kanak Nidhi says that he was the Raja's brother, and Hariballabh alleges that that he was the uncle of the chief. For two years he resisted the troops of Gorkha, and had collected a force of 22,000 men;

but Rana Bahadur, watching a favourable opportunity when most of these had retired to their homes, completely surprised the country, and acted with such vigour and cruelty, that no force durst afterwards assemble. A son of Sobhan, named Munsur Sahi, has fled for protection to the Taolakhar or Taklakhar Bhotiyas, and Hariballabh says, that the old chief is now at Lasa. He also says, that the Raja was carried to Kathmandu, where he died after some confinement. He was not used harshly, and was allowed two rupees a-day for his subsistence. A son of the Yumila chief, and acknowledged as the heir of the family, but whether son or nephew of Sobhan Sahi, I do not know, lives at Tulasipur, in the Vazir's country, along with the Dang Raja, his former vassal.

Yumila on the north is bounded by the great snowy ridge called there Humla, by which it is separated from the country of the Taolakhar or Taklakhar Bhotiyas, now certainly subject to China, and in the map of Hariballabh their capital is called Taklakot.

Near Taklakot, between two parallel ridges of Emodus covered with everlasting snow, Hariballabh places two lakes, Manasa Sarawar Vulgo Manasarowar, and Ravanhrad, which receives the water flowing from the former. On their west side is a vast peak named Kailasa, which the Hindus suppose to be the residence of the Gods. The valley, east and west from the lakes, and extending to a great width between the two ridges of the snowy mountains, is deeply covered with snow in winter, and then the shepherds retire lower down; but in summer it is covered with flocks, the pasture being short, close, and rich. A river flows from each end of the Ravanhrad, or rather from each lake. That going to the west is called the Satudra and Satrudra, and turning to the south forms what we call the Satluj. It must, however, be observed, that, according to Hariballabh, there rises from the northern ridge of that eastern part of the valley another river, which, as in the Chinese map of Thibet published in Duhalde, runs west parallel to the Satrudra. Hariballabh does not know its name. It was called to him the river of Ladak, as passing that city. From many other persons I have learned, that this river of Ladak passes north from Kasmira; and, if not the chief branch, is at least one of the greatest of those which form the Indus.

The river that flows to the east from the lakes is named the Karanali, and, according to Hariballabh, who has seen this part of its course, after flowing a short way in that direction, passes through the southern ridge of snowy mountains, and waters Yumila; but he does not know that part of its course, and has only heard that it passes on the west side of Dalu Basandra. Kanak Nidhi calls the river thus passing Dalu Basandra, the Sonabhadra; but Sadhu Ram told me, that its name is the Karanali, or Salasu, for many rivers of these parts have a variety of appellations, that is very perplexing to the geographer. He says, that west from Dalu Basandra, it is a river as wide as the Gandaki, where that river comes into the plain, which I have formerly described. Etawargiri says, that the Karanali passes near the salt mines of Yumila, and then turns west, passing north from Chhinachhin, in which case it must take a very large bend to the east from Ravanhrad, and then another to the west, before it reaches Dalu Basandra.

As connected by trade with Yumila, I may here mention, that the Chinese, in the part of Thibet, north-east from Manasarowar, and beyond the second range of Emodus, have a very valuable gold mine. It can only be wrought in summer, and those who wish to mine pay seven Mashes of gold for every solid cubit of mineral that they dig. They also give to the government all pieces of gold which they find that weigh more than three Mashas; all the smaller bits they keep to themselves. Thirteen Mashas are equal to a Furrokhabad rupee, that is, each contains between thirteen and fourteen grains.

CHAPTER SECOND.

OF THE COUNTRIES WEST FROM THE RIVER KALI.

Kumau; History, State.—Garhawal; History, State.—Sirmaur.—Twelve Lordships.—Besar.—Hanur.

KUMAU is a very considerable territory bordering with Duti on the east, the boundary being the Kali Nadi. On the west it has Garhawal or Gar, and it extends a considerable way into the plains of Bareli; but all that it has there is subject to the Company.

It is generally agreed, that the founder of the family of Kumau was Thor Chandra, a needy, but high born descendant of the family of the Moon, who, about 350 years ago, left Jhausi or Pratishthan, opposite to Allahabad, in quest of fortune. He was accompanied by a pure Brahman, equally necessitous, and named Jaydev, from whom the two Nidhis, my informants, claim a descent. According to Hariballabh, the two adventurers agreed that they should repair to the hills, and endeavour to procure service. If they succeeded, they should by degrees invite some comrades, and by their assistance, they expected to overpower their master, and seize his dominions, which were to be equally divided. They accordingly found service from an impure chief of the Jar or Magar cast, it is not worth while investigating which, my informant considering both equally vile. This fellow had a small territory, for which he paid tribute in peace to the Rajas of Karuvirpur; who, although of pure and high extraction, scandalously suffered their subjects to wallow in abomination. Having secured this man's favour, and invited some pure men like themselves, the two servants cut off their master, expelled the monsters his subjects, and settled the country with pure Hindus, building the town of Champawati, or Kurmachal, as it is called in the language of the Gods; but the word in the language of men has somehow been corrupted into Kumau.

The soldier, when not actuated by zeal for purity, was an honourable man; and, no sooner had he acquired this territory, than he offered the half of it to the priest; but Jaydev declined the troublesome office of government, and contented himself with stipulating for the hereditary office of register (Kunungoe) and steward (Zemindar) for all the estates, which the prowess of the Rajas might acquire. Thor Chandra was succeeded by his son Kamir C., whose son, Nirbhaga C., having died without legitimate heirs, the chief officers sent to Jhausi, and procured as a chief another needy descendant of the Moon. His whole revenues amounted to about 3000 rupees a-year, and like his predecessors, pure and impure, he paid tribute to the Rajas of Karuvirpur.

In this state the family continued, until the time of Bala Kalyan C., son of Kirti C., son of Bhishma C., son of Guru Gyangn C. This Kalyan married a daughter of the Raja of Duti, a collateral branch of the Karuvirpur family, and by her obtained Sor, as an addition to his inheritance. Their son, Rudra C., was a man of great abilities. In his time the family of his sovereign, the Karuvirpur king, was involved in dissensions, twenty competitors claiming the succession. Rudra, having a high character, was chosen by these unfortunate chiefs as umpire; and entered the capital under pretence of investigating their claims. When in full possession, he declared that they were all low fellows, descended only of Shalivahan, while he was a descendant of the illustrious Budha, and, therefore, seized on the sovereignty, giving each competitor a little land in a place called Manur in the Pergunah of Pali, where their descendants still remain, and are called Manuriya Rajputs. Rudra now built Almora, and made it the seat of his extended government. This was in the time of the Mogul Akbur, one of whose officers, having attacked Almora, was defeated, and Rudra advancing into the plain, obtained a jaygir eighty coses long and five wide, then overgrown with woods. The intelligent chief, however, brought inhabitants, and settled six Pergunahs, Rudrapur, Sabna, Belahari, Nanakamata, Kasipur, and Reher, which produced a revenue of 1,000,000 rupees; and in the first mentioned Pergunah he built a fort of the same name. He afterwards became a favourite of the kings, who granted him permission to coin money in the royal name, and Persian character. No other hill chief had a mint except Nepal, the Rajas of which have always coined money in their own name, and in the Nagri character. Rudra finally took Siragar from his kinsman the Raja of Duti, for he was one of those great men that do not hesitate about trifles. He was succeeded by his son Lakshmi, who was a saint, and had four sons. The three eldest, Dilip C. Vijay C. and Trimala C. succeeded each other, and had no male issue. Nila Singha, the youngest brother, left a son, Baz Bahadur, who succeeded his uncle Trimala, and was another man of great activity. He attacked the Yumila Raja, who after the overthrow of Karuvirpur, was probably the proper representative of Asanti, and who was acknowledged as liege lord by all the chiefs of the mountains. From this prince Baz Bahadur took Danpur, Joyar, and Dharma. Joyar was a very large territory, including Baropathi and

Munsiyari; and both it and Dharma, like the other territories of Yumila, were chiefly inhabited by Bhotiyas, and other impure monsters, who, on the conquest, were totally expelled or destroyed, and the rules of purity established. Jagat C., son of Gyangn C., son of Udyot C., the son of this Baz Bahadur, was, like his great-grandfather, a conqueror, and took Chaudas from Yumila, after which the family began to decline. His son, Devi C., had a dispute with Muhammed Shah, which was amicably settled by means of Raja Jaya Singha. He had no son, and was succeeded by Kalyan C. his grand-uncle, the youngest son of Udyata, C. This old man was succeeded by his son Dip, who had the misfortune to be born dumb, and to give himself entirely up to religious exercises, leaving the whole management of his affairs to his wife and officers. His first favourite was Jaya Krishna, a Brahman descended of Jaya Deva, the companion of Thor Chandra. This person, by the intrigues of the queen, (Rani,) was displaced, and the power transferred to Mohan Singha, a person of the chief's family, who was in command of the army. He soon displeased the lady, and, being a man of ungovernable passions, he retired to Dundiyu Khan, a Rohilla chief; and, having procured some assistance, returned and put the lady to death. Jaya Krishna now applied to Hafez, another chief of the Rohillas, who gave him some men, with whom he put Mohan to flight. This chief retired to Lakhnau, and watched there, until he learned that Jaya Krishna was employed in collecting the revenues of the country. He then, with a small band, advanced suddenly, and privately seized Almora, and, having sent the poor creature Dip, and his four sons, to the fortified hill of Siragar, he declared himself Raja, and, as usual, took the title of Chandra. His first care was to inveigle Jaya Krishna into his power, which he did by numerous assurances of friendship, and offers of employment. The Brahman was outwitted, and went into the castle of Kotaghat, where, as he advanced to embrace the Raja, who stood with open arms, a soldier struck off his head. Mohan then imprisoned Harsha Dev, the brother of Jaya Krishna; and, thinking himself firmly established, ordered Dip and his four sons to be thrown over the castle wall, which was done, and they were dashed to pieces. Jaya Deva, however, an uncle of Harsha Dev, went to Lalit Sa, Raja of Garhawal, and, having obtained 4000 men from him, drove out Mohan C.; but could not release his nephew, who being very warlike, was considered as of great importance, and was carried off by Mohan; soon after, however, he contrived to escape. The uncle and nephew then conferred the government on Pradyumna Sa, a younger son of their benefactor, the Raja of Garhawal, who took the title of Chandra, while the uncle was appointed (Nayeb) chief civil minister, and the nephew commander of the forces, (Bukhshi.) On the death of his father, Pradyumna, during three years, disputed for the succession of Garhawal with his elder brother Jayakirti; but without success. The elder brother, then dying without male issue, Pradyumna became undisputed owner of Garhawal and Kumau. He had a younger brother named Parakrama, of a very intriguing disposition, who, having been gained by Mohan Chandra, persuaded Pradyumna to dismiss Harsha Dev, who retired to the low country; and Kumau, being entrusted to weak hands, was recovered by Mohan Chandra, who held it for sixteen months. Harsha Dev could no longer suffer this, but attacked his enemy, and, having taken him and his son prisoners, he put them both to death. In this he vented his hatred on the father by a barbarous refinement of cruelty. Under pretence of not shedding royal blood, he kept his unfortunate rival without food, and daily beat him, until he expired. It is said that he suffered for seventeen days, but this seems incredible. The Brahman then placed on the throne a certain Siva Chandra, who was alleged to be of the family of Kumau, and acted as his chief minister. About this time the forces of Golam Kader having been dispersed by the Mahrattas, many of them were engaged by Lal Singha, whom some call the son, and others the brother of Mohan Chandra. With these troops this chief drove out Harsha, who fled to Garhawal. He there entered into an alliance with Parakrama, the Raja's brother, his former enemy, and both attacked and defeated Lal Singha, who had advanced into Garhawal to meet them. He was driven into Almora, where he contrived to form a treaty with Parakrama, by which Mahendra, the son of Mohan, was made Raja, and Harsha was placed in confinement. From this, however, he soon contrived to escape, and retired to the plains. Siva Chandra was allowed to escape, as having been a mere tool in the hands of the Brahman. In this state were affairs, when Damodar Pangre, the officer commanding the troops of Gorkha, sent his brother Jagajit and Amar Singha Thapa to attack the country. They were joined by Harsha Dev', and met with very little resistance. Lal Singha and Mahendra Chandra the Raja retired to Rudrapur, where Mahendra died, leaving a son named Pratap Singha. Their valuable estates in the low country are in the Company's possession, nor has it been determined to whom they will be given; for there are several competitors. Pratap claims as heir to the family, but his father was an usurper, although it would appear, that all other more direct lines of the family have now failed. Harsha claims as heir of Jaydev, who, by the agreement with Thor Chandra, should be Zemindar (collector) and Kanungoe (register) for the whole, availing himself of the interpretation, which has been given in our courts to the term Zemindar, (landlord.) The widow of

Siva Lal claims, as her husband, being deputy of Harsha, was in actual possession when the country was ceded by the Nawab. The widow of Lal Singha and Siva Lal are allowed pensions.

Almora on the Soyal contains, according to all accounts, about 1000 houses. According to Hariballabh, it is situated on the narrow ridge of a hill abounding in fine springs of water. Champawati, the ancient capital, called Kurmachal in the Sangskrita, may contain 200 or 300 houses, and is cooler than Almora. The only other towns are Ganggoli and Pali, each containing about 100 houses. In these towns the houses are built and roofed with stone, and several are two or three stories high. The population of the hills was estimated by Prati Nidhi at 50,000 families. All the impure tribes had been destroyed, except a very few Jars and Magars in Baropathi, that had been lately taken from Yumila, under which government these people enjoyed full toleration. The Brahmans are not numerous, all living a pure life, and abstaining from intercourse with the low tribes. The Rajputs form the most numerous class, but all, who are poor, except the descendants of Shalivahan, hold the plough. The Sudra tribes of cultivators are Ahir, Jat, Lodi, and Chauhan. Near Agra the Jats by other casts are reckoned the same with Ahirs; although, being there powerful, in their own territories they call themselves Rajputs. In the mountains they are considered as mere Sudras, and different from the Ahirs, an undoubted tribe of the plains, as are the Lodi; but I suspect, that the Jats and Chauhans of the mountains are original tribes converted to Hindu purity; for one of the Chauhan chiefs, at the time of the conquest of Gorkha, was still impure, although acknowledged to be of the same family with those who pretend to have come from Chitaur.

The mountains produced copper, lead, and iron, and the

Panar river produced gold; but no mine was of great value. The chief crop is summer rice, but there is also much wheat, and some barley. The parts conquered from Yumila are cold, but abound in pasture, and produce great flocks of sheep. The whole rents of the mountains, exclusive of lands granted to Brahmans, amounted to 125,000 rupees a-year, the whole of which, as usual west from the Kali river, was collected by the Raja's officers; but since the conquest, much has been granted to the army of Gorkha. The government is one of the best in the country, and with the title of Raja, is held by Brahma Saha, one of the Chautariyas.

There is much intercourse with the part of Thibet subject to China, which empire in the Khas dialect is called Hung. Between the countries there are three passes through the southern ridge of Emodus, Joyar, Dharma, and Beyas. The two last are the easiest, but they are inferior to Riti in Garhawal. Beyas is in a portion of Yumila that has been annexed to Almora, since the conquest by Gorkha.

The country now called Garhawal or Gar, at least in part, formerly belonged to a petty chief of low birth, but pure manners, who resided at Chandpur, and paid tribute to Karuvirpur. About 350 years ago, a Pangwar Rajput, named Ajayapal, came from the plains, and entered into the service of the chief of Chandpur, whom he soon after took occasion to expel. The descendants of Ajayapal paid the customary tribute to the prince of Karuvirpur, who, as usual in India, seems to have given himself no concern about these internal commotions among his tributaries. After Karuvirpur fell, the Rajas of Chandpur paid tribute to Almora; but, while Lakshmi Chandra held the latter government, Mahipat Sa, Raja of Garhawal, at the persuasion of a religious man, who promised success, declared himself independent. This person built Srinagar, and made it the capital of his dominions, on which account his descendants are usually known to Europeans as Rajas of Srinagar. This chief was succeeded by his son Syam Sa, who died without male issue, and was succeeded by Futeh Sa, his uncle's son. This chief incurred a great stain by delivering up to Aurungzeb one of that king's brothers, who had taken refuge in the mountains. As a reward for his treachery he received the Jaygir of Dun and Chandi, two low country estates. Futeh had two sons, Upendra and Dilip, and was succeeded by the former, who took from the chief of Besariya the countries of Ranigar and Barahat, on the upper parts of the Yamuna and Ganges rivers. When he died, his lady was pregnant, and no chief was appointed until the result was known, which shows that the government and succession were firmly established. The widow having been delivered of a daughter, Pradipa Sa, the son of Dilip, a boy five years old, succeeded quietly, and governed seventy-five years. He was an active prince, administered his affairs with great attention, and had several wars with Nuzuf Khan, who governed the petty remains of the Mogul empire. His son and successor was Lalit Sa, who, as above mentioned, made his younger son Raja of Kumau. Mention has also been made of the manner in which this son, named Pradyumna, succeeded his brother as Raja of Garhawal. After the conquest of Kumau, Jagajit Pangre and Amar Singha, the officers commanding the army of Gorkha, in conjunction with Harsha Dev, the turbulent Brahman often already mentioned, attacked Garhawal. They had fought two years, and were on the point of succeeding, when they were recalled by Bahadur Saha, the regent of Gorkha, in consequence of a Chinese army approaching the capital. The commanders of Gorkha, especially Jagajit, complied most reluctantly, and made a peace with Garhawal. The Brahman, their associate, now considering their affairs desperate, on being desired to accompany them, treated the request with insolence, asking who they were, that he should follow. They had, however, only retired a little way, when information was brought, that peace had been made with the Chinese, on which the Brahman immediately fled.

Garhawal enjoyed a respite, until Rana Bahadur returned from Banaras, when he sent Amar Singha Thapa with 3000 fusileers, and an equal number of irregulars, to extend his territories to the west. No pretext, I believe, was held out for the attack; indeed, so far as I can learn, the natives do not consider the holding out any pretence as at all necessary or proper in war, although, in treating with Europeans, they have now learned to make very appropriate observations on the subject. Rana Bahadur, on the contrary, when collecting this force, I am credibly informed, gave very publicly out, that it was destined to go either to Calcutta or Pekin, he had not exactly determined which; and had he considered the force adequate, there is no doubt that he would have made the attempt, although he was on very good terms with both governments. This violence, however, was suddenly directed against the helpless Pradyumna, who made little or no resistance; but with his brothers Parakrama and Pritama, and his son Sudarsan, retired to Dun, and from thence to Keni near Haridwar, in the territory then lately acquired by the Company. There, very contrary to the wishes of his brother Parakrama, the Raja sold the family throne for 150,000 rupees. This sum enabled him to raise some forces, with which the three brothers returned to Dun, and fought the army of Gorkha near Gurudhana. The Raja was killed, Parakrama escaped to Haridwar, and Pritama, having been shot through the foot, was taken prisoner, but is kindly used, and has married a daughter of Brahma Sahi, the governor of Almora. Sudarsan, the undoubted heir of the family, in 1814, was with Sir Edward Colebroke at Futehgar. He was then about twenty-six years of age, and has, it is said, good abilities; but was addicted to an expence ill suited to his means, which were very slender. His uncle Parakrama died without children, in the country of the Sikhs.

Chandi was taken from the family by Asof ud doulah, the Nawab Vazir. Dun, having been a Jaygir from Aurungzeb, should belong to the king at Dilli; but it has been seized by the government of Nepal. It produced a rent of 50,000 rupees a-year. The rent of the mountains amounted to 400,000 rupees, the whole levied by the Rajah's officers, but a large proportion has been granted to the military establishment by the government of Gorkha. There are three valuable mines of copper, the Raja's share of which was 76,000 rupees. Salt is imported from Thibet, with which there are three communications. One, a little west from Ganggotri, is difficult. The other two lead from the vicinity of Badrinath. That by Manu has no supply of fuel, but that by Riti is reckoned the best passage through Emodus, at least in these western parts. At Tapoban, towards Badrinath, is a hot spring. Rock crystal abounds in the vicinity of the snow.

The country near Emodus is very cold, and produces many sheep. The lower hills are warm, and produce most rice and wheat, but also many other crops.

Srinagar the capital is in a very hot valley, and contains about 2000 houses. There is no other town, but many celebrated places of worship, which seem to have been sacred among the Hindus for many ages. How these people came to establish places of worship in countries that, until of late, were occupied entirely by impure infidels, can, in my opinion, be only accounted for by supposing, that, when these places of worship became fashionable, the Hindus had not become pure, nor had they adopted the faith now reckoned orthodox. Four of the five places called Prayag, all celebrated as places of great sanctity for bathing, were in this principality, as is also the source of the most sacred of rivers, called therefore the Ganggotri, or source of the river. It comes from the southern face of the southern ridge of Emodus. Kedarnath is a temple dedicated to Siva, but the works are petty, and ruinous. Badrinath, dedicated to Vishnu, was lately rebuilt at a considerable expence by orders of Daulat Rao Sendhiya. Near the temple is the village called Kalap gram. The Hindus, who know nothing of the place except from books, imagine that many holy persons have retired to this place, where they have been living for many thousand years, in quiet expectation of better times. To pilgrims, who go there in expectation of meeting these personages, a cave is shown as the place of their residence; but as the cave is filled with snow, there is no fear of the good folks being disturbed, until these degenerate times pass away, and the age of gold is restored.

The whole original tribes have been expelled from this sacred territory.

West from Garhawal and the Yamuna, is the territory of Siramaura or Sirmaur, the capital of which is Nahan. It lately belonged to a family of the Raythaur tribe, which had held the country for about fifteen generations, and was descended from a younger son of the Jaysalmer family. The first Raja of Sirmaur, whom Hariballabh recollects, was Vijay Prakas, who married a daughter of Jagat Chandra of Kumau. He was succeeded by his son Pradipa Prakas, who, like his father, was a tame inoffensive man. His son Kirti Prakas succeeded when eight years old, and died in his twenty-sixth year; but during this period of youth he fought many battles with the Mogul officers, and took from them Larpur, Narayangar, Ramgar, and Pangjaur, all on the plains of India; but he left there untouched Rayapur, which belonged to a Chauhan, whose sister he had married. He would not consent to pay any tribute for these acquisitions, but obtained a grant of them in Jaygir from Ali Gouhur the Mogul, giving 100,000 rupees as a present. Turning then against his neighbour chiefs, he strengthened his frontier to the west by the conquest of Jagatgar, reckoned a very strong place, which had belonged to the Raja of Nurpur. He also attacked the Raja of Bilaspur, and wrested from his authority the superiority of twelve petty chiefs, who did not obtain the title of Raja, but were called Thakurs or Ranas. These had formerly paid tribute to the Raja of Bilaspur, and followed the standard of that chief in war; but these duties were now transferred to the chief of Sirmaur. This vigorous youth then attacked Garhawal, and endeavoured to wrest from its chief the fertile territory of Dun; but he died at Kalsi, after several fruitless battles had taken place between his brother Iswari Singha, and Lalit Sa, the chief of Garhawal. This young chief, by three wives, left four sons, and was succeeded by the eldest, Jagat Prakas, aged ten years. When in his fourteenth year, he set out for Kangra to marry the sister of Sangsar Chandra, the chief of that country; but on the way was met by the Raja of Bilaspur, his mortal enemy, who refused a passage through his territory. The youth, with the premature vigour of his family, instantly cut his way through his opponents, and married the lady. His brother-in-law wished to persuade him to return by the low country, and thus to avoid any contest; but the young hero disdained to show any mark of fear before his bride, and her brother giving an addition of 2000 men to his suite, they forced their way back. Having made a pilgrimage to Jaganath, Jagat Prakas determined to accomplish the conquest of Dun, which had been relinquished on his father's death, and he soon succeeded. He died at the age of 28 years, leaving no male issue, and was succeeded by his brother Dharma Prakas.

At this period Sangsar of Kangra, having become very violent, made an attack on the Rajas of Mundi and Bilaspur, who applied for assistance to Dharma of Sirmaur. This chief having received from them 200,000 rupees, and having been promised as much more, joined them with his forces, and the three Rajas advanced together to fight Futeh Chandra, the brother of Sangsar, who commanded the forces of Kangra. They were, however, entirely defeated, and Dharma fell in the battle. He was succeeded by his brother Karna Prakas. Sangsar now persuaded the Raja of Hanur to turn against his ally and chief, the Raja of Sirmaur, promising that he would render him independent, and place him at the head of the twelve chiefs that had been alienated from Bilaspur, and rendered tributary to Sirmaur. On this Karna invited to his assistance Amar Singha, the officer who commanded the forces of the Nepal government in Garhawal. This officer sent to his assistance Bhakti Thapa with 1000 fusileers, and these, united to the troops of Sirmaur, advanced to the west in search of their enemies. They were soon, however, compelled to retire by the united forces of Sangsar and Hanur. On this Sangsar entered into a negociation with Krishna Singha, the son of Iswari Singha, the uncle of Karna, and with his assistance plundered the family of that chief. He fled for assistance to Amar Singha, who advanced with his whole forces, and soon subdued Hanur, and the adjacent countries, leaving Karna in the possession of his estates.

Afterwards Amar Singha attacked Kangra; and, when he was compelled by Ranjit Singha, king of Lahaur, to make a disastrous retreat, he applied to Karna, requesting an interview.

The chief of Sirmaur, thinking the affairs of the Nepalese desperate, at least in that quarter, sent an insolent reply, on which he was immediately attacked by Ranajor, the son of Amar Singha, and fled without resistance. The troops of Gorkha then took possession of all his estates on the hills, while various chiefs seized on those upon the plain. His cousin Krishna retains Narayangar, which he seized, when he plundered his kinsman's family. Karna lives near Rayapur with the chief of that place, who is his relation. His wife and son have gone to Lodhyana, in hope of procuring assistance from the English.

When the Raythaurs arrived, the territory of Sirmaur was occupied by two tribes of Khas, called Bhats and Karets, of which the former was, as it still is, by far the most numerous, and they now form the greater part of the cultivators or Zemindars. Until the arrival of the Raythaurs, it is admitted that no Brahmans resided in the country; yet Hariballabh contends, that even then the Kanets and Bhats were not of the aboriginal infidel Khasiyas, but were descended of pure Sudras, who had come from the plains, on which their Gurus and Purohits resided, and made them occasional visits. These Bhats must not be confounded with the poets or parasites of the plains, and in their own country do not wear the thread of distinction; but some, who have gone to the low country, on finding the high rank which the Bhats there enjoy, have put on the thread, and call themselves poets.

The mountains of this state produced a rent of 70,000 or 80,000 rupees a-year. The low country gave 200,000. The chief crops on the mountains were rice and wheat. West from the Yamuna there are no mines of copper, and few even of iron; but one of these is in Sirmaur.

Nahan contained about 1000 houses, mostly built of stone, and in rather a cool situation. Kalsi, the only other town, contains about 100 houses.

Hariballabh does not remember the names and situations of all the twelve petty states governed by Thakurs or Ranas, who were tributary to Sirmaur, and followed its chief in war. The tribute was very inconsiderable. Among them were the following.

Dharmapur belonged to Dalel Singha, a Baghatiya Rajput, who was killed by the chief of Hanur. The lord (Thakur) did not live at Dharmapur, but the name of his capital has escaped the memory of Hariballabh. Taksal is the largest place in the country, and has about 200 houses. It is the principal mart for ginger and turmeric, which are produced most abundantly in the estates of the twelve lords, (Bara Thakurai,) and in Sirmaur.

The lordship of Arki, east from Dharmapur, belonged to a Gagat Singha, expelled by Amar Singha, who now has his head-quarters at the capital of this petty state, a town containing about 300 houses, besides the huts in the cantonments. His force consists of 3000 fusileers, and 1000 men armed with matchlocks, but they have a great body of followers, male and female, and these last are eager and expert plunderers.

The lordship of Kothar was very petty.

Mahalok was a little better.

Bhajji was still better, having an annual rental of 15,000 rupees.

Kengothal was worth about 50,000 rupees a-year.

Kumarsen paid annually 30,000 rupees.

Borbhakan paid 15,000 or 16,000.

Between the three last mentioned there was another lordship, of which Hariballabh does not recollect the name, nor does he recollect either the names or situations of the three remaining lordships.

North from the countries of these lords is Besar, a country of little value, but its chief was independent, and was called Raja. Many of his subjects were Bhotiyas, although he himself was a pure Rajput. The country is very cold, and produces many sheep. By the side of the Satrudra there is a very good route to Thibet, and much wool is imported that way. Rampur, the capital, contained between 400 and 500 houses. Anup Singha, who was lately Raja, died four or five years ago, leaving an infant son, who was immediately attacked by the troops of Gorkha. These seized on the capital; but the Bhotiyas carried their young chief to the fastnesses of the country, and reject the yoke of strangers.

I have already mentioned the Raja of Hanur, whose country bounds Sirmaur on the west, and whose rebellion and subsequent invasion of that state introduced the overwhelming power of Gorkha. The Rajas are of the Chandel tribe, and of the same family with the chiefs of Kumau and Kahalur. The earliest Raja that Hariballabh remembers was Bhup Chandra, who was a violent man, and held not only the country of Hanur on the mountains, but that of Palasi on the plains. This was worth 50,000 rupees a-year, while the mountains paid about twice as much. The chiefs did not pay any tribute, but in war they followed the standard of Sirmaur. Bhup Chandra was succeeded by his son Gaja Chandra, whose son Rama Chandra joined Kangra against Sirmaur, as already mentioned. On the approach of Amar Singha he retired to Palasi, which was saved by the interposition of Colonel Ochterlony, who threatened to interfere, and Amar Singha contented himself with the hills. Nalagar, which, until of late, was the capital of Hanur, contained about 500 houses; but Rama Chandra built a new town farther in the hills, and Nalagar was neglected. The new town he called after his own name, as he does also another town which he has built since he settled on the plain.

SUPPLEMENT TO THE ACCOUNT OF NEPAL.

SOME INFORMATION RESPECTING THE PETTY CHIEFS WHO STILL REMAIN INDEPENDENT TO THE WEST OF THE DOMINIONS OF NEPAL OR GORKHA.

Kangra.—History.—State.—Kahalur.—Bhomor.—Kotlahar.—Yasawal.—Datarpur.—Gular.—Nurpur.—Chamba.—Kullu.—Mundi.—Sukhet.

THE intelligence procured from Hariballabh extending somewhat farther west than the present dominions of Gorkha, but to no great distance, it may be given as a Supplement to the foregoing Account.

The country between the Satadru or Sutluj and Kasmira in ancient times belonged to Susarma, a chief of the family of the Moon, who was a principal ally (Paksha) of Durjadhan, competitor for the kingdom of India, at the commencement of this iron age. In the terrible battle, which settled the succession in the family of his adversaries, Susarma escaped, and his descendants long governed his country. The genealogy of this family is said to be contained in the Mahabharat, but is not to be found in the Sri Bhagwat, or other books from which I have had the Indian genealogies extracted. The Raja of Kangra pretends to be descended of this family, which, he alleges, has enjoyed uninterrupted possession of at least a part of its original estate, until the present day. The late Rajas, however, have been called Katauch Rajputs, for what reason I do not know; and the present chief is said to be desirous of being called a Chandel, for this tribe is generally admitted to be descended of the family of the Moon. Many others, however, allege, that the Katauch tribe sprang from the sweat of the goddess, spouse to Siva, when she was cut to pieces; and, when these were scattered by her husband and Vishnu, her thorax fell at Kangra, which has ever since been considered as holy; and once, probably, this descent was considered more honourable than that from the family of the Moon. No one, in fact, knows the real origin of the family, which, however, is generally admitted to be old, and to have consisted of fifty or sixty chiefs, of whom the first is usually said to have been a Bhup Chandra. Hariballabh does not remember any of his successors, until the time of Abhay Chandra. He had three sons, the eldest named Nirbhag C., and the youngest Ghaman Singha. The former had no son, and, when he died, his youngest brother was in the service of Pradipa of Garhawal, who was then at war with Siva Dev', the general of Kumau. This crafty Brahman gave the needy chief 700 Ashrufies of gold, and induced him to withdraw his men, and return to his own country. On his arrival he found his brother just dead, and nine or ten of his kinsmen squabbling about the succession. He therefore took off their heads, and ascended the throne, (Gadi.) He subdued several Rajas, such as Kottahar and Ghowasin, became a terror to all the petty chiefs in the vicinity, and removed the seat of government from Jaya Singhapur to Sujanpur, which he founded; for the fortress and town of Kangra had been long in the hands of the Muhammedans. He was succeeded by his son Tikayit Chandra, who, in his fourteenth year of age, had a son named Sangsar Chandra, the present chief. When eighteen years of age, Tikayit C. was caught by Khan Bahadur, who was Subahdar of Lahaur under Muhammed Shah. He was confined for some years, and then restored to liberty, but died at the age of twenty-five years, leaving the country to his young son. This youth became the most violent and formidable chief of his family, and recovered Kangra from the Muhammedans. All the neighbouring chiefs were then afraid, and he extended his conquests on the plains by seizing on the estate called Rajawara, which belonged to the king of Dilli. He removed the seat of government to Nadaun, but has many places of residence, especially a fine fortified garden at Alumnagar. I have already mentioned his dispute with Gorkha, during which Amar Singha besieged, or rather blockaded, the citadel of Kangra, for he was in possession of the town. He was opposed by Anirudra, the son of Sangsar. Bhakti Thapa besieged Sujanpur, which was defended by Man Singha, brother of Sangsar, and by Harsha Dev', the warlike Brahman of Kumau, often already mentioned. Sangsar himself, with a small body of chosen men, hovered round the besieging armies; but, these being likely to prevail, he invited to his assistance Ranjit Singha, who affects to be called king of Lahaur; and with his assistance the forces of Gorkha were repulsed with great loss. For this assistance, however, he paid dearly, as he ceded to Ranjit the fort and city of Kangra, and the fort of Kotta, with a territory of 50,000 rupees a-year, and all the petty chiefs now despise his authority, and respect the power of Lahaur. He still, nevertheless, retains a territory yielding from 900,000 to 1,000,000 rupees a-year.

The town of Kangra is open, and, before the attack by Amar Singha, contained about 2000 houses. Near it is the temple of the goddess, which is supposed to contain many rich ornaments of gold. The fort is the strongest in these parts. The situation is rather warm. Kotta, although inferior to Kangra, is considered as a stronghold of importance.

Sujanpur, which remains to Sangsar, contains about 2000 houses, and is surrounded by lines, which are said to be twelve coses in circumference, and besides the town, contain twenty-four villages, in which there may be 3000 houses.

Nadaun, the present capital, contains about 500 houses. Jwalamukhi was a considerable town, where many Gosaing merchants had settled; but during the disturbances it was plundered by the Raja of Gular, who had joined Amar Singha. At this place, where the tongue of the Goddess fell, in the dispersion of her members, above-mentioned, there is a small temple, perhaps twenty feet square. It is paved with large stones, and from a hole in one corner, perhaps two inches in diameter, there issues a constant flame, that at the lowest ebb rises about eighteen inches, but in the rainy season it issues with great violence, and flame bursts from several parts of the floor, and also from some places without the temple.

Although most parts of the country are high, the ascents from the plains below are easy, and the summits of the hills are level, so that a large proportion is fit for cultivation, and is well occupied. The poor live much on maize. Great quantities of rice are exported to Lahaur, and there is plenty of sugar-cane.

None of the infidel tribes remain. The most numerous cast is said to be that called Jat, to which not only the Ranjit of Lahaur belongs, but also Ranjit of Bharatpur. The tribe is considered pure, but in Kangra is not permitted to wear the thread of distinction, belonging to the military tribe.

Kahalur I have already mentioned as belonging to a branch of the Chandel family, that governed Kumau and Hanur. It was always able to resist Kangra, but has been occasionally squeezed by the Muhammedans, and by the Sikhs of Lahaur. Devi Chandra is the first Raja that Hariballabh remembers. So long as he lived, he was able to resist all his neighbours, and entered into a friendship with Prithwi Narayan of Gorkha, which has continued uninterrupted between their descendants, so that Maha Chandra, the son of Devi, lives under the protection of Amar Singha. The family at one time possessed Govindapur on the plain; but this was long ago seized by various petty Sikh chiefs. The country on the hills may produce 100,000 rupees a-year. Bilaspur, the capital, is the best town in these parts, and contains about 3000 houses, better built than usual. They consist entirely of stone, and are two or three stories high, with flat roofs. The air is very temperate, and snow falls occasionally in winter.

On the west side of the Satadru or Sutluj is one of these vallies called Dun, which is contained between the great range of mountains on the north, and a low ridge on the south. This valley is divided among many petty chiefs. Its east end, called Bhomor, belonged to a Rajput who had only the title of Rana: but, although he always leagues himself with some powerful chief, whom he follows in war, and from whom he receives protection, he may be called independent, as he pays no tribute. His revenue may be 8000 or 9000 rupees a-year.

West from Bhomor, the Dun, or valley, is for some way occupied by petty Sikh or Singha chiefs, who, like all those beyond the Satadru, are under the king of Lahaur.

Between these Singhas and the territory of Kangra, the hills are occupied by the petty state of Kottahar, which, as I have mentioned, was subdued by the chiefs of Kangra; but Mahipat, its owner, having joined Amar Singha, was by him replaced in his patrimony, which he retains. Although small, Kottahar is a fine country, and produces 50,000 or 60,000 rupees a-year. Raypur, the capital, contains between 200 and 300 houses.

West from Kottahar is the lordship of Yasawal, to which belong part of the hills, and part of the valley or Dun. For its size, it is exceedingly rich, as it produces about 200,000 rupees a-year. It belongs to Amed Singha, a pure Rajput, who is squeezed sometimes by Sangsar and sometimes by Ranjit, and is compelled to follow them in war. He resides at Rajgar or Rajpur, which is by nature strong, and contains about 2000 houses. It is colder than Nadaun. The chief possesses on the plain a fort called Setabgar.

West from Yasawal is the chief of Datarpur, who has also some territory in the valley and some on the hills. These may annually produce 40,000 rupees.

West from Datarpur is such another lordship, called Siva, the revenue of which may be 25,000 rupees a-year. Like the chief of Datarpur, the lord of Siva is squeezed by both Sangsar and Ranjit.

On the hills between these two petty chiefs and Kangra is Gular, whose chief is of the same family with Sangsar, but he pays tribute to Ranjit. His country is very productive, and pays about 250,000 rupees a-year. Haripur, his capital, contains from 1000 to 1500 houses, which are reckoned very well built.

West from Gular and Siva is Nurpur, the Raja of which possesses part of the hills, part of the Dun or valley, and part of the great Indian plain. What he has on the latter is called Pathankot, from the name of his tribe, for he is a Pathaniya Rajput, not a Pathan Muhammedan. Dalel Singha, the last chief, survived his son, and was succeeded by his grandson, Vir Singha, who married a daughter of Sangsar. His revenue may be 250,000 rupees a-year. Nurpur, the capital, contains about 2500 houses, among whom are some settlers from Kasmira, who have fifty looms employed in weaving shawls.

North from Nurpur is an extensive dominion, situated on both sides of the Rawi, and called Chamba. A long ridge of mountains, the summits of which are covered with perpetual snow, separates from the great ridge of Emodus, near the source of the Bepasa, or Bayas, and, running to the south-east, passes near Kangra, then crosses the Rawi, and finally bends to the north-west, towards Kasmira. This ridge, called Pariyat, in general forms the south-east boundary of Chamba; but, on its south side, the chief possesses a territory called Rillu. This was invaded by Sangsar, and Ray Singha, the chief of Chamba, was killed in its defence. The territory was restored to Iswari, the son of Ray, on condition of his paying annually 17,000 mans of rice. This tribute was transferred to Ranjit, along with the fortress of Kangra.

The parts of Chamba beyond the Pariyat mountains are very cold, and have several communications with Thibet, but Hariballabh knows that part by report alone.

Separated, in general, by the Pariyat mountains from Chamba, is the country of Kullu, watered in the centre by the Bayas, called Bepasa in the Sangskrita, but its territory extends to the Satadru of the sacred language, which, in the dialect of men, is called Satarudra. Kullu is extensive, but cold, mountainous, and barren, producing, however, many sheep. The grains which grow there are mostly phaphar, chuya, and uya. The chuya, from the description given, would seem to be the Holcus sorghum, although the coldness of the situation renders this doubtful. There is a very good communication between Kullu and Thibet; and the intercourse has been so free, that all alliances with the chief, although admitted to be a pure Rajput, are scouted by the purer inhabitants of the southern mountains. His name is Ratra Singha, the son of Pritama.

South from Kullu is Mundi, a smaller but better country, which possesses a mine of iron, and another of culinary salt, the latter of which is valuable. So far as I can understand the description, it is a rock salt, very full of impurities, so that one-half is lost in the processes of lixiviation and evaporation, which are requisite to fit it for use. The two mines produce annually a revenue of 150,000 rupees, and the lands produce as much. The present chief, named Iswari Sen, is a pure Rajput. Mundi, his capital, contains about 1000 houses, all of stone. Kamalgar, towards the southern frontier, is reckoned a very strong place, situated on a great hill.

Sukhet is a narrow territory, hemmed in between Mundi and the Satadru, which separates both from the dominions of Gorkha. The Raja Prakas Sen is related to the chiefs of Mundi, and Sangsar has married his sister. The country produces about 100,000 rupees a-year, but has no mines. Sukhet, the capital, may contain 500 houses. The Raja possesses a fort called Dahar, which defends him from the attacks of Kahalur.

REGISTER OF THE WEATHER,

FROM

FEBRUARY 1802

TO

MARCH 1803.

Astronomical Day.	PLACES.	Lat. N.	Fahrenheit's Thermometer. Noon.	3 Hrs.	9 Hrs.	16 Hrs.	Barometer. Noon.	3 Hours.	9 Hours.	16 Hours.	Winds by the Compass. Noon.	3 Hours.	9 Hours.	16 Hours.
1	Ghorasan	26°50′	76	79	61	54	29.58	29.52	29.51	29.48	S. 1	S. 1	W. 1	E. 1
2			76	77	62	53	29.62	29.56	29.57	29.57	S. 1	W. 1	W. 1	W. 1
3			72	76	62	55	29.67	29.60	29.59	29.58	S. 1	W. 1	W. 1	E. 1
4			73	77	63	58	29.72	29.65	29.64	29.64	SE. 1	W. ½	W. 1	E. 1
5			73	77	63	58	29.70	29.63	29.59	29.58	E. 1	E. 1	N. 1	E. 1
6			75	78	62	58	29.65	29.57	29.58	29.57	S. 2	E. 1	E. 1	E. 1
7			77	80	66	60	29.66	29.59	29.59	29.59	S. 1	SW. 1	E. 1	E. 1
8			77	80	66	61	29.65	29.61	29.59	29.58	SW. ½	SW. 1	E. 1	N. 1
9			79	82	71	68	29.67	29.64	29.63	29.62	E. 1	WSW. 1	E. 1	
10			76	83	69	63	29.65	29.63	29.63	29.60	NE. ½	SW. ½	NE. ½	
11			83	86	69	61	29.69	29.63	29.63	29.59	NW. 1	W. 2	W. 1	
12			80	86	71½	65½	29.71	29.65	29.69	29.67	E. 1	W. 1	0	E. 1
13			81	87	71	65	29.69	29.65	29.69	29.67	E. 1	E. 2	NE. 1	
14			79	84	68	59	29.77	29.71	29.69	29.67	NW. by N. 1	N. by W. 1	NW. by N. 1	
15			79	88	66	59	29.76	29.69	29.68	29.63	SW. 1	W. 2	W. 1	
16			81	88	70½	63½	29.68	29.60	29.57	29.54	W. 2	W. 3	W. 1	
17			77	83	68	57	29.63	29.57	29.58	29.61	W. 3	W. 2	W. 1	
18			80	83	65½	58½	29.71	29.67	29.64	29.64	E. by S. 1	E. by S. 1	E. ½	
19	Kachruya	26°53′	69	66½	59½	54	29.73	29.57	29.64	29.63	E. 1	E. 2	E. 1	
20			77	80	69	59	29.72	29.65	29.64	29.60	E. 1	E. by N. 1	E. 1	
21			80	84	67	55	29.64	29.55	29.53	29.48	W. 1	W. by N. 2	0	
22			79	81	66	53	29.56	29.49	29.51	29.49	SW. 1	W. 1	0	
23			78	79	65½	62	29.57	29.50	29.48	29.44	N. 1	SW. 1	0	
24			70	71	65½	62	29.56	29.54	29.52	29.50	E. 1	E. 1	E. 1	
25			75	77	65	56	29.58	29.49	29.50	29.49	SW. 1	SW. 2	0	
26			78	79	67	62	29.54	29.51	29.49	29.53	W. 1	W. 2	0	
27			74	78	62	58	29.65	29.61	29.68	29.64	E. 1	SE. 1	E. 2	
28			73	76	60	59	29.68	29.59	29.62	29.36	W. 2	W. 1	0	
Particular average,			76.68	80.02	64.87	59.06	29.6586	29.6092	29.5893	29.5807				
General average, 70.155							29.60945							

for February 1802.

OBSERVATIONS.

Moderate dew.	Few or no clouds.	Atmosphere hazy.	
Id	A few clouds.	id	Wind in the forenoon, E. 3.
Id	id	id	id
Id	No clouds.	id	id
Id	id	id	Wind in the forenoon, 2.
Id	A few clouds.	id	id
Id	id	id	id
Id	id	id	A few drops of rain in the morning.
Id	More clouds.	id	id
Id	Thick clouds in the afternoon. Clear in the morning. Atmosphere hazy.		
Id	A few clouds.	Atmosphere hazy.	
Id	id	id	A few drops of rain at night.
Id	Many clouds.	Atmosphere less hazy.	
Id	id	id	
Id	A few clouds.	Atmosphere clear in the forenoon.	
Id	Few or no clouds.	Atmosphere hazy.	
Little dew.	id	id	
Id	Many clouds.	id	
Heavy dew.	Cloudy afternoon, with rain at 3 o'clock.	Clear atmosphere in morning.	
Id	Few or no clouds.	Atmosphere hazy.	
Id	Some clouds.	id	
Id	id	id	Morning foggy.
Little dew. A cloudy morning, with a few drops of rain. Atmosphere hazy.			
Heavy rain from 14 to 16 hours, with little wind from the NW. accompanied by moderate thunder.			
Foggy morning. Atmosphere clear.			
Clouds and sunshine. Heavy rain with thunder from the NW. between 15 and 18 hours.			
Id		id	at 9 hours.
Id	Heavy dew.	id	Atmosphere hazy.

N. B.—In the columns of the winds 0 marks a calm, 1 denotes slight breezes, 2 moderate breezes, and 3 strong winds.

Astronomical Day.	PLACES.	Lat. N.	Fahrenheit's Thermometer. Noon.	3 Hrs.	9 Hrs.	16 Hrs.	Barometer. Noon.	3 Hours.	9 Hours.	16 Hours.	Winds. Noon.		3 Hours.		9 Hours.	
1	Kachruya	26°53′	77	80	68	59	29.70	29.64	29.64	29.58	E.	1	SW.	1	0	
2			79	81	68	57	29.61	29.54	29.51	29.51	E.	1	W.	1	0	
3			79	81	67	58	29.63	29.56	29.54	29.51	S.	1	S.	1	0	
4			78	81	69	57	29.63	29.56	29.55	29.49	N.	1	N.	1	E.	1
5			78	83	70	62	29.60	29.53	29.54	29.52	E.	1	E.	1	0	
6			84	86	70	65	29.63	29.59	29.54	29.57	E.	1	E.	½	0	
7			80	82	72	64	29.64	29.55	29.55	29.58	SW.	1	W.	1	E.	½
8			80	84	68	59	29.64	29.54	29.52	29.51	W.	1	W.	2	0	
9			82	85	73	59	29.52	29.44	29.46	29.42	NW.	1	N.	2	W.	2
10			82	86	70	56	29.51	29.45	29.48	29.50	W.	3	W.	3	W.	1
11			83	87	70	58	29.57	29.47	29.47	29.50	W. NW.	2	W. NW.	2	E.	1
12			82	86	70	63	29.60	29.52	29.52	29.50	E.	2	E.	1	0	
13			84	88	70	64	29.57	29.50	29.48	29.46	S.	1	SW.	1	0	
14	Bhagawanpur	26°55′	86	91	72	62	29.55	29.44	29.48	29.44	W.	1	W.	3	0	
15			84	89	71	59	29.56	29.51	29.51	29.48	W.	1	0		0	
16			86	90	69	59	29.60	29.52	29.51	29.48	W.	1	W.	1	0	
17	Kachruya	26°53′	84	90	78	62	29.56	29.48	29.48	29.48	W.	1	W.	1	0	
18	Ghorasan	26°50′	88	89	69	60	29.56	29.52	29.55	29.54	W.	3	W.	2	0	
19			86	91	74	60	29.56	29.53	29.55	29.54	W.	2	W.	1	0	
20			86½	91	76	64	29.65	29.60	29.58	29.57	W.	1	0		W.	1
21			86	90	72	68	29.66	29.58	29.56	29.54	W.	2	W.	1	0	
22			84	89	75	68	29.57	29.49	29.44	29.43	E. by S.	3	E. by S.	2	E.	1
23			83	86	73	70	29.46	29.38	36.38	29.38	E.	2	E.	2	E.	3
24			78	84	73	67	29.43	29.39	29.41	29.39	E.	3	E.	1	E.	1
25	Norkatiya	26°50′							29.42	29.42	E.	3	E.	2		
26			86	87	83	71	29.45	29.40	29.41	29.38	E.	2	0		0	
27	Dhonhara	26°55′	84	88	78	70	29.42	29.37	29.42	29.42	E.	2	E.	1	0	
28	Jukiyari	26°59′	86	90	75	70	29.48	29.44	29.42	29.41	E.	2	0		0	
29	Gar Pasara	27° 8′	86	91	78	68	29.41	29.30	29.32	29.29	E.	1	W.	3		
30	Bichhakor	27°16′		87	72	69		28.68	28.67	28.64					0	
31	Hethaura	27°26′			73	67			28.38	28.31	E.	1	0			
Particular average on the plain,			82.91	86.64	72.18	62.82	29.565	29.49	29.49	29.477						
Id for two last days,				90½	76½	69		29.37	29.37	29.35						
Particular average among the hills,				87	72½	68		28.68	28.525	28.475						
Particular average of the month,			82.9	86.8	72.11	65.41	29.565	29.08	28.93	28.98						
General average,				76.42				29.124								

for March 1802.

OBSERVATIONS.

Heavy dews.	Clouds and sunshine.	Atmosphere hazy, so that the hills are not visible.
Id	id	id
Id	id	id
Id	id	Atmosphere less hazy than usual. Thunder and a little rain at 22 hours.
No dew.	Fewer clouds than usual.	Atmosphere hazy.
Clouds and sunshine. From 11 to 13 hours a strong wind at NW. with much thunder and a little rain.		
Id	Heavy clouds about 9.	Atmosphere less hazy, so that the hills were visible.
Id	Little dew id	
Id	id	Atmosphere continued clear till the morning, afterwards hazy.
Id	Moderate dew.	Atmosphere hazy.
Id	id	id
Id	id	id
Id	id	id
Id	id	id
Id	Little dew.	Atmosphere hazy.
Id	Moderate dew.	id
Id	id	id
Id	id	id
Id	id	id
Id	Little dew.	id A few drops of rain at 16 hours.
Id	id	id
Id	id	id A few drops of rain at 5 hours.
Id	id	Sky clouded in the morning, but the atmosphere less hazy.
Id	id	id
Id	No dew.	Atmosphere hazy. Thermometer broken.
Id	id	id New Thermometer.
Id	id	id
Id	A little dew.	id
Id	No dew.	id
Id	id	id
Id	id	id

Astronomical Day.	PLACES.	Lat. N.	Fahrenheit's Thermometer.				Barometer.				Winds.			
			Noon.	3 Hrs.	9 Hrs.	16 Hrs.	Noon.	3 Hours.	9 Hours.	16 Hours.	Noon.	3 Hours.	9 Hours.	Sunrise.
1	Hethaura	27° 26′		80	69	60	28.56	28.49	28.43	28.42	E. 1	E. 1	E. 1	E. 1
2			80	85	73	63	28.46	28.36	28.32	28.29	E. 1	E. 1	0	E. 1
3			81	86	74	63	28.37	28.31	28.30	28.27	S. by W. 1	S. S. W. 1	N. 1	N. 2
4			78	86	74	68	28.27	28.21	28.18	28.18	E. 1	S. 1	N. W. 1	N. E. 1
5			81	81	76	63	28.24	28.16	28.22	28.19	0	0	N. 1	E. ½
6			82	85	73	64	28.27	28.22	28.26	28.21	0	S. 1	N. N. E. ½	S. W. 1
19	Kathmandu	27° 41′	79	81	67	59	25.38	25.29	25.29	25.28	S. W. 1	S. W. 2	S. W. 1	
20			83	82	63		25.35	25.39	25.45		S.W.byW. 1	S.W.byW. 1		
21			81	83	69	59	25.44	25.44	25.44	25.44				
22			83	83	75	64	25.47	25.47	25.47	25.47	W. 1	W. 1	0	N.N.W. 1
23			75	80	73	64	25.47	25.41	25.47	25.50	N. W. 1	W. 1	0	0
24			78	82	72	58	25.49	25.46	25.52	25.42	S. 1	S. W. 1		0
25			73	79	71	57	25.44	25.39	25.41	25.41	W. ½	W. ½	0	0
26			74	80	72	64	25.47	25.44	25.49	25.54	W. 1	W. 1	0	0
27			77	79	72	62	25.52	25.44	25.49	25.48	W. 1	W. 1		
28			75			62	25.50			25.44				E. 1
29			79	82	74	60	25.46	25.37	25.47	25.44	W. 1	W. 1	W. 1	W. 1
30			76	82	70	61	25.46	25.43	25.51	25.41			0	W. 1
Average of the first 6 days below the hills,			80.4	83.8	73.1	63.5	28.3616	28.2916	28.285	28.26				
General average below the hills, -				75	2			29	29.955					
Average of the last 12 days above the hills,			77.75	81.18	70.72	60.9	25.4541	25.4118	25.4555	25.439				
General average above the hills, -				72	63			25	44					

for April 1802.

OBSERVATIONS.			
Heavy dews, clouds, and sunshine.		Atmosphere thick and hazy.	
Little dew,	id	id	
Id	id	id	
Id	id	id	
Id	id	id.	A few drops of rain at 3 hours.
Id	id	id	
The mercury fell entirely below the scale, nor had I any convenience, during the journey to Kathmandu, to cut down the case of the barometer, nor to register the observations of the thermometer and winds.			
Clouds and sunshine.	Little dew.	Some showers on the hills.	
Id	At 7 hours a heavy shower of hail. Atmosphere hazy.		
Id	Much dew. Atmosphere hazy.		
Id	id	id	
Id	id	id	
Id	id	id.	Thunder and rain at 7 hours.
Id	id	id	
Id	id	id	
Id	id	id.	Thunder and some rain in the evening.
Id	id	id	
Id	id	id.	Thunder, with a threatening of rain in the evening.
Id	id	id	id

Astronomical Day.	PLACES.	Lat. N.	Fahrenheit's Thermometer. Noon.	3 Hrs.	9 Hrs.	16 Hrs.	Barometer. Noon.	3 Hours.	9 Hours.	16 Hours.	Winds. Noon.	3 Hours.	9 Hours.	Sunrise.
1	Kathmandu.	27° 41′	76	83	74	63	25.47	25.45	25.49	25.49	W. 1	0	0	W. 1
2			81	82	75	61	25.52	25.47	25.51	25.55	W. S. W. 1	S. 1	0	N. 1
3			80	83	74	64	25.53	25.53	25.48	25.51	W. 2	S. W. 2		W. 1
4			78		75	70	25.57		25.57	25.57	W. 2	W. 3	W. 3	0
5			76	82	72	61	25.52	25.43	25.56	25.51	W. 1	W. 2	0	0
6				76	69			25.49	25.47		W. 1	W. 2	0	
7			71	75	67	64	25.18	25.43	25.46	25.46			0	N. 1
8			72	74	69	64	25.54	25.52	25.52	25.54	N. 1	N. 2	0	N. 1
9			76	78	66	60	25.54	25.51	25.62	25.59	S.W.byW. 1	N. 3	E. 1	0
10			73	80	73	65	25.58	25.51	25.54	25.53	W. 1	W. 2	W. 1	N. 1
11			78	82	75	64	25.56	25.50	25.54	25.53	N. 1	W. 2	0	W. 1
12			69	76	71	63	25.56	25.50	25.51	25.51	W. 1	S.W.byS. 1	W 1	0
13			73	75	70	66	25.55	25.51	25.53	25.49	W. 1	S. E. 1	0	W. 1
14			75	79	66	62	25.57	25.47	25.51	25.52	W. 1	S. W. 1	0	0
15			69	68		61	25 53	25.44		25.45	W. 1	W. 1	W. 1	W. 1
16			73	77	65	60	25.44	25.36	25.36	25.36	S. W. 1	S.W.byW. 1	0	W. 1
17			72	71	66	60	25.51	25.34	25.38	25.41	W. 1	W.N.W. 1	S. W. 1	N.W.byW. 1
18			74	75	69	61	25.43	25.36	25.39	25 40	W. S. W. 1	W.S.W. 2		W. 1
19				79	75	64		25.40	25.37	25.41	W. N. W. 1	W. S. W. 1	0	S.W.byW. 1
20			78	83	72	65	25 47	25.42	25.45	25.43	W. 1	N.W.byW. 2	0	S.W.byW. 1
21			76	80	72	67	25.48	25.42	25.38	25.42	W. S. W. 1	S. W. 2	0	S. E. 1
22			80	78	73	66	25.42	25.36	25.31	25.34	S. E. 1	S. E. 2	W. 1	W.N.W. 1
23				80	73	64		25.29	25.33	25.31	N. N. W. 1	N. N. W. 2	0	W. 1
24			81	82	74	66	25 33	25.26	25.26	25.29	W. 1	W. 2	0	S.W.byW. 1
25			79	82	75	66	25.29	25.25	25.25	25.30	S.W.byW. 1	S.W.byW. 2	W. 1	W. S. W. 1
26			78	81		64	25.30	25.24	25.24	25.28	S. W. 1	S. W. 2	W. 1	0
27			80	85	74	68	25.34	25.28	25.28	25.28	S.W.byW. 1	S.W.byW. 1	0	S.W.byW. 1
28			80	83	73	66	25.32	25.25	25.25	25.32	W. 1	S.W.byW. 2	W. 1	S.W.byW. 1
29			75	80	72	67	25.34	25.33	25.33	25.37	W. S. W. 1	S.W.byW. 1	W. 1	S. W. 1
30					74	64			25.31	25.32				
31			80	81	74	66	25.37	25.39	25.34	25.33	S. W. 1	S. W. 2	0	0
	Particular average,		76	78.96	71.62	64.66	25.4652	25.4038	25.418	25.4306				
	General average,		72.81				25.4044							

for May 1802.

OBSERVATIONS.

Moderate dews. Atmosphere hazy. Clouds and sunshine.
Id id id Thunder in the evening.
Id id id
Id id id
Id Atmosphere clear in the morning. Heavy rain in the evening.
Atmosphere hazy. Heavy rain at night.
Atmosphere clear. The hills as usual covered with clouds, and partially visible.
Id Clouds and sunshine. Heavy dews.
Atmosphere hazy. id Thunder in the evening to the S. E.
Id id Moderate dew.
Atmosphere clear. Clouds with occasional sunshine. Thunder and rain at night.
Atmosphere hazy. Clouds and sunshine. Moderate dews.
Id id id Thunder in the evening.
Id id Much rain in the afternoon.
Considerable rain in the afternoon. A thick fog in the morning.
Id Morning clear.
A little rain in the afternoon. id Heavy dew.

Atmosphere clear. Clouds and sunshine. Heavy dew.
Id id id.
Id id Heavy rain from 14 to 16 hours.
Id id Dew.
Id id id.
Hazy. id A little rain at 10 hours.
Id id
Id id
Clear. id
Cloudy. Slight showers all night.
Clouds and sunshine. Atmosphere clear.
Id id A little rain in the afternoon.
Id id

Astronomical Day.	PLACES.	Lat. N.	Fahrenheit's Thermometer. Noon.	3 Hrs.	9 Hrs.	Dawn.	Barometer. Noon.	3 Hours.	9 Hours.	Dawn of Day.	Winds by the Compass. Noon.	3 Hours.	9 Hours.	Sunrise.
1	Kathmandu.	27°41′	80	85	76	65	25.34	25.37	25.36	25.35	WNW. 1	SW. by W. 3	0	W. ½ S. 1
2			81	84	76	66	25.35	25.30	25.24	25.30	W.SW. 1	WSW. 2	0	W. 1
3			80	84	75	66	25.35	25.31	25.33	25.34	WSW. 2	SW. by S. 3		
4			79	86	74	70	25.31	25.29	25.63	25.31				
5			79		72	68	25.40		25.38	25.41			0	SW. by W. 1
6			77	80		69	25.39	25.39		25.41	NW. by W. 1	NW. 1	W. 1	WSW. 1
7			76	81	76	71	25.43	25.38	25.38	25.37	W. 1	W. 1		
8			77	81	73	68	25.39	25.34	25.37	25.42			0	SE. 1
9			77	82	73	70	25.37	25.37	25.35	25.31	SE. 1	SE. by S. 1	SW. 1	S. 1
10			79	83	73	70	25.31	25.23	25.23	25.20	S. 1	SE. 1	W. 1	SW. by W. 1
11			78		73	68	25.22		25.12	25.12	SW. by W. 1	W. 1	0	SW. 1
12			76	75	70	68	25.10	25.08	25.06	25.05	S. 1	S. 1	0	W. 1
13			73	76	70	68	25.08	25.00	25.01	25.07	W. 1	W. 1	0	SE. by S. 1
14			73	74	69	68	25.03	25.02	25.11	25.10	SE. by S. 1	SE. by S. 1	0	W. 1
15			76	72	69	67	25.10	25.06	25.06	25.11	S. 1	S. 1	SW. by W. 1	SW. by W. 1
16			78	78	71	70	25.08	25.08	25.07	25.07	W. 1	W. 1	0	SW. 1
17			80	80	74	70	25 11	25.06	25.03	25.07	SW. 1	SW. 2	0	SW. by W. 1
18			81	77	70	68	25.07	25.04	25.05	24.95	SW. 1	SW. 1	0	SE. by S. 1
19			79	75	72	69	25.06	25.09	25.13	25.06	S. 1	S. 1	W. 1	S. 1
20			79	78	71	68	25.13	25.10	25.20	25,27	S. by W. 1	S. by W. 1	0	W. 1
21			76	79	73	69	25.09	25.18	25.21	25.18	W. 1	W. 1	0	SW. 1
22			76	74	70	68	25.17	25.15	25.14	25.11	S. 1	S. 1	0	SW. 1
23			75	72	70	69	25.17	25.20	25.14	25.08	W. 1	SW. by W. 1	0	E. 1
24			74	76	69	67	25.14	25.16	25.17	25.14	E. 1	S. by E. 1	0	SE. 1
25			74		70	68	25.17		25.22	25.14	SE. 1	SE. 1	0	SE. by S. 1
26			78	77	72	68	25.24	25.17	25.19	25.16	SE. 1	E. by S. 1	0	0
27			78	77	73	70	25.23	25.21	25.18	25.15	0	SE. 2	0	W. 1
28			78	79	75	70	25.17	25.13	25.14	25.17	E. 1	W. 2	W. 1	SW. by W. 1
29			78	80	74	70	25.15	25.13	25.12	25.12	W. 1	W. 2	W. 1	0
30			79	77	72	70	25.15	25.17	25.11	25.12	0	0	0	0
Average at each hour,			77.46	78.59	72.27	68.73	25.206	25.191	25.181	25.188				
General average,			74.26				25.195							

7

OBSERVATIONS.		
Atmosphere hazy.	Clouds and sunshine.	Thunder in the afternoon.
Id	id	
Id	id	
Id	id	
Id	id	Slight showers in the night.
Id	id	A very little rain at noon.
Id	id	A very little rain at night.
Id	id	Showers all day at intervals.
Id	id	Very slight showers.
Id	id	Much rain all night.
Atmosphere clear.	Mountains covered with clouds.	Id. Capt. Knox's bar. ½ inch higher than mine.
Id	id	Much rain. Clouds and sunshine.
Id	id	id Cloudy.
Id	id	id id
Id	id	id Sunshine in the forenoon.
Id	id	Little rain. Cloudy and sunshine.
Id	id	id id
Id	id	A good deal of rain. Cloudy.
Id	id	Rain in the afternoon. Clear morning.
Id	id	Much rain. Cloudy and sunshine.
Id	id	Some rain. id
Id	id	Much rain in the afternoon.
Id	id	Much rain. Cloudy.
Id	id	id id
Id	id	id Clear forenoon. Emodus visible.
Id	id	Much rain in the evening.
Id	id	Heavy showers.
Id	id	Very little rain. Clouds and sunshine.
Id	id	id id
Id	id	id id

Astronomical Day.	PLACES.	Lat. N.	Fahrenheit's Thermometer. Noon.	3 Hrs.	9 Hrs.	Dawn.	Barometer. Noon.	3 Hours.	9 Hours.	Dawn.	Pluviometer. Inches.	Winds. Noon.	3 Hours.	9 Hours.	Sunrise.
1	Kathmandu.	27°41′	79	80	72	70	25.20	25.18	25.22	25.26		0	0	0	E. ½
2			76	80	71	70	25.24	25.24	25.24	25.24		SE. 1	SE. 1	0	0
3				76	70	69		25.16	25.16	25.14		SE. by E. 1	S. by E. 1	0	0
4			80	78	72	69	25.17	25.14	25.13	25.13		0	W. by S. 1	0	NW. ½
5			76	78	74	68	25.12	25.12	25.16	25.17	0.12	NW. ½	W. ½	0	0
6			79	78	72	69	25.18	25.16	25.21	25.28	0.10	SW. ½	SW. 1	0	E. ½
7			78	80	75	70	25.16	25.18	25.19	25.16	0.00	E. ½	0	0	0
8			82	83	74	70	25.23	25.19	25.23	25.23	0.00	W. ½	W. ½	W. 1	0
9			79	80	73	70	25.24	25.16	25.16	25.16	0.72	W. 1	W. ½	0	0
10			80	76	74	71	25.16	25.13	25.17	25.08	0.62	W. ½	W. 1	0	E. ½
11			78	81	74	70	25.10	25.09	25.13	25.13	0.04	S. 1	W. 1	0	S. ½
12			79	75	73	70	25.14	25.16	25.10	25.10	0.84	S. 1	SE. ½	0	W. 1
13			80	80	74	70	25.11	25.08	25.08	25.10	0.28	W. 1	W. 1	0	W. ½
14			78	81	77	71	25.08	25.07	25.05	25.06	0.42	W. 1	W. 1	0	W. 1
15			79	84	77	70	25.07	25.05	25.08	25.05	1.75	W. 1	E. ½	0	E. ½
16			76	80		70	25.14	25.12		25.17	0.10	E. ½	E. ½	0	W. 1
17			82	80	73	72	25.18	25.15	25.15	25.17	0.37	W. 1	N. 2	0	0
18			77		72	72	25.22		25.15	25.14	0.00	S. ½	0	0	0
19			81	81	73	70	25.16	25.11	25.15	25.14	0.00	W. 1	W. 1	0	0
20			82	84	77	72	25.08	25.05	25.07	25.15	0.37	S. 1	S. 2	0	W. ½
21			81		76	68	25.10		25.15	25.21	0.12	W. ½	W. 1	0	0
22			78	78	72	71	25.16	25.13	25.16	25.12	0.11	W. 1	W. 2	0	W. ½
23			79	81	75	71	25.11	25.04	25.08	25.10	0.73	SW. 1	W. 2		
24			80	84	77	70	25.12	25.14	25.16	25.12	0.00			0	0
25			86	80			25.13	25.09			0.25	W. 1	W. 1	0	0
26			75	74	72	70	25.15	25.09	25.15	25.10	0.06	W. 1	W. 1	0	W. 1
27			76	80	72	70	25.12	25.10	25.08	25.10	0.00	W. 1	NW. 2	0	0
28			80	80	73	70	25.04	25.09	25.08	25.07	0.62	W. 1	W. 1	W. 1	SW. 1
29			74	78	73	71	25.07	25.05	25.05	25.05	0.70	W. 2	W. 2	0	0
30			75		74	70	25.05	25.00	25.06	25.05	0.00	0	W. 1	0	0
31			76		72	70	25.10		25.13	25.10	0.00	SW. 1	W. 1	0	W. 1
	Average,		78.5	80	73.55	70.13	25.1376	25.1131	25.1355	25.1348	8.32 in 27 days; of which 1.14 inches fell in the day time, and 7.18 inches in the night time.				
	General average,		75.54				25.13								

OBSERVATIONS.

During the whole of this month the atmosphere in the valley was clear, with a sky in general, when not raining, partly clouded, and partly admitting of sunshine. The clouds generally hung in patches upon the lower hills, and entirely hid the snowy mountains. I have marked every day that Emodus was visible. The pluviometer was erected on the *5th*. My barometer stood ¼ of an inch lower than Captain Knox's.

Showers.
Much rain in the afternoon.
Showers. Cloudy.
Id id
Id id
Emodus visible.

15. Emodus visible.

20. Emodus visible.
Id
Id

26. Emodus visible.
Thunder about 3. A waterspout seen.
Thunder about 4.

Astronomical Day.	PLACE.	Lat. N.	Fahrenheit's Thermometer. Noon.	3 Hrs.	9 Hrs.	Dawn.	Barometer. Noon.	3 Hrs.	9 Hrs.	Dawn.	Pluviometer. Inches.	Winds. Noon.	3 Hours.	9 Hours.	Sunrise.
1	Kathmandu.	27°41′	80	79	71	70	25.12	25.08	25.06	25.18	0.36	S. 1		0	0
2			76	74	70	68					0.46	SW. 1	SW. 5	W. 1	W. ½
3			75	74	71	69	24.96	24.92	24.92	24.93	0.23	0	0	0	W. 1
4			72	72	70	69	24.94	24.90	24.92	24.93	0.09	W. 1	W. 2	0	0
5			74	74	70	68	24.94	24.94	24.96	24.94	0.91	W. 2	W. 1	0	W. 2
6			71	73	70	68	24.99	24.94	24.94	24.94	0.46	W. 1	W. 1	W. 1	W. 1
7			74	76	74	71	24.92	24.86	24.86	24.77	0 00	W. 2	W. 2	0	SW. 1
8			73	75	72	70	24.90	24.87	24.92	24.88	0.00	W. by S. 1	W. 1	0	0
9			71	74	73	70	24.94	24.87	24.91	24.94	0.26	SW. 1	WSW. 1		
10			74	78	74	72	24.91	24.89	24.89	24.89	0.15			0	W. 1
11			74	73	72	70	24.94	24.92	24.90	24.90	0.30	SE. by S. 1	W. 1	W. 1	SW. 1
12				76	72	70		24.94	24.94	24.95	0.00	W. 1	W. 1	0	0
13			77	76	73	69	24.97	24.95	24.97	24.97	0.32	E. 1	E. by S. 1	E. 1	E. 1
14			74	73	68	69	24.97	24.94	25.02	25.01	1.95	SE. 1	SE. 1	0	E. 1
15			74	76	72	68	25.01	24.96	25.00	24.92	0.46	WSW. 1	WSW. 1	0	W. 1
16			74	74	70	67	25.05	25.02	25.08	25.14	1.80	W. 1	W. 1	0	NW. by W. 1
17			75	74	72	68	25.14	25.12	25.14	25.14	0 00	NW. by W. 1	WNW. 1	0	S. 1
18			74	76	72	70	25.12	25.08	25.03	25.04	0.00	SE. by S. 2	S. by W. 2	0	S. by W. 1
19			74	73	72	68	25.03	24.99	24.99	24.94	1.15	SW. by S. 2	W. by S. 1	W. 1	0
20			70	70	70	67	24.94	24.92	24.92	24.84	0.55	0	W. 1	W. by S. 1	0
21			72	71	69	69	24.92	24.89	24.93	24.93	0.92	E. 1	E. 1	0	0
22			70	70	70	67	24.94	24.94	24.95	25.01	0.05	0	E. 1	W. 1	W. ½
23			72	76	72	69	25.01	24.98	24.98	24.97	0.00			W. ½	W. 1
24			75	77	73	70	24.95	24.89	24.93	24.89	0.00	NW. 1	NW. by N. 1	E. 1	0
25			77	79	73	72	24.89	24.89	24.90	24.90	0.03	SW. by W. 1	W. 1	E. ½	0
26			73	71	69	68	25.00	24.98	24.98	25.05	0.00	WSW. 1	S. 1	0	0
27			73	78			25.01	24.97			0.00	SW. by S. 1	SW. by S. 1	W. ½	W. ½
28			76	72		70	25.00	24.92		24.93	0.35	SW. by S. 1	S. 2	E. ½	W. ½
29			76	78	74	72	24.96	24.92	24.96	24.97	0.05	S. 1	S. 1	0	0
30			77	76	69	68	24.99	24.93	24.94	24.99	0.32	S. 1	S. by E. ½	E. ½	W. 1
31			74	78	74	69	24.98	24.92	24.94	24.97	0.17	W. 1	S. ½	W. 1	
Particular average,			74.13	7.7 1	71.414	69.166	24.98	24.94	24.96	24.96	10.34 of which 4.57 fell at night.				
General average,			72.35				24.96								

OBSERVATIONS.

During the whole of this month, the atmosphere in the valley was clear, and when not raining, the sky was in part clear, and in part covered with clouds. These generally hung in patches on the lower hills, and entirely hid the snowy mountains. I have marked every day on which these were visible. The barometer was emptied, and new filled on the 2d, and stood afterwards a little lower, some air having probably got in, when we removed from Sambhu. A correction of 0.06 may be allowed in the intermediate time.

6. Cloudy all day.

25. Thunder in the afternoon. Emodus visible.

Thunder in the afternoon. Emodus visible.

Astronomical Day.	PLACE.	Lat. N.	Fahrenheit's Thermometer. Noon.	3 Hrs.	9 Hrs.	Dawn.	Barometer. Noon.	3 Hrs.	9 Hrs.	Dawn.	Pluviometer. Inches.	Winds. Noon.	3 Hours.	9 Hours.	Sunrise.
1	Kathmandu.	27°41′	74	76	72	70	24.94	24.91	24.92	24.93	0.00	W.S.W. 1	W. S. W. 1	0	0
2			75	76	71	69	24.91	24.92	24.92	24.96	0.12	W.N.W ½	W. N. W. 1	E. ½	W. by S. 1
3			73	76			24.96	24.94			0.82	W. ½	S. ½	W. ½	0
4					74	70			25.04	25.04	0.57	W. 1	W. S. W. ½	S. ½	0
5			77	76	73	68	25.00	24.94	24.95	24.97	0.13	S. E. ½	0	0	0
6			74	74	75	70	24.98	24.95	24.93	24.96	0.00	0	S. W. ½	W. ½	S.W.by S. ½
7			74	75	72	67	24.97	24.95	24.98	24.96	0.00	W.S.W. ½	S. W. 1	0	E. S. E. ½
8			75	77	72	70	25.03	25.01	25.05	25.03	0.00	E. S. E. 1	E. S. E. 1	0	W. ½
9			75	75	73	70	25 05	25.03	25.11	25.07	0.00	W. 1	W. 1	0	W. ½
10			74	78	74	71	25.08	25.04	25.07	25.04	0.00	W. ½	S. W. ½	0	S. W. ½
11			77	78	73	70	25.03	25.01	25 04	25.05	0.09	S. W. 1	S. W. 1		
12			76	77	74	70	25.06	24.98	24.97	24.96	0.25	W. ½	W. ½	0	S. W. 1
13			74	77	72	70	25.01	24.97	24.99	25.03	0.25	S. W. 1	S. W. 1	0	0
14			73	75	70	68	25.01	24.97	25.00	25.00	0 02	W. ½	W. ½	0	0
15			71	73	70	68	25.04	25.00	25.01	25.02	0.71	0	0	0	S. W. ½
16			74	76	72	68	25.03	24.98	25.06	25.01	0.04	S. W. ½	S. W. 1	W. ½	W. ½
17			72	74	70	68	25.06	25.01	25.04	25.02	0.30	N. W. 1	N. W. 1	S. W. ½	S.W.by W. 1
18			70	70	68	66	25.07	25.01	25.03	25 03	0.06	N. W. 1	N. W. 1	N. E. ½	E. ½
19			70	72	68	66	25.05	25.04	25.07	25.04	1.46	S. E. ½	S. E. 1	0	S. W. ½
20			72	74	69	65	25.03	25.00	25.01	25.05	0.30	S. W. ½	S. W. ½	0	0
21			74	74	70	67	25.06	24.97	25.07	25.04	0.00	S. W. 1	S.W.by W. 1	N. W. ½	N. W. 1
22			72	74	69	65	25 05	25.02	25.05	25.05	0.00	W. 1	W. 1	W. ½	W. S. W. ½
23			73	75	71	75	25.07	25.04	25.07	25 08	0.09	W. 1	S. W. 2	0	0
24			71	73	70	67	25.11	25.07	25.09	25.07	0.11	E. ½	E. ½	0	N. W. 1
25			70	72	69	66	25.08	25.04	25.06	25.03	0.12	N. W. 1	N. W. o 1	0	E. 3
26			67	68	66	63	25.12	25.06	25.09	25.11	0.39	E. 3	E. 2	E. ½	W. 1
27			69	74	70	67	25.12	25.08	25.10	25.10	0.00	W. 1	S. W. 2	W. ½	S. W. 1
28			72	76		65	25.14	25.10		25.14	0.00	S. W. 2	S. W. 2	0	N. W. 1
29			71	74		66	25.20	25.12		25.16	0.05	S. W. 1	S. W. 1	0	S. W. 1
30			73	74	69	66	25.14	25.10	25.11	25.09	0.11	S. W. 1	S.W.by S. ½	W. ½	S. W. 1
Particular average,			72.82	74.58	70.98	67.96	25.05	25.01	25.03	25.03	5.54 Total.				
General average,			71.585				25.03								

for SEPTEMBER 1802.

OBSERVATIONS.

During this month the clouds hung upon the hills, and in general hid the snowy mountains entirely. The atmosphere in the valley generally clear, with sunshine at times, interrupted by large clouds.

4. Much thunder at night.

7. Fog in the morning.
Thunder in the afternoon.

11. Thunder at night.

14. Thunder at night.

19. Thick fog in the morning.
Thunder in the evening.

23. A foggy morning.

26. A foggy morning. Emodus visible for an instant.

Emodus visible in the evening.

Astronomical Day.	PLACE.	Lat. N.	Fahrenheit's Thermometer. Noon.	3 Hrs.	9 Hrs.	Dawn.	Barometer. Noon.	3 Hrs.	9 Hrs.	Dawn.	Pluviometer. Inches.	Winds. Noon.	3 Hours.	9 Hours.	19 Hours.
1	Kathmandu.	27°41'	73	76	71	65	25.12	25.09	25.05	25.08	0.00	SW. 2	SW. 2	SW. by S ½	W. by S. 1
2			73	75	65	64	25.04	25.04	25.07	25.09	0.00	SW. 2	SW. by S. 2	O	O
3			69	72	69	64	25.11	25.07	25.08	25.13	0.97	SW. 1	SW. 2	O	W. ½
4			70	74	68	62	25.13	25.08	25.14	25.14	0.00	SW. by S. 1	SW. by S. 1	W. ½	W. by S. 1
5			70	72	66	62	25.17	25.11	25.19	25.20	0.00	SW. by W. 2	SW. by S. 3	SW. ½	O
6			72	75	69	66	25.19	25.15	25.19	25.17	0.97	WSW. 2	SW. by W. 2	O	E. ½
7			72	70	68	66	25.14	25.08	25.10	25.10	0.44	WSW. 1	SW. 1	E. ½	E. 1
8			64	65	65	64	25.17	25.12	25.14	25.19	0.95	E. 1	E. 1	O	E. 1
9			68	70	67	66	25.21	25.14	25.14	25.22	None during the remainder of the month.	W. 1	W. 2	O	W. by S. 1
10			71	70	67	61	25.17	25.15	25.19	25.22		W. by S. 2	W. by S. 3	W. ½	SW. 1
11			69	72	68	62	25.16	25.14	25.15	25.17		SW. 2	W. by S. 3	O	SW. 1
12			71	73	68	65	25.15	25.10	25.13	25.17				O	W. 2
13			69	73	68	62	25.17	25.14	25.16	25.16		W. 2	W. 3	W. ½	SE. 1
14			68		65	59	25.18		25.16	25.23		SE. 2	W. 2	E. 1	SE. 1
15			68	70	63	57	25.19	25.13	25.19	25.33		SE. by E. 2	SE. by S. 2		
16			65	68	63	60	25.26	25.17	25.26	25.34					
17			65	69	65	60	25.29	25.24	25.27	25.34				O	SW. by S. 1
18			66	69	63	61	25.28	25.23	25.23	25.24		SW. by S. 2	S.W. by S. 2	W. ½	SW. by S. 1
19			67	69	66	59	25.28	25.24	25.26	25.31		NW. by N. 2	NW. by W. 3	SE. ½	SE. by E. 2
20			66	74	65	59	25.24	25.19	25.22	25.28		SW. 2	SW. 2	O	SE. by S. 1
21				68	64	59		25.23	25.25	25.29		SE. by S. 1	SW. by S. 1	SW. ½	O
22			65	68	64	59	25.26	25.21	25.19	25.26		WSW. 1	WSW. 1	O	O
23			65	68	64	57	25.22	25.18	25.17	25.27		WSW. 1	W. by S. 2		
24			65	68	63	57	25.28	25.19	25.19	25.29					
25				68	63	59		25.20	25.20	25.27				O	O
26			65	66	63	58	25.23	25.18	25.25	25.27		NW. by N. 1	NNW. 1		
27			68	66	62	56	25.25	25.19	25.23	25.27				O	SE. by S. ½
28			62	65	60	57	25.24	25.19	25.23	25.28		NE. by E. ½	NW. 2	W. by N. ½	SW. by W. 1
29			63		61	58	25 26		25.22	25.28		SW. by W. 1	SW. by W. 1	WSW. ½	SE. by E. ½
30			64	66	62	58	25.23	25.19	25.24	25.26		WSW. 1	WSW. 2	O	SW. by W. ½
31			62	64	62	57	25.23	25.17	25.19	25.27		SW. by W. 1	W. 2	O	W. 1
Particular average,			67.4	72.25	64.55	60.32	25.20	25.16	25.32	25.22	3.33	Total.		11	
General average,			66.13				25.22								

OBSERVATIONS.

A little thunder.	
Emodus visible for a little in the evening.	
Thick fog in the morning.	
Id	Emodus visible in the forenoon.
Id	Thunder in the evening.
	Much thunder at night.
	Emodus visible in the morning.
	Id.
	Id and evening.
Thick fog in the morning.	
Id.	
Fog after sunrise.	
Id	Emodus visible in the morning.
No fog.	
Id	
Id	Emodus visible in the morning.
Fog after sunrise.	
Thick fog in the morning.	
Id	Emodus very clear.
Id	Id
Little fog.	Id
Foggy morning.	Id
Id	Id
Little fog.	
Id	Id
Id	Id
Id	Id
Id	Id
Considerable fog.	Id

Except during the fogs, the atmosphere in the valley was clear throughout this month. The sky was scattered with large clouds, which at times rested on the faces of the hills. The thermometer was hung up in an open room. When exposed to the open air at dawn, it sunk from 4 to 6 degrees lower than when in the room at noon in the open air, but, well shaded, it rose about 2 degrees higher than in the room.

Astronomical Day.	PLACE.	Lat. N.	Fahrenheit's Thermometer.				Barometer.				Pluviometer. Inches.	Winds.			
			Noon.	3 Hrs.	9 Hrs.	Dawn.	Noon.	3 Hrs.	9 Hrs.	Dawn.		Noon.	3 Hours.	9 Hours.	19 Hours.
1	Kathmandu.	27°41′	62	65	61	57	25.18	25.15	25.16	25.23	0.00	W. 1	W. 1	0	NE. by E. ½
2			63	65	62	57	25.20	25.18	25.22	25.29	0.00	WNW. 1	WNW. 1	0	0
3			64	65	63	60	25.26	25.19	25.24	25.27	0.00	W. by NW. 1	W. by N. 1	W. ½	W. 1
4			64	66	63	57	25.25	25.22	25.28	25.34	0.00	W. by S. 1	W. by N. 1	0	0
5			63	63		57	25.33	25.33		25.40	0.00	WNW. 1	WNW. 2	WSW. ½	0
6			64	65	62	56	25.33	25.27	25.33	25.35	0.00	W. 1	W. 1	0	0
7			62	65	62	56	25.33	25.25	25.27	25.32	0.00	NW. by W. 1	NW. 2		
8			62	64	62	57	25.30	25.24	25.26	25.30	0.04				
9			61		61	57	25.30		25.34	25.37	0.04			W. by N. ½	W. by N. ½
10			62	65	61	56	25.33	25.25	25.27	25.30	None during the remainder of the month.	NW. 1	NW. 1	0	0
11			61	64	61	56	25.29	25.24	25.26	25.37		W. by S. 1	WNW. 1	W. ½	0
12			62	63	61	55	25.34	25.28	25.31	25.40		0	W. ½		
13			61	64	60	54	25.34	25.28	25.34	25.45				W. ½	W. ½
14			60	63	61	54	25.37	25.31	25.31	25.37		W. by S. 2	W. by S. 2	0	0
15			60	62	60	54	25.34	25.29	25.27	25.37		W. 1	W. 2	W. ½	W. ½
16			60	62	59	53	25.36	25.26	25.32	25.40		SW. by W. 1	SW. 2	0	0
17			59	62	60	53	25.37	25.28	25.34	25.43		SW. 1	W. 1	WNW. ½	WNW. ½
18			60	63	59	53	25.30	25.25	25.27	25.31		NW. by W. 1	NW. by W. 1	0	0
19			60	62	58	53	25.27	25.23	25.25	25.26		N. by W. 1	NW. by W. 1	0	E. ½
20			56	60	57	50	25.30	25.24	25.28	25.35		W. 1	W. 2	W. ½	W. 1
21			55	59	56	51	25.33	25.26	25.32	25.38		NW. by W. 1	WNW. 1	0	W. ½
22			55	58	55	52	25.36	25.26	25.32	25.38		NW. 1	NW. ½	E. ½	E. ½
23			56	58	56	52	25.32	25.26	25.25	25.26		NE. ½	NE. by E. 1	0	E. ½
24			57	57	55	51	25.30	25.26	25.28	25.35		E. ½	W. ½	0	NE. ½
25			55		55	50	25.30		25.27	25.37		0	WNW. 2	0	E. ½
26			55	60	56	50	25.34	25.24	25.29	25.35		E. ½	W. 1		
27				59	57	52		25.26	25.33	25.37					
28			70	70	58	51	25.35	25.24	25.30	25.31					
29				72	57	54		25.20	25.25	25.25				0	0
30			72	70	58	50	25.22	25.17	25.22	25.27		NW. 1	NW. 2	0	E. ½
Particular average,			60.75	61.	59.24	53.93	25.31	25.24	25.28	25.34	00.8	Total.			
General average,			58,73				25,29								

OBSERVATIONS.

Foggy morning.	Emodus clear.
Little fog.	Emodus clouded.
Id	id
Thick fog.	Emodus clear.
Little fog.	id
Id	Emodus clouded.
Id	id
Much fog.	id
Id	Emodus clear.
Id	id
Id	id
Id	id
Id	id
Id	id
Little fog.	Emodus clouded.
Id	id
Much fog.	id
Id	id
Id	id
Id	Emodus clear.
Little fog.	id
Id	id
Id	Emodus clouded.
Some fog.	id
Much fog.	id
Id	id
Little fog.	id
Id	id
Id	id
Some fog.	id

The thermometer continued in the room, and six degrees must be substracted from that here given, to get the heat of the external air in the morning. Throughout the month, except in the foggy mornings, the atmosphere was clear, with a sky containing many clouds.

Astronomical Day.	PLACE.	Lat. N.	Fahrenheit's Thermometer.				Barometer.				Pluviometer. Inches.	Winds.			
			Noon.	3 Hrs.	9 Hrs.	Dawn.	Noon.	3 Hrs.	9 Hrs.	Dawn.		Noon.	3 Hours.	9 Hours.	19 Hours.
1	Kathmandu.	27°41′	70	68	54	50	25.23	25.18		25.27	No rain during this month.	NW.byW. 1	NW.byW. 1	O	E. ½
2			59	62	57	50	25.23	25.19	25.26	25.32		W. ½	W. 1	O	O
3			57	61	56	48	25.28	25.25	25.29	25.38		NW.by N. ½	NW.by N. 2	E. 1	W. ½
4			56	61	55	47	25.35	25.22	25.33	25.39		W. ½	W. 1	O	E. 1
5				60	55	46		25.28	25.26	25.31		NW. 1	NW.byW. 2	E. ½	O
6			54	59	53	49	25.25	25.20	25.24	25.28		W. ½	W. 2	O	O
7			55	57	54	50	25.24	25.19	25.23	25.29		NW.byW. ½	W. 2	O	O
8			54	56	53	46	25.25	25.17	25.32	25.28		O	O	W. ½	W. ½
9			53	58	50	41	25.28	25.24	25.28	25.37		NW.byW. 1	NW.byW. 1	O	O
10			53	57	50	42	25.28	25.21	25.32	25.36		W. 1	W. 2	W. ½	W. ½
11			51	55	50	41	25.31	25.21	25.30	25.36		WNW. 1	WNW. 1	SW. ½	SW. ½
12			50	54	50	41	25.27	25.22	25.21	25.30		W. 1	W. 1	O	O
13			51	57	50	41	25.23	25.17	25.22	25.33		SW. 1	SW. 2	O	O
14			51	57	49	41	25.25	25.22	25.27	25.30		O	W. 2	O	O
15			50	56	50	42	25.24	25.17	25.24	25.33		W. 1	W. 3	O	E. ½
16			50	54	49	41	25.29	25.24	25.28	25.38		W. 1	W. 2	W. ½	W. ½
17			50	55	48	41	25.32	25.26	25.37	25.46		NW.byN. 1	NW.byN. 2	O	O
18			52	57	49	44	25.38	25.33	25.40	25.46		W. ½	W. 1	O	O
19			51		50	45	25.41		25.37	25.44		W. ½	W. 2	O	O
20			53	56	53	43	25.37	25.31	25.38	25.46		W. ½	W. 1	O	E. ½
21			53	57	51	43	25.44	25.36	25.39	25.46		W. ½	W. 1	O	NE. ½
22			52	55	50	42	25.40	25.28	25.34	25.38		W. 1	W. 2	O	W. 1
23			50	57	49	41	25.38	25.27	25.36	25.39		W. 1	W. 3	O	O
24				55	50	41		25.25	25.34	25.47		W. 1	W. 2	O	O
25			51	57	49	41	25.39	25.32	25.42	25.47		W. 1	W. 2	O	O
26			52	57	49	40	25.41	25.32	25.42	25.40		SW. 1	SW. 2		
27			51	58	51	41	25.38	25.26	25.32	25.39					
28			51	57	51	45	25.33	25.26	25.29	25.26					
29			52	55	50	49	25.27	25.20	25.26	25.30					
30			54	57	52	47	25.26	25.21	25.27	25.34				O	O
31			50		52	46	25.28		25.26	25.33		W. 2	W.	O	O
	Particular average,		52.91	57.79	51.39	44.03	25.31	25.24	25.31	25.36					
	General average,		51.53				25.30								

for December 1802.

OBSERVATIONS.

The thermometer continued in the house in a room without a fire. Atmosphere as in the preceding month.

Little fog.	Emodus clouded.		
Id	id		
Id	id		
Much fog.	Emodus at times visible.		
Id	Emodus clear.		
Id	id		
Little fog.	Emodus clouded.		
Id	id		
Much fog.	id		
Id	Emodus clear.	Hoar frost.	Thermometer at dawn in the open air 31½°.
Id	id	No frost.	
Little fog.	id	Hoar frost.	Ther. exposed 33°. A fall of snow on the mountain above
Id	id	id	id 31½°. [Nayakot.
Much fog.	id	id	
Id	id	id	
Id	id	A little hoar frost.	
Id	id	id	
Id	id	No frost.	
Little fog.	Cloudy.	id	
Much fog.	id	id	
Id	Emodus clear	id	
Id	id	id	
Little fog.	id	Hoar frost.	
Id	id	id	
Some fog.	id	id	
Id	id	id	
Id	id	No frost.	
Id	Emodus clouded.	id	Thermometer at dawn exposed 44°.
Id	id	id	
Id	id	id	

Astronomical Day.	PLACE.	Lat. N.	Fahrenheit's Thermometer. Noon.	3 Hrs.	9 Hrs.	Dawn.	Barometer. Noon.	3 Hrs.	9 Hrs.	Dawn.	Pluviometer. Inches.	Winds. Noon.	3 Hours.	9 Hours.	19 Hours.
1	Kathmandu.	27°41′		56	49	32		25.21	25.27	25.29	No rain during this month but on the 24th day.	W. 2	W. 3	0	E. ½
2			49		49	38	25.28		25.35	25.45		SW. by W. 1	SW. by W. 2	0	0
3			50	55	50	38	25.35	25.26	25.33	25.41		W. 1	W. 1	0	0
4			51	55	51	35	25.35	25.26	25.30	25.36		NW. 1	NW. 1	0	0
5			52	55	51	34	25.31	25.25	25.27	25.33		W. 1	W. 1	0	0
6			50	55	50	38	25.27	25.18	25.27	25.25		W. 1	W. 2	0	0
7			50	56	51	38	25.22	25.16	25.18	25.22		NW. 1	NW. 1	0	0
8			55	58	52	42	25.24	25.15	25.24	25.32		0	0	0	0
9			51	57	52	42	25.31	25.23	25.31	25.34		W. 1	W. 3	0	0
10			51	58	51	36	25.35	25.26	25.32	25.42		N. by W. 1	NNW. 3	0	0
11			52	56	51	33	25.27	25.22	25.31	25.44		W. 2	W. 3	0	0
12			50	55	50	31	25.47	25.41	25.46	25.49		W. 1	W. 2	0	0
13			49	56	49	33		25.33	25.40	25.46		SW. by W. 1	SW. by W. 2	0	0
14			50	56	51	32	25.43	25.34	25.42	25.52		W. 2	W. 3	0	E. ½
15			50	54	50	35	25.45	25.41	25.49	25.52		W. 1	SW. by W. 2	0	0
16			49	55	49	36	25.47	25.48	25.43	25.43		0	NW. 1	0	0
17			50	53	48	35	25.39	25.44	25.40	25.39		0	NW. 1	0	0
18			50	52	51	35	25.34	25.28	25.30	25.39		W. 1	W. 4	0	E. ½
19			50	56	50	36	25.35	25.27	25.33	25.39		W. 1	W. 2	0	0
20				56	51	35		25.27	25.29	25.42		0	W. 1	0	0
21			51	55	51	38	25.38	25.33	25.29	25.42		NW. by W. 1	N. by W. 2	0	0
22			51	57	52	36	25.36	25.30	25.31	25.35		W. 2	W. 3	0	
23			51	55	53	45	25.33	25.28	25.27	25.27				0	0
24			51	51	50	40	25.28	25.23	25.24	25.25	0.44	W. 1	NW. 1	0	E. ½
25			51	53	50	42	25.21	25.18	25.16	25.24		E. 1	W. 1	0	SW. 1
26			51	55	50	40	25.25	25.25	25.31	25.34		SW. by S. 3		0	0
27			52	54	52	42	25.31	25.25	25.29	25.30		W. 1	W. 1	W. 1	SE. by E. 1
28			52	55	51	40	25.30	25.24	25.28	25.33		W. 1	NW. 1	0	E. ½
29			52	55	53	39	25.35	25.27	25.30	25.38		E. 1	NW. 1	0	SE. ½
30			52	57	52		25.32	25.25	25.27	25.28		W. 1	W. 3	0	0
31				59	54	40	25.25	25.23	25.23	25.28		W. 1	W. 2	0	E. ½
Particular average,			50.8	55.3	50.8	37.2	25.328	25.274	25.31	25.364	0.44 Total.				
General average,			48.1				25.32								

OBSERVATIONS.

The thermometer was exposed every morning till quite cooled. At other times it was kept in a cool open room. Sky and atmosphere as in the preceding months.

Thick fog in the morning.	Emodus clouded.	Hoar frost.
Id	id	No frost.
Id	id	id
Little fog.	id	id
Foggy morning.	Emodus clear.	A little frost.
Id	Emodus hazy, but visible at times.	No frost.
Id	id	id
Id	id	id
Id	id	id
Clear morning.	id	Slight hoar frost.
Foggy morning.	id	Hoar frost.
Little fog.	id	id
Id	id	id
Foggy morning.	id	id
Id	id	No frost.
Clear morning.	id	id
Foggy morning.	id	id
Id	id	id
Id	id	id
Id	id	id
Id	id	id
Id	id	id
Clear morning.	id	id Day clouded.
Snow on the tops of Shivapuri and Chandungiri. Hills clouded.		
Snow gone. No fog.	Emodus clouded.	
Little fog.	Emodus visible, but clouded in most parts.	
Id	Emodus clouded.	
Foggy morning.	id	
Id	Emodus clear.	
Id	Emodus clouded.	
Id	id	

Astronomical Day.	PLACE.	Lat. N.	Fahrenheit's Thermometer.				Barometer.				Pluviometer. Inches.	Winds.			
			Noon.	3 Hrs.	9 Hrs.	Dawn.	Noon.	3 Hrs.	9 Hrs.	Dawn.		Noon.	3 Hours.	9 Hours.	19 Hours.
1	Kathmandu.	27°41′		59	49	35		25.21	25.21	25.25	0	W. 1	W. 3	0	E. ½
2			53	57	54	39	25.26	25.20	25.27	25.30	0	W. 1	SW. 3	0	0
3			53	57	52	32	25.29	25.22	25.24	25.28	0	W. 1	W. 2	0	0
4			51	56	52	34	25.21	25.18	25.23	25.27	0	0	W. 2	0	0
5			52	57	52	37	25.25	25.19	25.23	25.35	0	NW. 1	W. 3	0	E. ½
6			52	57	52	37	25.28	25 23	25.26	25.33	0	0	SW. by W. 1	E. ½	0
7			52	58	51	40	25.29	25.22	25.24	25.31	0	W. 1	W. 2	0	0
8			51	53	51	39	25.31	25.26	25.24	25.28	0	0	W. 2	0	0
9			51	55	53	39	25.26	25.23	25.21	25.24	0	0	W. 2	0	0
10				58	51	33		25.20	25.19	25.27	0	W. 1	W. 3		
11			52	57	53	41	25.27	25 22	25 26	25.34	0			E. 1	E. 2
12			56		54		25.34		25.28	25.34	0	W. 1	W. 4	0	0
13			60	63	58	39	25.31	25.23	25.27	25.27	0	W. 2	W. 4	W. ½	W. 1
14				65	58	52		25.22	25.24	25.23	0	W. 2	W. 4	0	E. 1
15			56	57	55	50	25.21	25.21	25.24	25.22	0.54	W. 2	W. 2	0	E. 1
16			55	57	55	45	25.22	25 22	25.24	25.21	0.10	W. 1	W. 1	0	0
17				58	55	45		25.19	25.21	25.22	0	W. 1	W. 2	0	0
18			55	60	55	34	25.22	25.15	25.18	25.21	0	W. 1	W. 1	0	0
19			54	58	55	41	25.21	25.15	25.18	25.19	0	W. 1	W. 2	0	0
20			55	55	53	36	25.19	25.15	25.18	25.24	0	W. 1	W. 1	0	0
21			54	59	54	44	25.23	25.19	25.25	25.29	0	W. 1	W. 1	0	0
22				59	56	43		25.20	25.26	25.28	0	W. 1	W. 2	0	0
23			57	60	58	48	25.29	25.22	25.28	25.28	0	W. 1	SW. by W. 3	0	W. 1
24			59	63	59	44	25.28	25.24	25.29	25.36	0	W. 1	SW. by W. 3	E. ½	0
25			58	64	59	44	25.33	25.23	25.33	25.31	0	W. 1	W. 2	E. ½	0
26			61	61	57	47	25.33	25.26	25.34	25.37	1.15	W. 1	W. 3	E. ½	E. ½
27			52	52	50	41	25.44	25.32	25.34	25.31	0	E. 1	E. 2	0	0
28			53	58	56	44	25.32	25.26	25.28	25.25	0	W. 1	W. 2	0	0
	Particular average,		52.70	58.26	54.18	41.22	25.28	25.21	25.25	25.26	1.79 Total.				
	General average,		51.58				25.25								

OBSERVATIONS.

Sky and atmosphere as in the three preceding months. Thermometer exposed in the morning.

Thick fog in the morning.	Emodus clouded.	
Id	id	
No fog.	id	Hard frost in the morning.
Little fog.	id	Frosty morning.
Much fog.	id	No frost
Some fog.	id	
Thick fog.	id	
Some fog.	id	
Thick fog.	id	
No fog.	Emodus visible in the morning.	Hoar frost.
Id	id	
Id	Emodus clear at sunrise.	
Id	id	
Id	Emodus entirely hid.	No snow on the hills of Nepal.
Id	id	
Little fog.	id	
Id	Emodus at times visible.	
Id	Emodus clear.	Hoar frost.
Id	Emodus clear in the afternoon.	
Id	Emodus clear in the morning.	
Id	Emodus entirely hid.	
Id	id	
Id	id	
Much fog.	id	
Little fog.	Emodus clear at times.	
Hail in the afternoon.	Much snow at night on Chandungiri, &c.	
Thick fog in the morning.	Emodus clouded.	
Id	id	

N. B. The thermometer on the 6th was immersed into the spring below Hilchuck, and stood at 65°. In the open air, it had been previously at 52°.

Astronomical Day.	PLACE.	Lat. N.	Fahrenheit's Thermometer.				Barometer.				Pluviometer. Inches.	Winds.			
			Noon.	3 Hrs.	9 Hrs.	Dawn.	Noon.	3 Hrs.	9 Hrs.	Dawn.		Noon.	3 Hours.	9 Hours.	19 Hours.
1	Suburbs of Kathmandu.	27°41′	54	56	54	40	25.39	25.22	25.21	25.15	0	W. 1	W. 1	0	0
2				61	55	38		25.04	25.04	25.04	0	WNW. 1	WNW. 1	0	0
3			55	60	56	43	25.05	25.02	25.08	25.11	0	W. 1	W. 2	0	0
4			57	64	59	44	25.19	25.12	25.13	25.16	0	W. 1	W. 2	0	0
5			58	64	57	44	25.14	25.11	25.11	25.18	0	W. 1	W. 3	0	0
6			60	63	56	35	25.21	25.19	25.17	24.24	0	W. 2	W. 2	0	NW.byW. 1
7			57	64	58	38	25.24	25.19	25.21	25.25	0	W. 1	W. 2	0	0
8			59	68	58	42	25.26	25.18	25.20	25.29	0	W. 2	W. 3	0	0
9			58	63	60	40	25.33	25.26	25.28	25.35	0	NW.byW. 2	NW.byW. 3	0	E. 1
10			65	69	61	40	25.37	25.31	25.36	25.35	0	NW.byW. 2	NW.byW. 3	0	E. ½
11			62	67	60	37	25.27	25.22	25.23	25.23	0	W. 2	W. 3	0	0
12			61	68	63	42	25.29	25.22	25.25	25.25	0	E. 2	W. 4	0	E. ½
13			62	67	63	44	25.26	25.19	25.20	25.23	0	W. 1	W. 3	0	0
14			62	67	63	45	25.24	25.21	25.20	25.24	0	W. 1	W. 2	0	E. ½
15			63	66	62	44	25.27	25.25	25.27	25.28	0	SW.by W. 1	SW.by W. 2	0	0
16			63	69	64	49	25.24	25.19	25.20	25.22	0	W. 1	W. 2	0	0
Particular average,			59.70	64.75	59.3	41.5	25.25	25.1825	25.1962	25.2231					
General average,			56.2				25.21								

OBSERVATIONS.

Thick fog. Emodus clouded. Valley clear.

No fog. Emodus clear. In the morning a little hoar-frost on the straw, but none on grass.
Some fog. Emodus clouded.
Much fog. id.
Id. Emodus clear in the forenoon.
No fog. Hoar-frost. Emodus clear.
Id. Emodus clear.
Id. Emodus clouded.
Id. Emodus at times visible.
Id. id.
Id. id.
A little fog. Emodus clouded.
Id. id.
No fog. id.
Id. id.

CALCULATION OF THE ALTITUDES

OF SOME OF THE

SNOWY MOUNTAINS FROM THE VALLEY OF NEPAL.

BY COLONEL CRAWFORD.

Time of Observation.	Name of the Mountain.	Double Altitude as taken in the Mercury.	Double Altitude as corrected for the error in Sextant = 1.′ 18.″	Angle of Altitude.	Allowance for Terrestrial Refraction = $\frac{1}{18}$ distance.	Angle at the Station corrected for Terrestrial Refraction.	Angle at the Mountain's Top.	Base or Distance.	Height by Trigonometry.	Additional Height for the Earth's Curvature.	Height of the Mountain above the Station.	Thermometer.	Barometer.
								Miles Fur.	Feet Decis.	Feet Decis.	Feet Decis.		Inches D.
26th October 1802 at 3 hours P. M.	A	4.° 16.′ 00″	4.° 14.′ 42″	2.° 07.′ 21″	5.′ 39″	2.° 01.′ 42″	87.° 58.′ 18″	78. —	14,548.8	4,050	19,634.8	63°	25.18
	C	5. 37. 30	5. 36. 12	2. 48. 06	4. 55	2. 43. 11	87. 16. 49	68. 3	17,016.6	3,098	20,114.6		
	D	6. 47. 30	6. 46. 12	3. 23. 06	3. 41	3. 19. 25	86. 40. 35	51. —	15,637.2	1,727	17,364.2		
	E	6. 03. 25	6. 02. 07	3. 01. 03	2. 44	2. 58. 21	87. 01. 39	40. —	10,966.8	1,062.4	12,029.2		
	F	6. 18. 45	6. 17. 27	3. 08. 43	3. 15	3. 05. 28	86. 54. 32	45. 2	12,830.7	1,345.5	14,176.2		
	K	10. 09. 15	10. 07. 57	5. 03. 58	2. 10	5. 01. 48	84. 58. 12	30. 2	13,941.6	607.59	14,549.19		
	L Dhayabung.	10. 10. 00	10. 08. 42	5. 04. 21	2. 44	5. 01. 37	84. 58. 23	40. 7	18,900.	1,060.32	19,960.32		
	M	9. 07. 30	9. 06. 12	4. 33. 06	1. 53	4. 31. 13	85. 28. 47	26. —	10,890.1	448.86	11,346.97		

No correction for the state of the air has been attempted.

INDEX.

ABORIGINES, page 9, 23, 24, 25, 287, 305
Acham, a lordship, 280
Achar, a priest of the sect of Siva among the Newars, 29, 30
Adhikar, see Negi
Adhiyar people cultivating for a (half) share of the crop, 149
Adultery subject to fine, 161
Agalmatolite, 79
Agam Singha, hereditary chief of the Kirata tribe, 2. 54, 133, 140
Aggregate rocks, including granite, &c. 66, 76, 82, 203
Agnidanda, a family of Brahmans, 103
Agriculture, general state of, 64, 68, 73, 217, 221, 274, 275, 282, 298, 305, 312. See also for a detail, Cattle, Crops, Gardens, Grains, Implements, Labourers, Pasture, Produce, Rent, Tenures, Vegetables for the kitchen
Ahira or Cowherd, a dynasty, see Gupt
Ahir, a tribe or cast, 297
Air, temperature of, see Weather: degree of salubrity, see Ayul, and pages 65, 69, 71
Ajil Sen, a powerful chief, 129, 130
Alamnagar, a stronghold in Kangra, 311
Alangchang, a mart, 157
Alé, a tribe, 279
Alluvial matter, 80, 205
Almora, a principality and town, the former most commonly called Kumau, see also 112, 287, 293, 297, 298
Alpine region, 75, 87, &c.
Amaranthus, a species called Anardana or Phaphar, 275, 284, 315
Amar Singha Karyi, or Bara Amar Sigha, a chief of Gorkha, 19, 112, 259, 260, 300, 304, 307, 311, 312
Amar Singha Thapa, a general of Gorkha, father of Bhim Sen, 112, 176, 178, 179, 261, 266, 296, 299
Ambar Sen, first Raja of Palpa and Butaul, 170
Ammonite, a petrifaction, see Salagram
Ana, a money of account, 214
Anirudha, grandson of the god Krishna, 206
Anirudha, a chief of Kangra, 311
Antimony, the mineral, 78
Aniwar, a tribe of military Brahmans, 48, 164, 169
Architecture, 38, 210
Argha, a lordship, 172, 173, 238, 239, 263
Aristocracy or nobility, 108, 110, 255, 257
Arjal, a family of Brahmans, 103
Arki, one of the twelve lordships, and a town and military station, 306
Arms, military, 111, 112, 116, 148, 246
Army, see Arms, Company, Military
Arsenic, the mineral, 79
Artificers, 233
Arun river, 89, 91, 166
Asanti, Raja of Karuvirpur, leader of a Hindu colony, 12, 287, 293
Ashruffy, a coin, 214
Asoph ud Doulah, the Nawab Vazir, 173, 174
Astrology, or Jyotish, 251
Athabhai, see League
Ayul, an unhealthy air, 65, 194, 196, 199, 200

Badrinath, a temple, 301, 302
Baglungchaur, a town, 274
Bahadur Sahi, regent of Gorkha, 173, 174, 247–250, 271, 277, 281, 299
Baisi Raja, or twenty-two lordships, a part of the dominions of Gorkha, 268, 270, 276, 278, 279
Bala, a cast of Newars, 87
Balihang, a lordship, 171, 172, 264, 280
Balance of power, 283
Bandar, a small district, 172
Bandari, a collector of revenue, 113, 114
Bangra or Baryesu, called Bahauras and Bhauras by Colonel Kirkpatrick, priests of the Bouddha sect among the Newars, 29, 31, 219
Bangphi, a lordship, 270, 276, 280
Bangsi Raja, a Hindu chief, subject to the Company, 268
Baragarhi, a town and district, 167, 168
Barahat, a territory, 299
Barakadwar, a mart, 265
Barapul, a weight, 216
Bara Thakurai, or twelve lordships, a territory subject to Gorkha, 303, 304, 306, 307
Barley or Hordeum sativum, 226, 274, 282, 284, 298
Barometer, the instrument, its height, see Meteorological Tables at the end, and page 200
Baropathi, a territory, 293
Baryesu, see Bangra
Basnat, a tribe, 18, 28
Batar, a tribe, 164
Bayas river, see Bepasa
Baz Bahadur, a chief of Kumau, 293
Bear, the wild beast, 68
Belahari, a territory, 293
Belka, a lordship, 129
Bell metal, 232
Belortng, a mountain, 94
Beni means the junction of two rivers
Beniji or Benishahar, the town of Malebum, which, with Dhorali, the chief's residence, formed the capital of that lordship, 271, 274,
Bepasa or Bayas river, 315
Bera river, 195
Bera, a vegetable, see Solanum Melongena
Berberis, called Chootraphul, 85
Besar, a lordship, 307
Besariya, a lordship, 299
Beyas, a passage between the Snowy Mountains, 298
Bhairopati, a medicinal herb, 97
Bhajji, one of the twelve lordships, 306
Bhar, see Bhawar
Bharadar, the great council of state, and supreme court of justice, 103, 108
Bhat, a cast of Newars, 84
Bhat, a cast of Kasiyas, 305
Bhatgung, a principality, and its capital town, 209, 210, 211
Bhawani, see Devi and Tulasi
Bhawar or Bhar, a tribe, 47, 128, 164
Bhemagarhi, a town, 161
Bhimphedi, a station, 200
Bhim Sen, son of Pandu, first Hindu colonist, 9, 25, 167
Bhim Sen, a chief of Gorkha, 19, 108, 112, 176, 258, 260–262, 277
Bhingri, a lordship, 239, 268, 270
Bhitari Tarayi, a territory, 278
Bhomor, a lordship, 313
Bhot or Bhotan, the country occupied by Bhotiyas, including what Europeans call Bhotan and Thibet, 55–60, 90, 243
Bhotan, formerly Madra and Sailya, see these words, Deva Dharma Raja, and page 8
Bhotiyas, Hindus, so called from living near the frontier, 24, 215; see also Kath Bhotiyas, and Seyena Bhotiyas
Bhotiyas, a nation occupying Bhot, 25, 50–60, 118, 158, 165, 194, 242, 243, 248, 287, 288, 293, 307
Bhurjapatra, Bhuryapatra, } a medicinal herb, 97
Bhutkes, Bhutkesar, } a medicinal plant, 86, 98
Bichari, a judge, 102, 105, 150
Bichhakor, a customhouse, 196
Bidur Sahi, a chief of Gorkha, 261
Biga, a measure of land, 153, 154, 216
Bihadani, a duty on marriages, 161
Bikh, Bikhma, } a medicinal herb, 98, 99
Bilasi, a mart, 124
Bilaspur, Easter, see Dalu Dailek
Bilaspur, Wester, a lordship, 303, 304
Bilaspur, a town in Kahalur, 313
Binayak, first Raja of Butaul, 132, 170
Binayakpur, see Butaul

Birch tree, 83, 97
Birds, kinds of, 67, 95
Birkot, a lordship, 238, 239, 241
Birtha, a kind of melk land, 219
Bish, } a medicinal herb, 98, 99
Bishma, }
Bishtako, a tribe, 18, 28
Bist, see Karyi
Bisuli, a weight, 216
Bitalpa, a person holding land by a certain kind of tenure, 107, 219
Bitrawati river, 194
Bombax heptaphyllum or Simul tree, 68
Borax the drug, 214
Borbhakan, one of the twelve lordships, 306
Bos Bubalus, see Buffalo
Bos grunniens or cattle, the tails of which are called Chamari, Changwari, Chaungri, or Chauri, with different breeds of the same species, called Lulu and Jhogo, 76, 93, 217, 285
Bos Taurus, see Neat cattle
Bouddha, sect of, see Buddhas, and pages 10, 25, 30, 32, 40, 189, 208, 209
Bouddhama, a temple, 209, 211
Brahma, a deity, 32
Brahma, a sect and tribe, 189, 279
Brahmans
- Introduction into Nepal, &c. 10, 25, 305
- Manners, 16
- Privileges, 104, 179, 219, 234, 251
- Number, 242, 244, 252, 265, 266, 267, 269, 275, 277, 279, 281, 282, 286, 297
- Military, 48
- Of Mithila, 46

Brahmaputra river, 91, 214
Brahma Sahi, a chief of Gorkha, 254, 255, 261, 298, 301
Brahmutra or Brehmoter, lands held by a peculiar tenure, 219
Brass, the metal, 232
Breccia, a rock, 66
Brehmoter, see Brahmutra
Brick, 39, 233
Bridges, see Sangga and Ihola
Brim, a medicinal herb, 100
Brittiya, a person holding a kind of landed estate, 107, 219
Buddha, a deity or lawgiver of the Bouddha sect, 25, 29, 32, 56, 57, 190, 206
Budhkarna, a chief of the Kiratas, 140
Buffalo or Bos Bubalus, a kind of cattle, 76, 217
Bukhshi, a high military officer, 115
Burmah, a nation, 189
Burmah dynasty, see Varma
Burning rock, 312, see also Spring burning
Butaul or Binayakpur, a town and lordship, 132, 170, 180, 265, 274, 277

Caltha, a kind of plant, 99
Cannabis sativa, Charas, Gangja, Hemp, Ieea, or Subje, a plant, 226, 231
Capitation tax, see Rajangka and Sayer
Cardamon, a seed, 74
Casts, a hereditary division of professions, 16, &c. 30, &c. 234, 242, 265, 266, 267, 268, 274, 275, 277, 278, 279, 281, 282, 286, 297
Catechu, see Khayer and Mimosa
Cattle, see Bos grunniens, Buffalo, Goat, Horse, Neat, Sheep, Swine
Cedrella, a kind of tree called Tungd or Toon, 67
Chakor, } a bird, see Perdix rufa
Chakuri, }
Chakran, lands granted in fee for service, see Feodal
Cham, a lordship, 280
Chamari, see Bos grunniens
Chamba, a lordship, 315
Chamkal, a cast of Newars, 37
Champa, a tree, see Michelia
Champaranya, a lordship, often called Rajapur, or Rajpur, from its capital, see Rajapur
Champawati, a town, see Kumau
Chana, a grain, see Cicer arietinum
Chancelor, a high law officer, see Dharm'adikar
Chandangiri mountain, 204, 205
Chandi, a territory in Garhawal, 299, 301
Chandpur, a town and lordship, 298
Chandel Rajputs, a tribe, 268, 269, 307, 310
Changgu Narayan, a temple, 219
Changiya, a fortress, 157
Changra, see Goat
Changwari, see Bos grunniens
Charas, see Cannabis
Charity lands or Khairat zemin, see Melk
Chariyagarhi, a fortress, 165

Chaturbhuja Raja of Yumila, 15
Chaubisi, Chaubisiya, or twenty-four Rajas, a portion of the Gorkha territory, 145, 237, 268, 269, 270, 276, 278
Chaudanda, a town, 151
Chaudandi Raja, 146, 165
Chaudas, a territory, 294
Chaudhuri, an officer of government, 102, 105, 150, 152
Chauhan or Sisaudhiya tribe of Rajputs, 129, 130, 240, 297
Chaungri, Chaury, } see Bos grunniens
Chautariya or Choutra, called Hitan in Yumila, chief officer of state, 107, 108, 147, 255, 260, 261, 262, 287
Chayenpur, a province or large district, and its capital, 156
Chayenpur, a town on the San Kosi, 168
Chesnut tree, 83, 217
Chhawa Raja, the title among the Bengalese for the heir-apparent of Sikim, 120
Chhinachhin, a town, 283, 285
Chhipi, a cast of Newars, 37
Chilli, a lordship and town, 279
China and Chinese empire called Hung (Hun) by the Gorkhalese, 51, 122, 176, 248, 272, 288, 289, 298, 299; commerce with, 212
Chirata, a kind of Gentiana used in medicine, 85
Chiriyaghat hills and defile, 197
Chiriyamahal, a duty on birds, 68, 153, 163
Chisapani, a fortress, 168, 199, 201
Chitaur, colony from, 12, 15, 18, 20, 128, 129, 130, 178, 184, 240, 297
Chitlong, a town, 204
Chootraphul, see Berberis
Choutra, see Chautariya
Christians, 38
Chronology of the Hindus, 188
Chunra, 20
Chuya, a grain, perhaps the Holcus Sorghum, 315
Cicer arietinum, or Chana, a grain, 284
Cinnabar, a mineral, see Mercury
Civil power subordinate to the military, 109, see Establishment
Clay, 81, 83
Climate healthiness, see Air, Ayul; influence on the human appearance or colour, 60; state of, or weather, see Register at the end, and Weather
Clothing, see Dress
Coins, 154, 214, 215
Colebrooke, Colonel, 3
Colebrooke, H. T. Esq. 3
Collector of revenue, see Bandari
Colonies of Hindus, see Asanti, Bhim Sen, Chitaur, Thor Chandra
Colour of men, 60
Commerce, state of, see Customhouses, Porterage, and pages 104, 212, 243
Exports and imports, 124, 126, 157, 212, 284
Company, English East India, 143, 176, 177, 291
Company of troops, its establishment, 110, &c.
Convolvulus Batatas, Sakarkandh, or sweet potatoe, 230
Copper, the metal, 76, 203, 242, 264, 267, 269, 272, 275, 297, 301, 306
Copper manufacture, 232, 233
Corporal punishments, 103, 104
Corundum, a stone, 79, 267
Cotton, 64, 68, 74, 232
Cotton manufacture, 232
Court of the Raja, see Rajdani
Courts of justice, see Law
Crawford, Colonel Charles, his maps and drawings, 3, &c.
Crops of cultivated lands, 217, 222, &c.; see Produce, Grains
Crystal rock, 94, 195, 272, 301
Cuckoo, the bird, 203
Cucumber, the fruit, 229
Cultivation, extent of, see Agriculture
Cultivation by clearing forests, 68
Cultivation by the hoe, 274, 275
Customhouses, Golas, or Marts, 125, 126, 150, 152, 153, 156, 157, 161, 163, 164, 165, 168, 180, 218, 242, 265
Cynosurus, or Eleusine Corocanus, Maruya, or Pangdu Kodo, a grain, 226, 275
Cypressus, a tree, 97

Dahar, a fortress, 316
Daibyghaut, see Devighat
Dalbergia, a tree called Sisau, 67
Dalka, a town, 167
Dalu Basandra, burning springs, 281

Dalu Dailek, or Bilaspur, a lordship, 279, 280, 281
Dama, a coin and money, 214, 215
Damai, a cast, 20
Dami, a priest of the Magar tribe, 26
Damodar kund, a place in Thibet, 273
Damodar Pangre, an officer of Gorkha, 173, 175, 176, 248, 252, 254, 255, 257—259, 269, 296
Danakoti, a town, 274
Dang, a lordship and town, 238, 239, 277, 278, 288
Danpur, a territory, 293
Daphne, a tree called Siedburrooa, 85, 236
Darjiling, a fortress in Sikim, 119, 127, 157
Darogha, a judge, 102, 114
Darwe, a tribe, 279
Datarpur, a lordship, 314
Debt, recovery of, 104
Degarchi, a town of Thibet, residence of the Tishu Lama, see Tishu, and pages 57, 212, 213
Desa, in Hindu geography, denotes the 56 divisions of their country Bharatkhanda, 192
Desali, or Kamin, an officer of government, 102, 105, 113
Deva Dharma Raja, title of the prince of Bhotan, 56, 119, 120, 121, 122
Devatas, deities of an inferior rank, 32
Devi, Bhawani, Guhyiswari, Mahamaia, Parwati, Sakti, or Tulasi, a goddess, spouse of Siva, 193, 204, 310, 312
Devighat, or, according to Colonel Kirkpatrick, Daibyghaut, a town and place of pilgrimage, 193
Devikot mountain, 205
Dewan, chief minister of finance, 2, 148, 149, 150
Dewapatun, a town, 209, 212
Dewghat, a town and place of pilgrimage, 185
Dhaka, a town in Bengal, 212
Dhama, the holy land of Nepal, 192
Dhana, gifts for the remission of sins, 219
Dhangphiya, a bird, see Phasianus
Dharma, a territory and passage among the snowy mountains, 276, 280, 293, 298
Dharm'Adikar, or Chancelor, a high officer of law, 102, 103, 105, 114
Dharma Prakas, chief of Sirmaur, 304
Dharmapur, one of the twelve lordships, 306
Dharni, a weight, 216
Dhayabung, a town, 194
Dherna, a manner of recovering debt, 104
Dhewar, a tribe, 21
Dhimsa, a village, 194
Dhor, a lordship, 238, 239, 241
Dhoral, the castle of the chiefs of Malebum, 271
Dhui, a tribe of Newars, 36
Dhunchi, a village, 194
Dhupi, a tree, see Juniperus
Dhurkot, a lordship, 238, 240, 263, 266
Dilli, Mogul kings of, 299, 301, 303, 311, 312
Dimali, a tribe, see Mech
Dimali, a mart, see Siumali
Dimba Ray, chief of Malebum, 270
Dinajpur, a district, formerly Matsya, 7
Dip Chandra, a chief of Kumau, 294
Dipal, a town, 282
Diseases, 71
Ditha, a minister of justice, 105
Dolichos Mungo, Muk and Mugy May, or Mung, a grain, 227
Dolichos Soia, Gya, Bhotmas, or Musa, 228
Domestics, 234
Dress or clothing, 232
Drugs, 74, 85, 285
Duck, a bird, 223
Dudhkunda, a mart in Thibet, 166
Duhalde's account of China, 289
Dun, a large valley in the hilly region, 68, 313
Dun, a territory in Garhawal, 299, 301, 303
Dun, a territory west from the Satrudra, 313
Dungoda, a mineral concretion, 81
Durbar, a term adopted from the Muhammedans for the Raja's court, 108; see Rajdani
Duti, a lordship, 279, 282, 287, 292, 293
Duties on adultery, see Adultery
on birds, see Chiriyamahal
on boats, 163
on catechu, see Khayersal
on concubines, see Sagora
on goods imported, see Customhouse
on marriage, see Bihadani
on timber, see Kathmahal
Duyariya, chief and magistrate of a small extent of territory, 149, 150

Elephant, 63, 66, 218
Eleusine, a grain, see Cynosurus
Emodus mountain, see Himaliya
Ervum Lens, Mosu, or Mosuri, a grain, 228, 284
Erythrina monosperma, or Palas tree, 63
Establishment of civil government, 149, &c. 155, 162
Establishment, military, see Military
Estates, landed, management of, 220
Europeans, 246, 300

Fagara, a kind called Tinmue or Taizbul, 84
Fairs or Melas at Devighat, 193, at Dudhkunda, 165, at Kalesi, 165, at Nilkantha, 194, at Rerighat, 180
Fallow in agriculture, 281
Farms and gardens cultivated on the Raja's account, 217
Farmers who rent land to cultivate, 220
Farmers of rents and duties, 162, 163
Fenugreek, a pot herb, 229
Feodal tenure, or lands held in fee for service, called Chakran and Jaygir by the natives; see Jaygir, and pages 107, 150, 156, 163, 164, 212, 218
Fevers, 71
Fines imposed as a punishment or expiation, 103
Fines as a source of revenue, 103, 161, 164, 218
Fir tree, see Pinus picea
Fish, 65
Fluxes, 71
Food, 236
Forests, 64, 196, 197, 198, 200, 202, 217, 218
Foujdar, the military chief of a district or Taluk, 114
Fouzdar, the chief officer of revenue in a district or Taluk, 105, 150, 152, 155, 161
Fox, 63
Fruit, 73, 230
Fuel, 225
Futeh Sa, a chief of Garhawal, 299

Gajal, a lordship, 276, 280
Gajarkot, a lordship, 171, 184, 238, 239
Galkot, a lordship and town, perhaps the Ghoorikote of Kirkpatrick, 238, 239, 269, 275
Gandaki, Kali, Krishna, Narayani, or Saligrami river, 79, 91, 181, 272, 273
Gandharbha Sen, Raja of Palpa, 171
Gandhauk, capital of the part of Sikim remaining independent, 122
Gandi river, 244
Gang or Gram, a small division of territory, a village, a manor, 102, 113, 150, 155
Gangaye, a tribe, 156, 164
Ganges river sources, or Ganggotri, 3, 301, 302
Ganggoli, a town, 297
Ganggotri, see Ganges
Gangja, see Cannabis
Gar, see Garhawal
Garahang, a lordship, 238, 239, 241
Gardens, kitchen, 230, see also Fruit
Garhawal or Gar, a principality, often called Srinagar from its modern capital, 248, 283, 295, 298-302, 303
Garhi, a district or considerable portion of territory, 150
Garlic, the root, 228, 229
Gar Pasara, a fortress, 168, 196
Gar Samaran, a ruined city, once the capital of Mithila or Tirahut, 45, 49, 129, 188, 190, 191
Gautama, a deity of the Buddhas, 57
Gautamiya, a tribe, 270, 271
Gelpo, title of the chief of Sikim, 118
Gengdi, a town, 241
Gentiana, called Chirata, 85
Ghaman, chief of Kangra, 310
Gharti, a tribe, 18, 19, 28, 279
Ghiring, a lordship, 171, 184, 238, 239
Ghosts, worship of, 26
Ghowasin, a lordship, 310
Ginger root, 75, 229, 306
Giuseppe, Father, his account of Nepal, 7
Goat, common, 76, 217
Goat producing the shawl-wool or Changra, and its wool, 76, 93, 217
Gods of the Hindus, 288; see also Brahma, Devi, Gautama, Gorakhanath, Kangkali, Salagram, Siva, Tulasi, Temples, Vishnu
Goitre or swelled throat, 72, 87
Gola, see Customhouse
Gold, 76, 93, 272, 289, 298
Gomashtah, an officer of revenue, 103
Gootum, a lordship, 280
Gopal dynasty, or second family of Cowherd kings in Nepal, 188, 191, see Gupt

Gorakhanath, tutelar deity of the reigning family, 210, 211, 244
Gorakhpur district, once subject to Tirahut, 129
Gorayit, a messenger employed in the police and revenue departments, 155
Gordonia, a tree, 83
Gorkha, a lordship, 238, 242, 243
Gorkha Rajas extraction and genealogy, 26, 52, 240, 243, 262, 263
 policy, 64, 120, 172, 174, 175, 178, 179, 180, 239, 249, 278, 284, 300
 present power, 7, 117, &c.
 conquest of the Baisi and Chaubisi Rajas, 145, 173, 248, 269, 271
 conquest of Butaul, &c. 177
 conquest of Chaudandi, 146
 conquest of Garhawal and the countries to the west of the Ganges, 259, 299, 304, 307, 311
 conquest of Khidim, 171
 conquest of Kumau, 174, 296
 conquest of Makwanpur, 144, &c.
 conquest of Morang, 140, &c.
 conquest of Nepal, 145, 192, 245
 conquest of Palpa, 177, 261,
 conquest of Sikim, 120, &c. 248
 conquest of Yumila, 250, 287
Gosaignsthan, one of the chief peaks ot Emodus, 194
Got, a cast of Newars, 34
Gotoo, a cast of Newars, 37
Government, 101, &c. 287
Govindapur, a town, 313
Grains, see Amaranthus, Barley, Cynosurus, Dolichos, Ervum, Holcus, Paspalum, Phaseolus, Pisum, Rice, Sesamum, Uya, Wheat, Produce
Gram, see Gang
Granite, see Aggregate rocks
Guhyiswari, an idol and temple of Devi, 208
Gular, a lordship, 312, 314
Gulmi, a lordship and town, 171, 173, 174, 238, 239, 251, 263
Gunpowder, 164
Gupt or Ahira, that is, the (1st) cow-herd dynasty in Nepal, 188, 189, 190, 191, see Gopal
Guru, the spiritual guide of a Hindu, 211, 255
Gurung, a people, 25, 27, 28, 242, 274, 275, 287

Hakuya, a preparation of rice, 224
Hamo, see Sesamum
Hang, chief of the Kirata nation, 133, 146
Hang, chief of the Lapcha nation, 118, 121
Hanur, a lordship, 304, 307
Harbhang Rajas, a dynasty governing the Kiratas, 132
Hare the animal, 68
Hariballabh, his information concerning the countries west from the Kali river, 5
Hariharpur, a fortress, 168, 197
Haripur, capital of Gular, 314
Hari Singha, Raja of Mithila and Garsamaran, 190, 191
Harsha Deva, a turbulent Brahman, 295, 296, 299, 311
Hasthadal, a chief of Gorkha, 261
Hatiya, a mart, 157, 159
Hatuya, a fortress, 165
Hawoo tribe, 25
Hedang, a town, 157, 158, 165
Heir apparent, 107
Hemp, see Cannabis
Hethaura, an important station, 198
Hial, a cast of Newars, 36
Hilly country or region, 66, 125, 168, 197 199, 200
Himachul, Himadri, Himaleh, Himalichul, Himaliya, } Also called Humla, the Emodus of the ancients, 28, 62, 88-93, 124, 159, 164. 242, 243, 284, 288, 298, 301, 315
Hindus of the mountains, called Parbatiyas or Highlanders, Colonies, see Colony, and 9, &c. 23, 28, 165, 286, 287, 291, 302, 305
 Conversion, 38
 Intolerance, 23, 37, 293, 297, 302, 312, 315
 Manners, 21, 204, 208, 247
Hindustan, 91
Hindoo Coosh mountain, 92
Hingwalka bara Saral, see Yew tree

Hingwalka chhota Saral, see Pinus picea
Hitan, see Chautariya
Hodoya Bikh or Bish, a drug, 99
Hoe, the implement, 221
Hog deer, 68
Hog wild, 68
Holcus Sorghum, Kaungni, Muccai, or Muruli, a grain, 227, 231, see Chuya
Holly tree, 83
Hornbeam tree, 83
Hornstone rock, 66
Horse, 76, 217, 284
Houses, kind, 38, &c. 210, 241, 242, 263, 265, 266, 267, 268, 275, 277, 278, 281, 297, 313
Number, see Population
Taxed, 154, 162, 217
Humla, see Himaliya
Hung, see China.

Ichhang lima, a part of the snowy mountains, see Himaliya
Ika, see Sinapis
Implements of agriculture, 221, 226
Indus river, 91, 289
Information, sources of, 1, &c.
Inhabitants, 9, &c. see Aborigines, Population
Intoxication, 22, 25, 26, 35, 38, 55, 224, 226, see also Cannabis
Iron, blue earthy ore, a mineral, 81
Iron manufacture, 232
Iron mines, 76, 77, 264, 265, 266, 269, 272, 275, 278, 297, 306, 316
Irrigation, as a manure, 195, 203, 223
Ischæmum, called Sabé, a grass used for ropes, 64
Isma, a lordship, 238, 239, 263, 267
Izaradar or Renter, an officer of revenue, 105

Jackal, the wild beast, 68
Jagajit, a chief of the Pangre family, 296, 299
Jagannath, an idol's temple, 209
Jagat Chandra, a chief of Kumau, 294
Jagat Gar, a fortress, 303
Jagat Prakas, chief of Sirmaur, 303
Jahari lordship, 270, 276, 280
Jainti, a drug, 86
Jajarkot, lordship and town, 270, 276, 280, 283, 284, 286
Janaka Rajas, ancient chiefs of Mithila, 45, 161
Janaka Pur, their capital, 45, 161
Jar or Jariya tribe, 25, 28, 270, 291, 297
Jarapani, a mart, 277
Jat, a tribe, 297, 312
Jatamangsi, a drug, 97
Jausi, a tribe of illegitimate Brahmans, 17, 178, 275, 277, 279, 281, 282
Jausi, a tribe of Newars, 33
Jayadeva, see Jaydeva
Jaya Kirti, chief of Garhawal, 295
Jaya Krishna, a turbulent Brahman, 294
Jaya Singhapur, a town, 310
Jaydeva or Jayadeva, a Brahman of note, 291, 294
Jaygir, land held by feodal tenure for the performance of service, 107 155, 156, 164, 169, 212, 298, 299, 301, 303, see Feodal
Jaysalmer, a lordship in the Rajput country, 302
Jajurbedi Brahmans, a sect, 17
Jeea, see Cannabis
Jethabura, a chief officer of government, 107
Jhausi, a town on the Ganges, 291
Jhogo, see Bos grunniens
Jhola, a bridge made of rattan ropes, 27
Jhula, a drug, see Lichen
Jimri, see Rapti river
Jopu, a cast of Newars, 34
Joyar, a territory and passage among the snowy mountains, 293, 298
Jumnemundru, a tree, see Leontice
Juniperus, called Dhupi, a tree, 96
Juniperus, called Thumuriya Dhupi, a tree, 96
Jury, or Pangchayit, 102, 114
Jyotish, see Astrology
Jwalamukhi, a town, temple, and burning rock, 312

Kahalur, a lordship, 307, 312, 316
Kaigo, a pulse, see Pisum
Kailasa mountain, 90, 288
Kajy, an officer, see Karyi
Kakun, a grain, see Panicum italicum
Kalagong lordship, 280
Kalamakwani family, 263
Kalap gram, a cave famous in legend, 302

Kali river, there are two of this name, see Gandaki, and 282
Kaliya, see Secretary
Kalsi, a town, 303, 306
Kamalgar, a fortress, 316
Kamal Lochan, his maps, 4
Kami, a tribe, 20
Kamin, an inferior officer of government, see Desali
Kamiya Brahmans, 17
Kamrup, the district of Ranggapur and the adjacent part of Asam, 7, 119, 156
Kanak Nidhi Tiwari, his account and map of the Khas country, 4, 291
Kanet, a tribe, 305
Kangkali, a deity, 48
Kangkari, a fruit, 229
Kangra, a lordship, temple, and town, 304, 305, 309—312, 313
Kanguni, a grain, see Panicum italicum
Kankayi river, 124, 159
Kanungo, register in a Subah's office, 155
Karanali, Salasu, Sarayu, or Sonabhadra river, 5, 91, 289
Karara river, 197
Karki, tribe, 18, 28
Karmi, cast, 20, 36
Karna Prakas, chief of Sirmaur, 304, 305
Karphul tree, see Myrica
Karuvirpur, a principality and town, 12, 129, 291, 292, 293, 298
Karyi, Kazi, or, according to Kirkpatrick, Kajy, in Yumila called Bist, 102, 107, 108, 147, 259, 287
Kasachiet, a town, 209
Kasai, a cast of Newars, 37
Kasipur, a territory, 293
Kaski, a lordship, 27, 238, 239, 242
Kasmir, a country, 212
Kasuliya, a cast of Newars, 37
Katauch Rajputs, 310
Katha, a measure of land, 216
Kath Bhotiya, a dynasty of princes from Thibet, called also Burmahs or Varmas, 59, 189, 190, 191, 209
Kath Mahal, duties on timber, 153, 155, 163
Kathmandu, Kathmaro, { modern name of the capital of Nepal, and a principality, 209, 210, 211, 212
Kausiki river, see Kosi
Kawa karpola mountain, part of Himaliya, 124
Kazi, see Karyi
Kedarnath, a temple, 302
Kengothal, one of the twelve lordships, 306
Kerao, a grain, see Pisum
Kerung, or Kheero, a town and district of Thibet, 195, 272
Khachi, a lordship, 171, 173, 238, 239, 263, 265
Khaira, a tree, see Mimosa
Khanal, a family of Brahmans, 103
Khari, space between two rivers, 150
Kharka, tribe, 18, 28
Khas, the country between Nepal and the Kali river, with its aboriginal inhabitants, 4, 8, 18, 19, 23, 28, 281, 305
Khas, or Khasiya, a mixed breed between Hindu colonists and aborigines, 19, 156, 160, 164, 169, 178, 242, 244, 265, 266, 268, 270, 275, 277, 279, 282, 286
Khasant, part of the lordship of Malebum, 275
Khasant, another name for Saliyana
Khasbasha, language of the mountain Hindus, 16, 287
Khasiya, see Khas
Khatang, a district, 164, 166
Khati, a tribe, 287
Khatri, see Kshatri
Khawa, a cast or tribe, 20
Khayersal, duties on Catechu, 67, 153, 154, 155, 163
Kheero, see Kerung
Khet, or field, a measure of land, 216
Khidim, a small territory, 171, 181
Khor, a mart, 265
Khukri, a large knife or dagger, 111
Khungri, a lordship, 239, 268, 270
Khurchah, arbitrary exactions, under pretence of defraying expence, 105, 154
Khurdar, see Secretary
Khuzanchee, or treasurer, a chief officer of the Raja's household, 108
Kichak, a dynasty, see Kirata
Kichak, a people, see Kirata
Kichak jhar, a ruin, 152
King, see Raja
King supreme, 283
Kirata, or Kichak, a nation, 2, 7, 25, 53, 128, 132, 148, 160
Kirata, or Kichak, dynasty in Nepal, 132, 189, 191

Kirkpatrick, Colonel, his account of Nepal, 5, 217
Kirti Prakas, chief of Sirmaur, 302
Kirtipur, a town, 158, 205, 209, 211
Koch, or Rajbungzi, a tribe, 119, 125, 156
Kodo, a grain of two kinds, Pangdu and Sana, 226, 227
Kohrya, land, 231
Koncha, a kind of turf, 81, 223
Kosar, a cast of Newars, 37
Kosi, or Kausiki, river, 166. 195
Kothar, one of the twelve lordships, 306
Kotta, a fortress, 311, 312
Kottahar, a lordship, 310, 313
Kotwal, a beadle or messenger, 150
Kow, a cast of Newars, 37
Krishna river, see Gandaki
Kritimohun, a chief of Gorkha, 254
Kshatri, Kshatriya, or Khatri, a cast, 18, 52, 275
Kshir kangkri, a drug, 86
Kuchar, a part of Bhotan or Thibet, south from the highest Himaliya mountains, 90
Kullu, a lordship, 315
Kumarsen, one of the twelve lordships, 306
Kumau or Almora, a principality and town, called also Champawati and Kurmachal, 12, 13, 174, 261, 291-298
Kumbi, a fortress, 168
Kuppardar or storekeeper, 108
Kurarbas, a fortress, 168
Kurin Namki, chief of Sikim, 121
Kuriya, see Farmers who rent land
Kurmachul, see Kumau
Kurthi, a pulse, 282
Kutki, a drug, 100
Kutti, a province and town of Thibet, 121, 212

Labour, agricultural, 233, 234
Labour, rate of, 233
Ladak, a town in Thibet, 212, 289
Lahaur, (vulgo Lahore,) king or chief of, see Ranjit Singha, and 318
Lahuri Nepal, 202, 203, 204
Lalita Patun, a town and principality, 204, 209, 210, 211
Lalit Sa, chief of Garhawal, 295, 299, 303
Lal Singha, chief of Kumau, 295
Lama, an incarnation of a Buddha, and a priest of that sect in Thibet, 1, 25, 27, 52-57, 158, 287
Lama dangra, a chain of mountains, 167, 200
Lama, residing at Lassa, 10, 56, 58
Lama Tishu, see Tishu
Lamja, a mart, 165
Lamjun, a lordship, 238, 239, 243
Land measures, 153
Land rent, see Rent of land
Land, value by sale, 220
Langna, narrow vallies among the Alpine mountains, 28
Language of the Gods, that is, according to the Hindus, Sangskritta, 292
Language of men, that is, spoken language, 292
Gurung, 29
Jariya, 28
Khas or Parbatiya, 16
Kirata, 54
Limbu, 54
Magar, 25
Murmi, 52
Newar, 50
Parbutiya, see Khas
Lapcha, a people, 25, 55, 118
Lassa, a country in Thibet, 10, 56, 212, 213, see Lama
Laurel, } called Sinkauli, Sinkauri, and
Laurus, } Tejpat, 83, 84
Law, courts of, 102, &c. 114, 150, 155, 212
Laws, 101, &c. 150, see also Torture, Corporal punishment, Process, Fine, Prayaschitta, Panchayit, Police
Lead, the metal, 76, 78, 297
League for defence, called Athabhai, 239
League for defence, called Satbhai, 239
Leontice, a tree called Jumne Mundroo, 85
Leprosy, 72
Liberty, 108
Lichens, a drug called Jhul, 87
Limbu, a people, 25, 54, 118, 160, 164
Limestone, 66, 82
Limi, a town, 241
Lodi, a tribe, 297
Lohangga, founder of a dynasty, and its history, 132, 134, &c. 146, &c.
Lordships Twelve, a territory subject to Gorkha, see Bara Thakurai
Lulu, see Bos grunniens

Madarmali, the common silver coin, 215
Madder Indian, see Manjit

Madra, an ancient name for Bhotan, derived from a prince by whom that country called properly Sailya, was governed, 8
Magar, (Mungur of Kirkpatrick,) a people, 25, 28, 156, 160, 164, 169, 171, 178, 240, 244, 264, 291, 297
Mahadatta, Raja of Palpa, 170, 172, 250, 268
Mahalok, one of the twelve lordships, 306
Maha Maia, see Devi
Mahamandal, a peak of Himaliya, containing mines, 195
Mahatari, a district, 135, 160, 162, 168
Mahato, a petty officer, 102, see Mokkuddum
Mahes, a river, 193
Mahes Domohana, a town, 193
Mahipat Sa, chief of Garhawal, 298
Maingmo or Meyangma, part of the Kimaliya mountains, 89, 158, 160
Maize, a grain, 284, 312
Majhi, a tribe, 18, 21, 28, 279
Majhoya, a mart, 124
Makunda Sen, son of Rudra, Raja of Palpa, 131, 170
Makunda Sen, son of Udyata, Raja of Palpa, 170, &c. 245, 264, 268
Makwani, Makwanpur, a principality and district, 130, 132, 133, 144, 164, 167, 195, &c.
Makwanpur, a fortress, 168, 198
Mal family, chiefs of the Newar tribe, 29, 52, 187, 191
Mal family, chiefs of Malebum, 271
Malaneta, a lordship, 276, 280
Malay, a nation, 52
Malayagiri, a tree, 84
Malebamba, Malebum, called also Parbat, a lordship, 28, 238, 239, 245, 269, 275, see Mal
Malebum, a town, see Beni shahar
Malihang, a lordship, 269
Mana, a measure of grain, 216
Manal, a bird, see Meleagris
Manasa Sarawar, Manasarawar, a lake, 90, 288
Mandhata, Raja of Vijayapur, and his descendants, 139, &c.
Manik, Raja of Makwanpur, and his descendants, 144
Manjit or Indian madder, 74
Manners, dissoluteness, 72, 204
Manu, a passage among the snowy mountains, 301
Manufactures, 232, see also Bell metal, Brass, Cotton, Iron, Mint, Paper, Woollen
Manure, in agriculture, 223
Manuriya Rajputs, a tribe, 293
Maps, by Colonel Crawford, 3
Maps, by various natives, 2, 3, 4, 5, 124, 160
Marichangdi river, 244, 246
Markets, 152, 161, 164, 168, 220
Marts, for trade, see Customhouses
Maruya, a grain, see Cynosurus
Mas, May, or Mung, several kinds of pulse, see Dolichos and Phaseolus
Masha, a weight, 290
Mastang, a lordship in Thibet, 272, 273, 283
Matagari, a town, 281
Materia Medica of India, 100
Matsya, an ancient kingdom, now the district of Dinajpur, 7, 119
Matsyendranath, a deity, and his temple, 32, 211
May, a pulse, see Mas
Measures, 153, 154, 216
Mech or Dimali, a tribe, 119, 125, 156
Meleagris Satyra or Manal, a bird, 95, 285
Melk or charity land, or Khairat zemin, land held in perpetuity, which does not pay rent to the prince, 149, 179, 212, 216, see also Bitalpa and Brittiya
Menjoo Dev', a deity, (probably Manyu, son of Brahma,) 206
Mercury, the metal, 78, 264, 272
Meyangma, see Maingmo
Mica, a mineral, 94, 195, 272
Michelia or Champa, a tree, 83, 217
Military establishment or army, 110, 115, 148, 149, 246, 262, 298, 306, see Seapoy, Telangga
Military rank, higher than civil, 109
Military tenure, see Feodal
Mill water for grain, 221
Mimosa, called Khaira, 67
Minerals, 66, 76, 195, see Mines
Mines, see Copper, Corundum, Crystal, Gold, Iron, Lead, Mercury, Mica, Salt, Sulphur, Zinc, also 76, 154, 156, 164, 166, 169, 181, 184, 195, 218, 264, 275, 277, 306
Mint at Almora, 293, at Kathmandu, 213, 293

Mirgu, part of the snowy mountains, 89, 158, 159
Mitha, a root, 99
Mithila or Tirahut, an ancient kingdom, 156, 191
Mohan Singha, a chief of Kumau, 294
Mohur, a coin, 214, 215
Moburer, register in the Fouzdars office, 155
Mokuddum, a petty officer, called also Mahato, Pradhan, and Umra, 102, 113, 150, 153, 155
Money of accounts, 214, see Coin
Money, rent, 220
Moon, family of, 291
Morang, a lordship and district, 138, 151, &c.
Mosu, } a pulse, see Ervum Lens
Mosuri, }
Mountainous region, 69, 87, 168, 202
Muhammedans, see Musulman
Mujumdar, an officer of accounts, 102
Mukhola, salt mine, 286
Muktanath, hot springs, a place of pilgrimage, 79, 272
Mundi, a lordship and town, 304, 318
Mung, a pulse, see Mas
Mungur, a people, see Magar
Munsiyari, a territory, 293
Munsuf of Bahadurgunj, his information, 2
Muri, a measure of grain, 216
Murmi, a people, 25, 52, 59, 169
Musa, a fruit tree, called Plantain by the English, 230
Musa, a kind of pulse, see Dolichos
Music, 37, 111
Musikot, two lordships, 238, 239, 263, 266, 270, 276, 280
Musk, a drug, and the animal producing it, 94
Mustard, see Sinapis
Musulmans, properly Moslemin or Muhammedan, 38
Myrica, called Karphul, a tree, 85.

Nadaun, a town, 311, 312, 314
Nahan, a town, 302, 306
Nagarjun, a mountain, 205
Nag Bamba Mal, chief of Malebum, 270, 271
Nai, a cast, 20
Nalagar, a town, 308
Nanakamata, a territory, 293
Nandapur Tisuti, a lordship, 129
Narabhupal or Nribhupal, Raja of Gorkha, 244, 262
Naragarhi a town, 161
Narayan Das, a chief of Morang, 2
Narayani river, see Gandaki
Nau, a cast of Newars, 36
Nawab Singha chief of Dang, 278
Nawab Vazir, Muhammedan Prince of Oude or Ayodhya 277, 278, 301
Nawalpur, a town, 183
Nayakot, a lordship, and its capital, 238, 239, 241
Nayakot, a town of Nepal Proper, 194
Neat cattle, including oxen, (Bos taurus,) 76, 217
Neb, an inferior minister of a prince, 2, 147
Negi or Adhikar, an inferior officer of government, 114
Nepal Proper, conquest by the Gorkhalese, 7
  Definition, 7, 164, 167, 186, 192
  Description, 3, 80, 88, 205, &c.
  History, 187, &c.
  Name, 187, 192
  Originally a lake, 206
Newar, a people, 25, 29, &c. 48, 50, 59, 190, 191, 210, 225 229, 269
Nilkantha or Bara Nilkantha, a place of pilgrimage among the snow, 192, 194
Nirbikhi, } a root, 99
Nirbishi, }
Nitre or saltpetre, 164
Niyam Muni, (Nymuni of Kirkpatrick,) first king of Nepal, 187, 190
Nobility, see Aristocracy
Nribhupal, see Narabhupal
Nuggerkotie, tribe, 25
Nurpur, a lordship and town, 303, 314
Nymuni, see Niyam Muni.

Oak trees, 83, 202, 217
Oaths, 103
Orange, a fruit, 73, 230
Ordeal, trial by, 103, 104
Oriswa, a country, 46
Ox, see Neat cattle.

Padam chhal, a medicinal herb, 100
Pagan, Mr, his accounts of the country, 2
Paisah, a copper coin and money, 214, 215
Palaces, 210
Palas tree, see Erythrina
Pali, a district and town, 293, 297

Paliya, a people, 119
Palpa, a principality, 131, 170, &c. 238, 239, 245, 247, 251, 258
Pamar or Pangwar, a tribe, 240, 298
Panauni, river, 202
Panar river, 298
Pangchayit, a kind of jury, 102, 114
Pangdu Kodo, a grain, see Cynosurus
Pangre, a family of Brahmans, 103
Pangre, a noble family of Gorkha, 110, 254, 259, see also Damodar, Jagajit, and Ranjit
Pangtha, a family of Brahmans, 103
Pangwar, see Pamar
Panicum colonum, Tangri, or Kakun, a grain, 231
Panicum italicum, Kanguni, or Sami, a grain, 231, 275
Paper manufacture, 232
Papti, a part of the snowy mountains, 159
Parakeet, 67, 68
Parakrama, a turbulent chief, 295, 300
Parbat, a lordship, see Malebum
Parbatiya Basha or Khas Basha, the language spoken by the Parbatiya Hindus, 16
Parbatiya Hindu, a Hindu of the mountains, 11, 16, 210, 212
Pariyat mountains, 315
Parwati, see Devi
Pasara, a district, 168
Paspalum, called Sana Kodo, a grain, 227, 284
Pasture, 64, 75, 90, 204, 217, 288, 297
Pasupatinath, a temple of Siva, 208, 212, 219
Pathaniya, a tribe of Rajputs, 314
Pathankot, a territory, 314
Pathi, a measure of grain, 216
Pati or squad, a subdivision of a company of regular troops, 111
Patna, a city of Behar, 195, 212
Patwari, the clerk or register of a village, 155
Pauriyal, a tribe, 18
Pea, see Pisum
Peach tree, 73
Peasantry, 169
Perdix rufa, Chakor or Chakuri, a bird, 95, 235
Pergunah, a district or division of territory, 114, 150, 152, 153, 161, 162, 182
Phakali, a passage among the snowy mountains between Bhotan and Thibet, 127
Phakphok, part of the Himaliya mountains, 159
Phala, a mart, 166
Phalabam or New Dang, a town, 278
Phaphar, a grain, see Amaranthus
Phaseolus calcaratus, Roxb. Lata Rato and Ruta Mas or Hayngu May, a grain, 227
Phaseolus Minimoo Roxb. Urid, and Kala Mas or May, a grain, 227, 232, 284
Phaseolus ocultatus Roxb. Seta Mas, or Chika May, a grain, 227
Phaseolus racemosus Roxb. Lal Mung or Hayngu May, a grain, 227
Phasianus Impeyanus or Dhangphiya, a bird, 95, 285
Pilgrimage, 152, 161, 185, 192, 301, 302
Pine apple, 73, 230
Pine trees, 202, 217, see also Pinus
Pinus longifolia, Salla or long-leafed pine, a tree, 67, 197
Pinus strobus, or Weymouth pine, a tree, 83
Pinus picea, common spruce fir, or Hingwalka chhota Saral, 83, 96
Pisum arvense, Pea, Kerao, or Kaigo, 228, 284
Piuthana, a lordship, 231, 238, 268
Plain region subject to Nepal, see Tariyani
Plants, spontaneous, 63, 67, 83, 200
Pluviometer, see Register of the Weather at the end
Poin, a lordship, 238, 239, 269
Poison root, 55, 99
Pokang, a mart, 158, 159
Pokhara, a town and mart, 242
Police, 102, &c. 149, 212
Policy, see Gorkha
Population, 209, 242, 266, 267, 268, 269, 274, 275, 279, 297
Portaw, a province of Thibet, 121
Porters and porterage, 233
Potatoe, common, see Solanum
Potatoe, sweet, see Convolvulus
Pradhan, a petty officer, see Mokuddum
Pradipa Sa, a chief of Garhawal, 299, 310
Pradyumna Sa, a chief of Garhawal, 295, 299, 300
Praja, see Farmer who rents land to cultivate
Pratap Chandra, chief of Kumau, 296
Prati Nidhi Tiwari, his account of the Khas country, 4, 291

Prayag, five places of worship at the junctions of the principal branches of the Ganges, 302
Prayaschitta, an expiation or fine, 21, 103
Presents, a source of revenue, 106, 154
Prithwi Narayan, king of Gorkha, 141, 144, 171, 192, 211, 213, 214, 245, 262, 277
Prithwi Pal, Raja of Palpa, 174, 260
Process in law, 102
Produce of an acre, see Crops, and 216, 225
Prostitution, 235
Pujari, a priest who conducts the ceremonies of worship, 211, 219
Pulihu mountain, 205
Pun, a tribe, 279
Punishments, see Corporal, Fine, Prayaschitta
Puria, a tribe of Newars, 37
Purubi Brahmans, 17
Putaul, a tribe of Newars, 36

Queen, Rani, Maha Rani, or virgin spouse of a Raja, 105, 211, 212, 224, 235
Queen of Rana Bahadur, regent of Gorkha, 175, 212, 251, 252-258, 261, 264
Queen of Singha Pratap, regent of Gorkha, see Rajendra Lakshmi
Queen regent, concubine of Rana Bahadur, 251, 252-257

Radish root, 229
Rahal, a tribe, 287
Raja, the king, his authority and establishment, 102, 105, 147, 165, 219
Raja, a chief, often very petty, 261, 298
Rajangka, a kind of capitation or income tax, 106, 154, 156, 164, 169
Rajbungsi, a tribe, see Koch
Rajdani, the court of the king, 103
Rajendra Lakshmi, regent of Gorkha, 247
Rajgar or Rajpur, } a town, capital of Yasawal, 314
Rajpur or Champaranya, a lordship, 129, 131, 170, 172
Rajput, a tribe, see Chandel, Chauhan, Gautamiya, Katauch, Manuriya, Pathaniya, Raythaur, Samal, Shalivahana, Suryabangsi, also 15, 18, 19, 156, 160, 164, 169, 253, 266, 267, 269, 286, 297
Rama, ancestor of the Rajpur family, 170
Ramagar, a town in Hanur, 308
Ramajai Batacharji, his collections for the materials of this work, 1
Ramnagar, a district, 182
Rampur, chief town of Besar, 307
Rana or Thakur, a title inferior to Raja, a lord, 303, 313
Rana, a tribe, 18, 19
Rana Bahadur or Swamiji, king and regent of Gorkha, 174, 175, 213, 216, 247, 250-253, 258-261, 262, 264, 287, 300
Ranadhwar, a chief of Gorkha, 262
Ranajor, an officer of Gorkha, 305
Ranggapur, a district of Bengal, part of the ancient kingdom of Kamrup, 7
Rani, see Queen
Ranigar, a territory, 299
Ranjit Pangre, an officer of Nepal, 216
Ranjit Singha, the Sikh chieftain of Lahaur, 259, 305, 311, 312, 313, 314, 315
Rape seed, see Sinapis
Rapti or Jimri river, 268
Raputi river, 198, 199
Ratna Sen, Raja of Palpa, 177
Ravan Hrad lake, 288
Rawa, a fortress, 165
Rayapur, a lordship, 304, 305
Rayapur, a town, capital of Kottahar, 314
Raythaur, a family, chiefs of Jaysalmer and Sirmaur, 302
Reeds, 64
Register, an office in several courts, see Kanungo, Mohurir, Patwari, Suduriya
Reher, a territory, 293
Rent of arable land, 153, 161, 162, 211, 218, 220, 284
of houses, see House
of pasture, 153, 155, 162, 217
Rerighat, a town, 180, 264
Revenue, see Customs, Duties, Farms, Fines, Law courts of, Mines, Mint, Presents. Rajangka, Rent, Sayer, and also 105, 106, 112, 115, 149, 150, 153, 154, 156, 161, 164, 169, 211, 242, 243, 265, 267, 275, 277, 279, 293, 298, 301, 305, 307, 311, 313, 314, 316
Rhinoceros, 63
Rhododendrum, a tree, 97
Rice, 63, 65, 73, 74, 82, 217, 222, 265, 267, 282, 284, 297, 301, 305, 312, see also Hakuya, Takmare
Rillu, a territory, 315
Rising, a lordship, 171, 182, 184, 238, 239

Riti, a passage among the snowy mountains, 298, 301
Rivers in general, 65, 66, 89, 91, 195
Roads and routes in general, 180, 181, 220, 233, 265, 274, 280, 285, 286
Routes by Bareh from Kathmandu to the Low Country, 198
from Chatra on the Kosi to Nepal valley, 166
from Dudhkunda to Lengleng, 165
by Dudhkunda from the Kosi to Thibet, 165
from Dewghât to Nilkantha, 192–195
from the Gandaki to Nepal Proper, 183
by Gar Pasara from Kathmandu to the Low Country, 195
from Halesi to Lamja, 165
from Hethaura to the Low Country, 182
from Kathmandu to the Low Country by Gar Pasara, 195, by Bareh, 198
from the Kosi to Thibet by Lamja, 165, by Dudhkunda, ib.
from Lamja to Halesi, 165
from Lengleng to Dudhkunda, 165
from the Low Country to Hethaura, 182, to Kathmandu by Bareh, 198, by Gar Pasara, 195, to Siklik, 243
from Nepal valley to Chatra on the Kosi, 166, to Sivapur on the Gandaki, 183
from Nilkantha to Dewghat, 192–195, to Sivapur on the Gandaki, 193
from Pokang to Vijaypur, 157
from Siklik to the Low Country, 243
from Sivapur on the Gandaki to Nepal valley, 183, to Nilkantha and Thibet, 193
from Thibet to Chatra on the Kosi by Lamja, 165, by Dudhkunda, 165, to Sivapur on the Gandaki, 193
from Vijaypur to Pokang, 157
Roalpa, lordship, 280
Rohani, a tribe, 287
Rohuttut, a district, 168
Routes, see Roads
Rudra Chandra, a chief of Kumau, 292
Rudrapur, a fortress and territory, 293
Rudravir, a chief of Gorkha, 261
Rugun, a lordship, 270, 276, 280
Rup Chiring, a chief of Sikim, 119
Rupee, properly Rupiya, a coin, 154, 215. That of Calcutta worth nearly 25 pence at the mint price.
Rupini, a land measure, 216
Rupiya, see Rupee

Sa, Saha, or Sahi, a surname among the Rajputs of the Gorkha, Garhawal, Kalamakwani, and Shalivahana tribes, 262, 263, 282
Sabe, a kind of grass, see Ischæmum
Sabna, a territory, 293
Sacrifice, 236
Sacrifice, human, 35, 211, see also Samadi
Sadhu Ram Upadhyaya, his account and map of the Khas country, 4, 173
Sagora, a duty on each contract with a concubine, 161
Saha, Sahi, } see Sa
Sailya, a country, see Madra
Sakarkandh, see Convolvulus
Sakhuya, a tree, see Shoræa
Sakti, see Devi
Sakya, a teacher or prophet of the sect of Buddha, 10, 27, 29, 32, 56–58, 190, 191
Sal tree, see Shoræa
Salagram, a stone worshipped by the Hindus, 79, 273
Salagrami, a river, see Gandaki
Salasu river, see Karanali.
Salim, a cast of Newars, 36
Saliyana, a lordship, town, and government, 261, 270, 277, 278, 280
Salpa pahar, part of the Himaliya mountains, 160
Salt, culinary, 93, 214, 286, 301, 316
Sama, a grain, see Panicum
Samadi, the custom of burying alive, 138, 152
Samal, a tribe, 270, 278, 279
Samar Bahadur, his account of the Khas country, 4, 173
Samaran, see Gar Samaran
Sambhu, see Swayambhu
Sambhunath, see Swayambhunath
Samrigarhi, a fortress, 151

Sand, 80, 82
Sanders, red, or Lal Chandan, a tree, 85
Sandstone, 82
Sangga, a kind of wooden bridge, 274
Sanghu, a town, 209, 212
Sangkhasur, original lord of Nepal, 207
Sangsar Chandra, chief of Kangra, 303, 304, 310, 311, 314, 315, 316
Sankara Acharya, sect of, 30
Sankosi river, 166
Sanpati, a medicinal plant, 97
Saptari, a district, 135, 160, 168
Sarayu, a river, see Karanali
Sarisha, a grain, see Sinapis
Sarki, a cast, 18
Satadru river, see Satrudra
Satahung, a lordship, 238, 239, 241
Satatala, a territory, 276, 279, 280
Satbhai, see League
Satrudra, Satadru, or Sutluj river, 91, 288, 307, 315
Satya Raja, a dynasty governing the Kiratas, together with their residence, 133, 152
Sayer, or direct taxes, 153, 154, 156, 161, 162
Sayn, the name given by the Newars to the people of Thibet, &c. 56
Scorpion, the insect, 196
Seapoy, properly Sipahi, in Nepal applied to irregular armed men employed in the police and revenue, 106
Secretary, Kaliya, or Khurdar, 107, 108
Ser, a weight, that of Kathmandu weighing about 11,664 grains, that of Calcutta about 14,360, page 216
Serdar or Sirdar, one of the Baradar, or chief officers of government, 107, 257
Serdar, a very high military rank, 109, 151, 165
Serdar, a military officer among the Kiratas, 148, 149
Sesamum, Hamo, or Til, a seed used for oil, 223, 282
Seshant, a division of Malebum, 274
Seshant or Siklik, a mart and passage through the Himaliya mountains, 243
Setigangga, a river, 244, 282
Shalivahana Raja, and his descendants, the Shalivahana Rajputs, 12, 282, 287
Shawl goat, its wool, and shawls, 315, see also Goat
Sheep, tame, 75,214, 217, 274, 298,301,307
Sheep, wild, called Argali, 94
Sher Bahadur, a chief of Gorkha, 254, 260
Shivapuri or Siwapuri, a mountain, 205
Shops, 166
Shoræa robusta, Sal, or Sakhuya tree, 67, 198
Sial, a cast of Newars, 36
Sidhi Pratap, chief of Gulmi, 265
Siedburrooa, see Daphne
Sikh, a religious sect, 313, see also Ranjit Singha
Sikim, a principality, 1, 118, 119, 124, 126, 127, 140, 156, 157
Siklik, a mart, see Seshant
Silajit, a mineral, 80
Sili, a tribe, 18
Siling, see Sining
Silkauli, see Laurus
Silver, 76, see also Coin
Simul tree, see Bombax
Sinapis ramosa Roxb. or Ika, a grain, 228
Sinapis, called Sarisha or Turi, a kind of mustard or rape, 228
Sinduli, a fortress, 168, 199
Singgiya Bikh or Bish, 86, 98
Singha, a division of the Sikh sect, 313, see also Ranjit Singha
Singha Pratap, king of Gorkha, 171, 196, 246, 247
Sining or Siling, a town in China, 212
Sinkauri tree, see Laurus
Siragar, a territory, 293
Sirdar, see Serdar
Sirmaur, a lordship, 302–307
Sirnet, a family of Rajputs, 269
Sisau, a tree, see Dalbergia
Sisaudhiya, a tribe of Rajputs, see Chauhan
Sitakund, a burning spring near Chitagang, 273
Siumali or Dimali, a mart, 125
Siva, a deity, 32, 193, 208, 285, 302, 310, see also Kedarnath, Nilkantha, and Pasupatinath
Siva, sect of, or Sivamarga, which worships Siva as the chief deity, 29, 30
Siva, a lordship, 314
Siva Chandra, a chief of Kumau, 296
Siva Marga, see Siva
Siva Saha, chief of Gulmi, 264
Siwapuri or Shivapuri mountain, 205
Siwaraj, a territory, 268, 269

Siyena Bhotiya, a people, see Murmi
Slavery, 87, 234
Small-pox, 25
Smilax, a plant, 98
Smith, Mr, gave me information, 2
Snow, 69, 88, 89, 90, 234; see also Himaliya
Sobhan Sahi, chief of Yumila, 287
Solanum melongena, or Bera, a vegetable, 229
Solanum tuberosum, or common potatoe, 229
Sonabhadra river, see Karanali
Songat, a cast of Newars, 36
Sor, a territory, 292
Sorahbag, a ruin, 152
Spikenard, 98
Springs, burning, 194, 272, 281; see Burning rock
Springs, heat of, 197, 200, 203, 204, 205
Springs, warm, 194, 301
Subje, see Cannabis
Srinagar, present capital of Garhawal, often used for the whole principality, 299, 301
Srishtas, a cast of Newars, 33
Strata of minerals, 66
Subah, governor of a large district, zila, or province 104, 105, 109. 110, 149, 151, 154, 155, 160, 164, 167, 179, 183
Subahdar, a military officer, 110
Sri Krishna Sahi, a chief of Gorkha, 254, 262
Suduriya, a register of lands, 150
Sudarsan Sa, heir of Garhawal, 301
Sugar and sugar-cane, 228, 284, 312
Sujanpur, a town, 310, 312
Sukhet, a lordship and town, 316
Suki, a coin, 215
Sulphur, 78, 94, 272
Superstition, 33, 208
Survey of Nepal, in 1792, by Ranjit Pangre, 216
Suryabangsi, a tribe of Rajputs, 287
Susarma, an ancient chief of Kangra, 309
Sutluj river, see Satrudra
Swayambhu, or Sambhu, the Supreme being among the Bouddhas of Nepal, 32, 208
Swayambhunath, or Sambhunath, a temple of Swayambhu, 208, 211
Swine, 76
Syamphelang, part of the Himaliya mountains, 160
Syphilis, the disease, 71

Tadi, or Tazi, a river, 193
Taizbul, a tree, see Fagara
Takam, a town, 270
Taklakhar, or Taolakhar Bhotiya, a lordship, 288
Taklakot, a town, 288
Taksal, a mart, 306
Takmaro, a kind of rice, 88
Talc, a mineral, 79, 94
Taluk, a division of territory subordinate to a zila, 114, 152
Tamlingtar, a town, 158
Tamra khani, a village, 203
Tanahung, a lordship, 132, 145, 181, 238, 239
Tangni, a grain, see Panicum colonum
Tansen, a town and great military station, 179
Taolakhar, see Taklakhar
Tapoban, a hot spring, 301
Tarai, Tariyani, } or Hetoni, the low country, subject to Gorkha, 60, &c. 65, 125, 150, 163, 169
Tarki, a lordship, 238, 239, 240, 269
Taxes, direct, 153; see Sayer, also Revenue
Tazi river, see Tadi
Tejpat, a tree, see Laurus
Telangga, the regular soldiers, 110
Temperature, see Weather, and also Springs, and 69, 70, 197
Temples, 40, 208, 209, 210, 211, 219, 285, 286, 302, 311
Tenures of land, see Adhiyar, Feodal, Jaygir, Melk, Praja, Zemindar, and also 107, 112, 114, 149, 163, 164, 218—221
Tepai, a cast of Newars, 37
Terraces used in agriculture, 223
Thakakuti, a town, 273
Thakur, a title, see Rana
Thankot, a town, 204, 209
Thapa, a tribe, 18, 19, 28
Tharu, a tribe, 164, 169
Thermometer, see Register of the Weather at the end
Thibet, a country of great extent, north from India, see Degarchi, Kerung, Kutti, Ladak, Lassa, Mastang, Tishu Lama, and also 51, 52, 56, 89, 90, 91, 92, 121, 122, 123, 127, 156, 157, 164, 165, 180, 190, 191, 212, 289, 298, 301, 307, 315
Thor Chandra, a chief of Kumau, 12, 291
Thumuriya Dhupi, a tree, see Juniperus
Tibri, a fort and temple, 286
Tiger, 63
Tika, a mark of royalty placed on the forehead, 283

Tikayit Chandra, chief of Kangra, 310
Til, a grain, see Sesamum
Tilpur, a district, 170, 172
Timber, duties on, see Kathmahal
Timber, kinds, 63, 67, 83, 84, 217
Timmi, a town, 167, 209
Tinmue, a tree, see Fagara
Tirahut, a principality, 45, 129; see also Mithila
Tishu Lama, a supposed incarnation of God, spiritual guide of the Chinese emperor, 57, 248
Tista river, 127
Titi Piralu, a drug, 86
Tiurar Singha, a military officer of Gorkha, 120
Tobacco, 20
Toon, a tree, see Cedrella
Torture in criminal proceedings, 103, 257
Towns in general, 39
Transplanting rice, a festivity, 224
Travelling, 233
Trisulgangga river, 193, 244
Tufa calcareous, 66
Tula Sen, first Raja of Makwanpur, 130
Tulasi Bhawani, tutelar deity of Nepal, 210
Tulasipur, a territory, 278
Tungd, a tree, see Cedrella
Turi, a grain, see Sinapis
Turmeric, a root, 306
Tutenague, see Zinc
Twelve chiefs, a district subject to Gorkha, see Bara Thakurai
Twenty-four Rajas, a territory subject to Gorkha, see Chaubisi Raja
Twenty-two Rajas, a territory subject to Gorkha, see Baisi Raja

Uda, a cast of Newars, 34
Umra, a petty officer, see Mokuddum
Upadhyaya Brahmans, 17
Upendra Sa, chief of Garhawal, 299
Urid, a pulse, see Phaseolus
Uya, a kind of rice, see Rice
Uya, a grain, perhaps rye, 88, 274, 284, 315

Vagmati river, 205, 207, 208
Vairagi, a kind of religious mendicant, 246
Valeriana, an herb, 97
Vallies, see Nepal and Lahuri Nepal, and also 68, 69, 80, 87, 198, 274, 282, 284, 288, 313
Varaha Chhatra, or Kshetra, a place of worship, and its Mahanta or Priest, 134, 136, 137, 151
Varma, or Burmah, dynasty, 189, 190, 191
Vazir, a high officer of government, 102, 115
Vedas, doctrine of, 30, 208, 301
Vegetables for the kitchen, 228, 229
Vegetable productions, see Plants
Vijayapur, a town, capital of Morang, 133, 137, &c. 151
Vines, grape, 73
Vishnu, a deity, 32, 281, 302, 310
Visi, a measure of land, 112
Viswanath, a noble family, 110, 154

Wages, 233
Walnut tree, 83
War, 300
Water-spouts, 70
Weather, see Register at the end, Climate, Springs temperature of, and also 64, 71, 89, 196, 199, 203, 205, 242, 277, 284, 301, 307, 313, 314, 315
Weavers, 232
Webb, Mr, his survey, 4
Weights, 215, 290
Wheat, 226, 282, 297, 301, 305
Wool, 76, 307; see also Shawl
Woollen manufacture, 232
Women, condition of, 103

Yamapatri, a kind of melk land, 219
Yasawal, a lordship, 314
Yew tree, or Hingwalka bara Saral, 217
Yogimara, a town and military station, 183, 184, 193
Yuddha Vikram Sahi, king of Gorkha, 174, 251, 255, 260—262
Yumila, a principality, 15, 129, 174, 237, 239, 240 250 276, 280, 282, 293, 294, 298

Zedoary, a root, 99
Zemindar, a person holding land for rent, 112, 115, 149
Zemindar, a person managing the revenue of one or more landed estates, (Pergunahs,) 152, 292, 296
Zila, a considerable territory managed by a Subah, 151, 161, 162, 168
Zinc, Dasta, or Tutenague, a metal, 76, 195, 264, 272.

ERRATA,

Which it is hoped the Reader will correct, and in some part excuse, as, owing to the Author's residing at a distance from the Printer, the proof-sheets were once only revised, and this has been found totally inadequate to avoid numerous errors in printing so many foreign names.

Page 8 line 15, *for* Kasiyas *read* Khasiyas
11 — 8, *for* Vyas *read* Vayasa
29 — 17 and 18, *for* Lalita, Patan *read* Lalita-Patan
30 — 26, *for* Shivamarg *read* Sivamarg
46 — 19, *for* Laksham *read* Lakshman
— — 25, *for* Samaram *read* Samaran
55 — 11, *between* and *and* from *insert* east
56 — 29, *for* Budhs *read* Buddhas
67 — 10, *for* Khoira *read* Khaira
79 — 21, *for* Muktinath *read* Muktanath
88 — 23, the map intended to have been placed here, when this was printed, has been judged unnecessary, and the capital letters, denoting the different peaks alluded to, have been placed in the general map
90 — 10, *between* there *and* two *insert* are
91 — 11 and 24, *for* Karnali *read* Karanali, and *for* Manasarovara *read* Mansarawar
98 — 25, *for* Bikk *read* Bikh
102 — 12, *for* Mukudum *read* Mokuddum
115 — 16, *for* expence *read* expense
129 — 26, *for* Salgrami *read* Salagrami
144 — 22, *for* Kemkarna *read* Hemcarna
153 — 28 and 31, *for* bigah *read* biga
157 — 11 and 13, *for* Pakang *read* Pokang
160 — 30, *for* Kotang *read* Khatang
162 — 9, *for* bigah *read* biga
163 — 10, *for* kshatra *read* kshetra
165 — 6 and 12, *for* Kalesi *read* Halesi
170 — 2 and 17, *for* Mukunda *read* Makunda
171 — 3, *for* Rama *read* Rana
— — 7 and 22, *for* Kachi *read* Khachi
173 — 5, *for* so *read* to
— — 10, *for* Bakadur *read* Bahadur
— — 24, *for* Kachi *read* Khachi
174 — 22, *for* Yudda *read* Yuddha
190 — 13, *for* Letehmi *read* Letchmi

Page 191 line 4, *for* Buddha *read* Bouddha
193 — 9, *for* Bhenhongga *read* Bhenjhongga
195 — 23, *for* is *read* are
198 — 5, *for* and *read* which
199 — 26, *for* Chispani *read* Chisapani
— — 28, *for* Kethaura *read* Hetaura
207 — 13, *for* Anirudhra *read* Anirudha
209 — 23, *for* Timi *read* Timmi
212 — 5, *for* Guhyeswari *read* Guhyiswari
— — 17 and 28, *for* shal *read* shawl
— 19, 213 — 2, *for* Digarche *read* Degarche
216 — 7, *for* Pathil *read* Pathi
— — 27, *for* Katahs *read* Kathas
217 — 23, *for* shal *read* shawl
218 — 20, *for* feu *read* fee
219 — 3, *for* Baras *read* Bangras
— — 12, *for* Pasupanath *read* Pasupatinath
232 — 21, *for* shals *read* shawls
233 — 8, *for* Hethama *read* Hethaura
239 — 27, *for* Kachi *read* Khachi
246 — 6, *for* Marchangdi *read* Marichangdi
248 — 16, 249 — 17, *for* Digarchi *read* Degarchi
261 — 30, 262 — 1, *for* Kasthadal *read* Hasthadal
268 — 9, *for* Khungni *read* Khungri
270 — 9, *for* Jahuri, Baphi *read* Jahari, Bangphi
273 — 17, *for* Saligrami *read* Salagrami
274 — 19, *for* frot *read* fort
279 — 19, *for* Tishta *read* Tista
— — 22, *for* Banghpi *read* Bangphi
280 — 1, *for* Beesci *read* Baessi
— — 5, *for* Rugum *read* Rugun
286 — 21, *for* Manasarowar *read* Manasarawar
— — 31, *for* Satudra *read* Satadru
— — 32, *for* Satluj *read* Sutluj
292 — 14, *for* Kunungoe *read* Kanungo
300 — 9, *for* Thapa *read* Karyi
305 — 16, *for* Karets *read* Kanets
311 — 14, *for* Anirudra *read* Anirudha.

In the Press, and speedily will be Published, in Quarto,

AN

ACCOUNT OF THE FISHES

FOUND

IN THE RIVER GANGES

AND ITS BRANCHES.

BY FRANCIS HAMILTON, (FORMERLY BUCHANAN,) M. D.

FELLOW OF THE ROYAL SOCIETIES OF LONDON AND EDINBURGH; OF THE SOCIETY OF ANTIQUARIES; AND OF THE LINNÆAN AND ASIATICK SOCIETIES.

PART 1 OF A VIEW OF THE HIMALIYA MOUNTAINS

FROM OBA MOHISYU IN THE VALLEY OF NEPAL

A. *Bears from Oba Mohisyu N 77° E.*
a. *Top of Devikot*
b. *A mound near Kutunja*
c. *Another mound*
d. f. *A ridge coming from the S.E. towards Bhatgang*
e. *Lower corner of the valley of Nepal bearing S.E. by E.*

PART 4 OF A VIEW OF THE HIMALIYA MOUNTAINS

K. a Peak partly covered with snow bearing from Oba Mohizyu N 12° 22' E.
L. Dhayabung covered with perpetual snow appearing over K
M. a continuation of K has some snow for 6 months in the year
a. Kukani Mountain
b. Phulĉhok
c. Town of Jaganath

d. Ranikabag or the Queens garden where the Embassy resided
e. Part of Lalita Patana
f. Bura Nilkantha
g. Top of Sivapuri
h. Top of Dhunchi covered with perpetual snow

Edinburgh, Published by A. Constable & Co 1819.

PARTS OF A VIEW OF THE HIMALIYA MOUNTAINS

F. Bears from Oba Mohizyu N 38° 26′ E.
G. .... N 30° 44′ E.
H. .... N 29° 20′ E.
a. Top of Sivapuri
b. Bura Nilkantha
c. Kapila
d. Towns of Dewapatan and Pasupatinath
e. Lalita Patana
f. Wood of Gorakhanath
g. Jagatdara
h. Santakana
i. Temple of Narayana
k. Continuation of Sivapuri
l. Hills of Chautari
m. Hills of Sipa
n. Hill of Manikchor

Edinburgh Published by A. Constable & Co [illegible]

PART 2 OF A VIEW OF THE HIMALIYA MOUNTAINS

B. From Oba Mohizyu bears N 68° 10' E.
C. .... N 64° 20' E.
D. .... N 39° 05' E.
E. .... N 41° 30' E.
a. Top of Manikcher
b. Cascade in the Vagmati

c. Hills of Sipa
d. Changu Narayana Temple
e. Woody point near Changu Narayana
f. Timi town
g. Top of Devikot

PART 5 OF A VIEW OF THE HIMALIYA MOUNTAINS

N.	Mount Dhirku bearing from Oba Mozisyu N 24° 48 W.	e.	Small temple above Nilkantha
a.	Top of Nagarjun	f.	Bala Nilkantha
b.	Hill south from Nagarjun	g.	Maha Ranika Hawas
c.	Temple of Saraswati	h.	Hill of Marayko
d.	Temple of Sambunath	k.	Hill of Dalkaf
		l.	Hill of Kukani

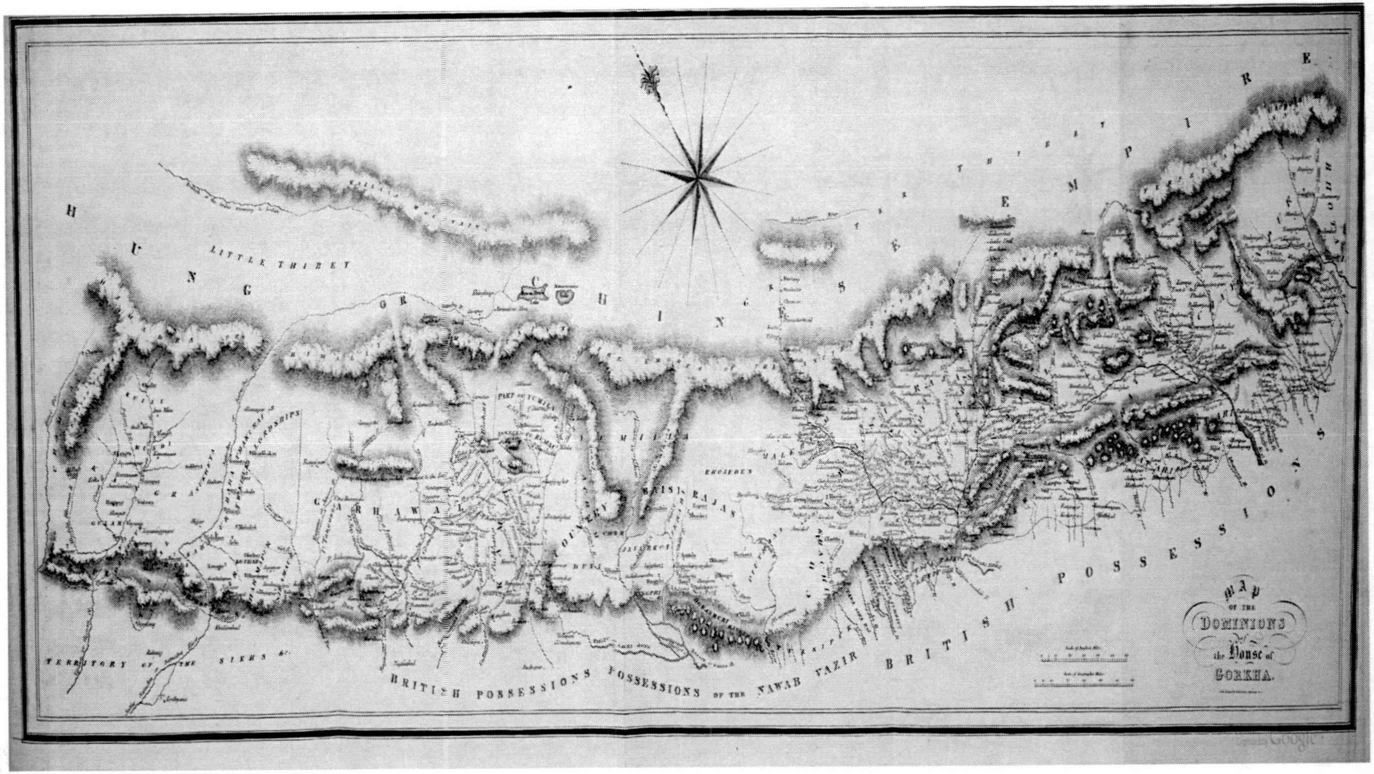

MAP OF THE DOMINIONS of the House of GORKHA.
HUNG
LITTLE THIBET
CHINESE EMPIRE
GARHAWAL
BRITISH POSSESSIONS
POSSESSIONS OF THE NAWAB VAZIR
BRITISH POSSESSIONS
TERRITORY OF THE SIKHS &c.